BUT NOW I SEE. ✝

THE GLASS SOLDIER

Not all of him shall die

Stan,

Best wishes,

Dave Farnworth

Big Sky Publishing Pty Ltd
PO Box 303, Newport, NSW 2106, Australia
Phone: 1300 364 611
Fax: (61 2) 9918 2396
Email: info@bigskypublishing.com.au
Web: www.bigskypublishing.com.au

Cover design and typesetting: Think Productions
Printed in China by Asia Pacific Offset Ltd

For Cataloguing-in-Publication entry see National Library of Australia.

Author: Don Farrands

Title: The Glass Soldier: Not all of him shall die

ISBN: 9781925520538

End Paper Image:
'I WAS BLIND BUT NOW I SEE'
Windows by Andrew and Peter Ferguson, sons of J Ferguson, grandsons of NH Ferguson.
Saint John the Evangelist Church, Soldiers Hill, Ballarat, Victoria.

THE GLASS SOLDIER

Not all of him shall die

BIG SKY PUBLISHING
www.bigskypublishing.com.au

DON FARRANDS

Contents

'Remarkable.... intensely personal'
- Barry Jones

...the Australian Imperial Force is not dead. That famous army of generous men marches still down the long lane of its country's history, with bands playing and rifles slung, with packs on shoulders, white dust on boots, and bayonet scabbards and entrenching tools flapping on countless thighs – as the French country folk and the fellaheen of Egypt knew it. What these men did nothing can alter now. The good and the bad, the greatness and smallness of their story will stand. Whatever of glory it contains nothing now can lessen. It rises, as it will always rise, above the mists of ages, a monument to great-hearted men; and, for their nation, a possession forever.

CEW Bean, *The AIF in France During the Allied Offensive, 1918: The Official History of Australia in the War of 1914–18*, 12 vols, Angus and Robertson, Sydney, 1942, Vol I, p 1096.

They move with their stretchers like boats on a slowly tossing sea, rising and falling with the shell riven contours of what was yesterday no man's land, slipping, sliding, with heels worn raw by the downward suck of the Somme mud. Slow and terribly sure through and over everything, like things that have got neither eyes to see terrible things nor ears to heed them … The fountains that sprout roaring at their feet fall back to the earth in a lacework of fragments—the smoke clears and they, momentarily obscured, are moving on before: a piece of mechanism guiltless of the weaknesses of weak flesh, one might say. But to say this is to rob their heroism of its due—of the credit that goes to inclinations conquered and panics subdued down in the privacy of the soul. It is to make their heroism look like a thing they find easy. No man of woman born could find it that. These men and all the men precipitated into the liquescent world of the line are not heroes from choice—they are heroes because someone has got to be heroic. It is to add insult to the injury of this world war to say that the men fighting it find it agreeable or go into it with light hearts.

Stretcher-Bearers by Ballarat-born war artist Will Dyson.

The Glass Soldier, the painting on the front cover, is by Suzy Papas Johnson-Thomson, granddaughter of NH Ferguson (www.facebook/suzyjohnsonart).

For images and material related to this book, and to contact the author, visit: www.glasssoldier.com.

Foreword

The author is a successful commercial barrister in Melbourne.

I knew his parents John and Jessica Farrands very well in the 1970s and 80s. Dr Farrands had been Australia's Chief Defence Scientist, then Secretary of the Commonwealth Department of Science for the Commonwealth Government, and Chair of the Australian Institute for Marine Science. I enjoyed working closely with him over many years and travelled overseas with them both.

In the 1960s, I taught at Dandenong High School (where, coincidentally, John Farrands and Jessica (nee) Ferguson had been students).

World War I, or The Great War as it used to be called, took many teachers and students to war. In Victoria, some 752 State school teachers volunteered to fight. One in five teachers did not return from war (at my old school alone, Melbourne High, many teachers volunteered and six did not return). For those with further interest, there is a book published in 1921 by the Victorian Education Department entitled *Record of War Service*, distributed free to every government school and teacher-soldier or their next of kin.

Of those teachers who returned from World War I, one was a young man from Ballarat, Nelson Ferguson. Before the war he taught art there. In the year Ferguson enlisted (in 1915), some 38 Victorian State teachers from the Department of Public Instruction, and a further 309 State School teachers, volunteered to serve in the Australian Imperial Force out of a total 1599 such teachers in that year. After the war, despite his disabilities from war, Ferguson taught at the Working Men's College in Melbourne, later RMIT.

In this book, Ferguson is referred to as 'the Glass Soldier'. That title comes from the rich and moving play by Hannie Rayson, *The Glass Soldier*. My wife and I went to its première in Melbourne in 2007. Jessica appears as a character in the play. A touchingly beautiful orchestral suite with the same name has been composed by Nigel Westlake, one of our national musical treasures. The suite has been recorded by the Melbourne Symphony Orchestra and performed by others, including the Australian Youth Orchestra. There is also a beautiful children's book, *The Promise*, by Derek Guille.

And now we have this remarkable book *The Glass Soldier*.

The author, grandson of Nelson Ferguson, traces his grandfather's life, starting as a young man in a young nation, following it to its end.

Ferguson's life was one of opportunity cut down by trauma and yet revived by providence.

Ferguson, a talented artist and musician, while stretcher-bearing in northern France as part of the Australian Imperial Force, was gassed during the famous battle at Villers-Bretonneux in April 1918. He suffered severe eye and lung trauma and remained disabled from those injuries until the late 1970s. Then, in the twilight of his life, by a surgeon's hand and the miracle of scientific learning, the AIF veteran received a corneal transplant, at the Heidelberg Repatriation Hospital for returned soldiers. The transplant restored his sight as if new. The hand of providence had delivered its reward for this man's lifelong courage against adversity.

Since retirement from Parliament I have been deeply involved in promoting measures to reduce blindness and vision loss as a high priority in public health. Vision2020 Australia, which I chaired for 12 years, part of an initiative of the World Health Organization and the International Agency for the Prevention of Blindness, has assisted in the early detection and treatment of serious eye diseases such as glaucoma (something I have suffered from myself, having also just had a successful cataract operation). Blinding trachoma is a serious condition in remote Indigenous communities. Many people remain unaware that 75 per cent of blindness or vision loss is preventable. Early detection is essential.

Vision2020Australia and other bodies assist in awareness, prevention and treatment of eye disorders. Their work is life-changing.

Ferguson's eye operation, significant for its time in Australia, was also life-changing. The Great War's stretcher-bearer was able to admire all of the spectacular and beautiful stained glass windows made in the backyard of his home by his son and son-in-law. He was the spirit of the windows. The reader of this book will understand why.

His spirit also lives on in the generations of artists and musicians who he taught and inspired, despite his disabilities. Ferguson's contribution to Australia did not stop with the end of the war; it continued until his death. He was a remarkable Australian. As the subtitle of this book suggests, not all of him shall die.

I commend this well-researched but intensely personal book to all, but in particular to the students of Australian and European history. They may see a deeper side to Australia and its development as a young nation, a greater understanding of disability, and have revealed to them a picture of courage and love not only during, but also after, war.

And for me there is a broader message in this book: with the necessary community support and the continuing miracle of modern science, much can in fact be achieved to support and overcome major disability (not only in the area of vision loss but of course more broadly). May this book remind us that we must all seek to apply our endeavours where we can towards that essential societal goal: of supporting disability. Like Ferguson's passion for art and music, so too must we remain passionate to assist those who need our care most.

Barry Jones AC FAA FAHA FTSE FASSA FRSA FRSV FACE FAIM

Preface

This book is about the colossal impact of World War I, experienced through the lens of an ordinary yet extraordinary man.

In the late 1960s my grandfather, then in his late seventies, sat with me in his small dining room in Karma Avenue, East Malvern, a suburb of Melbourne. I was not yet 10. It was his custom to wear a French beret and he wore it that day.

Pressed deep into a large old chair, he showed me a small box containing his World War I diaries and sketches. I had no idea what they represented or stood for.

Over 30 years later, when I was in my late forties, my mother, Jessica, told me she might keep the diaries and sketches from the war because they were important. I started reading them. This book, along with other major developments I describe below, is the result of that step.

It is a grand understatement that World War I (1914–18) caused immeasurable harm on a global scale. That is well known. Historians have explored in depth the causes of the war, the battles within it, and the eventful outcome. A number of scholars have also explored the treatment of returned soldiers by government and society generally.

While I touch on those things in this book, I seek to reveal a very different dimension: the peacetime contribution of returned soldiers, contextualised by their wartime experiences. I have sought to give voice to that issue through the lens of one Australian soldier in particular.

My grandfather, Nelson Harold Ferguson, was a stretcher-bearer in the 15th Field Ambulance, 5th Division, Australian Imperial Force (AIF). He joined the AIF in July 1915. He was a Ballarat boy catapulted onto a global stage without any real warning or preparation. He worked in four horrendous battles: at the Somme, Northern France (late 1916); at Bullecourt, Northern France (April and May 1917); at Ypres, Belgium (the Third Battle of Ypres, September/October 1917); and at Villers-Bretonneux, Northern France (April 1918). In April 1918, at the battle at Villers-Bretonneux, he was severely gassed, eyes traumatised, and lungs damaged.

There was a remarkable thing about this soldier. Although his contribution in the war was beyond what could be expected of anyone, he made an even greater one when he returned. It was intergenerational in effect. He was a true believer in peace, principally because, unlike the vast majority of us, he had seen war. There were tens of thousands of returned soldiers who did the same thing; they returned to Australia and got on with the job of building their community, peacefully. Not everyone was able, for obvious reasons, to do so, but those who were so able largely built the foundations of this great modern society we now enjoy. Their contributions collectively, and often individually, have been immense.

The grand canvas of my grandfather's life both during and after the war, now explored in this book, has also enabled me to raise other significant issues, including the role of leadership in war, the role of God and the role of recognition.

The reader will see that there are regular extracts from my grandfather's diary entries—these are all authentic. Furthermore, in the middle section of the book, I take the reader through Nelson's horrendous war experiences, referenced again from his diaries. Here, the reader will be given Nelson's own account of what was occurring and what he was doing during some of the major battles he took part in. The descriptions Nelson gave in his diary may not have always accorded precisely with the position of the battles and events depicted. That is the character of a private diary. Further, in the diary there are references to other AIF soldiers. I have included their names. This is not to impose distress on any relative of those soldiers, but rather to pay due respect to those diggers and to reflect the circumstances in question.

Although I engage metaphor, I have attempted to make this book as historically accurate as I can, through extensive historical research, as well as family recollection. However, the sheer size of the undertaking to deal with 100 years of history, albeit through the lens of one soldier, inevitably means that there may be errors in these pages. They are solely attributable to me. This is not an historian's journey.

The later part of this book focuses on the work done in a stained-glass window business in Melbourne run by my uncles, John and

Nick, from around 1952 to 1980. The business was run from my grandfather's backyard and he was the assistant. He did not make the windows. But it is certainly true that he was a guiding force in their creation. He was, according to one of my uncles, the 'spirit of the windows'. His mentorship and love of art was the prism through which masterpieces made by my uncles came about. My grandfather was, in that sense, truly 'the glass soldier'.

The study of war reveals a number of things. One in particular stands out for me. Armies remain embedded in our societies for one fatal reason: war is systemic, not episodic. It is peace which is episodic.

My ultimate hope is that the messages within the story of the Glass Soldier may assist future generations to understand war's immense destructive long-term power.

It is important for me to make a further observation and give important context. There are matters raised in these pages that may at times reflect poorly on certain armies and governments, in particular the British. This, however, may be explained by the context. It is true that the dominions, including Australia, were in perilous risk during World War I. But they were not, unlike the British (and the French), literally 'fighting for their whole nation'. If Germany had taken France, it was a short journey across the Channel to England. The British Government well knew that if the war could be kept on the European continent, and the Germans repelled from France, the island of England would remain safe. The methods and madness of the British army at certain times, which I touch on in this book (including the accompanying notes), must be seen (at least in part) in that very real context.

Finally, lest there be any doubt, it is not intended that this book enter the 'feel-good narrative' of World War I in which Australia romantically awoke as a nation and bronzed Australians returned to acclaimed world status as fighters. It is true that that sentiment is recorded in this book by reference to the written record of the time about what was happening to Australia and Australians. But to be clear, this is a book dead against the stupidity of war and the consequences of that stupidity. It tells the story of hope *despite* that stupidity.

I would like to thank the following people (not in any particular order) for their unique and significant contributions to this book and for their support and enthusiasm for it: Barry Jones, John Collee, Hannie Rayson, Nigel Westlake, Dr Paul Hicks, Martin Hubner, Peter Bick, Dr Tony Kjar, Geoff McGill, Ivan St Clair, Nigel McGuckian, Jenny Mitchell, Fay Woodhouse, Joseph Moore, Amie Churchill, Kevin Jones, Josephine Barnes, Jessica Ferguson, Suzy Papas Johnson-Thomson, James Farrands, Simon Griffith, Tebb Kusserow, Greg Blashki, and all the members of the Melbourne Villers-Bretonneux Brass Ensemble. I could not be more grateful, and I am deeply indebted to each of you.

My thanks also to Rosemary Peers, my editor. Her discipline and care has been extraordinary. Her great-uncle died in the Third Battle of Ypres. His name is on the enormous Menin Gate War Memorial in Belgium.

I would also like to thank Ian Macdonald, Catherine Burke and Karl Stewart for giving me the opportunity to better understand how and why the military conducts itself as it does, and to understand the work of leadership in war and during peacetime. Their book *Systems Leadership: Creating Positive Organizations* has been invaluable.

Don Farrands
Melbourne
B. Ec, LLB, AC, F Fin, GAIDC

June 2017

To my grandfather, Nelson Harold Ferguson

Honor virtutis praemium
(Esteem is the reward of virtue)

A Note on the War Diaries and Bible

NH Ferguson's war diaries, sketches and Bible are referenced in this book.

Nelson carried his Bible in his trench coat throughout the war. He posted some of his diary back to Australia and carried the rest. He also posted sketches and paintings home.

The diary is in many parts. One part is held together with an old large safety pin.

The diary is in narrative form, explaining where Nelson is, what he is doing, and what is happening around him. There is little reflection on his emotions or those of others. One reason for this may be that because he was posting his diary home, in sections, to his brother Roy (whom he called 'Mate' in the diary) others in the family, in particular Nelson's mother, Lucretia, might end up seeing the diary. It is a fair conclusion that the diary was accordingly written so as to protect (to the extent possible) the 'unintended reader'.

The diaries commence in Australia at the time Nelson joined the AIF in July 1915 and end upon his return to Australia in January 1919.

A Note on Nelson's Journey to War and Back

Nelson Ferguson was born and raised as a young man in Ballarat, Victoria, Australia, a prosperous goldmining town 70 miles (115 kilometres) north-west of Melbourne, Australia.

Nelson taught art at a school in Ballarat until his early twenties. He joined the AIF in July 1915, travelled to England, and was then sent to the Western Front in France, and to Belgium. He performed stretcher-bearing work in major battles in World War I: at the Somme, Northern France (late 1916); at Bullecourt, Northern France (April and May 1917); at Ypres, Belgium (the Third Battle of Ypres, September/October 1917); and at Villers-Bretonneux, Northern France (April 1918). He returned to Australia in early 1919.

Upon return to Australia, Nelson Ferguson lived in East Malvern, a suburb of Melbourne. He did not return to France but retained the utmost affection for its people.

Part I
Towards War

Part I
Towards War

The Cornet and Sussex by the Sea—March 1911

The large military brass band fanned itself across Ballarat's generous Engineers' Hall. The King of England calmly watched on, suspended from a nail.

The hall was now a hive of hectic activity: cases opened to glistening instruments; odd warm-up notes hit walls as scales scarpered up and down; music parts bustled onto stands.

A baton's tap brought silence. The 17th Rifle Brigade Brass Band, Ballarat readied itself. Young fit and strong Australians, with toughened hands from country work, and proud hearts from their musical heritage, stared up at the bandmaster, waiting for action.

The hall was off Ballarat's grand Main Street. Other cousin buildings pressed against it. They too had come from 1850s Australian gold-rush money.

By a willing horse, Victoria's main city of Melbourne was some five hours south-east. It was only three hours by reliable motor. And, according to the local timetable, only two hours by train.

Ten years earlier, the British Parliament had federated Australia as a new nation, a commonwealth of States, including Ballarat's State, Victoria. Britain's roots in the new nation ran deep. In May 1901, the Duke (later, King George V) and Duchess of Cornwall and York officially opened the first Federal Parliament. And an ex-convict gave the first parliamentarian's speech. Even after its birth, the nation proudly remained a Dominion of the British Empire (along with others such as New Zealand and Canada). And all Australians remained British subjects (and regarded themselves as such). When the queen died a month after federation, the whole nation sagged. Every brass band in Australia delivered mournful hymns.

Before federation, the territory covered by Victoria (named after Queen Victoria) had been a British colony for some 65 years. In 1836 it had only 230 white residents.

Since the early 19th century, wool had driven Victoria's strong economic growth (and, for that matter, across rest of Australia's). In 1822, Britain lowered the duty on wool from Australia; overnight, the nation could compete with German wool prices. By 1839, Victorian wool was reaching England. The opening of the Suez Canal in 1869 and a cable link later meant even more opportunities for trade, including wheat. By the late 1890s, wool was the nation's chief export, even with the severe drought of that time.

It was now 70 years since Britain had stopped dropping off her criminals in Victoria (and the rest of the mainland, but not Tasmania until much later, in 1853). But Australia's population had continued to grow (despite the emigration in the depression of the 1890s), including across the Ballarat region.

Now, in 1911, Victoria's white population was just edging over 1.3 million people (with 650 Aboriginals, down from 10,000 when Victoria was first settled). Ballarat itself now had nearly 50,000 people, servicing vast prosperous sheep and wheat-farming activity. It was the largest inland city in Australia.

The brass band sat stone-like awaiting the next command. The bandmaster shifted his grip on his pencil baton.

'Before we begin, gentlemen, may I introduce our new leader of the cornet section: Mr Nelson Ferguson.'

A short, fit, young man with an olive complexion rose to his feet. He smiled at his new colleagues, who smiled back. Nelson's bright silver cornet clinked against the shiny buttons of his brigade uniform.

'Thank you. I'm delighted to be here,' he said, nodding.

Nelson sat back down in the cornet section.

'As many of you know, this fine local was in Prout's Ballarat Band, the winner of the 1910 National Brass Band Eisteddfod. He is pretty handy with the willow and ball too—one of the quicks at the Ballarat East Cricket Club. And like some others here, he's now an art instructor at our School of Mines, in the Art Department.'

The bandmaster was right. Nelson was a star cornet player and had been part of winning brass bands in national eisteddfods from a young age. And it was also right that he was a talented young art instructor at the school. The school was the principal secondary educational institution in Ballarat. It conducted broad-based teaching, including mining, engineering, technical studies, and art classes. Nelson was now a second-generation Ballarat resident, heavily involved in music, art and sport across the town's community.

And now he was an integral part of the 17th Rifle Brigade Band itself. Brass bands were at the core of Ballarat's musical character. The town's national reputation was in holding (and often winning) annual brass-band competitions.

'Gentlemen, would you please all now welcome our new first cornet.'

The musicians tapped their instruments enthusiastically and cheered. Nelson was a strong addition and the band members knew it; his future solo performances might just put them into the finals for this year's national eisteddfod.

Nelson settled his sparkling silver-plated 1905 b-flat Boosey & Hawkes cornet on his lap. It was a first-class instrument, imported from the best source of brass instruments, England. Most of the marches played on it came from the mother country too.

'It's time to put you blokes to work,' announced the bandmaster. His steely stare pressed into the band. He had the necessary military leadership techniques to extract the best out of his musicians, which, if the band gave its best, would be duly recognised. His army leadership was uncompromising; if standards fell below the minimum required, there would be unnerving consequences. This afternoon's rehearsal was likely to put these traits on display.

A flourishing baton rose sharply and then stabbed the air, producing a clear and stable chord. Under the bandmaster's command, and with a drum line now at pace, the Ballarat 17th Rifle Brigade Band launched into one of the great British military marches: 'Sussex by the Sea'.

Despite the verve and crescendo, over the top of his music Nelson could see a deepening red fury on the bandmaster's face. The left arm fell abruptly and with it the march's momentum.

'Come on, you lot. This march must have a forward force. Like the troops for which it was written! Boys, it must empower. It must show whose side is on the go. I am afraid all I can hear is the sorry sounds of part-timers making part-time music. Do you have any idea how a military march should, in fact, be played?!'

The baton thrust towards the wall. 'Our king is appalled with you lot—as am I!'

The bandmaster looked straight at Nelson.

'I want to hear the cornet section only, and from the beginning. No, forget that, I want to hear the first cornets only. Ferguson, lead the way.'

Nelson immediately pressed his lips to the mouthpiece, as did the other section members.

The baton took aim at Nelson and then rose again. Held high for an unnerving amount of time, it then struck. Cornet upon cornet rang out across the band room. A blue-ribbon chord suddenly bounced off the walls.

As the balance of the band kicked in, a declaration could be heard over the top: 'Yes! The sound is powerful. Vigorous. Stirring. Keep going. Push forward, boys. Push!'

The final chord held long and strong until two swift arms guillotined it.

'Listen to me, boys. This sound has to take troops into battle. You can be sure it will have to do so one day. Play with the military purpose you have shown and this band will do the work the army expects of you.'

The Band's Fit

The band sat dumbstruck from the impact of one of the military's most powerful weapons: recognition.

'Ferguson, outstanding leadership of your section. Well done to all. Keep it up,' rewarded the bandmaster. 'Right, let's pick it up one more time.'

Nelson again pressed his lips to the mouthpiece and returned his focus to the sheet music, then the bandmaster.

'Before we begin again, please pay attention to what I am about to say.' The bandmaster looked determined. 'You are required to demonstrate the standards necessary to be an effective part of the Australian Army within the British Empire. This band is young, but its true history is one of Australia and Britain joined at the hip in defence, and for all other matters. I want you to remember that, boys. I want you all joined at the hip too!'

On the day Nelson was welcomed, the brass band had turned only one year old, as had the rifle brigade that it supported. But the history the bandmaster spoke of was long and deep. The origins of the brigade and its band and, for that matter, Nelson's membership of it, could be traced as far back as the 1880s; all the way back to king and country. When the new nation awoke in 1901, Ballarat men and those from all over Australia were fighting in the Boer War in aid of the motherland. Three Australians had won the highest British military award, the Victoria Cross for valour. Ten of the town's boys died in the conflict. The War Memorial next to the Town Hall said so.

In his bars' rest, Nelson quickly drained spit from his cornet, splashing the floor. He looked up to the king's gaze: it was not disapproving. The cornet returned to his lips.

The bandmaster's role was to make the band competent. The band's role was to stimulate a sense of purpose and pride in young Australian reserve soldiers from Ballarat. Like other rehearsals, today the bandmaster would demand a high work rate.

But there was a much larger task underway across Australia; the young nation had been developing for some years the systems and structures needed in order to be able to support Britain in war, should it ask. And these young reservists were now part of Australia's growing national reserve army.

'All right, let's take it again from the second-time bar, chaps. We are going to charge right to the end. With gusto!'

Ready Set—1912

'Pick that up,' barked the brigade sergeant, pointing to a large wooden barrel full of water.

'Yes sir,' said Nelson.

'Now bloody well carry it right across that bridge over there and down into that waterhole, then over to the other embankment. Then put the bloody thing on top of that pile. And I want it done alone and with haste, Ferguson.'

Nelson heaved the barrel onto his short but sturdy frame and marched off towards the bridge. He could see a huge pile on the far side. Salty sweat drained into his eyes as he pressed on under the sergeant's fierce gaze.

'Hurry up, Ferguson, you haven't got the whole bloody morning.'

Nelson soon found himself waist-deep in the mud of the stinking waterhole, driving himself forward to the next obstacle. He suddenly sank deeper, now at chest height, then launched himself out of it, heaving the barrel onto the bank. Nelson's chest searched for good country air.

'Ferguson, you're making some progress now! Remember, the army doesn't let up in the home straight! It drives forward!'

Nelson shouldered the barrel again, grinding his way to the end of the arduous task. He then strained to lift it above his head for one last time, jamming it on top of the pile.

A wry smile appeared. 'Now, go again.'

Support for the Empire

The waterhole exercise was being run by the combined operation of what had been the Ballarat 17th Rifle Brigade, now the 70th Infantry Brigade, and the associated Bendigo brigade. The militia group Nelson was part of had been re-formed, with the Ballarat East unit being allocated to the 70th Infantry Brigade.

The various exercises the young men had to undertake would make them fit, give them discipline, and get them used to teamwork. All of that might one day enable them to defeat an enemy. And save their own lives.

Nelson's military training was part of a national drive. In 1911, military training was instituted for all Australian boys born in 1894, and in the following year, boys aged 12 to 17 began compulsory training. The ultimate aim was to have a militia strength of 80,000 men in Australia by 1916. The government was on track to achieve this.

All this building of embedded community soldiers across the newborn nation of Australia was being driven by a number of influences: a natural inclination that the nation should have its own 'internal defence' force; Japan's defeat of Russia in 1904–05 and the threat she might pose in the future; and broad Empire support, encouraged by the motherland herself.

Britain and Australia's 'cooperation' in relation to defence matters was now well established.

In 1909, Australia's naval fleet was put under the Royal Navy and Australia agreed 'to take its share in the general defence of the Empire' (one in five people in Australia in 1901 had been born in England).

The following year, Lord Kitchener visited Australia, endorsing more military spending and creating a 'mobile striking force'. Australia then agreed its troops could be mobilised to proceed to 'certain overseas' ports.

And now in 1912, at a further conference on 'mutual assistance', Australia and New Zealand agreed to supply Britain with 12,000 men if need be. Australia's general defence scheme would shortly be 'endorsed' by the British Committee of Imperial Defence, discouraging mere 'local defence' and urging 'active defence'.

In Nelson's fitness and training, and those of thousands of other young Australians, lay the supreme military purpose.

The defeat of an enemy of the British Empire.

A Developing Storm—the Period to 1914

For Nelson, at 23, Ballarat seemed as safe as houses and was the perfect place to teach, to start a new family, and to enjoy music and sport. Ballarat was the largest inland city in Australia and enjoying much wealth. It had two daily papers, *The Star* and *The Courier*. It had an electric tram. It was part of the new prosperous and safe world of the Antipodes.

But on the other side of the world the picture was now completely different. There had been little to celebrate for a very long while. The European race to war could be traced back to the Franco-German conflict of 1871. Germany had defeated France, taking large parts of her as part of the prize of victory. The military leadership within Germany had since then signalled that European domination was the next goal.

And it was prepared and able to threaten Britain too. Since 1900, Germany had been building a naval force to rival the Royal Navy. Britain's supremacy at sea had been central military policy since the Battle of Trafalgar. From 1906, Britain's central foreign policy was to outbuild Germany in battleships.

On land, the scent of conflict was in the nostrils of European soldier and citizen everywhere. Both the German High Command and France had since 1911 been planning mobilisation on a vast scale, including the timetabling of thousands and thousands of trains across Europe to bring troops efficiently to battle.

And European countries had since the early 1900s developed huge civilian armies embedded into society, to be deployed when required should war break out. Compulsory training for European adolescents was widespread. By 1913, France was attempting to bring the number of its soldiers up to Germany's huge number. Hundreds of thousands of horses were also being trained for imminent war.

By 1914, the Europeans, Britain and Russia had ordered themselves into two camps: Germany, Austria and Italy on the one hand (the Triple Alliance); and France, Britain and Russia on the other (the Triple Entente).

Each camp had now developed a colossal vitality to engage in war on immediate notice. All of these nations were staring at each other, either planning for, or wondering whether there would be, war.

All that was needed was a flashpoint to start a global duel.

One that might just take Nelson out of the safety of rural Ballarat and into the teeth of combat in Europe.

Flashpoint—Mid-1914

On 28 June 1914, the spark for war was lit: the Austrian Archduke, Franz Ferdinand, and his wife, were shot dead. A month later, Austria-Hungary declared war on Serbia. Three days later, Germany sent Russia an ultimatum, declaring war on her the next day. Under the Franco–

Russian convention of 1892, if Germany attacked Russia, France had to defend her. France therefore mobilised against Germany and, on 3 August 1914, Germany declared war on France too. The intoxication of impending violence was about to be realised. Sharpened national differences would soon cut down the lives of millions of young willing (and some unwilling) men.

The next day, the heavily trained German cavalry crossed into Belgium. Border-breaching young soldiers all well trained and equipped to kill sat tall on magnificent horses. Under Germany's so-called Schlieffen Plan (first developed in 1908), Belgium would be Germany's entry point into France, with the intention of entering Paris within a short six weeks and securing a swift victory accordingly.

Deep in the night of 4 August 1914, Britain declared war on Germany. The steel-helmeted German army had invaded a small country, Belgium, unprovoked, and Britain told her allies (following a narrow Cabinet vote) it was not standing for it.

The British Parliament made no formal decision to go to war. The 'great crusade for democracy' would formally start not with fragile parliamentary judgement but rather by royal prerogative writs. At 10.35 pm at Buckingham Palace, acting as a tiny Privy Council, His Majesty King George V and three Lords (all un-elected) tipped Britain into war.

No European nation dilly-dallied. Military leaders seized earlier war-planning papers and began acting on them. Millions of men were now being mobilised across Europe for wholesale war.

So too were a staggering number of horses mobilised: one for every three soldiers. Germany alone mobilised 715,000 horses; Russia, over a million; and Austria, some 600,000. Farms had now been stripped of the very horsepower that sustained them. The Napoleonic notions of war were still very real and were now being enacted.

Some two weeks later, British troops in relatively small numbers crossed the English Channel in aid of France. As they bobbed in small boats, officers carried swords as wielded at Agincourt in 1415. The essentially unarmed and untrained island nation, with no real defence except its navy, was about to face the strongest manifestation of military power in human record. In the Kaiser's view the British troops amounted to a 'contemptible little army'.

And within those same two weeks, Britain illegally commenced a sea blockade of all food bound for Germany and, where possible, seized it. The enemy would be brought to its knees by all available means.

Germany was now embarking on a huge movement of trains to carry troops to destroy century-old buildings and kill other young men—some 2150 fifty-four wagon trains full of German troops now rattled over the bridges of the Rhine.

Those troops had now been tasked to conquer France quickly and then defeat the British Empire and her allies thereafter. Over a decade of preparation had now been unleashed.

Australia Joins In—July 1914

All of this maelstrom was an immeasurable distance from Nelson's weatherboard home at 52 Peel Street, Ballarat, Victoria.

Yet unbeknownst to the Fergusons or any other Australian family, on 30 July 1914, Britain urgently sent telegrams to Australia and the other dominions warning of imminent war. Germany sent a similar 'threatening war' proclamation.

The conflict was not now European; it was suddenly at the global end of the spectrum—with Australia being promptly pulled into it.

Days earlier, on 26 and 28 July 1914, without British Cabinet approval, Churchill concentrated the Royal Navy out to sea, positioned at war stations. Before Britain had asked for it, Australia's governor-general (commander-in-chief of all of Australia's military forces) 'unofficially' offered Australia's navy for Britain's purposes.

On 31 July 1914, Canada offered a force of men, and in Australia the opposition leader declared that, if elected, he would support the mother country to 'our last man and our last shilling'. New Zealand also offered support on the same day.

North-west of Nelson's hometown of Ballarat, in the town of Horsham, the Prime Minister of Australia, Joseph Cook, declared: 'It is no use to blink our obligations. If the Old Country is at war, so are we'. The Opposition soon matched that commitment to Empire.

Both sides of politics had now indentured young Australian sons to serve the British Empire by killing its enemy.

At 6 pm on 3 August 1914, the Australian Government offered 20,000 men who were yet to volunteer (out of a pool of some 45,000 young Australians who had received basic military training). But because Australia's citizen soldiers were largely composed of youths, it was decided a 'special force' of enlistments, chosen from elite volunteers across the whole population, would be created. According to official estimates, Australia might ultimately be able to give something like 820,000 men to the war effort from its population of five million. The Australian offer was made some 40 hours before the British Government announced it had declared war on Germany and was not in response to Germany's declaration of war on France.

British newspapers soon praised the dominion support, recording that 'Australia will fight for the Empire to the last'. This was true. Within the week, enlistments began at the Ballarat Drill Hall. On 7 August 1914, Nelson's Ballarat military regiment was sent to Fort Queenscliff, outside Melbourne, along with other country regiments. Three days later, official recruiting opened for what was now being called the 'Australian Imperial Force' (AIF). Elite young men from across Australia would shortly volunteer, then be selected for service abroad—only the nation's strongest and best would go to war.

On 1 November 1914, 20,000 such men, formed as the 1st Division of the AIF, sailed with 8000 horses from Western Australia, headed for war in aid of the British Empire and her allies.

But Nelson was not on the first shipload of young men making up the new AIF. It was not his turn for the 'adventure' of war.

Yet.

Art Instruction—Early April 1915

The Ballarat School of Mines marked the entrance to Ballarat. Like many other buildings, it was a product of gold-rush money (Victoria produced most of the gold mined in the rush).

The building housed the town's art school and, within it, a large number of students, trainee teachers, and permanent staff.

Nelson had been an 'art instructor' at the school since the age of 18. A Ballarat boy all his life, he was now waiting to be assigned elsewhere in Victoria as an art teacher. It was likely to take him from Ballarat. He hoped it would be in the lights of Melbourne.

By April 1915, no less than tens of thousands of young Australians had volunteered to assist the British Empire support France and Russia to defeat the enemy. Large numbers of Ballarat boys were now fighting. Many had been shot or wounded. Many would yet suffer those fates.

Nelson looked up at the large art studio's high ceilings and expansive windows. They were in fine condition and excellent for receiving a large light flow and therefore for delivering art instruction. The late-morning sun now occupied the studio. It arrived through old handmade windows set high in the room, their square panes each joined by substantial leadlight cross supports.

Nelson's students were not only from Ballarat but also from the greater goldfields region, including from another wealthy goldrush town quite nearby, Bendigo.

'I thought we might try something special today, class,' said Nelson enthusiastically. He held high an AIF hat. 'This is more difficult to draw than you might think. Its dimensions might just challenge you.'

Nelson carefully placed it on the desk at the front of the classroom. The light struck the 'Rising Sun' badge on the brim. The badge was the third pattern of the Rising Sun, introduced onto the hat in 1904. It carried a sun rising over a scroll inscribed with the words 'Australian Commonwealth Military Forces'. An earlier special version had been struck in 1902 for the coronation of King Edward VII of England.

The students pressed charcoal against paper.

'You have one hour to complete two sketches this morning. You need to draw from at least two angles to learn perspective.'

'Is this yours, Mr Ferguson?' asked a student.

'No,' said Nelson, 'I volunteered, but the AIF told me I was too short to fight.'

Nelson was right. For him, entering the conflict was not possible. He certainly met the AIF's age requirement of 19 to 38 years. But at 5 feet 5¼ inches, he was 3/4 of an inch too short to be 'one of the finest'. And with a chest measurement of 32½ inches, his trunk was also out by 1½ inches. The army upheld strict standards. True, a young boy could try to give a false age. But body size or height could not be fabricated.

Nelson quietly paced the classroom, studying the students' early workings.

'It's just a question of lightly developing the outline, and then refining the shadowing.'

Nelson passed quietly by another work in progress. 'Very good,' he said. 'You have shown the form, but always look for the substance of the object. There is a whole nation behind that hat. Care in your work will show respect for your subject and help reveal its character.'

Nelson moved to another student as he flipped the white paper on his easel. The leadlight in one of the windows began to impose the shadow of a cross on his page. Using the shadow as a frame of reference, the student's charcoal drew surely across the page, revealing the firm form of the brim.

'Class, I will give you some more time. Please try to complete your work by noon,' said Nelson.

Opportunity

Nelson quietly walked through the studio door. Boards creaked under heavy boots as he moved towards the Head of Art's office.

'Come in, Ferguson, I've been expecting you.'

Nelson stepped forward. Harbrow's office was sunlit and messy. Barricaded behind a clogged desk, Harbrow sat motionless, peering. His face held authority.

Harbrow looked up at his student teacher. The handsome face was calm, with a strong jawline. The summer had deposited a light tan. Nelson's twilight-brown eyes were large, clear and kind. Harbrow could see his office window in them.

Harbrow mechanically tapped an envelope on the desk. 'I'm afraid I have some news to relay to you, Nelson'.

'Yes sir.'

Harbrow slowly pulled the letter from its envelope. Earlier in the year he had taken Nelson up to Melbourne for an interview for a position as a full-time first-year art teacher in the State school system of Victoria. He now held the result. Harbrow unfolded the letter and stretched it to arm's length, diligently lowering his half-rimmed glasses.

Harbrow's face slowly produced a wry smile.

Dear Mr Harbrow, I am pleased to inform you that we wish to offer Mr Nelson Ferguson a position as an intern art teacher at our school commencing at the beginning of July this year, 1915. Would you please confirm his availability in due course. (Signed Principal, Warrnambool Junior Technical School, Warrnambool, Victoria)

'It's not quite Melbourne,' said Harbrow, 'but it's on the coast and you can train down to Melbourne in about four hours. Pretty close really.' Harbrow smiled and rose from his chair. Willing hands shook.

'I'm excited about this, sir.'

'You've been offered a place at a fine regional school, Nelson. You should take this up and count yourself lucky—you are one of only a select few from the school to receive an offer this year. The Department obviously thinks you have marked observational ability. I thought that when you first came here. And you have, as I expected, proven me correct I am delighted to say.'

Harbrow handed Nelson the letter. 'Show this to your folks Nelson—they will be very proud.'

'Thank you for all you have done for me, Mr Harbrow.'

'That is the responsibility and privilege of this fine school, and especially my privilege,' said Mr Harbrow.

Nelson looked down at the letter. He was full of mixed emotions: part excitement, part wonder, and part sadness to be leaving his hometown.

He returned the letter to its envelope. His future now rested in his shirt pocket.

'Go and tell your parents—they will be very proud I am sure.'

'I will. Thank you again, sir.'

'I know your mother will be sad you won't be going to Melbourne, but that is how it is—you have to take this up, it's a very good school and a good start for you for a long and distinguished career.'

'Yes, I'm fortunate to be given this chance.'

Mr Harbrow was not overstating it. The opportunity was a good one which could ultimately take the young art teacher far in the Victorian education system; young teachers who spent time in rural Victoria were well recognised for their dedication, commitment and broad experience. Currently only holding a temporary art instructor's position, Nelson knew he could not stay on at the school in Ballarat; the Warrnambool position would provide him with an excellent opportunity to start on the path he wished for: a long-term art teaching career with the Victorian education department.

But leaving his hometown of Ballarat meant leaving the close Ferguson family. And his teacher was right. There could be no doubt Nelson's mother would be proud of his achievement—but also sad to see him leave his home in Ballarat.

Leather Meets Willow

Nelson turned out of the school building, collecting his bicycle which was leaning against the wrought-iron gate. Straddling the seat, he realised the journey home with his Warrnambool news had to wait for one important commitment.

Dancing pedals powered through the back streets of Ballarat. The bucolic countryside opened itself to the young teacher. Old tyre tracks marked the journey's line along one of Ballarat's long dusty roads. The broad sweep of the Australian sunlight across the countryside was as bright as the adventure in Nelson's pocket.

As the bike shuddered across the cattle grate, Nelson could see a young man bobbing through long grass under labour.

It was Roy, Nelson's younger brother. Roy was pounding makeshift stumps into dry dirt with his bat.

The smell of woolly sheep lay in the golden paddock. A kookaburra perched on a fence pole laughed once, then flew off.

The long, dry summer grass tickled Roy's hand as he set and reset his batting grip. 'Come on Nel, you're late—time to play!' he called.

'I'm coming over.' Nelson's bike disappeared as he rested it in the grass and he picked up the well-worn ball. Cricket was the summer's ritual for the brothers; today it would continue.

Across from the pitch, Roy could see his enthusiastic counterpart for what would no doubt be a strong afternoon of brotherly mateship and teasing rivalry.

'Come on Nel,' called Roy again, 'let her rip. I'll go easy on you today'.

'We'll see about that!' declared Nelson.

Holding the ball tight, Nelson studied the pitch, then leant forward. A long enthusiastic run-in gathered further pace.

Roy gripped, and then re-gripped the bat; the pounding on the hard paddock quickened.

The willow raised itself high and volleyed the ball straight and high over Nelson's head, out beyond the paddock's distant barbed-wire fence.

'Great shot,' called Nelson, turning briskly to recover it. 'How did you get your eye in without me?'

The boys had been playing all summer and so it was a level of intuition coupled with a good dose of fairness which governed who would bat first, and the time to rotate thereafter. The spirit of the game was well respected between them; Roy's innings were longer but that was fine—the benefit of the doubt would always be with the younger brother.

The afternoon haze was gracious to the brothers. As they took turns time was lost. And sometimes the ball with it.

After many self-declared successes with bat and ball, and a fair exchange of innings, the afternoon's light began to tell them to call it a day and to head home for tea with the family. Mum always had it on the table at 6 pm sharp and it would be the same today.

'Nel, Mum will want us home very soon.'

'The Poms would declare "bad light" so we may as well,' called back Nelson.

Roy leant over and strained to pull the stumps from the baked Ballarat dirt. 'Nothing to aim at now, Nel,' called Roy, 'but how 'bout one more ball in my favour to get me over 50?'

'Right mate,' agreed Nelson.

Turning for his run-in again, Nelson moved down towards the pitch as if it was the first bowl of the day.

Roy could bat but this particular delivery had a speed and sureness to it; like a bullet, it went quick, straight and, against Roy's best bet, dead on target, just where the stumps had been.

Roy prised his head high and, with a twisting of the right shoulder and a straightening of the arms, heaved his bat at the ball.

The red dot arched long and high into Ballarat's sky.

'Bet that's a six,' yelled Roy.

'Bet it's not. But if it is, it's six and out over the fence!' cried Nelson.

Nelson about-faced, straining his eyes to see the projectile which had begun to disappear into the wide white clouds perched high over the pitch. Time stood still as the old cherry disappeared from sight. The sun temporarily struck Nelson's eyes, blinding him to where the ball might be.

'I reckon I've got it,' shouted Nelson in disbelief as the ball came back into vision. He immediately charged through the grass like a late messenger.

'This one's no chance for out,' shouted back Roy.

With keen sight and the willingness of a racehorse, Nelson dived under the ball, his left hand fully stretched.

'You can get this, Nel,' Roy shouted, cheering Nelson on.

'I bet you I can't!' gasped Nelson.

Nelson heaved himself towards the ball with one last surge. As paddock grass flew everywhere, the ball shot itself into Nelson's open hand.

And stayed there.

'Great catch, but still a six,' declared Roy.

'Great hit, but I'm afraid you're out!' Nelson shouted back, rolling through the paddock and ending on his back in laughter.

Roy ran, reached down, and pulled his brother up. Dust swallowed wide smiles.

'That was one of the best catches of the day, Nel. Hang on, maybe this summer.'

'Wish I could claim that one, Roy, but it was a fluke,' conceded Nelson.

'Nah,' said his brother. 'You lost it in the white clouds. But you chased it across from nowhere. It might have fallen into your hand, Nel, but that was no chance. God willed it, I reckon'.

'That may be right, Roy, but I could have used him earlier in the day!' said Nelson.

The teammates dusted themselves off. Roy tucked the old stumps under his armpit. Nelson spotted peeping handlebars and pushed his old bike upright.

The stroll home took the brothers down a narrow dusty track lined on each side with large mature oaks. The evening continued cooling. A flock of red-tailed black cockatoos formed, screeched loud, then glanced at the brothers. The birds flew in the direction of the track and then perched steady in the eucalypts.

By now the brothers were about two miles away from the Fergusons' weatherboard cottage in Ballarat.

Catching the Light

'Hang on,' said Nelson, stopping. He turned back and looked through the fence in the direction of the pitch. The sun's rays of light had covered the field with a late-afternoon golden haze. Nelson took the envelope from his shirt pocket, unfolded the letter and began sketching on the back.

'Roy, do you mind if I catch this light? It's beautiful. It'll only take a minute and I can finish it off later tonight.'

'Fine,' said Roy, 'but make it quick. We are just about past tea-time. I'm starving.'

Nelson sketched quickly but with care. His sure hand conveyed the field onto paper. He held a small pencil delicately and crafted a setting sun on the right lower edge of the page.

'That looks just like where we are,' said Roy.

'That's the idea, Roy. But it's just a start so I can build the scene in colour later,' said Nelson. 'I want to show my students some sketches at the school next week. As I keep telling them, capturing the outline and then the light is half the trick.'

'Yeh, and beating the bloody dark on our way home is a pretty good idea too—let's go, Nel'.

Quickly finishing the outline, the letter returned to its envelope and then to Nelson's pocket.

Catching Adventure

As they turned into their street, Roy flicked the ball in the air once more. 'We should tell Mum we're ready to play for Australia against the bloody Poms.'

'A lot of young chaps are already playing for Australia anyway, but against the Germans,' said Nelson. 'This war in Europe might just take plenty more of our mates there too.'

'Yes, I know,' said Roy. 'It sounds exciting; I'm going to find out more about it tomorrow. But it's on the other side of the world, Nel, and I think Mum and Dad are keeping that idea away from the dinner table, so maybe don't mention it. Unless I ask my mates at school, I can't seem to find too much about it or how to join up.'

Roy's country boot kicked another stone.

'But I know the army's in town, Nel—recruiting like mad. They want strong lads like us—well like *me*, Nel. They'll want me and they might even be interested in you, Nel.' Roy laughed.

'Yeh, perhaps they might if they fall short on numbers,' said Nelson. 'But anyway, you're too short, Roy. They're not going to let you volunteer.'

'We'll see about that. I reckon I can easily make myself look older—lots of my mates have got through that way,' replied Roy.

Nelson stopped suddenly, raising road dust. He turned to Roy. Nelson patted his shirt pocket. 'I've been offered teaching work full time in Warrnambool—Mr Harbrow gave me the offer letter today.'

'I thought you wanted to go to Melbourne,' said Roy.

'I did, but the Education Department reckons it has grander plans for me outside that city first.'

'Forget Warrnambool, Nel, wherever that is. Come to town with me tomorrow and we'll see whether the army will take both of us.' Roy thought it was time for some proper English: 'And let's join up with the Australian Imperial Force, old chap!'

'Very funny, Roy—war is no laughing matter. Harbrow's cousin is a senior officer in the British Army. He tells me the fighting has been appalling so far. We don't know what might be in store for those who join up.'

'But we could go bright and early to the Town Hall.'

'The place we're going is home for tea.' Nelson laughed. He added, 'If you really want to have a run at the idea, talk to Mum and Dad about it tonight at tea.'

'No way,' said Roy adamantly. 'I'm not up for that level of conflict! They'll stop me if I tell them what I want to do. My mates are either joining up with their parents' consent or joining up then they're telling their folks. Either way, they're bloody joining up, Nel.'

'Let's see,' said Nelson. 'Let's see what Mum and Dad say.'

The front door closed on the remaining summer light. The two brothers charged down the hall for a wash and family tucker.

Serious Family Concerns

James Ferguson turned into Peel Street, Ballarat. Large white and blue hydrangeas decorated the front verandah of the family's neat weatherboard cottage. James loved his hometown; he was a Ballarat boy, born there in 1874.

The train driver's boots were heavily worn but well kept and still strong. They came off slowly and took their usual resting place just inside the front door.

'I'm home, love,' he called down the hall.

'Good, the boys are just in too.'

Nelson's mother, Lucretia, was of European descent, born in 1869 in the small town of Smythesdale, 10 miles south of Ballarat. Her father was from Croatia but had become a naturalised citizen of the colony of Victoria in 1897. Lucretia was beautiful, as was her singing voice. Audiences at Ballarat's Her Majesty's Theatre, built in 1899, had heard it regularly. Lucretia had come from a long line of European artists and musicians. She drew her children in that direction whenever she could. All of her children, including Nelson, had responded to her encouragement and had natural talent as artists and musicians.

Lucretia carefully placed the bowls of soup on the table. Nelson and Roy were now joined by their siblings: young John aged 10, Hilda, 15, and Alice, 20.

'Dad, you should have seen Nel's catch out in the back paddock. It was a ripper,' said Roy. 'I reckon he could play for Australia.'

'I'm sure it was,' said his father.

'What happened on the track, Dad?' asked Roy.

'It was a long journey out to Learmonth, then back home in the afternoon. Then we went to the pub. The AIF was there recruiting lads by shouting beers.'

'A mate at school told me you can enlist this Monday outside the Town Hall,' said Roy.

'You won't be doing that,' said Lucretia firmly. 'You have better things to do. Anyway, the papers are saying the war will be over very soon.'

Nelson's father agreed. 'Roy, you must know you should not be joining up. Anyway your mother is right; this war will end soon enough. It'll be over before you get there, son. The papers all say so. Europe will return to normal and as far as this family is concerned this strife abroad is no business of ours.'

'But some of my mates have already joined up and others want to,' declared Roy. 'They say there's a lot left in this fight. And I've heard from a mate that the AIF might end up letting anyone in.'

'War is not for this family,' declared James.

'Yes,' agreed Lucretia. 'I don't want you going anywhere near it and certainly not near the army's recruitment activities. They have particular ways of getting the numbers up, and they're good at it.'

Lucretia looked at both boys with a mother's eyes. 'You have to build your lives. This war will only destroy them. I don't want to discuss it anymore and I don't want it mentioned in this house or between you.'

Roy glanced across to Nelson, then studied his soup.

Nelson took the envelope from his pocket. 'I've got some news, Mum and Dad. I've been offered a job in Warrnambool starting as soon as possible. Mr Harbrow gave it to me this morning.'

'That's wonderful news!' said Lucretia. Nelson's father reached across the table and placed his hand on Nelson's shoulder.

Lucretia beamed. For Lucretia, Warrnambool was as far away from the conflict in Europe as she could have hoped for.

'Yes, this is the best news, son.'

Gallipoli and the Anzacs—28 April 1915

On 28 April 1915, Nelson headed down to the newsagent in Ballarat's Main Street.

'One *Courier*, please sir,' requested Nelson.

Nelson flipped open the folded paper. A large lump formed in his throat. He flopped onto the street bench, gasping at the news from the war.

The headline on page 1 read:

'Attack at Dardenelles. Victorious Bombardment. Disembarkation of Troops. Large Force Established.'

The article told Nelson that Australian troops were now heavily involved in battle in Turkey as part of its effort in supporting Britain and its allies in their attempt to defeat the enemy.

Nelson read on. According to the newspaper, on 25 April 1915, Australian, New Zealand and other Entente forces had stormed the coastline of Gallipoli before sunrise, despite serious opposition from an enemy behind strong entrenchments.

The landing operations were completely successful, and before nightfall a large force of troops had been established ashore. The landing of the army continues.

'My God,' whispered Nelson, head in hands. 'Roy mustn't try to volunteer. Christ.'

The British strategy was to take control of the Dardanelles, and in turn to limit the enemy's main supply route to Russia where Germany had opened up an Eastern Front. Using the infantry to invade the adjacent peninsula of Gallipoli had arisen because the British Navy had failed to secure the Dardanelles some months earlier.

The Australians and New Zealanders taking to the shores on 25 April 1915 were known as 'Anzacs'. The name 'Anzac' had been born in a hotel in Cairo in 1914. Documents were being sent there to the 'A and NZ Army Corps', causing a British officer, Lieutenant AT White, to suggest the name Anzac. The leader of the Australian and New Zealand forces at the time, Lieutenant General Birdwood, also a British officer, decided to approve the term. At Gallipoli, Birdwood had requested that Australians and New Zealanders be known as

'Anzac' and that the primary landing place there be called Anzac Cove. Soon those who fought there were being called Anzacs.

After the landing, His Majesty the King told the Australian Government 'that Australian troops had indeed proved themselves worthy sons of the Empire'.

The day after Nelson had read the *Ballarat Courier*, 29 April 1915, the Assistant Minister for Defence told the Australian Parliament that 'the Government would send to the seat of war what the Imperial Government require'.

Later in the Gallipoli campaign, when bullets were not whizzing (and sometimes when they were) bronzed naked Australians dipped at the beaches—as they had done back home.

Upbeat Reports and Strong Sentiments—May 1915

Upbeat versions of how the young Australians at Gallipoli had fared were soon everywhere. In the *Town and Country Journal* of 12 May 1915, the following account of Gallipoli was given:

It was a great achievement to land in the dark on a coast where the enemy's strength was unknown, and, having driven the Turks back, to hold the country firmly, while reinforcements followed. Every one of those who are taking part in the action against the Turks will appreciate the words of General Birdwood, who said he could not sufficiently praise their courage, endurance, and soldierly qualities. Though the list of casualties has brought grief to many homes, there is consolation in the thought that all our men at the front are fighting gloriously for the defence of the Empire. Many more thousands of young men are giving their services, and in course of time will join their comrades in the battle line. And in the coming years the memory of all those who fought in the greatest war the world has ever seen, and in the severest crisis through which the Empire has ever passed, will be handed down from generation to generation with pardonable pride.

On the same day as the *Journal* had been published, a fellow teacher of Nelson's, Jeannie Dobson from Ballarat Agricultural High, wrote to the wounded in hospital abroad. The letter read:

Dear Australian Boys, every Australian woman's heart this week is thrilling with pride, with exaltation, and while her eyes fill with tears she springs up as I did when the story in this Saturday's *Argus* was finished and says, 'Thank God, I am an Australian'. Boys you have honoured our land; you, the novices, the untrained, the untaught in war's grim school, have done the deeds of veterans. Oh, how we honour you; how we glory in your matchless bravery, in your yet more wonderful fortitude, which the war correspondent says was evinced so marvellously as your boatloads of wounded cheered and waved amid their pain as you were rowed back to the vessels!

What gave you the courage for the heroic dash to the ridge, boys? British grit, Australians' nerve and determination to do or die, a bit of primeval man's love of a big fight against heavy odds.

God's help too, surely.

The school's motto was *Duty Always*.

In the letter the Ballarat teacher noted:

With God the ultimate issue rests. We can only leave you in His hands. Ask Him to soothe your pain, heal your bodies, recoup your lost strength, give you grace and help, that 'You may live to fight again, and to strike another blow.'

Australia's newspapers (as early as 1850 there were some 50 papers from Perth to Brisbane) soon published the letter. It was also published in British papers, described as 'stirring and touching'.

Right across the cities and towns of Australia including Ballarat, Australians had been anxious about how the young Australian soldiers would fare in battle. That anxiety had now vanished with the triumphant news of how the boys had handled themselves abroad.

'Come on,' encouraged Roy to his siblings sitting in the Ferguson family lounge room, 'it's time for this family to sing together.'

Roy had eagerly bought the newly written patriotic song from the newsagent: 'What Do You Think of Australia Now?' which had been written by Felix Le Roy with lyrics by JW Benson.

Lucretia looked ashen-faced at Roy. 'That's not a song for this house, Roy.'

'Come on Mum,' cried Roy. 'It's only a song.' Roy looked down, studying the sheet music.

They're missing from the Factory and they're missing from the Farm.

They're missing from the City Office too.

They heard the call of duty and they bravely shouldered arms,

Like ev'ry true Australian Son should do.

Far away from home and loved ones they have sailed across the sea,

To protect our King and country, and our glorious liberty.

Around the Rotunda—Warrnambool, Early July 1915

By July 1915, Nelson was living in the Victorian coastal town of Warrnambool. He had just begun teaching at the local junior technical school. The school had a long and proud record (schooling had been free, except for music tuition, and compulsory in Victoria since 1873).

The town was the birthplace of one of Australia's most famous songs. The tune had been played there at the 1894 horse races by the Warrnambool Militia Artillery Band, in the form of an old Scottish tune named 'The Bonnie Wood of Craigielea'. A month or so later, the Australian poet, Banjo Paterson, put words to it, calling it 'Waltzing Matilda'.

Nelson now found himself again with cornet in hand, this time under the new rotunda in the beautiful botanical gardens. But now the band was ready for a different tune: a military march in support of the AIF's current recruitment endeavours, a sound to give dignity to the job of collecting young men to kill others.

The gleaming buttons and badges of the Warrnambool A-grade brass band flashed themselves across the rotunda.

Warrnambool's rich architectural history was more than just fine local pubs and hotels. The rotunda (built in 1913 at a cost of £297) was a fine structure. It could house many a splendid band or other public event, and often did. Today was no exception.

The army's large green recruitment tent, diagonal to the rotunda, was makeshift by comparison. Its canvas walls flapped like sheets on a clothes line. In gaps, young men stretched out from it for about 100 yards. Army recruiting had been in full swing since shortly after the outbreak of war some 11 months earlier. The Australian Government had set demanding monthly targets, and they were (at least for now) being met.

This small coastal town was no exception; it had already volunteered a great number of its strong young men to assist the Empire fight the enemy. Many of the boys from Warrnambool, as with Nelson's own town of Ballarat, had volunteered early. The AIF's Gallipoli campaign had started some three months earlier; some of the boys in that campaign had already returned home. Of course the recruits today were not replacements; they were, according to the AIF, part of the 'consolidation' of the war effort.

Nelson held his shiny silver cornet high, waiting for the band to fire up again. As the baton swirled so too did 'Invercargill'. The strong sound volleyed out of the rotunda and into the generous garden area surrounding it. The context was now being set for a prosperous army recruitment drive.

As the band turned into the Coda, Nelson's cornet bell showed him more young local lads approaching and then joining the volunteers' line. Nelson could also see an AIF officer stepping up into the rotunda. He was fit and well kept.

'This bloke's got the army's most potent weapon,' whispered one trombone player to another. 'Yeh,' said the other, 'purpose.'

The officer stepped forward next to the band conductor just as the last note of the march struck. The bandmaster then placed his baton carefully on the lip of the music stand.

'Right, boys. Colonel Briggs of the AIF recruitment section will now say a few words.'

'Thank you, sir,' said Briggs, invading the rotunda. He paused, looking out over the young Australian potential recruits. With the full authority of the AIF, his large head slowly pivoted on his muscular neck. Laps held instruments stone still.

'Gentlemen, may I say you are doing a fine job assisting our work to recruit these splendid examples of the young local manhood within this town. By the end of last year, over 50,000 Australian men had enlisted to assist the Empire. Of course, more have enlisted since.'

'But this is, I am afraid, still significantly short of the further commitment Australia could make to mother England. According to our estimates, there are some 800,000 more eligible fighting men in this fine nation of some five million people. Those who sailed to Turkey and who are now fighting at Gallipoli are the fittest, strongest and most ardent in the land.' Briggs again paused. 'I have every reason to believe that you too may fall into that category.'

'Men, the point has come to consider your own positions.' Briggs surveyed the band slowly.

'I want the whole band now to rise and show this generous public how much its members are behind the war effort. By joining that volunteer line over there you will be demonstrating your commitment to the Empire's future.'

The officer took the baton and thrust it towards the recruitment tent.

'That steely glare under that bloody moustache is go'na put more blokes in France than any call to arms,' muttered the trombonist. 'Yeh,' said the other, 'that's the army's best chance by far.'

'As band members,' the colonel continued, 'you will, if you volunteer, in accordance with the longest of traditions of fighting men, likely be placed with the medical corps as stretcher-bearers.'

Nelson stared at the recruitment tent, then back at Briggs. He had just been told that his experience and profile fitted perfectly the role of the stretcher-bearer within an ambulance unit. A unit that might one day be in Europe as part of the Allies' war effort.

Bearer work was as deadly as infantry due to its close proximity to battle; bearers had to recover the sick and wounded from 'no-man's-land'—the ground between the two opposing armies. Frequently, bearers would be expected to work in full view of machine-gunners or artillery observers. They also had to perform strenuous duties on the battlefield. Both character and frame were pressed to the limit in the role.

'Thank you, Colonel. You heard him boys!' willed the bandmaster.

'Off you go then. We want that line as long as the British Government requires,' demanded Briggs.

Nelson cased his cornet and with the others spilled out of the rotunda and pooled near the volunteer tent.

Until this point, Nelson had no thought that the invitation to 'volunteer' would be offered. But the life-changing proposition just put to him had also been broadcast to all the public listening to the recruitment music.

Dutifully, one after the other, band members did the only honourable thing. The line into the tent was now growing like a snake out of its hole. Nelson fell in behind another cornet player, followed by one of the trombonists.

Time to Volunteer

After some time, Nelson stood in the middle of the flapping army tent, shivering in the wintery conditions.

Nelson stepped forward towards the recruitment officer sitting behind a long wooden trestle table.

'Name?'

'Nelson Harold Ferguson, sir.'

'Address?'

'Care of 52 Peel Street, Ballarat. I've only just started my teaching duties this month here at Warrnambool Junior Technical School,.'

The officer had a good long look at Nelson. 'I guess that's why we haven't seen you in this tent before, Ferguson,' snapped the officer.

'That's right, sir. But I'm also too short for the AIF. They told me that back in Ballarat. I'm only 5 feet 5 ¼ inches.'

'That may have been correct,' retorted the officer. 'But I am pleased to tell you that last month in its wisdom the National Recruitment Office determined that the height requirement would be appropriately adjusted. In the circumstances of Britain's war effort, and this nation's contribution to it, the minimum height requirement is now 5 feet 2. You now qualify, son.'

The recruitment officer was right. The AIF had now done what the British Army had done in late 1914—source more men by lowering the height standard. (In June 1915, it had also extended the range of eligible ages to 18–45 years.) The AIF had made its adjustment in June 1915. In the 10 months before doing so, approximately one-third of all volunteers had been knocked back because of the failure to meet the 'elite' requirements. Now, nearly a year into the war, the army had found itself pulling up short on the numbers it could send over to fight alongside the British Army.

The officer's demanding eyes looked up. 'I think you should consider yourself as having volunteered, Ferguson.'

'Very good, sir,' said Nelson.

Nelson suddenly felt dizzy and disoriented. He had been told he could not join the AIF because of his height. The Warrnambool teaching job had been taken on that basis. But the army had apparently, by one simple stroke of amended regulation, changed all that. And with it, perhaps the rest of Nelson's life.

'Write down your full details here, Ferguson. We'll organise a medical for you and then get you signed up formally. From the look of you, you're a fit and able young man and you'll surely be on one of our ships to Europe as soon as the AIF can arrange it.'

The shuffling line took Nelson to the next officer who gathered further details.

'Natural born. 23 years, 2 months. School teacher. Two years Education Department. Single. *Discharged from any part of His Majesty's Forces, with ignominy or as incorrigible and worthless or on account of conviction of felony, or dismissed with disgrace from the Navy?* No.'

'You're in the brass band, Ferguson, as I understand it,' said the officer. 'You can either enter the infantry or, more likely, you will be allocated to the medical corp. In any event, that is a matter for later. Here are the details of where you must go,' said the officer." 'But first please go to the tent adjacent to this one for a medical examination.'

With information sheet in hand, Nelson turned out of the tent and headed to the next one to be medically assessed.

Seeing the Required Distance

The examining officer wore a floor-length bleached-white coat. After first assessing Nelson from a distance, the officer looked over Nelson carefully, noting on a separate army form his age, height, chest measurement, complexion, eye colour, hair colour and religious denomination.

The officer then undertook a series of tests for some 20 minutes.

'One more test Ferguson,' instructed the officer.

'Would you now look at the chart on the wall and read the letters.'

Nelson then read the letters.

'That's the bloody bottom line, Ferguson. You are supposed to start with the large letters at the top. You can obviously see the required bloody distance.'

'Sorry sir'.

'Never mind, you have excellent vision—the best I have examined so far. The army needs blokes like you. A keen eye is a keen soldier. I have assessed you as fit for military service, Ferguson.'

The examining officer looked down, swiping his signature on the form. It read:

I have examined the above-named person, and find that he does not present any of the following conditions, viz:-

Scrofula; phthisis, syphilis, impaired constitution, defective intelligence, defects of vision, voice or hearing, hernia, haemorrhoids, varicose veins, beyond a limited extent, marked varicocele with unusually pendent testicle, inveterate cutaneous disease, chronic ulcers, traces of corporal punishment, or evidence of having been marked with the letters D or BC (tattoos imposed by the British Army signifying deserter or bad character), contracted or deformed chest, abnormal curvature of spine, or any other disease or physical defect calculated to unfit him for the duties of a soldier.

He can see the required distance with either eye; his heart and lungs are healthy; he has the free use of his joints and limbs; and he declares he is not subject to fits of any description.

I consider him fit for active service.

Signature of Examining Medical Officer.

An Oath to His Majesty

A short, pale-faced recruiting officer crouched over a scribbled form.

The head of the form read:

Australian Imperial Forces—Attestation Paper of Persons Enlisted for Service Abroad.

The officer wrote on the 'for unit' line: 'Special Medical Recruit, Harefield, England' and the date, 12 July 1915.

'Ferguson, in the first instance you will be assigned to the Convalescent Depot, Harefield Park Hospital, north of London, England, as a medical recruit. The hospital services injured Australians. That is what boys from your band will do. You are a special reinforcement—they are short-staffed.'

'Yes sir.'

The form spun towards Nelson.

'You are now required to take the Oath of Service to His Majesty the King. Before me, would you please hold this Bible in your right hand held high and now read aloud the following, then date and sign the oath.'

'I will.'

Nelson held the Bible to head height.

'I, Nelson Harold Ferguson, swear that I will well and truly serve our Sovereign Lord the King in the Australian Imperial Force until the end of the War, and a further period of four months thereafter unless sooner lawfully discharged, dismissed, or removed therefrom; and that I will resist His Majesty's enemies and cause His Majesty's peace to be kept and maintained; and that I will in all matters appertaining to my service, faithfully discharge my duty according to law. SO HELP ME GOD.'

The oath had rested patiently within the 3rd Schedule to the *Defence Act* since its enactment in 1903, two years after Australia's birth as a nation. The legal architecture built in that year in aid of the defence of Australia and the British Empire was now being put to active use, some 12 years later.

'You are required to be in Melbourne next month. The AIF will deliver you there, reconfirm your medical condition, and then you will commence basic training at Broadmeadows outside Melbourne, for a period of four months.'

'Very good, sir,' said Nelson.

'You should now inform the Education Department as soon as possible that this change of course is upon you. The army will do so concurrently.'

'I will,' said Nelson.

'You have done right by your country, and by His Majesty, young man. There is nothing further this office requires of you at this stage.'

'Before you take ease, Ferguson, I should explain three things to you. First, in the AIF I can assure you that you will always know what to do—because you will be told. Second, you will always know whether you are doing it well enough, because you will be told. And third, there is the question of your future in the force. This, the AIF cannot tell you, for obvious reasons. But I can give you this assurance lad: the AIF will look after you during the war with appropriate food, supplies and leadership.'

'Pleased to hear that, sir.'

One Further Commitment

'Will that be all for now?' asked Nelson.

The officer looked sternly at Ferguson.

'There is one further commitment the army makes, Ferguson. Should need be, it will also look after you at war's end. It will go on doing so for the rest of your life. Its obligation is to those who have given to it, and that undertaking is made by the whole of the Commonwealth itself.'

Nelson looked back at the officer. Sweat beaded above Nelson's wide-open eyes. Nelson could hear his pulse.

'I am grateful for that too, sir.'

'All right. You are dismissed, Private.'

Complete Control

As he walked out the door, Nelson realised that, at 23, the rest of his life was supposed to be a long time. The penny had suddenly dropped this might not be the case for him.

The voice in Nelson's head told him to have a new eye on what this adventure might deliver up, including the wonders of travel abroad. He would see European art and architecture first hand. The AIF would train him. He could sketch and paint the glorious churches of Europe. And he would be with his newfound mates.

But it would also be true that he would be far from Warrnambool, far from Ballarat, and far from Australia. As a member of a medical unit, battle would be his workplace and that work would be to recover and treat the injured and comfort the dying.

Nelson knew he could be lucky, but then again providence might not work his way; it could all come to an abrupt end at any time.

Bewildered by this turn of events and with chest thumping, Nelson looked back at the sign marked 'Recruitment Office'. He suddenly realised one vital thing.

The AIF now had complete control of his future, and was now deploying it.

Reporting Home—July 1915

Nelson shifted his grip on the handset. A telephone line from Warrnambool to Ballarat had been established since 1898.

'Hello Mum, it's me. I'm in Warrnambool.'

'Lovely to hear from you, son, are you all right? Has the teaching started yet?'

'Mum, I'm on my way to Broadmeadows for army training.'

Lucretia was suddenly breathless. 'What do you mean, dear?'

'The entire brass band has just joined up, Mum. Not sure what to make of it, Mum, but don't worry, they say the training is going to be really good. I'm going to be stationed at a convalescence hospital overseas. And I might be put into the medical corps or possibly the field ambulance. They say if that happens we'll be back from the battle line. I'm being sent for more training later. But first I'll be home to see you, Mum, so don't worry.'

'But the army rejected you, darling'.

'They did, Mum, but they reckon I'm eligible now. They want me to be part of it. Mum, I gave the king the oath yesterday.'

A mother's hand trembled. 'Come home as soon as you can Nelson. Come home.'

'I will, Mum,' assured Nelson.

A mother held the telephone and slowly turned. 'The army has taken our boy.'

PART 1

The War—to Mid-1915

Well before Nelson had taken the oath to the king in July 1915, World War I had taken a terrible turn. The German Army had begun with the high ambition of victory within just six weeks. Only weeks into the war, on land Germany was doing well and was only 22 miles from Paris. Things for the Allies were indeed desperate. All resources were being deployed to repel the enemy at the doorstep of France's capital. The military governor of that city had commandeered some 700 small taxis to transport thousands of French troops in record time to attack the right flank of the German invaders.

But the Germans had inexplicably withdrawn critical numbers from the front because of a perceived significant threat on the Eastern Front in Russia.

When the Germans realised they would be unable to take Paris, they went north, and each enemy then sought to turn the other's western flank to achieve a knockout blow. These manoeuvres in October and early November 1914 gave rise to the First Battle of Ypres, in Belgium. In October 1914 alone, the British Army sustained 58,000 casualties.

The thorns of war had spilt blood everywhere. By now huge numbers of soldiers had died: as at November 1914, one-third of the original British Imperial Forces were dead. These dead boys were not army blunders; they were the result of planned assaults on a fortified and dug-in enemy. The strategy of the 'planned attack' with huge casualties was now the mainstay of the British and French attack on the enemy.

And Britain's sea blockage was having devastating effects on Germany—more than 60 per cent of German merchant shipping had been impounded, leading to huge food shortages. Germans were asked to store canned meat, leading to *Schweinemord* (the slaughter of five million pigs).

The new year had remained grim. The Germans had made significant advances, capturing a vast 19,500 square miles of French and Belgium territory. The British had recovered a mere eight square miles, at a cost of 250,000 casualties.

Nelson had, by taking the oath, signed on to industrialised violence on the battlefields of Europe. The *Ballarat Courier* had been telling

Nelson for some time that because infantry charges had simply become events of carnage given the effectiveness of machine guns and grenades, the warring parties had 'dug in' - by building long deep trenches. Massive trench systems were now emerging across France. And it was not long before huge guns were being deployed to knock out the trenches, enabling young men to charge again at the enemy across treacherous open ground in the hope of taking territory before the enemy could put machine guns back into position.

The motto of Germany's highest military training school was that principles of strategy must never transcend common sense. Everyone was ignoring it.

In April 1915, the British Army marched to its doom at Loos, suffering one of the greatest military defeats in history. In May 1915, the Chancellor of the Exchequer in Britain had told the public that there was no doubt as to the result of the war, only its duration. But a quick and decisive victory by anyone was now completely illusory.

Although Nelson did not know it, the mindless actions on both sides were all now going to be focused in two places in Europe. The Commander-in-Chief of the British Army, Sir Douglas Haig, had made it clear in March 1915 that the Allies could not hope to win the war until the German Army had been defeated in the two places it counted most. If Nelson were to be in combat with the AIF in defence of the Empire, in all likelihood it would be in these very two countries.

France and Belgium.

Becoming a Soldier—July 1915

On 17 July 1915, five days after Nelson gave the oath to serve king and country, the warrant officer on behalf of the commanding officer of the 70th Infantry 'Ballarat Regiment' certified that Private N H Ferguson had returned 'all Arms and Equipment to his Regiment'.

Back in Melbourne, on 18 July 1915, the first repatriated wounded soldiers from Gallipoli began arriving. Those who could walk marched from the ship. Mates carried those who could not.

Wherever he went, Nelson could see the army's recruitment posters calling for others to pitch in as replacements. It read 'Come Lads. Give us a spell.'

The army soon had Nelson on the train to Broadmeadows. There, he would start his contribution to the war effort. He had already answered the poster's call. He would begin his six-week induction into the AIF.

The simple fact was that the army required every soldier to learn how to work closely with others, to understand their commands and moreover to have an understanding of the enemy; those learnings would be essential to survival.

The army told Nelson he would qualify as an Australian soldier before the end of 1915. He would then be given the AIF's slouch hat, with its proud 'rising sun' badge as drawn by Nelson's own students. And he would thereafter be deemed ready for service abroad.

As the AIF called it, he would be 'taken on strength'.

To Kill the Enemy, You Need to See It—July 1915

The battles now in Europe were requiring huge numbers of new and capable troops to replace dead and injured ones. The sufficient supply of young men was proving extremely difficult for all nations, particularly Britain.

That was not the only supply problem. Keeping hundreds of thousands of soldiers at fighting strength required the continuous production and supply of vast quantities of raw materials (such as oil) and industrial products (the Germans called this *Materialschlacht*).

The long distances of battle required high-grade optical products. Optics now played a crucial role both strategically and tactically, through the use of aerial reconnaissance cameras, periscopes, telescopic sights and binoculars.

Nelson's eyes had been put to stringent testing before he was eligible to swear the oath to the king. Nelson had passed with flying colours, assessed as having 20–20 vision. But a soldier without excellent optics was an ineffective or dead one.

By mid-1915, the British had begun to run out of these essential eye aids. A public appeal produced some 2000 pairs of binoculars but this was well short of requirements.

The British soon struck on the solution: supply would come from the best manufacturer of binoculars in the world, Germany. In exchange for products Germany was short on, such as rubber, it agreed to supply Britain with tens of thousands of binoculars. By the end of August 1915, the Germans had supplied Britain with some 32,000 binoculars, 20,000 of which were of the higher quality for British officers.

Although Nelson did not know it, the war had become an unstoppable and mad pursuit of victory no matter how much death might be involved and no matter how appalling arrangements for war might become.

The End of Leave—September 1915

As the Australian spring approached, Nelson took leave and spent it in Ballarat with his family.

Too soon it was time for Nelson to return to the remaining weeks of army training at Broadmeadows near Melbourne. He would embark for England before the end of the year.

Lucretia and Nelson stared down the track at the grand Ballarat railway station.

'I'm sure it will come soon, Mum.'

'I wish it wouldn't,' said Lucretia.

'It was so good to be home, Mum.'

'My darling boy, I have told you this before. Above all else, you must look after yourself. Think of your safety first. We want you home. You have already had a great start as a teacher. Your father and I want to see you back here soon and getting on with life.'

'Sure, Mum, me too. I'll be home before the end of this summer coming I reckon. That's what the army's told me. Anyway, they've also just told me that I'll definitely be starting at the Harefield hospital just outside London—that's miles from any fighting. That's where they fix Australian soldiers. That's the good work I want to do anyway.'

'Well as long as you stay in the medical corp, and not as a soldier, your father and I will not worry so much. Please stay away from the guns. I can't bear to think of you anywhere near them.'

'I'll do my best, Mum. I'll write to you and Dad as much as I can. I might even get some time to do some sketching or work with my paints. I'll send that too if the army lets me.'

'Only if you get the chance, darling.'

The train puffed closer. Lucretia gripped her son's hand.

'You must do what you have to do, my beautiful boy. But do it safely.'

'I will, Mum. But don't worry, I'll see you again when we sail off. The army can't tell me when that might be. The ships come in to Melbourne with returned soldiers and then go out, when needed, with fresh ones.'

Smoke billowed under the train's wheels as it screeched to a halt in front of a line of mothers with sons.

Nelson stepped up into the carriage along with dozens of other soldiers. The train's whistle sounded the start of the unknown.

Hands waved farewells to boarding volunteers. After a time, mothers' eyes watched a bullet-sized train being swallowed by the horizon.

Character Building—September 1915

Nelson was soon back at Broadmeadows learning how to be a wartime soldier. Despite his considerable compulsory military training before the war, the AIF was now 're-training' him—mainly by endless drills and exhausting physical exercise. This was largely directed at getting him ready to do things which in peacetime would be regarded as inconceivable.

And to do them without question. To act as told, despite fear.

The army well knew that Nelson's resolve, required for the real business of fighting, could only be built by a constant course of discipline and an unparalleled emphasis on service to comrade and country. Dealing with combat required character and the army had its unique ways to build Nelson's, and was now doing so.

Nelson's military training was not only to get him fit and strong. Since time immemorial military training like Nelson was now getting did a number of essential things: it built culture, preserved traditions of discipline, taught respect for authority and such behaviour under fire as would demonstrate courage and above all trust and love for comrade. Nelson's peacetime beliefs would in the course of army training be replaced by wartime ones: that authority and orders should not be questioned; that duty to comrade was higher than life itself; and that killing another person was an authorised act of warfare.

The behavioural standards which would be required of Nelson in the army would be concordant with the higher duty imposed on soldiers.

The army's work on Nelson was to build that necessary (but not sufficient) military resource for victorious armies.

The willing soldier.

A man who would fight until death, fight until wounded, or fight until ordered to stop.

Never again in his life would Nelson be part of an organisation with such a sharp-focused purpose: to defeat an enemy.

Community Support for the War—Socks and Other War Necessities—September 1915

But Nelson was not the only one doing the heavy lifting.

The war effort was supported across all community sectors. As Australia's Prime Minister, Joseph Cook, had noted in his diary: 'We have sprung at a bound at barbarism and despotism'.

Nelson's employer, the Education Department, had now established a Patriotic Fund and was holding fundraising activities. Teachers and students at Nelson's school and at other learning institutions were now selling badges in trams, buses, at railway stations and at rallies to raise money for the cause. Students in Nelson's classes and elsewhere now proudly pinned badges to their chests as symbols of contribution to the war effort.

Fundraising was ubiquitous across schools and other institutions. A patriotic concert at the old Stafford State School, Brisbane, was held in 1915. The children, dressed as nurses and soldiers, raised £52 for *The Courier* newspaper's Belgian fund.

The Red Cross also established a Belgian fund. In Nelson's hometown of Ballarat, it got support earlier in the year from the world-famous soprano, Dame Nellie Melba, who performed at the Coliseum, built in 1908 as a picture theatre.

The legal profession in Melbourne and elsewhere was also doing its bit. Earlier in the year JG Latham (later the Chief Justice of the High Court of Australia) on behalf of the Victorian Bar sent the Minister of Defence £505 that barristers had raised for the purchase of a motor ambulance for use in Europe.

And in Sydney the French–Australian League had commenced supplying 'comforts' to the troops abroad. By September 1915, some 33,000 items of clothing, such as shirts, knitted socks, pyjamas and dressing gowns had been made for the wounded. The labels read: 'Made in Australia by your friends'.

Not only the country folk in Nelson's hometown of Ballarat were raising funds—war effort support was an endeavour everywhere. A huge sheep sale in the rural town of Wagga Wagga produced £1000 for the war effort. In Newcastle, a city of New South Wales, £5000 was raised to pay for an extension to an orphanage in Normandy, France, to be called *Australie*.

From everything he had read in newspapers and heard on the radio, Nelson knew that the whole of Australia was now engaged in fervent support for Australia's contribution to the British Empire's goal of defeating Germany and its allies: from raising funds out of the pockets of the public; to rationing essentials (including chalk in classrooms at Nelson's old School of Mines); to knitting socks to keep soldiers' toes warm in Europe's deadly winters.

The *Karoola*—December 1915

From the war's outbreak, the Australian Government had taken full control of the economy, the labour force, and much of society. Legislation gave the executive arm of government virtually unlimited power to protect Australians, all the way from marshalling an army to restricting the sale of eggs.

Under the *Defence Act*, owners of vehicles, horses, mules, boats or other vessels, and any goods, were required to hand them over for military purposes if ordered (with compensation).

Using that power, the Commonwealth had been commissioning a significant number of large ships for the war effort. Their work was to carry young troops to and from Europe, as regularly and frequently as required. The troops' passage would usually pause at Egypt for supplies and for further training.

On 19 December 1915, rocking slowly at port, the *Karoola* sat ready to depart for England. She was a significant supply ship of 7391 tons with a cruising speed of 15 knots. She was now the No. 1 Hospital Ship of the AIF, requisitioned for war by the Commonwealth of Australia in May 1915. She had first embarked for Egypt carrying troops and general cargo in June 1915. While in England she had been converted to a hospital ship with beds for 463 patients.

Framed by a big blue bay adjacent to Melbourne, the large white crosses set against the *Karoola*'s hull told all her benevolent purpose.

A long line of troops moved slowly ant-like towards the main staircase bridging ship and pier. Nelson had learnt from his basic training at Broadmeadows that whatever the army did, it would be relatively well organised but could take a very long while, with long periods of idleness for no (or at least no observable) reason. He had learned, as a sergeant had shouted at him once, to 'hurry up and wait'. The simple but lengthy task of embarkation was falling straight into that category of task.

Nelson looked out across the army's tight control over the embarkation process. Some days earlier, some 500 wounded Australian soldiers had arrived in the bay and had been conveyed through the streets of Melbourne in motorcars before being taken to base hospital. The public was overwhelmingly enthusiastic, the streets thronging with people. One of the first to land was Corporal Moorhead, who had lost an arm and a leg at Gallipoli. Fifty-six motorcars were provided by the local automobile club and were waiting by the pier at Port Melbourne. The returned heroes were driven through the city in comfort. A number of girls and youths had invaded the vehicles, sitting on the soldiers' knees, and even on fragile car hoods. Both soldiers and car owners protested this; the men because of their injured limbs; and the motorists because of the damage to the cars. The police had been instructed to prevent joy riding.

'Mum, they're calling me to join the queue onto the ship,' said Nelson.

Lucretia gripped her son's hand. 'I suppose you had better go, dear.'

'This boat looks pretty sturdy, Mum. It might be a hospital ship but it's got some pretty big guns on the stern. Don't worry. They told us the Germans won't even fire on us with that big white cross.'

Nelson pointed to the side of the ship. A mother's hand pressed tighter. 'You must be sure to look after yourself, son—do that, above all else.'

'Thanks, Mum, I will. But I'm going to help the blokes injured in battle. I won't be caught up in the fighting—the army has already told me that. I can't be looking after the wounded if I'm injured myself. Don't worry, Mum and Dad. This job is the right one for me.'

Bound hands released and Nelson turned towards the hospital ship.

Nelson's boots shuffled slowly, close to others, towards the staircase reaching onto the boat. The task was undemanding but the summer's sun had sweat pooling on soldiers' foreheads.

Nelson looked back towards Port Melbourne. He could now see over 1000 soldiers about to be sent to harm's way.

The *Karoola* would be Nelson's home for the next six weeks. He had been told his initial pay would be five shillings per week. But like all soldiers, three shillings would be 'deferred' and only 'issuable' on completion of service with the Expeditionary Force.

Large numbers of family members now milled close to the ship as if waiting to board themselves. Soldiers caught streamers and kisses along the high railings. Nelson spotted Roy waving wildly at him next to Mum and Dad. As he waved back, he caught a red unravelling streamer. He could see Roy mouth 'Great catch'. Nelson mouthed back 'Yes, six but not out'.

Nelson uncased his box brownie, looked directly down into it, and took a snap of the thronging families. He could see his own nestled among them. He then checked in his coat for the small Bible his mother had given him earlier in the week. He patted the sacred book twice.

He also checked for his new diary. It was there too. Nelson had earlier pencilled in it:

Please return this to 52 Peel Street, Ballarat, Victoria, should it be found on my body.

Nelson held his hand high for some time, gave one final wave, and with the others turned into the corridor of the top deck.

After the *Karoola* had travelled about three hours down Port Phillip Bay, Nelson passed the holiday town of Sorrento, just before 'the Heads', Bass Strait, and the ocean beyond. More than a year earlier, on 5 August 1914, the British, and in turn Australia, had declared war on Germany. Some three hours and 45 minutes into the conflict, Australia had fired the first shot from Coastal Artillery Gun Emplacement No. 6 at Fort Nepean. The shot had prevented the German merchant vessel, SS *Pfalz*, from escaping Port Phillip Bay to the open seas.

Now the international anger Nelson was heading for would be sending its own shot across his bow.

And likely much worse.

The Great Australian Bight

The *Karoola* pressed onwards and out of Port Phillip Bay, turning west towards England, and war.

It hugged the coast of the magnificent Great Australian Bight, with its hundreds of miles of broad yellow Australian beaches, then journeyed on to Perth in Western Australia.

In the late 1820s, the British, fearing that France would make a colony in Western Australia, had founded Perth. France ultimately decided to ignore Australia. As a consequence, until its birth in 1901, Australia was the sole possession of Britain.

When he arrived there on 23 December 1915, Nelson disembarked the *Karoola* and soon boarded a train at the dock. It took him straight into the city and sightseeing.

Perth was hot but not unpleasant. Nelson pencilled in his diary: 'Perth a glorious pleasure resort'.

Shortly after Nelson had re-embarked, the *Karoola* headed west and out to sea. The last Australian lighthouse blinked at him one last time.

Nelson wrote in his diary: 'Beginning to feel that friends and home are a long way off'.

The 1915 report of the Public Service Commissioner of Victoria addressed to His Excellency the Governor in Council for the State of Victoria commenced with the list of persons on the permanent staff of the Victorian Public Service. It included those from the Department of 'Public Instruction' who now formed part of the Expeditionary Forces as at 31 December 1915.

The name 'N H Ferguson' was one of the 38 teachers so listed from the Department of Public Instruction. These men were part of a total of 309 volunteers for active duty from Victorian State Departments. In addition, 307 State School teachers volunteered for active service. The 1915 report paid tribute to the teachers and other volunteers: 'All honour is due to these officers and teachers for their patriotism and courage in going forth to brave the dangers and horrors of war, and we mourn the loss of many who have already given their lives.'

The Close of 1915—An Early Heavy Toll

By 19 December 1915, Nelson had sailed for England. Unbeknownst to him, on that same day the AIF began evacuating the last of its men from the disaster that had been the 'Gallipoli campaign' in Turkey.

The AIF successfully evacuated all by the next day. Brudenell White, the author of the mobilisation plans for Australia's initial contribution to the war effort, had magnificently planned and supervised the evacuation of some 80,000 men. His plan, a tactical masterpiece, had stolen the enemy's attention, having them believe that the Australians were merely preparing for Gallipoli's winter.

During the eight months of the campaign, the Anzacs had shown incalculable acts of bravery. One of Nelson's co-reservists in the 70th Infantry Ballarat Regiment back in July 1914 was William Dunstan. Dunstan had fought at the Battle of Lone Pine on Gallipoli. During the course of the action on 9 August 1915, Dunstan was temporally blinded by an explosion and was evacuated and treated for head and eye injuries. For his conspicuous acts of bravery in the face of the enemy, Dunstan received the Empire's highest honour for acts of valour in the face of the enemy, the Victoria Cross (introduced as a war medal in 1856).

The anabranch of AIF activity which had been Gallipoli was now over as AIF troops began to be re-assigned to the Western Front in France. The war was continuing to rage there and would no doubt escalate. At this stage, the Germans were the masters of the battlefield.

The war had already placed a heavy toll on all, including the leadership of each national army. Because of the carnage of British troops on the Western Front, their leader, Sir John French, had now been replaced by Sir Douglas Haig. Haig was given the clearest 'special task' by Lord Kitchener: to drive the enemy from Belgium and France. A self-assured man, Haig would draw on a profound source, encouraging his chaplains to preach the cause of war for the good of humanity.

The French General Marshall Petain had decided that given the resourcing of the combatants, beating Germany would not be possible until it had been exhausted, both militarily and morally. He therefore ordered that there should be limited but regular operations against it, with a possible breakthrough planned later to reach the enemy's communications. It had been learnt that attempting to overwhelm Germany by massive artillery strike merely nullified the element of surprise.

It followed that for the next year or so at least, attrition would be the Allies' overarching strategy on the Western Front, with sporadic abortive assaults. This inevitably meant large numbers of hungry, cold or dead soldiers on both sides. Between August 1914 and December 1915, 2.5 million British men had volunteered only to end up part of the horrendous carnage across vast and appalling landscapes of mud, busted cities and towns, and countries deliberately shredding entire generations of young men.

That Other Foreign Place

As Nelson continued on the *Karoola* towards Europe, wireless messages were read to him and the other troops on deck, telling them about the war. The news was hard to piece together. But there was a much greater puzzle: Nelson was still trying to understand how it was that one day he had been playing his cornet under a rotunda, and on what seemed like the next day, he was on a huge hospital ship sailing for England.

Nelson's path to the slaughter of the Western Front was now set. Britain and France desperately needed as many young Australians as possible to help break Germany's deep hold on large parts of France and prevent the fruition of its desire to push yet deeper. All those who could fight or help, including those from the dominions, would ultimately be called on to do so. In Australia's case, it would only ever be volunteers.

But first, medical work of the kind Nelson would be doing required specific training. He was now on his way to receive it. The AIF had special facilities in England for this very purpose. They would provide Nelson with his next stop along the inexorable journey towards that other foreign place.

The theatre of war.

A 'Call to Arms'—23 December 1915

Four days after Nelson had set sail, Roy stepped out of the Ferguson family home in Ballarat, spotting various envelopes resting in the letterbox.

The box also had a large government leaflet in it. The heading read:
'DEFENCE OF AUSTRALIA AND THE EMPIRE'
'THE CALL TO ARMS'

'This is my chance,' Roy whispered to himself. He turned for the kitchen. 'Mum, the government wants me to fight.' Roy handed Lucretia the leaflet. 'Look at that. I have to go.'

The leaflet was from the Prime Minister of Australia. It set out that: The present state of the War calls imperatively for vigorous action. The soldiers of Australia have covered themselves in imperishable glory, but, in order that they may strike a more effective blow against the enemy, it is necessary that their numbers should be largely increased.

The leaflet noted that, in addition to the monthly quota of 16,000 Australian men, the government had decided to raise a further 50,000 recruits.

All Roy had to do was to write 'E' on the accompanying 'recruiting check slip' and his name and address, then send it to the Ballarat Recruiting Committee. The letter 'R' stood for 'refusal', but no 'inquisitorial questions' would be raised on that account.

The Prime Minister thanked Roy and the other addressees in advance for their 'anticipated patriotic response'.

'Mum, surely I can't let the Prime Minister down.'

'You certainly can, and you certainly will,' said Lucretia.

The Prime Minister had earlier written to the Australian public stating that the AIF had already 'carved for Australia a niche in the Temple of the Immortals'. He noted that destiny had now given the young men of Australia 'a great opportunity'.

Gallipoli and Frostbite—28 January 1916

It was now over a month since Nelson had left Melbourne on the *Karoola*. She steamed steadily towards England. Nelson's next port of call would be at the Mediterranean city of Egypt, Alexandria.

On 28 January 1916, Nelson disembarked the *Karoola* to take in the ancient city. A sandstorm had just begun so Nelson took a rocking tram to another hospital ship, the *HMT Nevasa*. *HMT Nevasa* was larger than the *Karoola*, and a little quicker. In August 1914 she had been taken over by the British Government and converted to a troopship, and from January 1915 she had become a 660-bed hospital ship.

When Nelson got on the *HMT Nevasa*, soldier talk took him straight to war. He pencilled in his diary:

A bonnie hospital ship bigger than the *Karoola*, splendid, roomy quarters, and good food. Met our reinforcement Nurses who were staying in Cairo. Spent the whole day in the port alongside the pier. Took on 500 wounded frostbitten from Gallipoli.

This is the busiest port I have ever seen. At night, lights from the ships look like Melbourne lights from Newport. A welcome bed with glorious white sheets, after a period of Egyptian sand.

A quiet day spent most of the time talking to wounded Tommies. By the court martials and bombardment by the British which the

French stopped later, I am satisfied Britain does not play the game. Tommies say that Australians much better than Englishmen but they are glad they are not fighting the Gurkhas who bayonet the wounded. One chap told about 200 of our survivors out of 1,500 on Gallipoli.

After spending time on the *HMT Nevasa*, Nelson returned to the *Karoola* and it soon set out again for England. He was now well on his way to the medical training the AIF had planned for him and work at the Australian rehabilitation hospital at Harefield in England. Harefield had special facilities for this and Nelson would, of course, receive 'on the job' experience in patching up soldiers so the army could do either of two things with them: return them to the front as soon as possible for more fighting, or send them home if they were not fit or able to fight again.

Another Call to Arms—31 January 1916

The Prime Minister was not the only one calling Roy 'to arms'.

On 31 January 1916, the *Ballarat Star* contained a 'call to arms' from the Mayor of Ballarat. In it, the mayor asked young men to most seriously consider their duty to 'Commonwealth and Empire'. The mayor noted that 'we are at the throes of the most stupendous conflict in all history'. The mayor called out to Roy and the other Ballarat men who had not yet volunteered:

We appeal to your high, sense of honour, sacrifice and patriotism. The Empire demands that every man this day will do his duty. You will do yours by enlisting now.

A week earlier, the British government had decided that a 'call to arms' would not be adequate to deal with the appalling losses from the first six months of the war which had decimated the fighting power of the British Army. The government there introduced conscription, to apply from May 1916, requiring all eligible men to fight.

Harefield Hospital—February 1916

A train ride from London, followed by an army motor vehicle, took Nelson north into the English countryside. A British biplane flew over.

The pilot spotted the vehicle turn into a small country lane, heading towards a house. Nelson looked up towards the sound as the plane pierced the underbelly of England's clouded heavens.

Just north of London, Harefield Park was large and stately. In November 1914, two Australians resident in the United Kingdom, Mr and Mrs Billyard-Leake, had offered it up as a convalescent facility for the wounded soldiers of the AIF.

The property comprised the main house, a plain three-storey brick structure, some outbuildings, and ample grounds. The AIF initially thought it could accommodate some 50 soldiers under winter conditions and 150 during spring and summer. But by the time Nelson arrived in 1916, Harefield was already accommodating nearly 1000 beds, with a large number of nursing and ancillary support staff.

Under the UK Director of Recreation and Study, the hospital regularly issued a small magazine, the *Harefield Park Boomerang*.

As the motor vehicle pulled up outside the hospital, Nelson could see a line of hospital wagons and a number of AIF troops assisting wounded soldiers into the main lobby of the hospital.

'Good evening. I understand you are Private Ferguson, just off the *Karoola*. Welcome to Harefield,' smiled an officer waiting to greet approaching vehicles.

'Yes, I'm from Ballarat,' said Nelson, stepping out of the motor vehicle.

'Very good. You will be trained here, Ferguson, then you may be transported to France for active duty. Please register at the front office behind me and then you will be escorted to your quarters. A group of injured Australian soldiers has just come in and we will have you observe how we take them in and deal with them. They will include gas victims. Those bloody Huns have used gas again recently. You may find what you see troubling at first, Ferguson, but with training you will do good work, you will help many, and you may ultimately, if not immediately, find it rewarding.'

'I will do my best, sir.'

He knew that the Germans had previously used gas but now he was seeing the weapon's product. The Germans had first used gas nearly a year earlier on 22 April 2015 at Ypres in Belgium, deploying more than

150 tons of lethal chlorine gas against two French colonial divisions. Instead of receiving a German infantry attack, gas had wafted across no-man's-land and into the French trenches, devastating the troops and their morale. Two days later, the Germans launched a second gas attack, this time against a Canadian Division, pushing the Allies further back. By reason of these attacks and the heavy pressing forward movement of the enemy, by May 1915, the Allies had retreated to the town of Ypres.

As Nelson walked into Harefield, he could see, hear and smell a world unknown to him in his hometown of Ballarat.

The hospital was militarily neat, disciplined, clean and well supplied. Its hygienic processes and clinical systems were for healing.

But as Nelson would come to realise, not all damage was repairable.

The Paralysis Ward—29 February 1916

At 1400 hours Nelson reported for duty and was immediately assigned to the Paralysis Ward.

The white-walled ward had 30 beds in one long room with a high ceiling and extensive dark drapery. Dim yellow lights dotted the middle of the ward.

Nelson walked down its centre, flanked by beds and broken men. He had not been told of paralysis from war, had never seen it, and had not received any training to care for it. He did not know why these young men were paralysed or how it had occurred other than that it was said they might be 'shell shocked' by war.

The look of the damaged men made him feel sick. His stomach churned badly and he entered a cold sweat. He was not sure whether the flickering of the ward's lights was mechanical or a figment of his imagination. As a young boy, after a billy-cart accident, he had seen the inside of the Ballarat local hospital. His mind told him these men were in the best place they could be, having come out of the worst. His eyes were not so sure.

Prior to 'supervising' the ward, Nelson had been ordered to ensure the soldiers did not harm themselves by involuntary limb movement. This was in fact unlikely; the hospital had sought to calm them by heavy sedation for the evening.

After four and a half long hours, Nelson came off duty. One occupant of the ward had cried the whole of Nelson's shift. The soldier's weeping washed over the ward—and all over Nelson.

After tea, Nelson sat shivering by the fire in his dormitory but he enjoyed the solitude until bedtime. The flames were bright but the fire produced what seemed to Nelson to be little more than the heat of a match as the chimney had been over-vented and was jammed that way. Now shivering hard, Nelson pulled the thin army blanket up onto his shoulders. He was colder than he had ever been in his whole life. He had lost the feeling in his toes. The 'adventure' had started as a nightmare.

But from down the corridor, Nelson could hear a digger quietly whistling Nelson's favourite band tune: 'The Minstrel Boy'. It had become the unofficial anthem of the AIF; every soldier knew it; most whistled it. Nelson had played it many times in Prout's Championship Brass Band back in Ballarat, and many times too in the high- standard 70th Rifle Brigade Band. For a moment the tune conveyed him back home. He could hear his own humming as accompaniment, both in unison and occasionally in harmony.

'Not bad'.

Nelson pencilled into his diary: 'Hate Harefield and its hospital. Glad to keep away from paralysed patients. One cried all day.'

He then wrote home: 'Things are all right here.'

Free Instruction for Returned Soldiers—February 1916

The first meeting for the year of the Ballarat School of Mines Council was shortly to commence. Its agenda had previously included aspects of the impact of the war on the town of Ballarat and the contribution that could be made to help returned soldiers.

Councillors hurriedly took their seats for the meeting.

'I now declare the meeting open,' said the chair. 'We have now had a large number of our boys return from Europe, many of whom, as you all know, have been badly damaged. It seems to me that we ought to be assisting these returned soldiers in any way we can.'

'I agree,' said a councillor. 'I think we should be making the School of Mines available for instruction if that would assist the returned soldiers.'

The room nodded.

'I agree,' said the chair. 'May I propose the following.'

'That all applications by returned soldiers for free instruction at the School of Mines will be favourably considered. All in favour say Aye.'

'Aye,' said the room.

'Secretary, would you please let the other educational institutions in the region know of the resolution and invite them to consider following this initiative.'

In due course Nelson's old school in Ballarat, the School of Mines, became highly involved with repatriation classes for soldiers returning to Ballarat. Classes covered fitting and turning, woodworking, electroplate work, electrical wiring, and commercial subjects. Getting returned soldiers back on their feet was now a primary and continuing responsibility for the whole town.

The Operating Theatre—10 March 1916

'Ferguson, you are here at Harefield to learn as much and as quickly as you can to help our boys. Feel free to get in as close as you need to so you can see how it all works,' said the surgeon.

Nelson shuffled forward.

'Who is next?' asked the surgeon.

The soldier was lifted onto the operating table.

'How long has the limb been like this?'

'Two or three days at most, sir.'

'Well let's press on; I think we still have time.'

Nelson pushed closer to the operating table. The assistant handed the surgeon a steel saw.

The anaesthetic would put the digger still and keep him that way until the limb had been removed. The theatre's numbing technique was to apply chloroform by way of droplets into a single-layer gauze mask placed above the soldier's face, which after a minute or so would be lowered and placed on the face itself. A second mask followed into which ether was administered until the gauze of that mask became saturated. Soldiers sometimes struggled and had to be held down, but in the main they were ready for surgery within several minutes.

These anaesthetics came with significant adverse effects: among other things, both contributed actively to shock and exhaustion because of the depression of blood circulation. It was known that the treatment also damaged the liver and other organs.

Shrapnel had sat ugly in the soldier's leg and had been removed on a hospital ship. But now the leg had become infected and needed cleaning or to come off. Through AIF commitment, and with relative army efficiency, the digger had quickly been brought back in for emergency surgery. He was only alive because of new blood transfusion techniques developed as a direct result of modern warfare.

'Will he come out all right from this?' asked Nelson.

'That depends on his constitution rather than anything we might do. In cases like this we first see how much we can get out and how much repair the leg will take. In this case, that won't work, and so, if we don't take the leg off, he is likely to die.'

The saw sliced the leg. Nelson had seen a number of amputations earlier in the night and knew that the procedure would be silent until the saw struck bone. A deep chill suddenly went through his body. The saw appeared on the other side. The rank smell of the chloroform brought a sickly response in Nelson's stomach.

'We're done. Wrap the limb. Hopefully, he'll make it,' declared the surgeon. The soldier was shuffled off onto another table which was then wheeled out.

The theatre's doors swung open for another soldier. Nelson took one end of the table and pulled it under the light. The patient had ingested heavy quantities of gas into his lungs; he was strongly sedated but moaning. Nelson levered him onto the table.

'This Brit is a special case we need to look at. He is not actually here for his lungs. He's here to see what we might be able to do for eye trauma from the gas,' noted the surgeon. The hospital had just opened an eye ward for diggers injured in battle.

Nelson peeled off the bandages and peered into the soldier's face. One eye was relatively clear but the other was heavily damaged and leaking yellow muck.

'He's received heavy damage but what is really troubling is the eye infection and distress following the attack. We may have to take it out and cure the area,' said the surgeon.

The doors swung open again and another medical officer approached the table. He looked closely into the damaged eye, conferring closely with the surgeon.

The discussion had real military purpose. The army was short on numbers and needed experienced soldiers to keep fighting if they could. Many of the damaged troops would, if and when they had recuperated, be sent to the Western Front in France. If a soldier could be made productive again, that was the army's best course.

'I think we might put this man under further observation before we attempt anything too permanent tonight. Private, take him to Ward E and we will have another look at him in the morning.'

Nelson pulled the soldier's arm as other assistants pushed him off the table and onto another trolley.

'Take the end of the trolley, Ferguson, and move him out to the ward. We have quite a few to get through yet.'

Nelson rolled his patient into the centre of Harefield. A trolley wheel wobbled all the way. Ward E held all the Australian troops the medical staff were not quite sure what to do with; they were deemed appropriate for 'further observation'. Gas cases with heavy eye damage were within that category. The squeaking trolley wheel fell silent and Nelson assisted the patient onto his bed.

'You'll be all right, mate,' said Nelson. 'I'll come and check on you a little later'.

Nelson tucked a blanket gently around the patient.

Time to Apply for France—Mid-March 1916

'This can't go on,' said Nelson to himself. 'I need to help these blokes early in battle, not later.'

Nelson stepped out of the main building at Harefield and walked some distance in the snow towards the army's records office. There he asked if he could apply for a transfer to the field ambulance and in due course take up duty in France at the front.

The officer told him his application would be thrown out because he would shortly be seconded to the Deputy Director of Medical Services, AIF.

That meant more time at Harefield and England. At least for the time being.

It was now mid-March 1916. At that stage no Australian had yet seen action on the Western Front in France. But all at Harefield knew it would not be long. Nelson had received word that extensive preparation of the wards would shortly occur as the AIF was now expecting to receive heavy casualties. Unofficial estimates were in the order of 900, given that the Anzacs would soon be in action in France. As a consequence, Nelson was also informed that no 'ambulance men' would leave for France until further notice.

A New Field Ambulance—30 March 1916

By the end of March 1916, Nelson was still doing office duties at Harefield, with occasional shifts in the operating theatre. The army also had him on various other tasks all over the hospital system at Harefield.

An officer approached the front desk of administration. 'Ferguson, I understand you have previously applied for the field ambulance.'

'Yes I have, sir, but no luck so far, sir.'

'Well word is that the 15th Field Ambulance that was formed at Tel-el-Kebir, Egypt, in February 1916 for the AIF's 5th Division, will now be assisting the 15th Brigade within that division. I'm told it was formed from C Sections of the 5th and 8th Field Ambulances who have already fought in Egypt. They're a good mob and you should consider applying. They're on their way to the Western Front right now.'

This was good news. Nelson had been rejected because he was needed at Harefield. He had been keen to get to France. And with the 15th Brigade heading for the Western Front, there was a real prospect of being able to join the 15th Field Ambulance.

'Thank you, sir. I'm going to apply.'

'Well you had better do it quickly—lots of our boys want to go.'

That night Nelson wrote in his diary: 'Prospect of going away very bright.'

This was true. But war is the province of uncertainty. And with an expected stream of wounded Anzacs soon to be coming in from the Western Front, it was also true that there remained doubt whether Nelson would ultimately make it to France. As Nelson knew, by reason of the oath he had given, and the hierarchy of the army, the AIF could do anything with him at any time. It had demonstrated that handsomely since he had joined up in July 1915. His fate as a private in the AIF remained completely unknown to him.

Nelson would have to wait for whatever turn of events the war would deliver. But his odyssey to the battlefields of France and Belgium was well in train.

London Celebrates Gallipoli's Knights—25 April 1916

In the early hours of the now officially named 'Anzac Day', Nelson received a leave pass to travel to London to share in huge celebrations. The first Anzac Day services had already commenced in New Zealand, followed by those in Australia. It was now London's turn.

Now at Charing Cross Station, Nelson pushed through his fellow British subjects and headed down Fleet Street towards the Westminster district. Seventeen hundred Anzacs were due to march before their sovereigns, the king and queen. It would be the first great assembly of wounded since that memorable day one year earlier.

As Nelson passed by the London newspaper firms, he saw large posters headed 'The Knights of Gallipoli'.

Nelson followed the Anzac disciples towards the formal grounds of Buckingham Palace. His instincts took him to the best vantage spot at the dawn of a new legend.

From an elevated point, Nelson looked down over a large and glinting Anzac brass band now swinging into the centre of the road by the Westminster courts, just past Australia House in Fleet Street. Arms pushed large Union Jack flags back and forth. The whole of London was now cheering the Australian soldiers on for their new reputation at Gallipoli in the name of the Empire. Australian flags dotted here and there. Out of the proud bells of brass instruments Australian military marches now filled the crowd's ears.

In amazement Nelson scanned the bright sunny afternoon's display of British gratitude, fine Australian troops, and well-recognised tunes.

Nelson began to whistle and tap his right foot. Britain's sun worked on his Australian tan. His eyes enjoyed the patterns of respect and recognition for service now being recorded in waving flags and streaking streamers.

Over at Westminster Abbey, King George V and Queen Mary attended a special Anzac Day service, as did Australia's Prime Minsiter and Generals.

At Suez Canal, Brigadier General John Monash, of the Fourth Brigade, AIF, had already turned out the whole brigade for a short service. Monash had devised a special set of blue and red ribbons, denoting service at Gallipoli. These were handed out to the eligible. This was followed by cricket matches, and in the afternoon the canal provided the perfect venue for a swimming carnival. Some 15,000 soldiers went for a dip.

Of those who fought in the AIF at Gallipoli, at least three out of ten were immigrants, born in Britain.

A 'Fresh Lustre' on the British Arms—25 April 1916

Roy was like a dot in the large Ballarat crowd being rained on. All business in the city and the broader area had been suspended. Ballarat trams were depoted.

Roy looked up at the Soldiers Statue in Sturt Street. He had been told by the *Ballarat Star* that:

Anzac Day is to be observed today, it being just twelve months since the Australian troops made their wonderful landing at Gallipoli.

'Damn,' said Roy to himself, 'I knew I should have volunteered. Nel will be having such a good time.'

Roy looked up and pushed into the crowd. Weeping mothers stood in Ballarat's winter.

But in other parts of Ballarat things differed. Other celebrations and gatherings were now occurring in the town in a solemn but optimistic sense. The State school held a special ceremony, the full-sized Union Jack flag (of the Empire) flying high above children receiving sweets.

Elsewhere in the nation, the *Sydney Morning Herald* printed the king's message to Australians:

> Tell my people of Australia that today I am joining with them in their solemn tribute to the memorial of their heroes who died in Gallipoli.
>
> They gave their lives for a supreme cause in gallant comradeship with the rest of my sailors and soldiers who fought and died with them. Their valour and fortitude have shed fresh lustre on the British arms. May those who mourn their loss find comfort in the conviction that they did not die in vain, but that their sacrifice has drawn our peoples more closely together, and added strength and glory to the Empire.

On the same day, the Australian Defence Minister's message published in newspapers noted that in this peaceful land, with no history of conflict, the word 'war' jarred the ears of Australians. The minister noted that the German challenge to the mother country found 233,720 Australian sons, who had wrenched themselves from their parents, wives and friends, to answer the call of their country and to fight the Empire's battles on distant shores.

The minister foreshadowed that for generations to come, the story of the entry of the Australian troops to the European battlefield would ring in the ears of all English-speaking nations: 'We can regard the future with a calm confidence in the military prowess of our soldiers.'

The papers told Australians to solemnly commemorate the great deed which made the whole world ring with the peon of praise for Australian valour. In Sydney, all trains were ordered to stop at 9 o'clock, at which time passengers were to give three cheers to the King, the Empire, and the Anzacs.

The States and local towns commemorated their heroes. But the Commonwealth of Australia held no Gallipoli event in 1916.

Stretcher Drill and a Surprise—19 May 1916

By late May 1916, although Nelson had not been officially told he would be able to join the Field Ambulance, he had already started stretcher-bearing drills at Harefield.

After several strenuous hours, those on the drill, including Nelson, were drenched with sweat and all done in.

They soon poured into the orderlies' canteen. Warm soup and army chatter were in plentiful supply.

'Hey Ferguson! Telephone call for you.'

'For me?'

'Yeh, a chap wants to talk to you.'

Nelson crossed the canteen, strode down the corridor, and picked up the phone.

'Nelson, it's me Peter. I'm at Wandsworth Hospital just outside London.'

Peter was a mate from Ballarat. He had just come in from the Western Front—wounded in the arm.

'Amazing. Bonza to hear from you, Peter.'

'It's good to hear your voice, Nel. I am wondering if you are going to be in London at all over the next few days?'

'I'm not due to be, but I'll ask for some leave and if they let me I'll take the train down there. I might be able to visit you tomorrow.'

'That would be fantastic,' said Peter.

At 5.00 am the next day, Nelson was part of the kit inspection routine. At 6.00 am he undertook a route march and then had breakfast.

As soon as he came off duty at 10.00 am, Nelson ran to Northwood station. When he got to London he took a taxi to Wandsworth General Hospital, arriving at 2.00 pm.

The Wandsworth General Hospital was a military institution. It had started life in 1859 as the Victoria Patriotic Asylum for orphan daughters of soldiers, sailors and marines, endowed from the Patriotic Fund of the Crimean War. Although Nelson did not know it, two orderlies at the hospital were Tom Roberts and Arthur Streeton, Australian artists who would later become world famous.

The administration office directed Nelson to Peter's ward. Nelson turned through the door of the ward. Peter was fast asleep.

Nelson gently rocked Peter's left arm. 'I'm here, mate.'

Peter slowly roused and the two embraced.

'I've just been brought back here from the front.'

'Yes I was told. I see your arm'.

'It's bloody sore I can tell you. The bullet went through here. If they didn't give me morphine, I reckon I'd be on the ceiling.'

Nelson smiled. 'At least you're here on the mend and not in a trench, Pete.'

The two spent the afternoon talking like mad. Afternoon tea was brought to the patient and guest.

'For what you've been through, I reckon you look strong and well.'

'I might look it Nel but it's bloody awful on the front. There's no let up. The conditions are shocking. The rats outnumber the bloody troops in some of our trenches. The damage I've seen to our boys is unspeakable.'

'Peter, I've applied for the field ambulance and I've been told the prospects of going away are bright.'

'Well Nel, if you end up going, try to keep your chin up and your head down. The front is a barbaric place where men are asked to do things no man should. And they bloody do it. Over and over again.'

'Well I reckon the Aussies need medical help so I'm going to try and get there if I can. That's if the AIF makes up its mind whether to let me!'

The two mates laughed, before bidding each other farewell. Nelson ran for the train bound for Harefield. He was assisting AIF soldiers repatriated to England to be patched up and returned to the Western Front—if they could be. The AIF could see no reason to move him from that essential task.

At least at this stage.

The Battle of the Somme—July 1916

Back in July 1915, when Nelson first enlisted, Allied leaders decided that only concerted and simultaneous attacks on the Germans would deprive them of their strategic advantages. And they had also decided that this should be done on the Somme, France. (The name is derived from the Celtic word for 'tranquillity'.) But in February 1916, the Germans launched a massive attack at Verdun, causing large French (and German) casualties. By July 1916, the battle at Verdun had been running for several months but there was no sign of it ending. The French Army was exhausted and in parts mutinous. Since 1914, at least some 2.5 million French soldiers had been killed or wounded. The army was now numb from war.

The Allies decided to reconfigure and upscale the Somme offensive, which would make the Germans fight on two fronts (at Verdun and on the Somme) and give the French Army some relief. The British knew that massive numbers of men would be needed for the Somme offensive. They summoned Australian and New Zealand divisions to buttress numbers.

Over the last week of June 1916, and in anticipation of a huge infantry assault, the British unleashed one and half million shells on the Germans. Nearly half a million men gathered on an 18-mile front, a quarter of whom would attack on 1 July 1916 with a seven to one advantage.

On 1 July 1916, the British charged at the Germans, initiated by a football kicked over the front line. By the end of that day, 60,000 British soldiers were either dead or wounded. Haig noted that the number could not be considered 'severe'. It was merely part of a 'wearing down' process.

On 19 July 1916, north of the Somme offensive, the Battle of Fromelles commenced. The British Expeditionary Force, together with two divisions of the AIF (the 5th Australian Division for infantry and the 4th Australian Division for artillery) attacked the Germans, designed to draw German forces from the Somme. Although not used at Gallipoli, the Australians were issued with steel helmets for a different kind of warfare: mass destruction by mass artillery fire. The preparatory bombardment of the Germans by the Allies was ineffective and German machine guns swayed through the Anzacs and the British troops. The attack would be the worst in Australia's entire military history. The 5th Australian Division suffered 5533 casualties. As a consequence, it could not attack the enemy for many months.

On 23 July 1916, the second Somme Offensive commenced, the Battle of Pozieres. The 1st Australian Division attacked and captured the German-occupied village of Pozieres, securing some 1000 yards. But this created a bulge in the British line, allowing German artillery to shell the Australian positions heavily from multiple sides. The 1st Division suffered 5285 casualties over five days. In the following days, the 1st, 2nd, and 4th divisions came in and out of the line, suffering heavy casualties like those at the Battle of Fromelles.

Nelson was told back at Harefield that the bloodiest battle of the war was now well underway in France.

What he did not know was when he would be inside the raging madness.

Time for France—September 1916

After months of carnage on the Somme, the Allies' offensive was producing only one winner: war itself. That meant lots of damage suffered by all parties, and lots of need for recovery.

Between May and early September 1916, Nelson continued working at Harefield, helping the wounded. He regularly applied for the field ambulance—that would get him to France.

But by 4 September 1916, he had, according to his diary, 'given up hope' of going to France as a stretcher-bearer, so he decided to apply for the artillery.

A few days after applying, Nelson was told Australians were being withdrawn from the trenches on the Western Front because of heavy losses. He thought that might be a good sign that replacements would be needed.

The next day, Nelson was told the artillery had accepted him and that he should be ready to move at any time.

Within two hours of receiving the news, Nelson was on his way to Ludgershall, 16 miles north-east of Salisbury. This was a major gathering place for Anzacs due to be transferred to the Western Front. All sorts of units were getting ready to make the journey to France via the English Channel crossing.

Nelson lined up at the supply tent to receive his equipment and further instructions.

'Name!' shouted the sergeant.

'Private Ferguson, sir.'

'I am about to issue you with essential equipment for the next phase of your life as a soldier!'

'Yes sir.'

'You are now being provided with three wooden boards to sleep on, two blankets, a bowl and your very own plate.'

'Yes sir.'

'Move over to the tent on your left to sign for your new hat, Ferguson.'

'Yes sir.'

After collecting the 'essential' equipment, Nelson was then marched to his assigned 30-man hut where he laid his boards out, three inches from the dirt, and lay down. He wrote in his diary: 'Not too impressed but too long a soldier to be down hearted.'

The next day, Nelson was taken to the Australian headquarters at Tidworth. Just as the impressive headquarters Australian brass band struck up, Nelson was told he would be taken back to camp.

A hard night on the boards meant no sleep and not enough bedclothes meant constant cold.

The Australian Medical Corp—September 1916

By this time, Nelson had had long periods in operating theatres, had undertaken stretcher drills, and had received significant medical training including bandaging training. He was ready to serve, and ready for France.

After reveille in the camp at 6.00 am, Nelson commenced a route march at 6.30 am which ended at 8.00 am. A tasty but inadequate breakfast was followed by a medical inspection.

'You have passed the medical, Private, and I have decided to put you into the Australian Medical Corp'.

'Thanks very much sir, I was hoping to join the Field Ambulance.'

'We'll worry about that later, Ferguson. For the time being you are required to report to the Australian Medical Corp immediately.'

On Sunday, 17 September 1916, Nelson was part of a church parade and then sent on a 16-mile route march. Back at the huge camp where he was now staying, he was told it would be broken up into units for deployment in France. He was also told he could join the 39th Brass Band if he wished to.

At 2.00 pm on 19 September 1916, Nelson was warned of the draft to France with the Australian Medical Corp. He was immediately inoculated and told to be ready to go at any time. He was issued with ammunition and new boots. He was told he would be going in what he was standing up in plus 20 lbs of supplies, and no change of clothes.

Nelson had reached the end of one book of his diary. He wrote on the last page:

Dear Mate, I enclose this on the eve of going to France. I am sending it to you to keep till I come home. Don't show it to anyone else. Have started another for France and I hope you get this safely.

At 3.30 pm, the camp commandant made a 'full kit' inspection. The colonel then gave a farewell speech. Nelson was then issued with iodine ampoules. They were for pre-operative skin preparation and to help reduce bacteria that might cause infections. It would be his job as stretcher-bearer to halt serious haemorrhaging by use of a tourniquet or other means, to fix splints to broken bones, and to apply dressings to wounds. For those who could not be patched at the battlefield, if possible he would, with another bearer, carry the injured soldier back to one of the Advanced Dressing Stations. For those dying, Nelson would make them as comfortable as they could be in their final time.

Nelson was then told he would be marching off to Tidworth and would then catch a train to London, then on to France. His journey to the slaughterhouse of the Western Front was now well underway.

Waterloo Station and Beyond—20 September 1916

On arriving at Waterloo Station in London at 2.00 o'clock in the morning, Nelson immediately marched straight to Victoria Station. Red Cross ladies fed him on the station platform. He then lay down on the cold stone pavement and slept until 3.45 am. As he dozed, Nelson could see several AIF drafts arrive during the night, receiving the same treatment.

By 5.45 am Nelson was on the train to Folkestone. He arrived there at 8.00 am. The train took the soldiers right to the pier. From his carriage Nelson could see it jutting into the English Channel.

Nelson and the other Anzacs got off the train and spent several hours on the beach. The glorious warm day framed a majestic calm sea. Apart from the coarse stones under foot, it reminded Nelson of the seaside town of Queenscliff on Port Phillip Bay near Melbourne. He wrote in his diary: 'Folkestone beach a bright break in a monotonous military career'.

In the distance, Nelson could see the rolling transports on the English Channel, patiently waiting to take him and his new mates away to a new foreign experience.

The peril of the Western Front, France.

A First Night in France

At 10.30 am, Nelson and the others boarded the transport. She set cautiously out across the English Channel, housed between two huge British destroyers. At full speed they planed over calm Channel seas.

At 12.30 pm, Nelson looked toward the horizon and could see the French coast as the transport headed for Boulogne. It took about one hour to get the soldiers off the transport. Nelson and the other soldiers then marched down old cobblestone roads to the AIF's rest camp on the edge of Boulogne.

Set against fine French weather, the countryside looked glorious but the locals looked like they had been through a great deal. Nelson noted in his diary: 'Poverty showed itself among the French.'

As he approached the camp, young girls from the town greeted the Anzacs with energetic waves and bright European smiles.

Nelson's eyes were wide open from the adventure of the last two days but he was nevertheless now worn out. His new military boots were as hard as nails and were giving him much grief. But with his head now pressing against the floor, he soon entered a fitful sleep.

This would be Nelson's first night in an invaded nation, France. It was now a country where millions of young men were trying to kill and maim each other using industrial-scale machinery and weapons, deploying hundreds of years of military doctrine. It was a country where the civilian population had been displaced. Where their towns had been blown to pieces. Where schools and churches were not off limits. Where huge numbers of young men were trying to kill each other using discipline.

But more than anything else, it had become a country where the end of war was beyond sight.

And for Nelson, battle was just at its beginning.

The Biscuit Tin and Sacred Papers

Roy briskly walked up to the Ballarat Post Office at the end of Peel Street.

'They said there was a parcel for me from my brother in France. I am Roy Ferguson.'

'Very good,' said the clerk, turning to the back room.

'R. Ferguson. Yes, here it is.'

The clerk returned with a small brown parcel.

'Please sign here.'

Roy stepped out of the post office and back towards the family home. After a short distance he stopped in the street and opened the parcel.

Among torn bits of French newspapers sat a small book.

'It's Nel's diary,' Roy said to himself. 'I'll put it in the old biscuit tin in the shed for safekeeping till after this bloody war is over and Nel is back.'

Part II
In War

Part II

In War

Training for Gas—26 September 1916

The reveille was always early: 5.30 am. Nelson and the others were then told to fall in, however physical training soon started, followed by a parade.

At 9.00 am Nelson was directed to the gas lecture theatre. He was then taken to an outside trench that the AIF had dug specifically for gas training purposes. Chlorine and phosgene at the deadly levels the Germans were using was then injected into the trench.

Nelson looked down into the deep claustrophobic trench about 50 yards long.

On the order, he then ran into the sarcophagus-like tunnel, hurrying through the gas inside. The gas was virtually invisible and therefore deceptive as to effect except for its smell if it leaked through the gas mask.

To Nelson's surprise, apart from the faintest irritation to his cheeks, his mask and gas helmet worked well. Nelson stomped his way to the other end of the trench.

'I hope we don't have to do that at the front,' Nelson muttered to himself.

'Shut up with that back chat, Private. You're slowing the training line. Move on immediately.'

Nelson joined the back of the caterpillar-moving line for another run through the gas.

As he shuffled closer to the trench once more, a cold and clammy sweat beaded on Nelson's forehead. He quickly wiped it off with his forearm and took a number of deep breaths. His chest suddenly felt tight. His heart rang loud in his ears. The gas mask instantly fogged up. The line shuffled further forward.

The next soldier appeared out the other side of the trench coughing loudly.

'That's bullshit, Private,' shouted the officer. 'You are bloody fine. Keep moving! Just remember to keep the bloody mask on at all times.'

'What if I take it off, Sarg?'

'Under no circumstances must you do that. This gas toys with the wind. If you take off the mask the gas will burn your eyes and cripple your lungs. You will be a dead man quickly. Or as good as, Private. We put masks on mules and they don't try to take them off—they're bloody smart enough to keep them on. Got that, Private?'

'Yes sir,' spluttered the soldier. 'I'll keep it on.'

When all had been through the trench several times, the sergeant lined up the trainees.

'You might wish to remember this little ditty, boys,' shouted the sergeant.

If a whiff of gas you smell,

Bang your gong like bloody hell,

On with your googly,

Up with your gun—ready to meet the bloody Hun.

A trainee sniggered. 'We don't have a gong, Sarg.'

'Of course you don't. You'll be using mouth-to-mouth communication. If you think you're funny, Private, we'll see how much laughing there is when you're out there for real.'

'We'll train again tomorrow morning. There will be no bludging on the flag like I've just seen. You're dismissed.'

Nelson went back to his tent, his issued gas mask dangling around his neck. He wondered when he would have to confront a gas pit of the kind he had just been 'trained' to deal with. In accordance with army practice, Nelson sat down and waited for orders for the front.

Volunteers Needed

At 2.00 pm, Nelson heard loud shouting.

'Volunteers for the front! Volunteers for the front!'

Nelson and his mate Jock held up their hands.

'Right, you're in,' continued the caller.

At once Nelson was issued with another gas helmet. But this time three days' rations were also thrown in. He was told he would move off with the others at 3.00 am and would commence his journey towards the front.

A large red cross on a white square of cloth was hurriedly stitched onto Nelson's khaki-clad left arm.

'This will keep you safe, Private. The Huns aren't supposed to fire at you with that on.'

'That's a great relief,' said the soldier next to Nelson. 'The Huns must have bloody good eyesight to spot this badge on the battlefield.'

'Don't be stupid,' called the sergeant, 'you'll be carrying a white flag too.'

As dusk arrived, Nelson entered another fitful sleep. At 2.00 am a stranger's voice whispered: 'Time to go, Private.'

He dressed in the dark and went over to the tea being served at the cookhouse. By 3 am he and the others were ready to depart but waited around for about an hour.

At 4.00 am, in the far distance Nelson could see reflections of explosions and gunfire which looked to him like lightning. He marched through the huge hospital camp with the others and shortly arrived at Etaples train station which was adjacent to the camp. The hospital camp at Etaples took in large numbers of wounded Australians from the Western Front who would recuperate there or be sent on to England for further treatment. From here he entrained with the others. The train was full of Aussies, Tommies, and a few big guns. It soon headed out to collect yet more Allied soldiers, travelling back to Boulogne, then on to Calais, and then ultimately east towards Estaires, close to the front line of battle.

As the train approached Estaires, Nelson was told he would soon be at the 5th Division's headquarters of the AIF, at a place called Le Nouveau Monde, near Estaires. Dusk fell again. The constant travel and anxiety as he approached the front had exhausted him totally.

This would be Nelson's very first night up the line. In his diary, he pencilled:

Fairly quiet all night except for occasional machine guns and little heavy artillery. A slight bombardment on left through the night but I was too sleepy to wake for it.

Until near the end of September 1916 Nelson had daily gas drills, kit inspections, marches and parades. But no carries yet.

A New Mate—29 September 1916

In early 1916, a further Australian recruitment drive had now raised the troops necessary to replace the losses at Gallipoli. The AIF in Egypt had grown to four divisions and these were then transferred to the Western Front. At home a 5th Division had been raised and was also now in France.

Nelson was again taken to the 5th Division's headquarters just back from the front. The morning there was filled with questions about his experience at Harefield. The army then told him he could be called to the front for stretcher-bearing at any time, and that he should be at the ready.

Nelson remained ready and within whistle call all day, playing cards and patiently waiting. The evening passed quietly. He went to bed at 8.00 pm.

But at 10.30 pm, he was woken suddenly.

A car immediately took him to the 15th Field Ambulance depot stationed up the road. As he approached the camp, Nelson pencilled 'Nouveau Monde' in his diary, the name of the small town to the east of Estaires in France, 150 miles due north of Paris and about 20 miles south of Ypres in Belgium.

The 15th was part of the 5th Division of the AIF, formed in February 1916 as part of the expansion of the AIF's infantry brigades. Both the 14th and 15th Brigades had been added, and with the 15th Brigade, the 15th Field Ambulance was formed. The 15th Brigade of the 5th Division comprised of the 57th, 58th, 59th and 60th Battalions, all from Victoria.

The car drove off. A large roar came from nearby. Suddenly a fuming motorbike pulled up alongside Nelson.

'G'day, I've been told to introduce you to the 15th's camp and show you round. That means of course we're off to the pub. It's late but things will just be firing up.'

The broad Australian accent came from a tall well-framed rider.

Through the rider's goggles, Nelson could see a mischievous streak in a pair of friendly eyes.

'Great. Good to meet you. I'm happy to start there,' accepted Nelson.

'You should be. Everyone's likely to get pretty loosened up by the French grog. We may as well be part of it.'

'Fine, where's the pub?' asked Nelson.

'It's a little way off. Hence the motor, old chap.'

'I didn't know the AIF had motorbikes,' responded Nelson.

'They don't. I've "borrowed" this one for the evening.'

'Very good, let's go,' said Nelson.

Nelson climbed on and the men disappeared in fumes.

Through the boggy French fields the driver pressed the engine hard as they made their way down a country road. It took them to a small French town back from the front. The bike's dull light sprayed a yellow flicker as it bounced its way up the cobbled road.

Nelson tapped the driver's shoulder. 'Hey steady, I want to see the war out!'

'Don't worry mate, stick with me, and you just might!'

The motor cut as the bike pulled up at the hotel.

'I'm from the 15th Field Ambulance. We've decided to welcome the new boys, including your good self, to life at this part of the front.'

'Great to be part of it,' said Nelson.

'Good-oh. The grog here's likely to be acceptable but some of the patrons won't be. Let's open up with a beer, shall we?'

'Sounds good,' said Nelson.

'By the way, my name's Norman Scholz. Yeh, I know it's a German name. It's true my parents were born on enemy soil but the boys here know I'm an Aussie—born north of Adelaide. All the boys here call me Pomp. And yes I know you're Ferguson, one of our new members of the 15th.'

'Happy to meet you, Pomp, and happy to be here.'

'Happy to meet me!' said Pomp. 'No-one's bloody happy to meet anyone at this flam'in hell-hole part of the world.'

'Call me Nelson or Harold if you want to—I don't mind. I've just come up towards the front line in the last few days.'

'I think you're a "Fergo" if anything. You can tell me all about yourself over some liquid refreshment, Fergo.'

Pomp pushed open the hotel door. The noise from raucous patrons filled Nelson's and Pomp's ears. The pub swarmed with Anzacs, a few locals, and no sobers.

Nelson looked across the room. Pomp's prediction was right: the diggers were all pissed and falling about the place.

'What are you drinking?!' called Pomp.

'The beer you mentioned sounds pretty good,' said Nelson.

'No worries, and this one's my shout.'

'Thanks cobber.'

'No worries. We'll have a great evening, Fergo. This place is going off like fire crackers.'

Nelson looked around and could see a number of the 15th Field Ambulance patches on arms.

Pomp pressed a beer into Nelson's hand and leaned closer to his left ear.

'If you can carry one end of a stretcher any distance, you're doing better than most of these bludgers!'

Nelson laughed. But not as loudly as Pomp.

Pomp ran his rough hands through his thick dark-brown hair. His ocean-blue eyes beamed at Nelson. He was, as he said, from South Australia (a colony first established in 1836), a highly progressive State of Australia (leading the world in granting votes for women). The size of four United Kingdoms.

Now 24 years of age, and a strapping lad, Pomp had left his coach and trolley building job and volunteered from Riverton (about 100 miles north of Adelaide) in June 1915. He had spent nearly two years in the Commonwealth Cadets prior to volunteering for the AIF. Pomp's younger brother, Harold Scholz, had sought exemption from service on the grounds that it was 'expedient to the national interest' for him to continue in the family's blacksmith business. No conscription for overseas service meant this was not strictly necessary but it was considered desirable should Harold be asked why he was not abroad.

At 5 feet 7 inches, and with a chest size of 36 inches, Pomp was indeed a strapping man and had met the 'elite' requirements of the AIF from the outset. He had originally enlisted in the infantry, but had been moved to the 8th Field Ambulance when in France. On 24 February 1916 the AIF had transferred him over to the 15th Field Ambulance.

Pomp had form: back in April 1916 he had been charged with refusing to obey an order from a non-commanding officer. But he was a strong and loyal soldier, and an essential mate on the other end of a heavy stretcher.

Pomp's parents were from Poland and had emigrated to South Australia. His father had become a naturalised citizen. Until Federation of Australia in 1901, a naturalised person in one colony was not automatically naturalised for the purposes of another colony. Therefore, if Pomp's father crossed into Victoria, he would be deemed an enemy alien in that State; a well-recognised complaint among the German locals in South Australia.

Nelson and Pomp made their way through the packed pub to the bar and elbowed a beer together. Then another.

'From what I've seen so far, we're all in for some rough action,' called Nelson.

'Mate, I was transferred over from the 8th and I've been in the bloody 15th since near the beginning of this year and I can tell you we'll be carrying that bloody stretcher for a very long time. Or may be for a very short time—the way the Huns have been behaving.'

Nelson well knew the 15th was part of the advancing 5th Division of the AIF. And he also knew Pomp's new prediction was likely to be right.

'Hey,' called Pomp now standing on the bar, 'how about the "Old Bull and Bush"?' shouted Pomp across the whole of the pub.

'Bloody good idea!' shouted back an Australian digger.

The pub erupted with cheers and more poured beers. A potted version of the first verse of the song spilled out. While Nelson's home

State of Victoria had just passed laws requiring pubs to close early, if these diggers had anything to do with it this pub would be staying open till dawn.

'Stick with me, Fergo, and we'll both be all right.'

'I will,' said Nelson, '*tres bon.*'

Stars and Darkness

After the night's induction, Nelson stumbled out of the hotel to head back to camp with Pomp. As the new mates motored back, Nelson wondered at the French countryside now lit by brightly coloured German star shells.

The two mates had started with a motorbike ride across the French countryside, followed by some rowdy beers and song. But their likely next adventures would be much darker and more perilous than they could bear to imagine.

The September 1916 entry in the 15th Field Ambulance War Diary recorded:

Medical work during the month was quiet. A daily average of only 40 cases was treated at the Advanced Dressing Station. On average, 30 of these were medical cases, the remainder being casualties. Admitted 526. Evacuated to Casualty Clearing Station 213. Transferred to DRS 254.

The general classification of cases was as follows.

Shell shock 10 Wounds 107 Injuries accidental 37 Pulmonary disease 30 Diarrheal 7 Other Intestinal 30 Influenza 75 Tonsillitis 23 Infections 19 Venereal Disease 7 Miscellaneous 131 Rheumatism 39

The Task at Hand—End of September 1916

At 5 am Nelson and Pomp stood to attention out in the open along with the others in a number of units within the 15th Field Ambulance. Although it was still summer, the early clear French air chilled young pencil-like soldiers.

The major spoke to the unit:

Men, on this fine morning I welcome you all. We have some new members of the 15th and so I welcome you in particular.

We have gone through what could be described as a relatively steady patch of work in the last two months as we make our way further into the Somme in support of the 15th Brigade and 5th Division.

It will come as no surprise to you that there are some very challenging days and months up ahead. It may have commenced in July but the battle for this Somme area is far from over and may continue for some time for all we know. We must respect the enemy. But we must also hate and defeat it. You are at once servants of humanity and of hatred.

Let it be known men that I am extremely proud of the work you have been doing. The righteous are as bold as a lion and you are that. You have maintained the privilege of wearing the 'rising sun' on your brim and I want you to always remember that the sun will rise for the cause we fight for.

And you have the unique privilege of the Red Cross on the left arm which calls you to a higher order of task.

I have seen in this field ambulance superb examples of the hero within man. The currency of the army is courage and I have seen this field ambulance spend it time and time again in battle. It is rightly esteemed as the first of human values—for it is the value that guarantees all others. I have seen self-interest immediately abandoned for comrades. That is how we operate in this unit and it is now the 15th's tradition.

I want you always to remember this, men. The task is to bring back a man so he may re-enter the theatre of war when once again able to defeat the Hun. Not only does that provide a further resource, it also provides encouragement to others that there will be help where there is trouble.

But I know, as you know, that there will be men who you cannot bring back. For them, we must do God's work of making our comrades as comfortable as possible until the end. Those men must in their final moments not only be shown compassion for their plight but also a full recognition that their contribution was not in vain but rather was significant and regarded as gallant.

The major looked out at pink-cheeked young Australians.

Finally men, when you are doing your work in the field, always remember the words in St John's Gospel.

'Let not your heart be troubled, neither let it be afraid.' You are doing God's work.

You are dismissed.

As bearers, Nelson and Pomp were essential cogs in the wheels of a complicated system of military machinery. And at the fighting end of that machinery, they were vital to the success of the war effort. For without them and those in similar roles, there would be an intrinsic deficiency. There simply would not be enough men to attack the enemy in order to achieve the overriding goal of any army.

Victory.

The Town of Estaires—14 October 1916

Although Nelson was not far from the Somme and the major theatre of battle, the military command was not yet ready to put him there. For now at least, he remained some distance from the front, just outside Estaires.

Reveille was again early: this time at 6 am. After it, Nelson decided to wash in the river, La Lys, followed by breakfast.

Nelson then cleaned out his billet – he had been put up in a small part of a large school within Estaires. Every classroom had a crucifix in it. By 8 am, Nelson could see that some classes were already commencing. The young children were dressed in black and the boys wore black aprons. The *estaminet* (café) was in the same building, the '*Pensione de demoiselles*'.

At 9 am, Nelson was ordered to march down to the train station to unload stretchers and medical equipment from the wagons.

On the way to the Estaires station, he passed a funeral flowing out of the local church. The mourners were in black. The coffin-bearers were all women.

The next day, Sunday, Nelson looked over the church. He wrote in his diary: 'Church great. The Roman Catholic windows are a feature.'

Much Closer to Battle Now—17 October 1916

At 1.30 pm, the 15th Field Ambulance was called up to be ready for the front. Packs were arranged and at 2.15 pm, Nelson and the others were given their first rum issue. Although Nelson did not yet know it, rum would be given to stretcher-bearers regularly before and after action on the Western Front. It was by then an established AIF practice. The Australians had been given it on 25 April 1915 as the moon sank and rowboats journeyed towards the cliffs at Gallipoli. (The *Defence Act 1909 (Cmth)* prohibited the supply of spirituous liquors to persons at any camp or fort or post, but only during training times. The issue of rum to Nelson was therefore perfectly legal.)

After all had assembled, the soldiers marched out along dark streets that (according to Nelson's diary) 'resounded' by the nails in their synchronised boots on French cobblestones.

The soldiers arrived in a square where they were packed in groups of 30 in Army Service Corps wagons to be taken to the front via Baileau, Calais, St-Omer, Boulogne, arriving at Pont-Remy about 4 pm. Along the way, Nelson could see much of France's old trucks and old railway stock had been lost to the Germans.

After disembarking, fatigue parties were put together and work continued until 5.30 pm after which time coffee and biscuits were handed out. After a short break, Nelson and the others picked up their packs and started a 10-mile march that continued until 9 pm. A few of the men collapsed despite two spells of five and seven minutes each. By this time, it was pitch dark along the valley with its long avenue of trees.

Suddenly the marching stopped. The men were issued with a second round of rum. Some 200 yards up the road, Nelson could see a farmhouse. It was his billet for the night along with the other mates in the 15th. Plenty of straw meant a soft and warm bed.

The next day Nelson wrote in his diary: 'Soundest sleep I ever had.'

Time to Vote—18 October 1916

Nelson woke in the French countryside at about 8 am and lay in the hay until 9 am. Dazed by the night's exhausting marches, he began to realise he was being billeted in a substantial French farm.

He headed down to C Section and had breakfast on a stump in the drizzle. A sergeant handed him a form to fill out.

'Here, take this. We all have to do it. Your family back home has to do it too. So get on with it and I want the form returned promptly, Ferguson.'

It was the vote to decide whether Australians could be conscripted into the AIF; that is, made to fight without volunteering. The Australian Government wanted to make it compulsory to join the army. Although it had the power to draft soldiers and send them abroad, it had decided to put the idea to the Australian people by referendum. This included Nelson and the others fighting abroad.

Shivering hard, Nelson looked towards the bog and the battlefield stretching out in front of him, wondering whether men should be required to die that way.

Nelson marked the form.

'I hope you bloody marked it the right way, Ferguson,' shouted the sergeant.

'Yes sir, I have voted according to conscience.'

'Well there will be a lot more young dead blokes before there are fewer if we don't get this over the line.'

Ultimately, those within the AIF voted for compulsion, but only by a slim majority of 13,000. The nation of Australia would, however, vote otherwise.

Things Now Serious—The Last Week of October 1916

Nelson was now 16 miles from the Somme and in a major theatre of war. A transport took him to Albert through Amiens, followed by a 15-mile march to Fricourt, north-east of Amiens. Fricourt had been taken by the Allies in early July 1916.

When Nelson arrived at dusk, he was given water and then a cup of tea. Meals could not be provided because the transported food did not arrive until 11 pm.

Things were serious—the front was just up ahead. Nelson could now see it. Smell it. Feel it. War was finally right in front of him and would soon surround him. The hairs on the back of his neck and all up and down his arms stood to attention as if ordered.

Nelson wrote in his diary: 'Could see shells bursting on half horizon & continuous barking of guns woke me often in the night.'

The next morning was freezing, consistent with a bright and clear French sky. Big Allied surveillance balloons reached to the blue sky high above Nelson. They were to gather information on German artillery positions. But they were constantly being pulled down by the AIF on account of the Huns approaching, with many aeroplanes zipping back and forth in the air. On the ground, everywhere Nelson looked there were thousands of horses. The heavy bombardment seemed to be coming from all quarters. The canvas of military endeavour was as broad as the kingdoms being attacked and defended.

In the middle of the morning Nelson was put on duty in the operating theatre. There were four men on four operating tables at a time. The first was a brain case, the next an arm.

Nelson was put off duty at 4.30 pm but told to be ready for duty all night. Rations for the bearers were limited due to the poor roads and heavy traffic up and down them. The 15th Field Ambulance's War Diary recorded that the difficulty for the bearers was almost insufferable. The diary noted that reports from bearers:

show the terrible and arduous nature of the work. All ranks are almost continuously exposed to the weather which has been very severe. No shelters are obtainable at some posts and the men are in consequence suffering from the unusual exposure as well as from the fact that it is almost impossible to obtain fuel and cook food.

That night Nelson was not needed for further stretcher-bearing of damaged soldiers (called 'carries') in urgent need of medical attention, as the 95th did not hand over. Nelson rose the next morning to be put on routine tasks, and in the evening he and a mate walked across the shell holes made from the recent artillery attacks. They became visible by the light of German shots.

It rained the whole next day, with no bombardment and no clamber by the troop over the trenches towards the enemy (known as 'hop-overs'). Nelson had been assigned to night duty and so he went for a walk in the rain and the mud. He pressed forward towards the front line and soon found himself in disused German trenches which had been fearfully battered by the Allied artillery. The surrounding landscape was a mass of shell holes and twisted iron made by dud shells and bombs. Nelson ventured further and found himself in a German dugout. It was comfortable and clean and, to his surprise, had Aussies living in it. The dugout also had a dead German in it surrounded by photos and letters, which the Anzacs had left alone.

Nelson walked further on. The church in front of him had been turned into a Red Cross comfort store, servicing displaced citizens.

When he returned to camp, he was put into the 'preparing tent'. It readied soldiers for the surgeon's work on the operating theatre. The shift lasted 12 hours. A heavy depression fell over Nelson as he listened to and watched the fearful cases on the large bloodied table.

He worked all night and went to bed at 8.00 am. Before sleep he wrote in his diary: 'Tired from continual bearing and smell of blood.'

Shells screaming directly overhead woke Nelson at 4.30 pm. They were landing in the town of Albert, some two miles behind him.

He went on duty again at 7.00 pm, as he had the night before. A heavy and fearful bombardment by the British commenced at 5.00 am. A 'hop-over' was expected but in fact did not come off and so Nelson went to bed. When he woke at 2.20 pm, he walked to the railhead and saw part of an armoured train and a 12-inch gun firing away.

At night, things were not such a rush; only one case died on his stretcher. The wound was not that bad but the soldier lost so much blood that he died despite Nelson's saline injection.

The next day, Nelson again woke in the afternoon and began his night shift. Six ambulance chaps became exhausted just as shell shock and gas cases needed carrying to the Advanced Dressing Station (ADS).

The cases had initially been taken by 'regimental bearers' who were part of fighting units right up at the front. If wounded could not walk (on average some 50 per cent of the time that was so) then the regimental bearers would take the wounded as soon as possible to a Regimental Aid Post (RAP) where a regimental medical officer would seek to assuage pain, permit rest, provide sustenance, and triage (sort) them depending on the severity of wounds. RAPs were usually in a dug-out or communication trench and sometimes in a shell hole close to the front. If the soldier could be fixed up there and then, he would be put back at the front. If he could not, a card or ticket describing his wounds would be attached, and field ambulance bearers would then take the 'carry' (the wounded soldier as he was referred to in the field) to the better equipped Advanced Dressing Station (ADS). The ADS would usually be some 400 yards from the front. The station was usually a tent or series of tents. If the soldier could not be treated there due to the severity of the wounds, he would be taken (usually by wheeled transport) to a Casualty Clearing Station (CCS), the first point at which surgery could be undertaken if necessary. CCSs were usually near roads or railway lines so that the soldier could, if needed, be transported to an Australian General Hospital in France (there were three). The CCSs, like the RAPs and the ADSs, had to be capable of being moved quickly in the event of an enemy advance or attack. The British Army had some 70 CCSs in France, three of which belonged to the Australian Medical Corps.

At the ADS Nelson was now at, one of the gas cases sat up on the stretcher, then fell back dead.

The preceding days had not only been shocking and terrible, but there was not enough food to go around; Nelson was given one piece of bread for the day. He jotted in his diary: 'Chaps taking biscuits from the pockets of the dead.'

Things were getting worse still. A proclamation was given that, at a given hour, all roads would be closed to all traffic except gun limbers (a two-wheeled cart supporting the movement of artillery); not even ambulance personnel would be permitted through. Nelson was suddenly very worried; everything had become exceedingly quiet. The supposed attack would be along a 20-mile front, involving a vast number of men for the hop-over.

The next day rain pelted down and neither side could do much to shake the other. Nelson wrote in his diary: 'Rain hampers all.' It abated in the afternoon so Nelson went for a walk. Nelson could see German shells bursting on the ridge ahead of him. He was staggered to see a new monster of warfare: the tank. The British had employed them for the first time in the Battle of the Somme. They were, at least at this stage, more experimental than effective but still they terrified all the troops. Only thirty-two were used and this was not enough to achieve any significant breakthrough.

Nelson walked back to Albert. He stopped outside the main doors of the church in the centre of the town. Nelson looked up. The statue on top had been blown over and was hanging down. From this precarious angle, the Virgin Mary looked down the street, holding baby Jesus in her arms.

Two days later, after heavy rain, Nelson began trying to dry his clothes between carries. There was little or no food; certainly not enough bread for three days.

Nelson wrote in his diary: 'A stew at 11 at night saved our lives.'

The field ambulances had not fared well from the prior weeks of work. From the 6th, 14th and 15th Field Ambulances, 60 members had been evacuated from shell shock, cold and exhaustion.

At 3.00 am, Pomp and Nelson, who had been paired for stretcher work, clambered up over the top of the trench. With stretcher in hand, they began their journey into and across no-man's-land. Two other bearers in the squad (part of a unit) had been assigned to the work too. Stretchers were about six feet long with wooden poles down each side. A man lifted each corner. Stretchers were heavy. With an injured soldier on them, the bearers would take great physical strain for long periods.

The artillery had just ceased barking and the distant moaning of the wounded was now being received into the Australian trenches.

The trenches were impassable in parts for these stretcher-bearers, so the men had been carrying over the surface of the battlefield. But the ground there was so slippery that Pomp and Nelson could scarcely keep from falling over while carrying, and in some places the mud was so gluey and deep that it was as much as they could do to just walk without being able to even raise the stretcher.

At this point, the condition of the battlefield in the area Pomp and Nelson were in rendered it necessary for the AIF to set up over 400 bearers and five relay posts across some 4000 yards, with relief for the bearers being given at regular intervals.

'Get over there and help those two,' shouted the corporal. Four men went over to Pomp and Nelson and started supporting them. The men lifted a wounded soldier onto the stretcher and the six bearers began carrying the patient to the ADS.

Pomp and Nelson finally arrived at the post. Their patient was in shock and very cold. The journey took several hours.

The Spade

When Pomp and Nelson arrived back at the ADS, they were exhausted. They dragged the stretcher into the tent and put the 'carry' in the care of others. They staggered outside and folded in the mud.

'Get back out there!' shouted the sergeant from the flap of the tent.

'We're all done in, sorry,' said Pomp.

The sergeant's face turned blood-red.

'Piffle. If you don't move off, you will be charged with failing to obey an order.'

Pomp and Nelson looked at each other in disbelief.

'We've been carrying for hours in this mud,' shouted Pomp. 'We saved as many as we could, Sergeant, but we have nothing left. If you make Fergo go out there again, I'll knock your flaming block off. And much worse.'

Pomp's eyes raged. His huge frame reached for a trench spade, both fists clenched with the will of a champion axeman. The sergeant moved forward. Pomp pushed closer, the spade now high, its edge aimed straight at the sergeant's head.

The two men stared at each other with blind fury, each waiting for the other's move.

'We'll get on our way, Sergeant,' said Nelson.

Pomp dropped the spade.

'It's not bloody right, Fergo. This bloke's a fuckwit. He doesn't know what we've been through.'

'He could never know, Pomp. But one man killing another isn't going to help the diggers out there.'

Pomp glared at the sergeant. 'We can only do our best and no more—that's it,' said Pomp. 'If you ask us again, I'll finish what you started.'

The bearers pulled their stretcher from the stinking mud and climbed back over the trench once more towards endless slippery terrain.

The Sledge

As Pomp and Nelson headed out for further carries, they passed a group of huddled men.

'Hey boys, you should be using this.'

Pomp and Nelson looked down. A sledge had been built from canvas and long poles, meaning men could be at the front instead of each end of a stretcher.

'Bloody brilliant,' said Pomp.

The sledge had been conceived and designed by Warrant Officer Arthur Evan Roberts, a farmer from Warragul in Victoria. Roberts had been in the 13th Light Horse as a sergeant prior to the outbreak of war. He had used sledges on his own farm back home like the one he had designed for the front. The sledge had initially been built using the fork of a tree but this was found to attract too much suction in the mud and so it had been modified.

'We've already saved a few chaps using this contraption,' said another bearer. 'His leg was blown off and without this we couldn't have got him back to the ADS in time—it took less than one hour to get him there.'

The carry by stretcher-bearers using the sledge would ultimately be reduced to only two hours between battle and the ADS. The sledge was never officially endorsed by the AIF. It was an 'unauthorised but productive system' like countless other systems developed by soldiers during wartime.

Shell Shock Cases Still Coming In

For the month of October 1916, the War Diary of the 15th Field Ambulance reported reduced casualties. Only seven soldiers had been gassed, 240 wounded, and 109 suffered shell shock. The diary listed other cases treated and then noted the following:

The above list calls for no comment except in the case of shell shock cases. The great majority of these patients were Imperial Troops, the Australian Troops being singularly free.

Hop-overs—November 1916

By early November 1916, Nelson and Pomp had been constantly up in the front line performing carries each night. German aeroplanes regularly dropped bombs near them. On one night, bombs had been dropped just 200 yards from Nelson and Pomp. This shook them badly; it killed eight, wounded 10, and lamed four horses.

On 1 November 1916, Nelson looked over the battlefield to see German prisoners being taken and kept under loose AIF guard.

According to Nelson's diary, a captured German officer was 'petted' by Australian troops, who offered him a cigarette and a drink.

Carries remained difficult; although the land was now drying up, the mud was still past the knees. This meant hop-overs were not possible, at least just not yet.

On 2 November 1916, one of Nelson's mates, Alfred Hopkins of the 15th Field Ambulance, died of wounds.

On 5 November 1916, the 1st Division of the AIF hopped over with the 2nd in support. The first and second attempts were failures but it was now believed that the AIF was holding a ridge on the approach to Bapaume, but with many Australians wounded.

Nelson and Pomp were 'put on carries' all through the battle. On one occasion, just as they approached the ADS, the soldier on their stretcher died. The bearers put the soldier into the tent. Soldiers at the door of the tent peered in, then continued with their game of draughts.

On 12 November 1916, Nelson and Pomp came under severe shellfire. Officers of the AIF bolted down the road and sergeants scattered. In the distance, further up the road, huge explosions could be heard; a French ammunition dump was going up in clouds of smoke. The noise lasted nearly a quarter of an hour.

Two days later, there was another 'hop-over' and some 60,000 AIF infantrymen held the ridge close to Bapaume. As they hopped over, so too did the Germans. Some 200 of the enemy threw up their hands and became prisoners.

Nelson went down to the German trenches to have a look. They were lined with grey duckboards, well kept and dry.

Snow and Trench Foot—November 1916

On 18 November, Nelson woke to snow-covered ground. The unbearable cold cut right through him, invading his bones.

The winter was now the main enemy. It was one of the coldest in 40 years. Men from the Australian 5th Division were now wearing woollen mittens and sheepskin vests. Throughout 1916, Australian wool-farmers had donated enough hides to make half a million vests for frozen diggers in Northern France.

Nelson was told to unload a train-full of wounded. His ears filled with their screaming up and down the carriages.

When he came back to his tent to rest, he found himself totally exhausted. He had now been at the front for several months and had been performing 'carries' on a daily basis. Nelson rested before getting up to prepare himself for his turn in medical support.

'I reckon they'll make us go out again soon,' said Pomp.

'Yeh, I can't see anything changing,' said Nelson.

'We should bloody well tell them to bugger off completely,' said Pomp angrily.

'Even if they told us to go out, I don't think I could make it this time, Pomp. My feet are gone. They ache. I reckon I'm coming down with trench foot,' said Nelson.

Nelson pulled his boots off. His feet were greyish-white and swollen.

'Bloody hell, Fergo, they look shocking. Sorry, mate, but they stink like dead rats. We'd better take you down to camp for that. I've heard they have some ointment you can smear on.'

Pomp helped Nelson down to the dressing area. When they arrived, a medico put whale oil on Nelson's feet to get them going again. This was supposed to provide relief against trench foot. Orders had earlier been made that:

FEET: The feet of all personnel marching out will be rubbed with
whale oil on the evening of 20th inst and a clean pair of socks put on.

'You're lucky, Private, we can sort this out before you're out of action
for months with "trench foot",' said the doctor.

Trench foot was a severe ailment which plagued large numbers of
soldiers, caused by feet remaining damp or wet for long periods.

'Some luck, doc,' said Pomp, steering Nelson's feet back into the
old boots.

As Nelson and Pomp sat there waiting for the treatment to have
some effect, guns remained busy and continuous nearby.

The Valley of 1000 Guns—November 1916

When Nelson returned to his position back from the front, he began
cooking the evening meal. He and Pomp were now in Delville Wood.
The Germans began shelling overhead.

Nelson and Pomp went out the next day for carries and continued
stretcher-bearing right through the night. The two mates were
absolutely done in.

As the next day began with a grey dawn the sound of shelling got
closer. 'Hurry along, Pomp,' cried Nelson. 'These shells are getting
very, very close.'

'Very close, they're bloody well on us now!' called Pomp.

As he spoke, boards laid to enable troops to walk above the mud
of the battlefield (known as 'duckboards') failed under foot and a shell
landed nearby, covering the boys in mud. The stretcher tipped and the
'carry' also then fell into the mud.

The bearers were now knee deep in the mud, trying to right the
stretcher, collect the patient, and return to the duckboards.

As they struggled on, further stretcher-bearers arrived and gave
relief. Nelson and Pomp returned to their dugout and collapsed, glad
to get away from the shelling. But it was not long before they were
ordered out again. As they passed the battery at No. 1 station, shells
from big distant guns came on them. None of the shells landed close
and so the bearers clambered along in the mud and rain. Knees, backs
and shoulders were now gone.

On 20 November 1916, Nelson and Pomp marched to Bernafay Wood. The boys found tents there and flopped down into them. The beds in them were wet but the bearers slept till the morning. Nelson tried to get up but collapsed and went back to bed.

He was stronger the next day and wrote in his diary: 'Pleased to get away from the valley of 1000 guns.'

The Allies had pushed hard since the Battle of the Somme had commenced in July 1916. Nelson had been part of it since late September. It was now the end of November. The Allies had gained ground and held the line to Clery (on the Somme), Sailly-Saillisel, Gueudecourt, Le Sars and Beaumont-Hamel. The Germans had reached the limit of their endurance for the time being, and had fled back to the so-called Hindenburg Line for protection. The Line was a long and heavily reinforced system of trenches which the Germans had been constructing since September 1916, from Arras to Laffaux, near Soissons on the Ais, in anticipation of further Anglo-French attacks planned for 1917.

Both sides knew those attacks were inevitable, as would be the eventual result: damaged and dead soldiers in large numbers on both sides yet no side giving up.

Apart from continuing to build the Hindenburg Line, the Germans were now also seeking to boost the number of Germans dedicated to warfare and killing. In the month Nelson was in the valley of the 1000 guns, November 1916, the German parliament introduced the Auxiliary Service Law (*Hilfsdienstgesetz*) under which all Germans aged 16–50 would be required to undertake compulsory service. Practically the whole German adult male population was now a war participant.

Infected Eyes—11 December 1916

By now Nelson was virtually dead on his damaged and near trench-rotten feet.

But Nelson was not the only one suffering. The medical report for the 15th Field Ambulance stated:

The great preponderance of trench foot cases was a marked feature of the diseases arising in Australian troops, 520 being passed through during the month. Influenza number 237.

The report noted that troops were also suffering from bronchitis (with associated loss of voice), chronic pneumonia and lung infections.

In the early part of December Nelson was trying to recover from exhaustion and illness but was constantly in and out of bed, as were many in his unit. He prepared himself regularly for the trenches but was often assigned as baggage guard because of illness.

On 5 December he spent a long day mostly in bed, during which he had to guard two German prisoners. This was not unusual; the wounded and sick were regularly appointed as guards so that fighting men could return to the front.

In the next week, things got worse. Nelson's eyes became infected.

'The night's been a misery Pomp. I can't get on the other end of our stretcher like this. I reckon I'll fall off the duckboards every time, mate.'

'You're not going anywhere with those flaming red sunspots for eyes on your dial, Fergo. We've got to get you some treatment and more bloody rest.'

But Nelson's eyes were not sufficient reason to avoid carrying. Pomp and Nelson were given orders to go out and find the wounded. They did so but not much bearing was required so they managed the day out.

The next day Nelson and Pomp's post was abandoned by their unit and so all dugouts were pulled down and material was carted back from the front.

Nelson could not keep anything down and dry-retched all morning. He spent the rest of the day in a damp bed.

More Snow and Duckboards

By the middle of December 1916, after some rest it was Nelson's turn again for the trenches. In the almost unbearable early cold on the morning of Saturday 16 December 1916, Nelson and Pomp undertook fatigues work (cleaning and maintenance at camp) until 11.00 am, then had some lunch.

At 1.00 pm, the bearers had to fall in to start their journey towards 'advanced posts'. It was again snowing on them. All the bearers lined up with heavy packs. Nelson stood with the others in the freezing conditions, waiting for orders.

After some time, Nelson, Pomp and the others were ordered out and began marching from Bernafay. Nelson began to warm up and he soon entered the duckboard section. He passed fresh shell holes and a few dead horses. The walk along the duckboards was in close single file as snow fell all around. Strangely, Nelson could see the romantic nature of his conditions.

Nelson wrote in this diary:

The pack marches along duckboards in close single file with white snow falling all around, feeling nice and warm, so happy. The duckboards finish so now walk in mud towards Deville Wood. Plenty of shells coming over but passing very high and towards the sugar factory.

As they approached the new No. 2 post, the officer in front of Nelson shot inside the post box and then disappeared from Nelson's view. Nelson and the other bearers were given no instructions, so they stood in the falling snow for some 20 minutes waiting for the officer to return. On his return, the officer told the bearers they would be setting out further, for No. 3 post.

As they approached No. 3 post, the bearers were told to make camp. They scraped off the snow from their kit and crawled into a dugout, all six of them. A fire would not start—it was too wet—so the soldiers had bread and cheese for dinner rather than anything cooked or warm.

By 5.00 pm it was dark, so the soldiers lay down to sleep in the dugout.

At 6.00 pm, Nelson was woken and told to take a sheet of iron to the ADS hospital. As Nelson made his way down the track he was shelled at, but not all the time.

By now, Nelson was just two ridges from the German lines. It was too dark for him to get his bearings. He became lost but eventually found his way back onto the duckboards.

When he returned to the dugout for sleep, he was again woken, this time at 9.00 pm, and ordered to take a walking case to No. 2 pillbox (a concrete dug-in guard post, normally filled with loopholes from which to fire weapons—the name 'pillbox' was given by the troops because the guard post looked like a medical pillbox sold at the time).

The firing of shells out of a military battery (a number of artillery guns collected together for strategic or tactical reasons) made Nelson's path difficult because shells were landing in the area he was now in. He decided to place himself and his patient in a nearby dugout. After some time, Nelson and his patient left the dugout but just as they recommenced their journey, enemy shrapnel from the artillery fire landed just by them.

So Nelson and his patient returned to the dugout and lay there listening to the shrapnel bursting about them, as the shelling from the battery continued for 20 minutes.

Eventually Nelson and his patient left the dugout and continued with their journey, soon arriving at No. 2 pillbox. Nelson told his patient to rest against the wall, and checked on him again before heading off to the soup kitchen nearby, where he had tea. He then set out for the long, lonely homeward journey. As he travelled, for some reason the enemy decided to stop shelling.

Nelson was relieved from duty after passing Delville Wood. All throughout the journey, Nelson had not passed a single soul.

Although he was pleased to get back to his dugout, he slept poorly due to the wet and the cold. But he was grateful not to have been interrupted further that night.

Rumours of Peace Talks

The next day, Sunday, the warring parties held artillery duels all day. Nelson sat up in his dugout with all his clothes wrapped around him to keep warm. He got a loan of a primus and made himself some tea, followed by bread, butter and jam for breakfast. During breakfast, a soldier who had just returned from leave approached him.

'G'day mate. Mind if I join you for a brew of tea?'

'Sure,' said Nelson.

'Thanks. I've just come back from leave. I've heard those bloody Huns are all done in and want peace.'

'Maybe,' said Nelson, 'but from where I sit it doesn't sound like they're ready for that yet. The recent quiet of the last few hours just means the guns are resting, or being taken somewhere else I reckon. I saw some caterpillars backing up to take guns away just then. Thank God for that, these 18-pounders are a curse.'

'Yeh,' said the digger. 'Let's hope we are heading for peaceful times.'

The digger's hope was real. The AIF was pulling out of the area and the next day Nelson began a march that saw him draw back from the big guns and the terror of carries.

Eventually Nelson met up with the 24th Division Company and took up lighter work at the collecting station maintained by it. He was fed well and now living in much better conditions than he had for many months. His pencil placed this in his diary: 'Feeding well with Y corps collecting station. Having good time living in bonza huts.'

As far as Nelson's immediate circumstances were concerned, there was room for optimism.

But at the Empire level, things were very different. Lloyd George himself had in the same month declared: 'We are going to lose this war.'

Christmas Pudding—December 1916

On Christmas Eve 1916 Nelson and his mates received boxes of goodies, including tins of lollies, peanuts and walnuts, a handkerchief, a pipe and some tobacco. Puddings were also handed out, one for every two soldiers.

It was temporarily quiet and peaceful. The troops talked about the way Christmas had been spent at home before the war.

The rumours Nelson and his mates had heard about peace had been true. For at least the previous two months there had been serious attempts by the warring nations to end the war, brokered by America.

But two long months of brinkmanship by the Allies and the Germans had produced no result. The Allies had rejected Germany's offer in mid-December 1916 'to open negotiations'. In late 1916, Haig had asked the British Government for a further 500,000 fighting men, even though hundreds of thousands of men had already died in France. The military machine always had the trump card: to deny men to the Generals would be to contribute to defeat. In December 1916, the British War Cabinet approved compulsory military service.

Earlier in the war, Germany had suspended its unlimited submarine warfare, but now the German High Command was pressing for its resumption, for two reasons. First, the burden of food shortages in Germany had become intolerable. Second, Germany estimated that if it could sink 600,000 tons of enemy shipping per month, Britain would surrender in six months.

Germany's desire to 'starve' Britain out of the war by these means was not only driven by Britain's successful starving of the German people so far. It was also motivated by the Allies' raw superiority of fighting power over Germany—Britain and France now had more men (190 divisions versus 154 divisions), heavy guns, machine guns and other equipment than Germany.

And Germany's plans were being enacted now in the face of one shocking fact— that if Germany sank even one neutral vessel, it would breach the undertaking it had given to America in May 1916, which would result in America declaring war on it.

The perennial difficulty of war, that no-one knows when it is going to end, meant that the warring nations had to continue to pace themselves. The failure to see reason by either side meant more carnage of young men.

And for Nelson and Pomp it meant one thing in particular. They would be put back into the hell of battleground, soon and indefinitely.

The New Year and the Flu—January 1917

At 5.00 am on New Year's Day, Nelson left Amiens and began walking to Albert for a day's leave. Not far from Amiens, he waited by a large shell hole in a wall of a building until lorries took him 19 miles up the road to the outskirts of Albert. Nelson took some time to find the main street. It bore no resemblance to the war-torn villages he had become used to. There were no shell holes or destroyed shops, although many were closed. As he passed through the main street, he admired the beautiful black dresses of the women, and the fine French coats on the men.

Nelson stepped into a restaurant and ordered breakfast, then took a tram ride until 2.00 pm. He stopped off at Albert's massive cathedral, which was weather-beaten but not war-damaged. It had been largely protected by sandbags, and the Germans' greater priorities.

He had afternoon tea (costing 15 francs) in another restaurant. After his brief break, it was time to return to camp and so Nelson caught another lorry home. He wrote in his diary: 'Amiens not up to expectations but a fine break from devastation.'

After his return to camp, Nelson was told he would be motored to Dernancourt. As he rested that evening, Nelson began to feel unwell. The symptoms were of influenza. Chills. A rasping throat. And heavy stiffness in the joints. But, more than anything, heavy malaise.

The next morning he paraded sick. Although he had been given some medicine, after a few hours he was excused from duty as he could not stand up. He went to bed ill and exhausted. For several days the flu knocked him out.

As soon as Nelson turned the corner with the flu, he was put back on duty. He was told to go out and look for any sick or wounded diggers.

By this time, the mid-January snow and frost had turned the ground to cement. Nelson looked down at his frozen boots; he could not feel his feet. His ankles were blue and walking was only barely possible.

Despite all this, Nelson went out the farthest he had been towards the German lines, providing first aid to the soldiers in the trenches.

On the way back he was stopped twice by shells, with many Taubes coming over. Taubes were German planes, developed by an Austrian, Igo Etrich, in 1909. Taubes made up about half the German aircraft force. They would travel long distances. In fact, one had bombed Paris in the first month of the war.

The heavy shelling just behind him was now in many places lifting the very duckboards Nelson was tramping on as he made his way to and from the front line. As he approached the last leg of the duckboards, Nelson could see men dead on each side of them, killed by artillery and machine gun fire.

He pinched himself to see whether he was in fact dreaming.

When he got back to camp, Nelson was astonished to see two AIF stretcher-bearers barefooted, carrying a digger back to safety. Their damaging frozen boots were tied to the end of their stretcher.

In the late evening, Nelson went for a footbath at the medical tent. His feet had now been wet for days. He was again at serious risk of trench foot.

The bath temporarily improved the feeling in the feet. During the treatment, Nelson noted in his diary that according to the army's thermometer the weather outside the tent had reached minus 18 degrees Fahrenheit (minus 28 degrees Celsius).

Given his condition, the AIF was likely to remove Nelson from the battle area. However, if they did not, he would potentially become involved in further heavy engagements. The German manpower shortage on the Western Front had become acute near the end of 1916, and the Germans had now transferred large numbers of troops from Russia. By late January 1917 a total of a staggering 133 German divisions were now positioned to continue the fighting on the Western Front. If Nelson remained where he was, he would be part of further and continuous major battles.

The inevitable next offensive by either side would see a heavy escalation of the wounded and the ill, requiring yet further toil by bearers and others in extreme conditions. There might be early signs of a retreat by the Germans, but they would no doubt be on the offensive again in the not too distant future.

As a fighting force, the Germans remained formidable. The Allied leadership well knew it. Nelson and Pomp saw it.

The Opening of the British Parliament— 7 February 1917

On 7 February 1917, His Majesty King George V, who had signed the royal prerogative writs putting Britain (and as a consequence Australia) into war, opened the British Parliament in London in person. It was the first since November 1914.

The usual pageantry and courtly guests were not present. Instead was a modest and sombre parade to the palace, the king in a plain carriage, accompanied by officers from the armies of the Empire.

The Gentlemen Usher of the Black Rod of the British Parliament made the following announcement: 'The King commands this

Honourable House to attend immediately at the House of Peers to hear His Majesty's Gracious Speech from the Throne read.'

This was a proud moment for the citizens of Ballarat. At the ceremony, a Ballarat boy, Mervyn Herbert, acted as escort to the king. He was one of the Gallipoli Knights, having been one of the first to land at Gallipoli on 25 April 1915, injured there two days later, and evacuated on 28 April 1915.

In His Majesty's Speech, the king noted:

My Armies have conducted successful operations not only in Europe but in Egypt, Mesopotamia, and East Africa, and they are fully prepared to renew the great struggle, in close and cordial co-operation with my Allies, on every field. I trust that their united efforts will carry the successes already won to a victorious conclusion.

I have invited representatives of My Dominions and of My Indian Empire, which have borne so glorious a share in the struggle, to confer with My Ministers on important questions of common interest relating to the war. The step so taken will, I trust, conduce to the establishment of closer relations between all parts of My Empire.

Displacing usual dignitaries in the Royal Gallery, the king had invited over 300 wounded non-commissioned officers and men from the colonial armed forces (including those from the AIF), who joined in the cheering of the king when directed.

Back in Parliament, a parliamentary officer in formal court dress begged leave to offer humble thanks for the king's speech. He then noted Wordsworth's words in 1803 that, as Britain stood ready against Napoleon's planned invasion, 'Britain is in One Breath' against the enemy.

In answer to the king's speech, the Admiral of the Fleet, Sir H Meux noted: 'Once it is known that you are fighting for the right, you cannot be defeated, for righteousness is immortal.'

Gas Cases—February 1917

Back in the trenches on the Western Front, despite the appalling conditions Nelson and Pomp had been working in and the work rate required, at least according to the Australian Medical Corps, they were still 'at strength'. They were therefore considered fit and able to continue their work of bearing the wounded back to ADSs as required.

On 13 February 1917, Nelson was warned that the Germans in his region would use gas. The enemy had in fact sent it to the right of the area which had been expected to be targeted. Nelson and Pomp moved into the area of the gas to assist with carries of those now damaged from its toxic effect.

The next day, the Germans sent gas over again. Nelson and Pomp worked all night transporting the gas cases back to safety. Gas had caught the 32nd Battalion near the so-called Rose trench (trenches were given names for specific identification). Two of the gassed soldiers died from it.

The Germans had also worked out where the Allied munitions dump was. They began shelling it aggressively. Huge explosions surrounded the two bearers, followed by gas shelling. Nelson and Pomp hurried back in case the wind changed to avoid being caught in the poison.

The next day, cases of late gas poisoning started coming in and Nelson and Pomp began assisting as best they could. The poisoning made young men sicker than the mates had seen.

As soon as their duties finished, Nelson got into his damp bed. He had been working day after day in the mist and rain and had been staying in wet dugouts without knowing the day or date. He was now totally exhausted.

Sketching Time—February 1917

On 23 February 1917, Nelson and Pomp were about to lay on their bunks in the muddy dugout when they were warned that there were five cases needing carrying. The mates sat outside the dugout and waited for further orders. They sat there with cold feet and mud to their thighs for some time.

But no news of the carries arrived so the two mates went back down into the dugout, took their boots off, and got under some wet blankets. They were awoken at 1.30 am, put their slings and helmets on, and carried a stretcher out of the dugout, ready for more work.

On arrival at the trenches, they put a wounded soldier onto the stretcher and began the trip back. Their dull torch limited the number of times they fell over while carrying. According to Nelson's diary, the patient talked 'wonderlingly' at first but by the end of the carry Nelson could not rouse him.

By this stage, the bearers were again up to their thighs in mud. Nelson could not tell if he and Pomp were on the track or not. Because of the heavy mist, Fritz's flares were not assisting the two mates to see what was happening in front of them. The journey of five miles back took them about two hours.

When Nelson and Pomp reached the safety of their dugout, they rolled into bed drenched in salty sweat and pig dirty.

The damp bed was not helped by the spring night which was clear, making it particularly cold. And it was now getting colder.

But sleep was still possible and the two mates took advantage of it until now well into the afternoon. For once the officers sensibly left the bearers alone to recover from physical and mental exhaustion.

In the late afternoon the distant guns fell silent, waking the bearers.

'I'm just going out to do some more sketching, Pomp.'

'You want me to come too?'

'No, I should be fine Pomp—get some more rest, mate.'

Nelson pulled on his trench coat. Some months earlier he had cut the end of it off so it would not get wet and boggy in the mud, and so it wouldn't weigh 40 pounds in the rain. No officer had held it against him for doing so. The inside pocket held a small tin box of brushes and watercolour paints.

He pushed out towards the setting sun and sat down behind a broken wooden fence. He opened the tin and pulled out a small piece of paper he had collected in the local town.

The heavy rumble of guns in front of him had Nelson's tin swiftly back in his trench coat. The spare brush in it rattled.

After pausing for some time, the guns fell silent again and Nelson returned to the task. A lark gave Nelson company by its call from the left.

Across the base of the work the broken trees and scarred landscape soon began to emerge. Nelson then applied a watery pink and golden blaze of sunset across a pale blue French sky.

Just as the watercolour was coming together nicely, Nelson suddenly heard heavy footsteps behind him quick at pace.

'Come on mate!' shouted Pomp. 'We've been called to a carry and it's bloody unsafe out here anyway, Fergo.'

'Righto Pomp, I'm on my way now.'

Nelson turned over the small cardboard he had been drawing on and hurriedly pencilled:

Second attempt at sunset behind a broken wooden fence. We got a carry just as I got this far, therefore I could not fill in the barbed wire and stakes to make the foreground interesting. The evenings here are glorious but just as they fall into night the fire opens.

The Germans Retreat—March 1917

By the middle of March 1917, the Germans were in retreat in the section in which Nelson and Pomp had been carrying. Nelson had heard rumours that they had retreated as far back as Cambrai. In fact this was already the case. On 17 March 1917, the town of Bapaume, which was one of the objectives set for the July 1916 assault, was finally captured by the Allies.

AIF patrols had been sent out to determine the extent of the retreat. Patrols had also entered Bapaume. In the coming weeks, the 8th and 15th Brigades of the AIF would re-enter Bapaume.

Nelson and Pomp did so too. The houses there had been mostly reduced to ruins. All of them seemed to have cellars and a few boys from the AIF went exploring for useful items but the Germans had left only broken beds and heaps of bricks all over the place.

In the main street, Nelson and Pomp passed an AIF official photographer, taking photos of a few generals high on horseback.

Sharp chins, polished leather, and shiny buttons on fresh uniforms glinted in front of rich manes. In the distance, Nelson could hear the occasional shot by a big retreating German gun. And he could see the ruined train station in the distance; the trains were smashed to pieces too, now lying sideways.

Blood-red Water

When Nelson and Pomp entered onto Albert Road, it was full of AIF transports which were heading towards the retreating German forces.

As they followed the advancing AIF, they passed by German positions. Nelson and Pomp crawled through barbed wire that had been part of Bapaume German defences. The two mates then reached the German lines and followed enemy-made sunken roads, with dugouts on the left and right.

Many bodies, mostly Australian, lay within 40 yards of the trenches they passed. Nelson recorded this in his diary: 'As we passed by, rain began to fall and the shell holes began to fill with water reddened with blood.'

As the bearers reached open territory, a large area was strewn with the dead, all horribly mutilated, and with one chap face down.

'This is an absolute nightmare,' said Nelson, shaking.

'Come on,' called Pomp, 'we have to keep moving, Fergo.'

Pomp immediately fell waist-deep into a stinking pit. Nelson grabbed a strong muddy hand and pulled hard. Pomp clambered out.

'Don't worry, Pomp, we're good now. We're not sticking around here. But I'm sticking close by you, mate.'

Breathless, Pomp wheezed. 'Wouldn't have it any other way, Fergo.'

The two pressed on in the driving rain and heavy mud until they reached the town of Gueudecourt. Nelson scribbled in his diary that it was the most ruined place he had yet seen in France.

In the coming week, Nelson and Pomp helped out in retaking the region and were part of the organising of medical facilities.

Sunday Service—25 March 1917

By late March 1917, the two mates had reached Meaulte, a small town just south of Albert. On Sunday, 25 March 1917, Nelson sat in the church service for a chap he knew who had been blown up in so-called Thistle trench.

When Nelson came out of the service, civilians were pulling carts of all shapes down the road and making their way back into their wrecked houses.

At the end of March, he wrote in his diary: 'Seems like peace time, have not seen or heard shells for days.'

Health Concerns with New Recruits—March 1917
Nelson had been accepted into the army because of the AIF's 'adjustment' in June 1915 to its height and chest requirements. The measure between initial ineligibility to fight and warfare was for Nelson a mere 3/4 of an inch.

By a series of significant further reductions in standards since Nelson had joined up, the AIF had now recruited further large numbers of young Australian volunteers for the European and African campaigns.

However, AIF commanding officers in the field were becoming increasingly concerned about the health of recruits coming to England. The AIF was having severe doubts about whether recruiting so-called 'B' class soldiers was actually worth it. In fact, even before seeing battle, large numbers of Australian troops were now being shipped back to Australia virtually as soon as arriving in England, deemed unfit for war.

Unlike Nelson and the others in England and on the Western Front, these men were not even given the 'opportunity' of battle.

Bullecourt and the Resurrection—April 1917
In early April 1917, Nelson and Pomp travelled by train to Albert.

By rubbing the carriage's foggy glass window Nelson could see a wet and smashed up terrain taking light snow. The bearers' destination was Bullecourt, north of Bapaume, and north-east of the vital strategic town of Amiens with its railway link to Paris and therefore military supplies.

Elsewhere, at Arras, in an area that had seen much battle known as Vimy Ridge, the British had again tried a head-on assault to break the German line. This was a major offensive: the British deployed 14 divisions, the Canadians four, supported by 2817 heavy guns and 48 tanks. Pushing forward for five days straight, the British and Canadians gained some 7000 yards and took some 10,000 German prisoners. That distance cost 160,000 killed and wounded young men.

The boys arrived in Bullecourt on Easter Sunday, 8 April. They soon formed part of a large parade of troops in front of the town's fine church. It was now time for glorious sunshine across lovely green fields, with only a few shell holes here and there to tell of the events of the night before. There had been a heavy bombardment into Bapaume, and Bullecourt had been within the roar of guns.

Nelson took the Bible from his trench coat. He thumbed through it to Matthew 28:1 and began reading the preface:

Christ's resurrection is declared by an angel to the women. He himself appeareth unto them. The high priests give the soldiers money to say that he was stolen out of his sepulchre. Christ appeareth to his disciples, and sendeth them to baptise and teach all nations.

The First Battle of Bullecourt—11 April 1917

On the night before 11 April 1917, Nelson noted in his diary that rough weather was washing across the area around Bullecourt, a town some 10 miles north-east from Bapaume, and that night alarms had continued calling Nelson and Pomp to be at the ready on an hour's notice.

Nelson's C Section had to get up and load wagons at midnight in the snow but they did not move out for some unknown reason.

In the morning of 11 April, the first battle of Bullecourt commenced. The 4th Division of the AIF attacked German trenches east of the village. The AIF's plan was that the division would advance some two miles north, take the village of Hendecourt which was one and a half miles north-east of Bullecourt. Usually, this kind of operation would be supported by a prior artillery bombardment of the German trenches. Not this time—the Anzacs attacked without such a bombardment having occurred. Nevertheless, the Anzacs took two German trenches. Nelson noted in his diary that the 4th Division had entered the Hindenburg Line, with the 15th Brigade to follow up. But the German counter-attacks regained the ground made by the Australians. The battle was a disaster for the Allies, with some 3000 men lost.

By mid-April, the 15th Field Ambulance, including Nelson and Pomp, had been marched down to Bapaume. The weather was too cold and wet for Nelson to sketch and shelling was in any event frequent, particularly along the Bapaume Road.

Nelson and Pomp were soon split up and for some time did not know each other's whereabouts. Nelson received news Pomp was at the Casualty Clearing Station and was very ill. In fact it was even worse, Pomp was now in hospital sick, unable to carry.

On 20 April 1917, Nelson arrived in Pozieres from Bapaume. He had been in the fighting of the Somme for six months now. Nelson smiled as he left that ghastly region behind.

The battle for the town of Pozieres, on the Albert–Bapaume Road, and the ridge upon which it stood, had taken place some 10 months earlier. The town had been a German stronghold. Between 13 and 17 July 1916, the Fourth Army of the British forces had sought to take the town and in the process it had been reduced to rubble. Shortly after, the accountability for the attack on Pozieres by the Allies had been transferred to the British Reserve Army, to which were attached three Australian divisions of the 1st Anzac Corps, which had begun moving from the Armentières sector.

Over the course of the next month, remorseless bombing, attacking and counter-attacking occurred in and around Pozieres, with the Germans and in turn the Allies suffering some limited success and many failures until, by mid-August 1916, at vast cost of life and injury including to the Australians, the Allies had retaken the town.

Below Army Standards—23 April 1917

On 23 April 1917, a new non-commissioned officer was appointed to Nelson's unit. In the afternoon, Nelson and the others were given a lecture on discipline. This was followed by a gruelling drill.

The new officer then lined up Nelson's section.

'As you all know, we are coming up to Anzac Day. Yet all I see in front of me is rabble and an un-kept lot! That's what I have concluded!'

The unit stood silent and exhausted.

The officer went slowly down the line of men.

'You, what's your name?'

'Ferguson, sir.'

'Why haven't you fucking shaved, Private? Don't you understand the army has high standards?!'

'I will ensure it happens every morning, sir.'

'I should bloody well hope so, Private. You are a fucking disgrace. We can't win this war if you can't even do the simplest of tasks. Do you know anything about discipline?!'

'I know what is expected of me.'

'Well you might know that, Private, but you sure haven't bloody well demonstrated it!

'If I see any of this sort of undisciplined behaviour again, I will go through the lot of you like a dose of salts. You are dismissed.' In front of this officer, all of Nelson's recent months in battlefields had counted for nothing—Nelson's misconduct, failing to shave, had fallen below standards.

But things were not too bad overall—Pomp had been released from hospital and would soon rejoin Nelson's unit.

A Second Anzac Day Arrives—25 April 1917

On Anzac Day, 25 April 1917, Nelson wrote in his diary:

Officers did their best for the men on Anzac Day. Walked to mine crater of July 16th 1916 with Buck. Took photos. No chance of sketching lately.

Nelson got out his box brownie camera. Through it he looked down into a huge crater—there was no time to sketch it. He peered into the enormous hole made by one large shell and wondered just how big the guns could end up.

On the same day, 25 April 1917, the HMAS A70 *Ballarat*, an AIF troopship, sailed in the English Channel. It weighed 11,120 tons and had an average cruising speed of 14 knots. It had been owned by the P & O SN Co, London, before being requisitioned by the Commonwealth of Australia for war purposes.

Just as 1600 men from the 24th Reinforcements Regiment sat down to lunch to celebrate Anzac Day, a German torpedo struck the side of the ship, fatally wounding it. It sank the next day. She was one of 15 Australian troopships lost to enemy fire out of a total of 74 which had been commissioned for war service.

A Parcel—May 1917

A knock at the front door took Lucretia down the hallway.

'I am delivering this on behalf of the Australian Imperial Force ma'am,' said the bicycle boy. 'Would you please sign for it here?'

'Yes, certainly. Thank you for delivering it.' Lucretia returned to the kitchen. She sat alone at the table, staring at the parcel.

Fingers cautiously unwound string until the parcel's contents sat open in front of Lucretia.

Between two heavy cardboard sheets Lucretia could see blue and pink.

Slowly she extracted the only thing she could find between the cardboard sheets.

Lucretia began reading the pencilled message on it: 'Second attempt at sunset behind a broken wooden fence…'

Lucretia then turned it over, revealing a partly completed sketch.

'Oh my God.'

Palms met face then a whisper.

'Nelson, where are you, my beautiful boy?'

Always Time for Australian Rules Football— the Beginning of May 1917

By the beginning of May 1917, across Nelson's area the weather had considerably improved. The fighting had largely abated.

The AIF were now organising plenty of sport for the troops, including the unique game of Australian Rules football. The game had developed in Melbourne in the 1850s during the goldrush, as a mixture of various other football codes, and with some local Aboriginal influence, derived from the game called *Marngrook*. The game had been hugely popular back in Australia for a long while —as far back as 1886, some 34,000 had attended a match by the lake in South Melbourne. And it was hugely popular among the troops abroad (an Australian football had been kicked by Anzacs at

Gallipoli). But now, with the war raging, Australian Rules football had been scaled back heavily—amateur competitions at home were abandoned for the duration of the war. And at the professional level, only four teams played during 1916 (Carlton, Collingwood, Fitzroy and Richmond).

A keen aspect of the Australian rules game was long kicking of the ball, as Nelson was now doing, marked high at the other end, and with fast and open running by a squad of some 18 players. In the Aboriginal game played close to Melbourne, the ball, made from possum skin containing charcoal from a fire, was tied up with sinews from a kangaroo's tail. (In eastern Victoria the ball was a kangaroo's scrotum stuffed with grass.)

It was now spring in France and the playing of Australian football was therefore somewhat out of season—in Nelson's hometown of Ballarat (and elsewhere in the State of Victoria for that matter), the game was played in winter as one means of keeping cricketers fit.

The AIF had put Nelson into the rover position. Unlike other positions where the player has to stay in a particular area, the rover is generally of smaller stock, quick, whose role is to chase the ball around as it is kicked all over the park. Heavy demands therefore were placed on Nelson throughout the match.

The Australians were always hungry for football. According to Nelson's diary, even when games were not on, the evenings were still consumed by 'glorious long football practice'.

The AIF also held athletics competitions for the troops. Nelson 'admitted' in his diary he had been beaten in the hundred yards, but had performed well in the winning relay team. There was also good boxing to be done at the 'pioneers' camp'. There was also 'tug-o-war', but the performance of the ambulance combined team was messed up when the 14th Brigade was taken into the line.

The troops had now had quite a bit of physical exercise in the warmer weather and were by now relatively relaxed. But, as was usual, the standing order for the week was to be ready to go at 20 minutes' notice.

The Second Battle of Bullecourt—More Shelling, More Carries—7 May 1917

That notice in fact came. A bearer from the 15th Field Ambulance came into Nelson's tent, shaken.

'The news is not too good,' said the bearer.

'Are we off then?' asked Nelson.

'Yes,' said the bearer, 'there are casualties all over the place. This is another bloody big one.'

The bearer was referring to yet another major battle the Anzacs were now in: the second battle of Bullecourt. It had commenced early in the morning of 3 May 1917. Part of the battle's objective was to retake the German trenches which had been temporarily taken but not held in the first battle of Bullecourt which had commenced a month earlier.

Nelson and Pomp were immediately sent out into the front line.

After passing the ADS, Nelson's squad was shelled heavily until it came to a second sunken road, some 300 yards behind the line. Two men from the squad died getting to this position.

Nelson and the bearers with him lay on the 'communication' road, just behind the railway line. Nelson tried to dig out a hole for himself but there was not enough room to fit in it. He lay in the partially completed hole as feared German bombs landed around him all night. He made several carries through each barrage when he could.

Nelson's pencil scratched out the position he was now in:

Much sniping and shells kept us in the trench on the way back. Saw Scotties hop over. Picked up. Cruel shelling of squads who behaved splendidly. Got back to road, easier this time, many dead about. Almost walking over them. Little to eat or drink. Lost 6 up to the first 12 hours in. Detained at the first sunken road outside the village, pleased not to face the barrage again. More hit. Relief came at 8 am so left sunken road at 10 am. Shelling not so heavy now. Passed the 6th field ambulance going in. We stopped at the motor post to collect our strays and muster. We marched to Vaulx dressing station. Starting to rain, no equipment came out with only a haversack. Took bus from Vaulx to B-notre point, went to bed with a mate at 2 pm.

Pause to Paint—9 May 1917

A few days later, 9 May, Nelson marched to Favreuil, just north of Bapaume. The weather had improved dramatically and Nelson and his mates sat about in the sunshine half dressed, relaxing. An AIF general came by and praised the troops.

Things were looking up generally; Nelson had ordered paints the day before, which had now arrived. He and another painter in the 15th Field Ambulance, Adrian Feint, decided to spend the afternoon sketching the ruins of the town. They had been told they would be going up the line at 7 am the next morning for a 'stunt' (a battle). While painting, they could see aeroplanes landing in the adjacent big green field.

Feint had studied at Sydney Art School from 1912 under Julian Ashton and Elioth Gruner. He had enlisted in 1916 at the age of 22, and had come into the 15th Field Ambulance in February 1917. Feint was not an official war artist but painted and sketched regularly while on the front.

War artists were not known before 1917. An expatriate Australian artist living in London, Will Dyson, had petitioned the Australian Government to permit him to travel to where the Australians were fighting on the Western Front. In 1917, Dyson was made the first Australian official war artist and accompanied the AIF, recording soldier activities.

Other Australian artists also undertook commissions on the front lines to record the Australian experience of war. Some enlisted soldiers were artists themselves and were appointed official war artists also.

Nelson was not a war artist, either official or unofficial. His collection of works would be a private one; he had been diligently sending his sketches back home for some time now, whenever this was possible. Many of them were in fact now arriving in Ballarat in remarkably good condition, cherished by family.

A Foul Smell from the Dead—May 1917

On 10 May 1917, Nelson marched with the other troops to the line at the front.

He was later sent back to the sunken road he had come from. During the evening he had to huddle amidst a terrific bombardment. The troops, including Nelson, could hardly assemble or hear themselves speak because of the terrific bombardment. Nelson and his mates ran from one road to another and over the top of trenches in fours. The phosphorus and smoke was fearful and the disorder of battle caused them to arrive at the ADS very late, at about 11 pm. When he got there, Fritz saw Nelson and the others by flares high in the sky and the Australians were again shelled.

After midnight, Nelson was relieved by the 6th, and so found shelter till the hop-over came at 4 am, requiring him to return to duty.

After more carries, Nelson could not sleep as the shelling remained too close. A hot strong and foul smell from the dead sat in the roads. The terrific bombardment lasted all night with shells landing right in the road Nelson was sheltering in.

The next day, Nelson started carrying at about 4.30 am and this continued until 12 pm without stop. There were some close escapes but the last trip did not involve carrying through the barrage. Machine guns and snipers worried Nelson and his mates all through the return trips. A couple of field ambulance squads were knocked out and were unable to cope with the cases. Feint's squad received a great number of casualties.

Later in the day, the 14th reinforced the troops and after 3 pm the artillery became active, mostly AIF's work. Large numbers of troops were wounded, and there were some 200 prisoners to manage. Fritz had surrendered freely when the AIF had got under its artillery. Aeroplanes flew overhead all day. At night, Nelson slept on the side of the road as there was no dugout available to him.

Disaster at Night—15 May 1917

On 15 May 1917, the bombardment remained terrible all night; it was so bad that Nelson, Pomp and the others could not get any of the wounded out. Fritz then hopped over the trenches but was soon bombed back into them.

Eventually, Nelson and Pomp went out for carries. One of their patients was knocked off the end of his stretcher. Snipers targeted the bearers all the way back. Gas shelling came over the bearers all night. The night was disastrous for the 15th Field Ambulance. MacFadden had been wounded, Snowy was killed by a shell which exploded near his dugout, both legs blown off. Westwood now had exposed lungs. White had his arm almost blown off and Minty was 'funked' (severely frightened).

During the night the 15th was relieved by the 6th, and Nelson went to the Advanced Casualty Station (ACS) and then carried soldiers to the wagons until about 6 am. By this time, Nelson had had a clear run for some time; Fritz had not fired on him and the Australians had not fired on Fritz.

Snowy's body was then brought to the SAP, then to the Advanced Dressing Station in the evening. His mates then buried him. Arnold Westwood (Westie), from Bairnsdale, Victoria, was placed beside him. Nelson was impressed by the compassionate service. He sketched the preacher using charcoal and an old bit of paper. He had been told that Snowy had died almost instantly at the RAP. Snowy was Harold Walter Hornby, from Carlton, Melbourne, aged 22. After the service, Nelson struggled 'home' in the dark about 2 am.

Shells Overhead—16 May 1917

On 16 May 1917, it rained all day. Nelson spent the whole day in bed. He had not slept or eaten for three days. From his bed, he could see more wounded and more shock victims being evacuated, with only nine now left in Section A. Sections B and C had more than that.

After recuperating from the previous day, Nelson and Feint went out to Favreuil sketching. The rain had cleared and it was a glorious day with spring colour everywhere. The front was all quiet now as Fritz (the Germans) had evacuated his positions. The two men continued sketching into the afternoon.

That night, Nelson and others were required to undertake more gas drills. Heavy whistling filled the air. Nelson looked up. Massive shells were coming straight over Nelson's unit.

Victory at Bullecourt—17 May 1917

On 17 May 1917, the second battle of Bullecourt ended with the Germans admitting defeat; they had stopped seeking to regain lost ground. Of the around 150,000 men from both sides who had fought the battle, some 18,000 British and Australians, and 11,000 Germans, had been killed or wounded.

Despite being right in the middle of it, Nelson and Pomp had survived yet another bloody conflict.

Now it was quiet on the front, Nelson went with Feint to Favrieul to sketch. Nelson noted in his diary that the French countryside had the 'glorious colour of spring'.

Now Bullets Overhead—21 May 1917

But the peace and quiet did not last long.

A few days later, on 21 May 1917, Nelson was again back at the front line carrying. He got up at 2 am and moved out at 3 am. There was heavy shelling up the road. He arrived at the ADS at daylight.

After a spell of coffee at the ADS, he moved to a sunken road where machine guns started firing all around him. The roads near the battlefield had been 'sunken' by the army so that troops, vehicles and equipment would be better protected against enemy fire. He and his squad crowded in a shell hole. Bullets spat over Nelson's head. One by one, Nelson and the others sprinted 100 yards to the RAP then quickly along the railway. During the first carry, aeroplanes flew very low and the soldiers were under constant shell and machine gun fire. Eight tanks appeared and went over at once.

An Avenue of Honour—June 1917

Back in Australia, there were early signs that the country knew the war could not go on forever. Many soldiers had already returned home and were now attempting to rehabilitate themselves into citizen life with the help of their loved ones and the community.

On 3 June 1917, the town of Ballarat planted the first 1000 trees as an Avenue of Honour along the Ballarat Burrumbeet Road. Mrs WD (Tilly) Thompson, a director of the local clothing manufacturer,

E Lucas & Co, had conceived the idea. The staff of the factory did the planting.

The intention was to build an avenue that would contain one tree for every serving member of the AIF from Ballarat and the surrounding region. The trees were being planted in a row on either side of the main road out of town, approximately 35 to 40 feet apart and set back from the carriageway some 15 to 20 feet.

Although it was not known when the war would end, the people of Ballarat were nevertheless now in the process of building a permanent memorial to the immense contribution to peace that the local men and women were seeking to make. When completed, the Avenue of Honour would be a permanent memorial to the contribution its soldiers, sailors and nurses were making, and would continue to make, until war's end.

One of the trees yet to be planted would be for Nelson, whether or not he returned home.

If he did not, it would bear his name with a single star.

Sport and Church Behind the Front—June 1917

In early June 1917, Nelson spent time away from battle in the town of Amiens and the surrounding region. He admired the Amiens cathedral, took a tram ride, and spent time bargaining in the town's shops. He could buy paints there and did so.

With that, Nelson soon completed his second watercolour for the war, along with much sketching of the French countryside. He showed his work to Adrien Feint who told Nelson he liked it.

But there was also an important commitment to keep. Back in Albert, cricket had been arranged with the 14th Brigade. Nelson had his first hit with the bat since his time with Roy back in Ballarat, now more than two years ago.

No-one told Nelson where he might be going next, but the glorious summer days and cricket evenings had taken that question far from his mind. Nelson posted letters to Harefield mates, and sketches back home. Recreation and rest was being taken up for all it was worth.

But on 13 June 1917 Nelson was told his unit would be moving off the next day. The unit got up at 5.15 am and moved off at 8 am through Albert, to Contay, about 10 miles due west of Albert.

After a hot march, Nelson and the troops arrived at a splendid place, with a long sports ground and high trees surrounding it. Many slept out on the grass, playing cricket after lights out under the northern hemisphere dusk. The cricket match early in the day had given Nelson a good bowling average for which he was pretty pleased.

A few days later, Nelson could hear church bells and a band parading through the trees surrounding the church. He figured it must be Sunday.

By the end of June, there had been several weeks of sport, sketching and resting. Nelson sent another spool of film to Amiens to be developed, and posted six sketches of Contay to the family.

The sport continued into early July. The AIF had organised a divisional sporting competition. It was a fine turnout with much military flare. The 15th won the ambulance competition.

On 6 July, Nelson walked to Henecourt and on to its 18th-century chateau with a couple of mates, George and Dick, taking in the countryside and the wonderful avenues lined with trees.

When he arrived, a large brass band was in full spirit. Nelson could see significant army leadership in residence. Lieutenant General Birdwood, the commander of the Australian and New Zealand troops on the Western Front, had set up residence in the chateau.

On 8 July, Nelson was put through more drill. In the evening, the AIF put on a great concert, featuring the 'Rising Sun Entertainers'.

But none of the last few days could top what was to happen in a week's time.

An Important Visitor to the Battleground— 12 July 1917

In early July 1917, Nelson was told that the Allies had been victorious at Messines Ridge, in Belgium. The battle for that ridge was a prelude to a much larger battle which the Allies would commence at the end of July 1917, the Third Battle of Ypres.

On 12 July 1917, Nelson and a large number of other AIF troops gathered at Henecourt Wood and awaited the arrival of their most special guest.

As Nelson looked out over the field behind the front, the man Nelson had given the oath to exactly two years earlier, King George V of England, emerged with a special party accompanying him. The king had come from England to congratulate the Allies, including the Australians, on the victory at Messines Ridge in Belgium in June 1917.

The king inspected a splendid demonstration of military fitness by the AIF. As planes flew over, young Australians climbed over large vertical obstacles with little effort, demonstrating their intrinsic athletic ability. This was followed by a splendid 30 minutes of military demonstrations, including artillery fire.

From close quarters, Nelson marvelled at the large numbers of staff accompanying His Majesty on his inspection of the Australian troops. Anzac throats delivered three cheers as the king passed by.

Mustard Gas, the New Weapon—12 July 1917

On this same celebratory day, German shells fired mustard gas for the first time in the war. Other gas had been used earlier but now the 'king of gas' had been released. The British called it mustard gas because of its odour. Both the British and the French had considered using it but it was rejected because it lacked toxicity. However, toxicologists at the Kaiser Wilhelm Institute had experimented with monkeys in 1916 and had shown that it could linger long after shells delivering it had burst, rendering the gas an effective defensive weapon against attack. Tests in 1917 were conducted on hundreds of cats and dogs. The Germans believed the Allies were brewing a major offensive in the second half of 1917. The use of mustard gas on 12 July 1917 therefore kicked off trials of this new defensive weapon. The gas was expected to be an effective lung-irritant. Its later use in battle would prove it excellent for producing non-lethal casualties—ones who would tie up many resources and therefore dilute enemy energy. The first shells would be marked with a yellow cross.

The genius of mustard gas was that it lacked immediate effect and therefore troops did not keep their gas masks on and did not appreciate the danger of remaining in the vicinity of the shells.

In the evening following the king's inspection of the Anzacs, elsewhere, near Poperinge (in the Ypres region in Belgium) and beyond, the Germans fired 50,000 mustard gas shells.

The Germans bombarded the Ypres area every night with mustard gas, keeping British guns silent, and forestalling (so the Germans thought) a forthcoming offensive. Thousands of soldiers were maimed or killed by the shelling. Yet worse was still to come—and right in Nelson's direction.

The Vase Shop and Happier Times—July 1917

On 13 July 1917, Nelson took off to Amiens, a trip conferred on him by the army for winning numerous competitions earlier in the month. He was astounded to see the city had a vase shop.

'*Bonjour* madame,' said Nelson.

'*Bonjour*,' said the assistant. 'I speak English to you?'

'Thank you,' said Nelson, 'that would be good.

How are things in Amiens?'

'Not too bad. But we fear for what might happen soon.'

'We are here to help if we can.'

'Thank God for the Australians,' said the assistant.

'And thank God for the goodwill of the French people,' said Nelson. '*Au revoir* madame.'

'*Dieu vous benisse*, soldier,' said the assistant. 'God bless.'

'Thank you,' said Nelson and then turned for the door.

'Please wait,' said the assistant, 'I have something for you.'

She pulled a small bag from under the counter and placed a blue beret on it.

'I am sad to say it is no longer needed here, but I would like you to have it,' whispered the assistant.

Nelson strode forward to the counter.

'Thank you,' said Nelson, 'I am not sure I can take it.'

'Please.

When you wear it, you will think of this place.'

'I will,' said Nelson, 'I shall never forget the French, just as they will no doubt never forget the Australians. Thank you again, madame.'

Towards Belgium

Nelson turned out of the store and into the main street of Amiens. He stopped after a few steps and put on the beret. He could hear 'religious music' down the other end of the street, near the church. The city was full of colour and interest, including gardens, canals with boats, and beautiful buildings.

After tea at the Railway Hotel, Nelson set out for home, about 15 miles away. He walked for six miles and then picked up a motor at Franvellier, with three miles then to walk to complete the journey. According to his diary he arrived at 12.15 am, '*tres* fatigued'.

On 18 July 1917, Nelson was told there would be much action shortly, including a hard march he would have to take north towards Ypres. He was told no cameras would be permitted from now on. Nelson dispensed with his.

The journey north did not eventuate until the end of July. Nelson had slipped on the road late at night and his knee was seriously swollen. He could do nothing until it healed. While waiting in Amiens, he received films that had been processed, but they were not his. The rest gave Nelson time to sketch and, importantly, to post the works home.

Nelson knew he would soon be heading north to Belgium. He had been told there would be a 'significant engagement' with the Germans there and that things could get very bad.

Nelson wrote in his diary: 'Goodbye to the best camp and happiest time ever had.'

The first leg of Nelson's journey to Belgium was a three-hour march, followed by yet another long train ride. The army was excellent at keeping him on the move towards strategic and important battlefields.

Nelson knew that for the next six months the army would be likely to place him within the most arduous and horrendous periods of fighting World War I could muster. Carries would therefore be at the centre of battle and at the epicentre of risk. Nelson knew this would all happen in the area north-east of Ypres.

Like all his mates, that is all he knew.

The Third Battle of Ypres, Belgium—31 July 1917

On 31 July 1917, the so-called Third Battle of Ypres opened. The British assault would, according to British General Haig's plan, break through German defences, including those around the Ypres salient which bulged the British front line.

The overall objective of the battle would be to advance to Passchendaele Ridge, then to capture the Belgian coast up to the Dutch frontier. With the control of that frontier, a chief aim would be met, to destroy German submarine bases at the ports of Ostend, Zeebugge and elsewhere. German U-boats were waging unlimited war on Allied shipping as part of the war of starvation Britain and Germany were imposing on their civilian populations. The British blockades had caused mass food shortages in Germany. On any day in Vienna, 250,000 people (in 800 queues) would line for food.

The Allies were now taking action to stop Germany torpedoing ships with vital food supplies for Britain. And the Allied strategy of pressing north-east of Ypres would also ultimately rout the German Hun from Belgium, a significant step towards victory on the Western Front and the overall war.

Over the course of the week prior to 31 July 1917, the British fired four million shells at the enemy in order to prepare the ground for British infantry charges.

On the night of 31 July 1917, rain began to fall. It would continue to rain for months, the worst weather in 40 years. The effect was profound on the fighting; everything turned to mud as the battlefield drainage failed due to the unrelenting bombardment.

Towards Ypres and Refugees from Battle

At the opening of the battle Nelson was on a train further south. He could see pretty farms across the countryside. He noted in his diary that they seemed bigger than those in more southern France.

He arrived at Steenvorde about 10 am and saw hundreds of soldiers everywhere and trains by the dozen, with heavy truck traffic everywhere.

When he detrained, Nelson was given cocoa at the YMCA and then marched to within two miles of Hazbrouck, a small town west of Armentieres, just south of the French border with Belgium.

At 8 pm, the refugees from Hazbrouck started pouring in, the town having been heavily shelled by the Germans over the previous days.

Nelson was shocked by the terrible plight of the women and children; they ran down the road in family groups, bound for nowhere. Nelson wrote in his diary: 'Have seen pictures of them but never so fearfully impressed.'

On the first day of August, Nelson packed loads of equipment onto trains in the rain and then went home to a wet billet. On his way home, Nelson saw three Australian chaps accidentally fall into a manure heap, one right to the neck. He helped them out as best he could.

The change from the sunny and restful time of July had now gotten to Nelson. He wrote in his diary: 'Long time since so down in dumps, winter seems to have fallen on us in a day.'

The Germans had now been pushed back some five miles from where Nelson was positioned, but the refugees were still coming in from Hazbrouck in the heavy rain which did not let up all day. Many of them had no overcoats and were just carrying a handkerchief of valuables. Nelson thought a possible surprise attack by the Germans had spooked the villagers, as many women were still lavishly powdered up. An old man with no legs hobbled along the road as best he could. Nelson's diary recorded the image:'This is one of the hard scenes of this war.'

More Drills and Training for Battle—August 1917

By early August 1917, Nelson was living the first anniversary of his prior visit to the region. He was taken on a route march to Oxclare, within 8 miles of Cassel, west of Ypres. The scenery was simply stunning with glorious misty mountains and beautifully coloured fields. The country homes were, according to Nelson's diary, 'flash and coloured mostly red and white'. The windmills were most picturesque. The people in the town spoke more Flemish than French.

But the days were filled with much hard training and many gas drills, so Nelson had little time for painting, except at night.

Pomp was now on leave in the United Kingdom. Nelson had given Pomp another filled volume of his diary to post home to Roy.

For most of the rest of August, Nelson continued with drills and training in preparation for further work in battle.

Australian Beaches—Late August 1917

In late August 1917 Nelson was put on a train to Boulogne, his first French town when coming to the continent in 1916. Nelson took a long walk along the local beach and the Boulogne esplanade. He wrote in his diary: 'Glorious beaches, if only I was in Australia.' While on the beach, Nelson met one of the 'khaki girls' he had earlier seen at the AIF camp. He met her again the next day and they walked around the main monument in the town.

Nelson enjoyed these diversions. He knew that what was soon to come would be a total nightmare.

The Cornet and the Minstrel Boy—August 1917

Over the last days of August, Nelson, Pomp (who was back from leave) and the others in the 15th were officially directed that their recent further training was for a specific purpose and they would shortly be going into a significant period of battle. They would be part of a huge push by the Allies to drive the Germans from the region around Ypres, Belgium.

But it would not be happening just yet and so Pomp and Nelson took one last opportunity to rest and relax.

There was only one place to do it: the small pub on the outskirts of town.

They were soon joined by others from their squad and from the 15th Field Ambulance's other units.

'One more round, then back to camp, chaps,' called the sergeant.

'Yeh, and one more thing before that,' called Pomp.' It's time for Fergo to give us a tune.'

'Yeh!!' shouted the pub. 'Come on!'

'But I don't have my cornet,' said Nelson.

'You do now,' said Pomp, pointing.

The barman handed Nelson a cornet. The bell was dinted and the instrument looked all knocked up like it had lived in the trenches for some time.

Nelson raised the cornet to his chest and pressed down on the valves only to find, to his surprise, that they in fact worked, at least to some extent.

'Come on Fergo, it's got to be "The Minstrel Boy" surely!' shouted Pomp.

The rest of the pub agreed; loud cheers and stomping army boots called on the command to be met.

Nelson put the cornet to his lips. The pub fell silent. As soldiers pressed forward, mournful first notes sounded. The music reminded the soldiers of their mates, and of the melancholy fields they had fought with them in, and which earlier in the year had been filled with blood-red poppies.

As Nelson sounded the end of the first verse, he could hear Pomp's loud call break the air: 'Come on boys, from the top!!'

Across the foreign country lanes and fields surrounding the pub, locals could hear the open throats of Australians:

The minstrel boy to the war is gone,
In the ranks of death you'll find him;
His father's sword he hath girded on,
And his wild harp slung behind him;
'Land of Song!' said the warrior bard,
'Though all the world betrays thee,
One sword, at least, thy rights shall guard,
One faithful harp shall praise thee!'

Further towards the Front—September 1917

During the first week of September the nursing sisters invited Nelson and his squad on the Monday evening for some entertainment. Nelson wrote in his diary:

The Matron and Sisters there gave us a night which touched our hearts and made us feel like real heroes, giving us the kindest treatment.

The next day Nelson was told that his division had gone into the front line. He knew nothing else of what was going on.

Movement towards the front was soon apparent. When Nelson went back down to the beach the next day, it was packed with thousands of troops who were entering the water together. It was a spectacular sight, back-dropped by many warships and transports in the English Channel. Nelson could see British destroyers patrolling up and down.

The next day Nelson was told to return to his unit. He thought this was an unfortunate turn of events because the rest and relaxation was much shorter than had occurred in July and the weather had been nothing like it had been in the more southern part of France.

Nelson had promised earlier to say goodbye to the nurses but before he knew it he was again on a train at 11.30 am. Rumours were being repeated that his unit would be in the front line of a major initiative.

The next morning, Nelson's squad had their kit inspected and his boots were mended in preparation for front-line work.

But as had become customary, the wait to join the line was again filled with football, this time against the French workers in the evening.

And Nelson thought they were pretty good too.

Bayonets Sharpened—Mid-September 1917

By 13 September 1917, things were very serious. The boys knew battle was imminent. Nelson wrote in his diary: 'Infantry sharpening bayonets.'

'Thank God Roy's not here,' said Nelson to himself. 'This is a nightmare within a nightmare.'

It was not long before Nelson was marching to an Allied brigade train and on his way across the Belgium border and into that country's territory towards well-planned wholesale brutal violence.

He arrived at his billet at 3 am. There were so many soldiers there was no room to lie down so he slept outside. He was once again in the land of crowded billets and congested traffic, with the 70th only some 300 yards away.

He was told he would be stopping there about six days with the first and second divisions going into battle that night. Nelson wrote in his diary:

Everything is so congested it reminds me of the Somme last year. Good thing it is not raining. The boys arrange themselves into squads. We are supposed to take a wood which has been taken before but cannot be held.

The Storm of Battle Arrives—Late September 1917

It was now some seven weeks since the Third Battle of Ypres had commenced on 31 July 1917 by massive British bombardment. The AIF had not yet actively participated in the series of rolling, limited and costly offensives, but now its turn was due.

The AIF had been assigned to offensives to take place in the Menin Road (the first objective), the Polygon Wood (the next objective) and Passchendaele areas (the ultimate objective). Only two and a half miles separated the last two. Over that distance, the mightiest armies ever gathered would unleash unspeakable levels of firepower on young men.

The first of these objectives, along the Menin Road east of Ypres, was scheduled to commence on 20 September 1917. Nelson and Pomp would be part of it.

On 20 September 1917, Nelson got in a motor vehicle about 5.30 pm, headed for the front line. Hours before, British guns had unleashed horrendous violence on the Germans.

Nelson arrived near Ypres at almost dusk, which he thought was a 'wonderful sight' as the hall in the town was being silhouetted out of a red sky. Nelson could see and hear a terrific barrage of AIF guns on his right. He and the others were full of excitement as they wound their way between motor cars and ambulances in the streets of Ypres. Fritz was supposed to be massing for a winter attack but the Germans had been caught out.

After some further journeying, Nelson arrived at the dressing station at Hellfire Corner, west of Ypres. It intersected the Menin Road, an important supply route, and was therefore under constant surveillance and shellfire from the Germans.

Nelson's squad set out to unload their stretchers, then stood close to a ruined wall for three-quarters of an hour, then loaded up again and moved further forward.

While at the next place, big shells began to land in the streets, one striking a motor transport that set it on fire. All the ruins of the town were reflected red in the midst of artillery fire, ambulances and a training squad carrying the wounded back. There was great excitement all about with men rushing away from the fire. There was damage everywhere but Nelson could not estimate the losses being suffered. He was told that a colonel of the 5th Field Ambulance had been killed earlier in the day at the very spot Nelson was now at.

Nelson then got onto a motor vehicle as part of a more general move of his squad and they travelled through country resembling Delville Wood, north-east of Amiens. The canopy of the trees had been lost along Menin Road so the Allies had screened the road with canvas to conceal movement up and down it.

By this time, Fritz was sending star shells and Nelson could see the whole surrounding landscape brightly lit. He got out of the motor vehicle. The 14th Field Ambulance remained there while the 15th settled further forward at a guide post and as a consequence became the next relay towards the front for injured troops. While there, Nelson was told that Charlie Felton had been wounded. There was then a terrific bombardment all the time with only a little reply by Fritz so Nelson did not get 'the wind up' to start collecting the Australians who had been wounded.

A second guide then found Nelson's squad and tried to place them in a tunnel for safety but there was no room so the squad found another dugout to hide in. But the mouth of the dugout in which Nelson and the others were staying was broken. A shell arrived right by it, killing the twenty-five year-old Herbert Harry Daley of the 15th Field Ambulance. Nelson was told that four of the 14th Field

Ambulance had also been killed along the track on which Nelson's squad was travelling.

Nelson's squad remained in the dugout for about a quarter of an hour and then eight squads were picked to clear the wounded from the 3rd and 15th Brigades. Progress to the next post was very slow through Glencorse Wood. Bodies in awful condition were lying everywhere, mixed up with shell holes and barbed wire.

Mangled Bodies

After some time, the AIF's shelling cooled down and there was very little shelling from Fritz. This gave Nelson and his squad the chance to find the post they were looking for. Nelson could see wounded lying in all the shell holes and he could hear them moaning horribly.

At 2.20 am the squad got one soldier each on a stretcher and started back but it was terribly slow through having to keep close together for fear of getting lost. The terrible cut-up ground studded with stakes and barbed wire made the carrying extremely difficult. Long tapes had been put up to guide bearers to the ADSs. After several attempts to find the ADS using the taping to it, all the bearers arrived and discharged their patients safely.

Nelson and his squad then rested for about one hour and at daybreak headed out for the 10th Battalion at the No. 9 RAP in the middle of Glencorse Wood. When they arrived, the concrete formation that was the post itself was in a terrible state and strewn with mangled bodies, including one German soldier lying in a hole with an Australian. Most of the wounded lying about were German soldiers.

Nelson and his squad did the trip to the No. 9 RAP and back twice before 10 am. Suddenly bullets rained down on Nelson; a German aeroplane was firing its machine gun and the artillery activity of the enemy began again. While resting in a dugout, Nelson was told that Cullen had been wounded as had four others of the 15th Field Ambulance. While there, he was introduced to Sydney Parsons and Wallace Tucker. Parsons (2nd Field Ambulance) was killed some two hours later.

Gas Masks On

Soon poison gas poured over Nelson's squad. All of the crew put their masks on for about a quarter of an hour. Nelson and the rest of the squad wheezed heavily into their masks but by order kept them on.

Although Nelson's eyes became slightly irritated, the mask did its job of protecting his eyes and lungs from major damage.

During the night, after some time recovering from the earlier strenuous activity, Nelson and his squad made another three trips to Clapham Junction, then another out to the 3rd Brigade to collect the wounded and then another to the 9th at daylight, which was misty at first but this soon lifted. By this stage, Symonds, Fenton (who would die the following year) and Buck had been wounded. Nelson saw a mate off for relief; he had also been wounded in the chest and arm while in the tunnel.

At 8 am, after two days of bearing with no rest, relief finally came.

Although Nelson did not know it, in the period between 20 and 21 September 1917 where Nelson had been bearing, three brothers from Five Dock, New South Wales (and all serving in the 17th Battalion) were killed at Polygon Wood: Private Theo Seabrook (24), Lieutenant William Seabrook (21), and Private George Seabrook (25).

The Fighting Intensifies—22 September 1917

But things did not let up for Nelson. Two days later, on 22 September 1917, Nelson and his squad made their way back to the ADS outside Ypres where they could rest. He had hidden some equipment in a shell hole on the way and he tried to recover it but it had been ratted (taken by others). When he got to the ADS he was given coffee, bread and jam. It was the third bit of food since his squad had gone out to the trenches some days earlier. There had been food in the trenches up at the front but the sights and smells of battle made Nelson feel too sick to eat.

During the day, the enemy's long-range guns were firing. Nelson and his squad went along the torn road, passed the howitzers and Hellfire Corner quietly, where much ammunition and stores had been destroyed. The light railway for carrying munitions was now in a terrible state. Nelson waited about half an hour for a lorry to take him further. About 14 soldiers were supposed to be withdrawn and put into the stunts (battles) Nelson's squad would be part of, as the bearers had been over 60 hours in battle and were in a bad state. According to Nelson's diary, many had 'the wind up them'.

The lorry came at last and Nelson scored a ride. Nelson gave the driver his Fritz water bottle.

After about an hour's ride, Nelson arrived at a camp between Reningelst and Poperinge in Belgium.

Nelson recorded in his diary:

A hearty dinner then wash, shave and feel splendid except that shoulders a bit sore. Got word that Dick has had metal removed and Cullen going next on table … Got Dick's coat, he was operated on at Canadian CCS outside Poperinge. One chap gets late shell shock and Kershaw became disabled. Supper at the little estaminet with Arthur and Buck, then to bed in a hut at 7 pm, twenty of us.

The next day, Nelson was called at 7 am in a hurry and taken with his squad in lorries to an ADS outside Ypres. There were many aeroplanes about and the batteries were pelting all day from the ruins of the town. Both A and B Sections of the 8th Field Ambulance moved up closer to the battle ground but Nelson's 15th Field Ambulance remained at the ramparts for the night.

The next day, 23 out of 25 of Nelson's squad had shocking diarrhoea, as did a number of B Section bearers, and all became unable to move. They spent the day at the ramparts.

Later, Nelson was well enough to get up. He walked around Ypres, until the shelling came again. Fritz began putting over stray shells to find the Allies' big guns. Nelson found some French stamps among the ruins and he put these in his pocket.

When Nelson returned to the ADS he was told that six more of the 14th had been wounded, and nine killed.

By this time the weather had improved significantly. Nelson and his squad lay outside the dugout in the sun. There they ate their 48 hours' rations of bully beef and biscuits.

PART 2

A Death Trap—25 September 1917

Between 20 and 25 September 1917, casualties were enormous. The British casualties alone were 20,255. But Allied gains were thought to be significant and every Allied unit in France and Belgium was at the ready to exploit any turning point in the war. British cavalry divisions were ready to charge on order.

At 4.30 am on the 25th, Nelson and his squad again marched out to the trenches, this time through the dark streets of Ypres.

They got out to the ADS but the rest of the trip was not possible as the road had been blocked. There was a terrible congestion of trams and lorries along a minor road.

Fritz was now shelling the area heavily and caught a lorry convoy in front of Nelson. He could in fact see that every lorry in the line had been struck and each was flaring up horribly. The shelling included mustard gas in large quantities.

At daybreak, Nelson could see the enemy's planes and balloons, which accounted for the good shooting.

Nelson arrived at the tunnel at 'Clapham Junction'. He had been there several weeks earlier. The shelling was still very bad. From there he started doing a few carries, taking the wounded back to the ADS. At this point Nelson found himself in the most trouble he had been in during the whole of the war so far. His diary recorded it in these terms:

Afternoon a trip to Inverness corpse with Sims, reached under terrific fire barrage along the ridge. Kept inside strong point for two hours. Sims squad makes a rush. Doctor would not let us go, as there were direct hits on the pillbox and in the doorway, which caught on fire from flares. Two were killed inside it—the Doctor was wounded at last. To save a patient we make a rush and get through terrible barrage intense shelling which sets fire to corpses in many places. Reached next post feeling much shaken. Clarke was wounded. Got a long spell after that. Doctor sent a note by us to prevent bearers coming up as the track became a 'death trap'.

At 11 pm, Nelson was sent out again to the same post, as the shelling had subsided. But during the trip out Nelson completely lost the track as the area was all broken up and completely unrecognisable.

As shells studded about the area, Nelson and another bearer returned one wounded chap, but not as part of the 15th, which had disengaged from them due to the chaos.

Nelson again set out, this time with another squad, to clear the wounded from the spot the bearers had been in, but could not find it. After wandering about Glencorse Wood, the squad arrived where they were supposed to be.

They took shelter for a while until Fritz shot an Allied tank which then flared up, giving away their position. Nelson could see wounded were lying all over the place in terrible condition. He had a difficult return trip to the ADS again as he became lost and wandered about over shell holes and country which had been staked and covered in wire. His trousers and puttees (cloth wrapped around ankle and knee for protection) were torn badly and he and the other bearers fell over several times. On one carry back, Nelson and the other bearer threw the soldier over onto the ground as he had been wounded too badly to be saved.

As Nelson got to the post he was looking for, six tanks moved up to attack. At daybreak there was yet another hop-over for the third and final objective, the final ridge being sought. All of the 58th and 60th Brigades just got in in time. A tank went over a machine gun position crushing and killing the team. It also crushed the AIF's tunnel in part.

On 25 September 1917, the following entry was made in the War Diary of the 15th Field Ambulance: James Hoy McClenaghan 'killed in action'.

Blown to Pieces—26 September 1917

At 5.50 am, Anzacs rose under a British barrage of artillery and hopped over to take Polygon Wood. A dense wall of dust and smoke poured over the Germans like an Australian bushfire. The hop-over was successful but, according to Nelson's diary, nearly spoiled by others. The Australians took their objective by skirmishing with enemy soldiers.

Many ashen-faced prisoners came through and Nelson could see them being raided for their watches. The prisoners then had to carry the wounded and to help out the walking wounded too.

By just before 10 am, Polygon Wood was held by the Anzacs, driven by Pompey Elliot's 15th Brigade. The Anzacs would shortly dig in so as to overlook the next valley. Another 'victory' line had been drawn.

At about 11 am, Nelson was sent out for further carries. The conditions were quite all right going out, but suddenly he was caught under concentrated fire upon return, all of which was big shelling. Nelson rushed for shelter under a railway bank. He had lost his other bearer on the shift, Buck.

Nelson stayed in a shell hole for about 20 minutes and then returned to look for Buck. He feared Buck had been blown to pieces, but later found him at a tank post.

The two bearers returned to duty, undertaking terrible carry work all afternoon. Nelson saw Hind from the 15th back at the tunnel. He was told that Arthur Joyce (aged 19) and James McClenaghan (aged 27) had been killed at 5 pm the day before on the Menin Road, Ypres. (In fact Joyce would die some days later, on 2 October 1917.) While stretcher-bearing down the line at Polygon Wood, Quirk had his leg almost off and would shortly die (the 15th Field Ambulance War Diary records him as dying from wounds at 9.40 pm and therefore 'struck off strength'). Olfield had been wounded in the face. Symonds had also been wounded (and therefore also taken off strength).

Big shells were landing about the place all afternoon and two more patients were killed while bearers were changing.

Nelson's diary recorded the mayhem going on: 'Big shells half bury the dead about our post. Then terrible piercing sound before explosions.'

At about 8 pm the fighting ceased and Nelson was told to rest until 12 pm. He and his squad were left to get some sleep in the dugout. It was rather quiet all night but the dugout had been left in a fearful state by the 3rd brigade; the horrible sweat and smell of the dugout, together with the flies, made it unbearable.

The capture of Polygon Wood was a complete victory but at a huge cost of 15,375 British casualties, 1215 being killed. The 4th Australian Division suffered 1717 casualties and the 5th Australian Division had 5471 dead and wounded in the period 26–28 September 1917. Those young men were the resources for the capture of just a few miles.

Relief came at 6 am and Nelson and his squad left the dugout. As Nelson looked back over the battlefield, he could see the bombardment had reduced the Polygon Wood to shattered stumps.

Nelson had been in and part of the carnage and had been called on regularly to pick up the pieces of battle, that is, the men who had been injured and maimed during it.

Nine Victoria Crosses were the product of one day's fighting.

Some 2750 yards had been gained by the Allies at a cost of some 36,000 casualties across both sides, some of whom Nelson and Pomp had carried to safety.

On the evening of 26 September 1917, the Prime Minister of England dined with Haig 60 miles south-west of Ypres. Haig told the Prime Minister the enemy was considerably shaken and had suffered considerable wastage and its manpower would run out next May or June.

The British newspaper *The Times* told the British public that the British and Empire Armies were 'in the best of spirits'.

Yet More Gas—28 September 1917

During the next two days, Nelson rested at the army laundry back from the front. No bombs were dropped on it but Nelson could still see many Taubes over Ypres.

Back at the British headquarters, Haig wrote in his diary: 'I am of opinion that the enemy is tottering, and that a good vigorous blow might lead to decisive results.'

The next morning Nelson was unexpectedly called at about 4.30 am. He set out for the trenches at 5 am after some bread and cold meat at the rampart.

He was marched to the ADS, which was quiet, in striking contrast to his earlier experiences there. Nelson set up a home in a shell hole and started enjoying the autumn morning. There had been all sorts of rumours that Fritz was evacuating on account of his silence. Nelson did a few carries to the crater nearby but they were all uneventful.

At 11 am, a few shells came over and Nelson had to take shelter in another stinking big dugout. But things stayed relatively quiet for some time and working parties ran up and down the supply roads and light railways. Nelson could see ammunition mules everywhere, delivering bullets and shells to the Australians.

In the distance, Nelson could also still see Fritz's pig-like balloons. And his Taubes were duelling with Allied planes all the while.

During the afternoon, Nelson watched the Allied artillery put up a wonderful barrage on Nelson's left, directed at that part of the ridge that the Allies had not yet taken.

In the evening things became more serious for Nelson.

Fritz put over a mixture of gas, shrapnel and shelling towards Nelson's location. Casualties began arriving and Nelson and Pomp were required to do a few carries. A horrible struggle to protect the wounded began.

At 11 o'clock, the gas made its presence felt. Nelson's diary recorded it in this way:

Many coming over and much gas about. Start with helmets on but could not see so I pulled my mask off, but still holding my mouth clip to keep us on the track. Breathing difficult so changed it many times. Gas was thicker in certain areas. Buck became sick and the mob became windy but we had a very good patient who could look after himself. Eventually, we got to the crater and came back without anything. We got a bit scattered on the way back to the post. Heavy bomb lands very close and grave danger of being hit and left behind as all much excited. So we sat quietly still wearing masks.

Nelson and his squad eventually made it back to the tunnel, but it took a few direct hits that put the wind up everyone. Nelson was struck by the fact that the rails forming part of the roof of the tunnel made a peculiar ringing sound when hit by the shells.

The next day Private Herb Mallyon of the 15th Field Ambulance was killed in action on the Menin Road, Ypres and therefore struck off strength. On that day, Private A Francis was wounded (gassed), evacuated and therefore also struck off strength.

The Menin Road—30 September 1917

The gas shelling had by now abated.

Everyone was generally astounded that the Germans were not taking the opportunity of the clear day to shell the large convoys of Allied soldiers and munitions going up the Menin Road towards Ypres.

But the earlier days' events had caused much injury and death. Nelson's diary had rightly recorded that Herb Mallyon had been killed the day before, and Sharp was now shell shocked.

Nelson was making his way up the Menin Road when, suddenly, a Taube passed over and dropped bombs, scattering the troops, lighting up a lorry and killing six horses.

This part of Hellfire Corner was continually being shelled, so Nelson and his squad headed out cross-country, hiding in shell holes because of the Taubes overhead. The Taubes were flying low. Nelson looked up and could see Fritz's crosses on their underbellies.

Nelson soon reached Menin Gate, where he met Stock and Mac. They set out for Ypres as part of a long column of soldiers, taking shelter regularly on the ramparts.

Nelson could see more Taubes coming over regularly. Suddenly one came straight over him. It passed over, then dropped its bombs on the front of the column of soldiers. Men scattered in all directions, somersaulting over the sandbags. Nelson and his squad made for the ramparts by various side streets. Bombs were getting many soldiers and as Nelson got to the ramparts yet more bombs were being dropped.

The soldiers stayed there until 11.30 pm and were then bundled into motor vehicles that set out for camp. When they arrived Taubes were still under attack. Nelson could see a Taube above him, this time fixed in the silvery beam of the Allied searchlights. Everyone in the camp scattered, especially the Chinese men camped over the road.

When the Taubes had flown over, Nelson went to bed in a cold night. He lay in bed sweating in the cold, listening to the silence.

The entry in the 15th Field Ambulance War Diary for the end of September 1917 read: 'The casualties sustained by this unit during this month have not been excessive for the work performed and under the conditions current.'

Ragged Clothes and Sandbagging—1 October 1917

An exhausted sleep freed Nelson from the previous unbroken 96 hours in the trenches. Upon waking, all beards in the squad were required to be removed, but Nelson and the others' ragged clothes had to stay on as there was nothing to change into.

After a lie-in, Nelson and the others paraded at 2 pm, followed by hard work sandbagging the camp against bomb attack. Nelson was told this would give it optimum protection.

Nelson worked until it was almost dark. In the evening there was a form of entertainment from the Chinese men, and a band, but not a good one. The British had deployed Chinese men to help with the horses; they were being paid virtually nothing to do so.

In the evening, Nelson stepped out of his tent to admire the pastel sky. He and Buck walked along the road and watched the planes from a distance.

Later at night, the Taubes dropped bombs nearby, although not on the camp itself, but Nelson's hut still shook.

The next day, 2 October 1917, Arthur Joyce of the 15th Field Ambulance died. He was 19. He was killed while carrying the wounded from the front line. He was buried opposite the shell crater where he died, on the Menin Road, Ypres. A cross what erected over his grave bearing his number, name and unit.

Mud—3 October 1917

At midday Nelson was warned yet again for the trenches and at 2 pm he and the others set out for the journey forward, towards the battle which would occur at Broodseinde north-east of Polygon Wood. Taking Broodseinde from the Germans was the next objective towards the Passchendaele objective.

Before heading for the trenches, Nelson spent a little time in the church army tent writing letters, and was then put into a lorry and marched up to the Corduroy Road section of the front. It started to rain. Nelson's squad was told to head out to the tunnel and look for cases to return to the ADS. Along the way there were many dead horses and overturned vehicles.

Many wounded were lying out in the open as a result of the 1st and 2nd Division's stunt but there was absolutely no way to get to them, so Nelson and the others turned back. He soon discovered an old cookhouse. He stayed there from 2.20 am to 4 am in terrible, freezing conditions. By 4 am he was on his way back to the Hellfire Corner track to the RAP. Nelson passed a ruined pillbox and saw a German soldier sitting beside a dead Australian soldier. The dead around were horribly mangled.

Nelson did seven carries in total and cleared the post area by 1 pm.

All about there was terrible mud from the rain. Nelson noted in his diary that everyone was now drenched to their thighs.

The conditions were appalling. Nelson's feet and legs were now wet through and would stay that way. There was nothing to eat either.

From what Nelson had been told he expected he would soon leave the battle area. But this did not happen—he was sent back to the tunnel. He sat inside it while Fritz shelled it all afternoon. But late in the day, for some reason, the Germans left those huddled in the tunnel alone.

When Nelson and the other Australians left the tunnel, they found dead Germans strewn about everywhere. The Australians searched their bodies and found iron crosses and cigars.

Recognition—Time for Medals—3 October 1917

In early October 1917, a number of honours and awards were recommended for members of the 15th Field Ambulance for the work done in late September and early October 1917: Private R C Felton, Bar to Military Medal; Private E Morley, Military Medal; Lance Corporal DG Moore, Military Medal; Private AF Davis, Military Medal; Private JT Rees, Military Medal; Private AJ Graham, Military Medal; Major RF Craig, Distinguished Service Order; Sergeant ES Mara, Distinguished Conduct Medal; Lance Corporal CW Goyder, Distinguished Conduct Medal; Private H Hanby, Military Medal; Warrant Officer Class 1 JT Goodhall, Meritorious Service Medal; Private AF Lemon, Military Medal; Captain SG Gibson, Military Cross; Lieutenant Colonel JMY Steward, Distinguished Service Medal; Private MS Goyder, Military Medal; Lieutenant Colonel JMY Mitchell, Distinguished Service Order.

It was the AIF's judgement that Pomp and Nelson's endeavours in September 1917 did not warrant the awarding of any medal.

The Battle of Broodseinde—First Week of October 1917

Nelson was eventually sent to the ADS near Menin Gate, given some rum, and this time a decent place to sleep.

But just as he thought he might be taken out of the battle area, he was awoken at 4 am and taken by lorry to the front, given a stretcher, straps and a blanket, and ordered to go straight out to collect the injured.

The battle-wounded who Nelson would collect were fresh casualties from the next phase of the Allies' push to Passchendaele: the battle at Broodseinde north-east of Polygon Wood on 4 October 1917. Huge dumps of medical supplies, stretchers and blankets had already been taken up forward and ADSs established.

The battle had started at dawn. A huge British barrage opened, the worst for Germany in all of 1917. The endeavour was to snuff out all enemy life. Earlier heavy rain was now easing. The New Zealand and three Australian divisions, fighting together for the first time, had been chosen to lead the attack across a front of 2000 yards.

By 8 am, the Anzacs had made great gains, the enemy fleeing in all directions. The AIF's leader, Monash, cabled Melbourne: 'Division again brilliantly victorious in greatest battle of the war.' Nine Victoria Crosses would soon be awarded, including to some Australians.

The British 5th and 2nd Armies also captured their objectives, aided by tanks, taking thousands of prisoners. British papers called it the most complete success achieved by the British Army so far on the Western Front (despite 20,000 killed or wounded).

The Allies were now well on their way to their key objective: Passchendaele.

Now at the pillbox and preparing to undertake as many carries as possible, shells landed around Nelson and there were very close hits to the structure itself. Nelson decided to stay at the pillbox overnight. It was now bucketing with rain and would stay that way for some time. Nelson took his boots and socks off because they were soaked, and shared one blanket with the four other bearers in the pillbox. The men stayed wet and cold all night.

Hellfire Corner—October 1917

Nelson was eventually ordered to return to Hellfire Corner. He wrote in his diary: 'Night at Helles too rough, dark, and too much gas to carry at night. Fritz gives us drum fire almost all day.'

The next day, 16 October 1917, the Germans put much gas over Nelson's location and gas bombardments continued every three hours during the night. The tunnel Nelson was staying in was evacuated. Pearce was gassed and many 14th Field Ambulance bearers were mostly carrying gas patients. They could smell gas all along their carries. Nelson's diary betrayed the sheer gravity of the risk at hand: 'Day spent trying to protect against this place.'

Nelson noted in his diary that officers had been killed: the Assistant Director Medical Services (ADMS) and Major Bullen. Major Bullen had been wounded by a shell between Zonnebeke and Polygon Wood on the Broodseinde Ridge at a pillbox (a concrete dug-in guard post) on Helles Track. The pillbox was two miles from the front line and was being used as a dressing station. He died some two hours later from wounds. Just prior to being hit, Bullen was outside the pillbox telling his men to keep down. Bullen's body was taken to Ypres and he was buried with full military honours. Others who were killed by the shell were buried in one grave behind the pillbox, four crosses being erected on it.

Some Sketching between Shelling— October 1917

Now, several days later, back from the front, Nelson walked to an old church in Ypres with Sergeant Mara, having shared Pomp's parcels and the food taken from a dugout.

In the morning, Nelson was not required for the trenches, so he went out sketching. But in the afternoon, he sat under cover as Fritz had a big gun and was shooting huge shells regularly, although some were duds.

The trenches were not far away and the next morning, after reveille at 4.15 am, Nelson was marched to the ADS, and he and Pomp were then allotted a position, which happened to be Hellfire Corner again. He set out along the duckboards. Nelson's diary recorded: 'Quiet and brisk autumn day, too beautiful for fighting.'

There was no gas but plenty of mayhem with heavy bombardment during the afternoon, including shelling by Fritz, this time using Allied shells. In the evening, Nelson and Pomp went to bed near a dugout entrance until they moved to a rampart dugout after it started raining.

It was now getting dark by around 4 pm each day.

Further Offensives and Objectives—October 1917

The Allied successes had emboldened Haig. Despite resistance from other leaders, he insisted the Allies should push on and take Passchendaele. Huge numbers of exhausted men pushed on in October's worst ever rains. On 12 October 1917 the New Zealanders suffered their worst day in military history attempting to take the Passchendaele Ridge. So too had the other Allied armies taken appalling losses, initiated by officer whistle-blow.

From 31 July 1917 until now, Nelson's endeavours, and those of tens of thousands of Allied soldiers, had been instigated to meet the objective of taking Passchendaele and in turn controlling northern ports in Belgium used by German U-boats wreaking havoc on food and other supplies to Britain.

But as early as 23 September 1917, and despite the huge loss of life, it became obvious those endeavours were futile—Haig had cancelled the amphibious attack on the Belgian coast, rendering it impossible for the Allies to win the Belgian coast in 1917. Although Nelson did not know it, he had been part of the Allies' splendid victories at Polygon Wood and Broodseinde for little strategic reason.

More Recognition—End October 1917

By the end of October 1917, the Third Battle of Ypres, including at Passchendaele, had left more than 300,000 British and dominion troops either dead, wounded, sick or frozen.

On 28 October 1917, the 15th Field Ambulance was relieved by 2nd Division activity and Nelson, Pomp and the others made their way out of the battle area quickly. As they walked down the Roman road they were continually shelled.

On 30 October 1917, the men assembled at the ADS. There they were told a number of new military medals would be awarded.

One to Lance Corporal R Wood, Military Medal; one to Captain WL Smith, Military Cross; one to Corporal OA Cropley, Military Medal; Private LC Ludbrooke, Military Medal; Major PA Mapleston, Distinguished Service Order; Sergeant L Johns (4th Field Ambulance attached to 15th Field Ambulance), Military Medal; Sergeant AJ Morris (8th Field Ambulance attached to 15th Field Ambulance), Military Medal.

Chests pushed forward. Medals were then pinned.

'Boys, well done by all. You are dismissed,' said the major.

Congratulations rang out.

A medalled infantryman approached Nelson and Pomp.

'I feel bad you blokes got nothing,' said the soldier.

'That's fine,' said Nelson. 'We are all in it, mate. Pomp and I are yet to earn it.'

The soldier laughed. 'I reckon you've earned it times over, cobber. You blokes have saved half the Australian Army. And some lazy Poms too for good measure.'

Nelson and Pomp laughed back.

'If they keep us out here any longer,' said Pomp, 'we might just prove you right!'

After the ceremony, the two mates took a motor car to their old camp, where they brushed up and took the only recognition on offer: some army tucker and a nip of rum.

A Deadly Phase

The months of September and October 1917 had been extremely hard on the 15th Field Ambulance.

Of Nelson and Pomp's mates, the following members would not make it further in the war: George I'Anson died 24 September 1917 (aged 26), Herbert Mallyon died on 29 September 1917 (aged 23), James McClenaghan died 25 September 1917 (aged 27), Roy Quirk died on 27 September 1917, Arthur Joyce died 2 October 1917 (aged 19), Norman John Bullen died 16 October 1917 (aged 30), William Wheldon died 25 October 1917 (killed first day up the line by a shell which wounded him above the heart and left shoulder).

Many more from the 15th Field Ambulance had fallen in earlier battles and would fall in later ones.

Painting and an American Show—8 November 1917

During the first week of November 1917 Nelson had been pulled back into Poperinge, Belgium, and was now resting in that region for some days. He painted in the afternoons. In the evenings he took in various concerts and shows, including concert parties put on by the AIF for the troops.

On 8 November 1917, Nelson went to a show the Americans were putting on in Poperinge. American troops had stayed out of the war until April 1917 (when German submarines attacked commercial shipping despite an undertaking to America not to do so. Germany's submarines had been extraordinarily successful—for the month of March alone it had sunk 169 British and 204 other nations' ships). Now the Americans were starting to arrive in France in greater numbers. But it would take some considerable time to muster the huge American force that would ultimately descend on the battlefields of the Western Front by mid-1918.

The speedy arrival of the Americans was heavily anticipated by the Allies, if not considered essential to victory and the cessation of hostilities.

Inside this global context there remained only one vital question in Nelson's mind—could he continue to hold his position as stretcher-bearer in the 15th Field Ambulance without being blown to pieces or severely damaged in the course of trying to rescue and assist the wounded. He was asking himself that question frequently.

Nelson knew luck could last only so long.

A Futile Offensive—November 1917

By 10 November 1917, the battles for Passchendaele had been fought. The last of them, led by Canadian and British soldiers, ended with the capture of Passchendaele and higher ground beyond it. Contributing to the success was the first use of wireless communication rather than pigeons, dogs and runners. The technology of the battlefield had come of age.

The village itself was completely ruined. Amidst shattered stained glass, Christ in fragments lay everywhere about the wrecked church within the town.

The key military objectives Nelson had been part of had now been accomplished, but for no tactical or strategic advantage. A week after the Allies took Passchendaele back from the Germans, Haig decided any further offensive should be discontinued at once as the positions gained fell short of what he had wanted before the winter.

Pomp and Nelson and countless British and dominion troops had taken the full brunt of key campaigns in the Third Battle of Ypres.

And they had done so for no lasting reason.

Leave to London—November 1917

By late 1917, both the Allies and the Germans' morale had hit rock bottom. Court martials in the AIF were now at 400 for October and November 1917. The ferocious fight power of the AIF had seemingly left it heavily degraded by the Herculean efforts of the Australians across the Third Battle of Ypres between July and November 1917.

After long periods in the trenches bearing the wounded with Pomp as part of the Third Battle of Ypres, the army finally gave Nelson leave. On 14 November 1917, he left France, boarded a boat to cross the Channel, and on arriving in England headed straight for London.

When Nelson arrived he was surrounded by a public who could no longer be deflected by government and media messages that things were fine. They were not. Tens of thousands of young men were now amputees. Full-bodied local cricket teams now played 'Arms & Legs' sides. Hideous battle wounds were now part of public attention.

On his first day in London, 16 November, Nelson went to A & F Denny, 47 The Strand, Reeves, Charing Cross, where he bought some etching books, including two for Adrien, his war artist mate. After that he left his films at Kodak. The film processing shop told him they would be ready after the 21st.

Nelson then visited various art galleries in Leicester Square before heading off to Kensington for dinner.

For the time being, the horrors of battle seemed a million miles away.

And there was good news in London. Nelson had been told that the AIF was recruiting for further war artists from its ranks. He obtained a form on which he could make application. It read:

Applications are invited from members of the AIF to fill vacancies for appointment as Artists under the Australian war records section, Administrative Headquarters, AIF, London. The appointments will be distributed as follows:

One member will be attached to the medical section at administration, Headquarters, AIF

One member will be attached to Headquarters, Australian Corps.

One member will be attached to Headquarters, each Division of the AIF.

Artists will be subject to the control of war records section but they may be required for camouflage duties under such conditions as may be issued by general order.

Necessary equipment and materials will be issued by the Australian war records section.

All artistic work produced by the artists will be property of the Australian government. Artists will not be permitted to undertake work for any other authority or person nor for their personal gain.

Successful applicants will be appointed for a period of five months, with present rank, and on appointment may be granted honorary rank, and on the general list with pay according to rank.

Applications must be submitted before 15 March 1918, addressed to the officer in charge of Australian war records section, administration, Headquarters, AIF, 30 Horsefary Road, London SW1, accompanied by specimens of work and accompanied with the record of war service of the applicant.

'I should apply for that if I get the chance,' Nelson told himself.

The sketchbooks he had just bought were now essential items. They were to be taken back to the Western Front so that Nelson could produce the specimens of work for his application. His last day of leave would have him in France by 29 November 1917.

Another Attempt to Conscript Australians— December 1917

In December 1917, the Australian Government again asked Nelson and his family to vote on whether Australian men should be forced to fight for the Empire. The eligible voters from a population of 4.75 million people said no. As a consequence, no further AIF Division would be sent to France to add to the existing five divisions.

Grateful Thanks from the Australian Front — Christmas 1917

'Mum, have a look at what I've just picked up from the newsagent.' called Roy from the front door.

Roy bounded down the hall and placed his new purchase on the kitchen table. Lucretia turned from the sink and joined him.

Roy turned open the first page. 'It says here that profits from the sale of this booklet will be devoted to the Australian Soldiers' Patriotic Fund.'

Roy turned to the next page. On it was an Introduction.

Roy read aloud:

We are now approaching our fourth Christmas at war, and let us hope it may be the last one during which we shall find ourselves fighting. We hope this book will convey to those whom we left behind in Australia, and who we know are thinking of us, some idea of the surroundings on the battle fronts of the Australians, and which carries with it our wholehearted hopes of good wishes for those at home.

With it, I feel I have the privilege of sending my grateful thanks to all for their past work, and my best of good wishes to every member of the A.I.F. for the future.

FRANCE, 28 September 1917.

The Introduction was signed by WR Birdwood. Born in India and educated in England, he had led the Anzacs at Gallipoli, had assumed command of the 1 ANZAC Corps between 1916–17, and commanded the Australian Corps formed in November 1917 (from the AIF's five divisions).

'Hey Mum, let's have a look at the photos inside.'

Lucretia and Roy slowly turned the pages of the booklet. They revealed horrific pictures of trenches, damaged soldiers, battles at Pozieres and elsewhere, mud at the Somme, shrapnel bursts over stretcher-bearers, a brass band playing at the capture of Bapaume, the ruins of churches at Ypres, scenes at an Advanced Dressing Station, hundreds of shells for large guns, German prisoners of war, tens of thousands of empty shells piled high, and scenes from the Third Battle of Ypres.

'I feel sick,' said Lucretia. 'Put that away Roy, what are you doing bringing that home?'

'Christ, Mum,' said Roy. 'We haven't heard from Nel in ages. I hope he wasn't in any of that.'

Towards Villers-Bretonneux—March 1918

In March 1918, the Germans launched the 'Spring Offensive' on the Western Front. The immediate objective was to break through the Allied lines and defeat the British Army. This was partly enabled by the collapse of Russia (the Germans and Russians had signed an armistice in December 1917), permitting vast numbers of German troops (15 divisions) to flow from east to west. By the end of 1917, Germany had 154 divisions and about 8000 extra guns on the Western Front. In contrast, the British Army was now significantly below 'establishment' level, but the combined British and French Armies still outnumbered the Germans by 1.2 million soldiers, with around 400,000 more rifles.

The March offensive was also partly to seek to obtain a strategic advantage before the arrival of large numbers of American troops. And it was also a last-ditch effort to use Germany's depleted resources to maximum effect. Berlin had already exhausted her metal reserves, had depleted domestic metal supplies, and had drawn on every other source possible (to add to the madness of the war, the old Prussian Synod had donated 10,312 church bells to make weapons).

In late March, the Germans attacked across a 74-mile front on the Somme. Amiens, north of Paris, was now in danger of falling. The Germans fired 1,160,000 shells in five hours and half a million mortar rounds, across an area of 150 square miles.

The Germans had a specific area in mind: they were heading towards the small town of Villers-Bretonneux, which, if taken, would be a key strategic position from which to take Amiens. From that town, Amiens could be seen 12 miles away. If the Germans were to take Amiens, they would disengage its railway and blow the city to pieces. The Allies would soon bring infantry and artillery down into that region in order to repel the Germans if possible.

Nelson and Pomp, still up in Belgium, could well be sent into the Villers-Bretonneux region with the 5th Division.

If that occurred, they would be part of yet more deadly combat.

The Wisdom of Solomon—April 1918

But the Germans were not only attacking the Somme. In late March 1918, the Germany Army fired its first shells out of the mouth of the *Paris-Geschütz*, its 'Paris Gun'. The largest gun in the history of warfare to date, it was 69 feet long, with a calibre of eight inches. The shells, weighing 234 lbs, were fired on Paris from a forest in Coucy, some 81 miles away.

Like the mustard gas Nelson was continually being threatened by, the gun was not used to destroy the city; it was fired to destroy French morale. A crew of 80 men were engaged to fire it, surrounded by batteries of army artillery so that the 'chorus' of destruction would make it difficult for the Allies to pinpoint the gun's location. Each shell took three minutes to reach Paris, the first human-made objects to enter the stratosphere. (Shells from the gun had a maximum altitude of 26 miles.)

On 29 March 1918, one of the 183 shells fired from the gun landed on the St-Gervais-et-St-Protais Church in Paris. The church had been built between 1494 and 1657. The ornate church included a 1533 intricate stained-glass window by Jean Chastellain, 'The Wisdom of Solomon'.

The shelling from the Paris Gun had collapsed the roof during a Good Friday service, killing 88 people and wounding 68 others.

Gas or No Gas—April 1918

By now, Nelson and Pomp had had multiple gas scares themselves and had carried countless gas victims from the battlefield to ADSs. Gas had become one of the key and effective weapons on both sides. Both sides knew its value but also its shocking results.

In the first week of April 1918, the leadership of the International Red Cross could no longer accept its role as the carer of gas-damaged young men. It now sought to prevent poisonous gas from being used at all against troops and civilians.

The French said they would agree if the Germans did too.

But Churchill was furious with the Red Cross. The deployment of poisonous gas was, according to Churchill, more favourable to the Allies because the prevailing wind was from the west. In a letter dated 6 April 1918, the British Minister for Munitions, Winston Churchill, told his French equivalent that the prohibition being sought on the use of poisonous gas was not to the Allies' advantage and that in any event he did not trust the word of the Germans.

In the letter, Churchill told the French Minister that Churchill was, to the contrary, 'in favour of the greatest possible development of gas warfare, and of the fullest utilisation of the winds, which favour us so much more than the enemy.'

Churchill's view prevailed. In the month of April, over one-third of the shells fired by the British were for the release of gas. In the next few months, gas production would increase by over 100 per cent.

For Nelson, this defeat of common sense could be catastrophic—if the British were going to fire large numbers of gas shells, so too would the Germans.

The strategy by both sides of using gas to maim, displace and demoralise soldiers was about to reach its crescendo.

Right where Nelson and Pomp were heading.

Villers-Bretonneux—April 1918

In early April 1918, the Germans launched an attack on Villers-Bretonneux. Allied defences repelled it but the enemy was close to success until a major counter-attack on 4 April by the 9th Australian Infantry Brigade and British troops. The town remained in Allied hands.

But as part of a 15th Field Ambulance briefing, Nelson and Pomp were told there would soon be yet another major contest for Villers-Bretonneux. German guns had apparently been 'registering' on the roads around Villers-Bretonneux.

This meant guns were being calibrated for a heavy and well-aimed bombardment expected to commence shortly. There was yet more evidence of impending battle: the red planes of Richthofen's 'circus', and the Red Baron himself, had been seen and heard high overhead.

On 9 April 1918, evacuation arrangements were made for the forward posts of eight AIF battalions. The posts were to be cleared back to the ADS at Aubigny by the 15th Field Ambulance motor transport. Two additional Ford ambulances had been requested and supplied. Four Sunbeam ambulances were also ordered with complete reliefs of drivers, who were given 48 hours' rations. Horse ambulances were to be used for conveying the walking wounded to Daours, four miles north-west of Villers-Bretonneux.

Pomp had been told he would be assigned to that work but he did not know when he would be separated from Nelson. Until separated, the two mates were heading into the new eye of the storm of war—the town of Villers-Bretonneux itself.

A Rich Red Vein—April 1918

In the late afternoon of 9 April 1918, Nelson and Pomp walked towards Villers-Bretonneux. Up ahead they could see the town's large church, still standing but badly damaged by bomb blasts.

As they approached the church in the mist, the mates walked alone. Pomp ran up the stone stairs. The large wooden door creaked partly open. Pomp then shouldered it. Two heads turned and the men stepped inside to look.

Gazing towards the roof, they could see large parts taken out by shellfire and other extensive damage. At the other end of the church, parish hymn books lay strewn across recent rubble. Some of the stained-glass windows still stood in their lead housings. Along the aisle, glass shards crackled under their boots.

To the left of the nave, Nelson headed straight towards a large red and blue window. Studying it with care, he could see that the lead in the windows had held against the raging conflict which had surrounded the church for the last month.

As he stumbled forward, a large wooden beam above him broke out of its housing and large pieces of the roof began to crash at the far end of the church. The cacophony caused a small flock of white birds to scatter through the church, whizzing over Nelson's and Pomp's heads. A large hole in the roof sucked them out.

'Christ Fergo, I thought the Huns had dropped a mustard gas shell right on us. I thought we were history, mate. Let's go!' shouted Pomp.

Nelson stood still in case any movement or further noise might cause further insult to the church.

He took his Bible from his trench coat and thumbed through it, looking for a page. Taking his sketch pencil from his ear, Nelson carefully marked down the side of a passage near the end of his Bible.

Suddenly a large beam creaked and heavy dust billowed from the ceiling. Nelson dropped his Bible.

'Come on, Fergo, we're goners in here. We've got to go!' cried Pomp.

Nelson quickly bent down to pick up the sacred book. It was now buried in the rubble and falling debris.

'I'm coming, Pomp.' Nelson scratched around, pushing his hand hard under a large piece of broken coloured glass, gashing his hand badly. He reefed the Bible out and jammed it into his trench coat.

'Come on, Fergo. This place is about to give way. I'm not joking.'

Nelson urgently wrapped his field ambulance armband around his hand and clambered his way towards the only remaining window in the church. To his amazement it was full of rich etchings on the glass. He could see the hands of Jesus. Open and calm as if cradling peace. A white dove rested above them.

Suddenly, the sun escaped from French clouds. A glorious wide bright torch penetrated the stained-glass window. Nelson stood motionless, bathed in a rich blood-red vein of light.

'Bloody hell. Come on Fergo!' called Pomp, 'I'm telling you we're history in here if Fritz lands one.'

The bearers stumbled over the rubble to get out, ready to steady each other if need be. Against the wall of the church, Pomp stirruped his hands, taking his mate's boot. Nelson's lungs gasped cold French air. He then lurched himself out of one of the window openings using an old beam. Pomp did the same.

As they took off down the old Roman road, Nelson's wide eyes focused back on the church. In the distance he could see beyond it bright flashes from bursting artillery guns engaged on the other side of the valley.

Both men knew it was now extremely dangerous to stay. Each side was now giving warning that major offensives were on the way.

Further north about 60 miles, a major development of that very kind had already taken place. On the evening of 7 April 1918, back in the area of Estaires (where Nelson had first come into the 15th Field Ambulance in September 1916), the Germans were bombarding the southern part of the Allied line between Armentières and Festubert. The barrage continued until dawn on 9 April 1918. The German Sixth Army then attacked with a whole eight divisions. The Germans eventually broke through 9.3 miles (15 kilometres) of front and advanced up to five miles (eight kilometres), with the most advanced units reaching into Estaires. There they were finally halted by British reserve divisions.

Severe damage was inflicted on the church at Estaires, including the magnificent Catholic Church. Its huge stained-glass windows Nelson had admired some 18 months earlier were now shattered pieces of the colour spectrum strewn across grey rubble.

The Gas Attack—17 April 1918

By mid-April, the two mates had been together for some 18 months on stretcher ends, and had shared many of the AIF campaigns across the Somme and in the Third Battle of Ypres.

The bearers were now part of yet another strategy on the Somme—a significant move by the British forces, AIF and other Allied forces to halt possible further German gains across the region of the Somme that Nelson and Pomp were now stationed in. But while the Allies still held Villers-Bretonneux, the Germans were keen to take it and continue a push on to Amiens, then Paris. The Germans were now more than two and a half years behind their 'six-week' victory over France and were desperate to make large gains quickly to maintain the hope of victory.

On Wednesday, 17 April 1918, the region around the town of Villers-Bretonneux was covered in mist and cold light rain.

At 3 am, Nelson and Section B of the 15th Field Ambulance gathered in the old Roman road outside the town, anxiously waiting for conflict, then immediate orders. Bearers crouched long and still, shivering.

Pomp was not at the other end of Nelson's stretcher; he had just been ordered back to Daours for repair work in the operating theatres.

'All right, we want you and the others in the section to be at the ready for carries when the Hun attacks across this area,' said the sergeant.

But the attack did not come. Although the Australians did not know it, the Germans were in fact in an earlier and more deadly phase of operation.

That phase began at about 4 am when the Germans sent thousands of mustard gas shells over the whole of the Villers-Bretonneux region. It had come to be known as the 'king of the gases' because it had reached the top of the merit order for its effectiveness in maiming soldiers.

Gas shelling had been used as a weapon of terror by the Germans, French and British Armies since 1915. Initially the Germans had used chlorine as the primary agent, and later phosgene, but more recently mustard gas had proven the most effective. It produced blindness, swelling of the eyes and eyelids, vomiting, and burns and blisters to the skin. The primary purpose of the activity was to demoralise and injure. If used widely, the gas could take down a large number of soldiers and require a further large number to care for them. This was perfect for a follow-up large-scale assault. The use of gas was in fact a war crime as it violated the *1899 Hague Declaration Concerning*

Asphyxiating Gases and the *1907 Hague Convention on Land Warfare*, which prohibited the use of 'poison or poisoned weapons' in warfare. Both sides flouted the Convention. As the Romans had observed centuries earlier, 'the law falls silent in the presence of weapons'.

The mustard-gas shelling continued until around noon. The gas was yellow-brown and had been given its name because the odour resembled mustard plants. The AIF had known from at least 1916 that the gas was heavy and hung low over the ground like a mist, lodging in woods, hollows, trenches, shelters and cellars. Its genius was that it would hang around, waiting for unsuspecting soldiers to come into its path.

Conditions for use of gas were now ideal: wind not more than four and a half miles per hour, fog and gentle rain, and descending air currents.

Gas Masks Ordered to be Removed—17 April 1918

The adjacent village was now taking heavy casualties, as was the immediate neighbourhood of the Roman road.

Nelson and the other bearers were urgently put into action and began carrying the villagers and others affected to the nearest dressing station. This continued for some hours across the early morning and into midday.

By midday the weather had not improved and mist and rain continued to ruin visibility and effective operations.

By now Nelson and the others had been wearing their gas masks for several hours. While the masks were said to provide 'complete protection' from gas, many of the bearers were stumbling and slowing down under the load of the evacuation work. Visibility through the mask was near zero. That was the nature of its design and operation.

'If you can't see, just take the fucking things off,' shouted the lieutenant. 'Take it off now!'

Nelson followed the order. He pulled his mask down off his eyes, pressing it awkwardly hard up against his nose so it would not move under heavy carry. He then heaved up the end of the stretcher and the bearers lurched further towards the clearing station.

Chaps Gassed Everywhere—17 April 1918

Around 2.00 pm, the wind lifted, now blowing the low-lying mustard gas over the whole of B Section bearer squads posted at the right-hand RAP.

Nelson immediately smelt the sickly fumes of the mustard gas, and then more of it. He desperately tried to replace his mask but it was too late. A sharp and sickening barb suddenly jabbed Nelson's eyes, then his lungs and armpits. Nelson and the other bearer immediately dropped their carry and fell about the place. Fingers tore eyes, chests heaved, the two Australian soldiers lay contorted upon the foreign soil. Gas burned the enemy with hate.

In the aviary of the town's chateau, birds dropped, asphyxiated by the gas.

B Section's incapacity was immediate. It had to be evacuated to the Central Main Dressing Station and then replaced.

Between 2.00 pm and midnight, instead of bearing others, Nelson and the other bearers themselves were couriered backwards from the front some 13 miles.

Under Australian Army medical supervision, ½oz of 5% soda bicarb was placed into mouths, and 1% soda bicarb into the eyes. Each man was given a pad of cotton wool soaked in 1% soda bicarb to apply to his eyes in order to prevent rubbing with the fingers.

The Commanding Officer of the 15th Field Ambulance made the following entry in the ambulance's War Diary for 17 April 1918: 'treatment very efficacious'.

Nelson's pencil made its own account:

Fritz opens with a heavy gas bombardment at 4.30 going till 9. Chaps gassed everywhere in the village. We begin to feel it and all begin to vomit badly. I went for relief but unable to get back. Very weak and retching all the time. Mara brings Arthur on the stretcher and the rest assist each other out. Now about one o'clock, a couple of hundred gassed lying in sunken road waiting transport. Motor takes us to Aubigny. Jack Rees fixed up my belongings there and Blaikie washed and bound up my eyes. Another motor ride to MDS where a Doctor again fixed our eyes and put a kind of chloroform mask on us. Seemed to wait here about three hours but they stopped the vomiting. Then another jolty motor ride to Casualty Clearing Station.

The events of the week had drastically changed one stretcher-bearer's life, with the possibility it was permanent. All Nelson knew was that he and his mates had been badly damaged by the insidious gas and were doing what they could to survive its horrendous effects.

Uniforms were now being stripped from gassed soldiers and replaced with Red Cross pyjamas and socks labelled *Made in Australia by your friends.*

Goggles Sought Too Late – April 1918

On 18 April 1918, Captain ST Appleford, Australian Army Medical Corps, prepared a memorandum to the Commanding Officer of the 15th Field Ambulance, explaining what had happened to Nelson and the others:

I examined and interrogated about 40 gassed cases (all stretcher cases) at the A.D.S at Aubigny … The eyes in every case were affected and caused intense pain. The lids were swollen, the conjunctival red and injected. There was copious lachrymation. Vomiting occurred in all cases and at frequent intervals. The 5% soln. of Sod. Bicarb was immediately rejected. The vomiting composed generally of bile and mucus, in the worst cases of practically pure bile. Coughing was general and troublesome. Headache was generally intense. Pulse always soft and rapid averaging about 104. In one case the rate was 120 … The majority of the patients wore their masks continuously for three hours and then took them off because they were told they could do so; some by their Sergeants; others received the order from those next them i.e. the order was passed along. Officer… stated that he gave that order to his men. He was not very communicative and was very ill…These men … seemed confident they could have worn the masks much longer had they not received the order to remove them …All these cases were gassed in or around VILLERS-BRETONNEUX.

On 20 April 1918, the Commanding Officer of the 15th Field Ambulance sent a secret report to the headquarters of the 5th Australian

Division. He noted that those left within the 15th Field Ambulance would on relief move to Les Alencons, north-east of Amiens, to open up a divisional collecting station there. The report further asked for the supply of 100 stretchers and 200 blankets as a reserve supply, that the current ADS had become 'untenable', and that 'sufficient comforts had been obtained to meet all emergencies.' By hand, the commanding officer further wrote: 'Please arrange for three wheeled stretchers from the 8th Field Ambulance.'

In the field, combat and disparate activity continued across the Somme. On 21 April 1918, the flamboyant 'Red Baron', the German flying ace, with some 80 victories to his name, and holder of Germany's highest military honour, was shot down north-east of Villers-Bretonneux. The Australian Medical Corps was the first to reach the famous German pilot, who told them he was 'kaputt'.

On 23 April 1918, the Commanding Officer of the 15th Field Ambulance wrote to the Assistant Director Medical Services (ADMS), 5th Aust Division, AIF:

I beg to recommend that anti-gas goggles be supplied for the Bearer Sub-Division of this Ambulance.

The S.B.R. mask cannot be worn by Bearers when working in a shelled area at night both on account of inability to see sufficiently and also on account of the heat generated inside the face mask. Even in very weak concentration sufficient to necessitate breathing through the SBR, such as occurs after shelling by Mustard Gas, the exposure of the eyes results in excessive lachrymation with affection of the Nasal and Pharyngeal mucous membranes, salivation and swallowing of excretions. In a very short space of time vomiting results and the Bearer is a casualty.

I am sending you this recommendation in accordance with a conversation to the DDMS Aust Corps.

For your necessary action please.

Lieut Colonel

Commanding Officer, 15th Australian Field Ambulance A.I.F

The next day, the eve of Anzac Day, the Lieutenant Colonel received the following response: 'Arrangements have been made to supply suitable goggles to the Field Ambulances.'

For Nelson and the others all this was too late.

The Germans' use of mustard gas had now reached its fortissimo. Since late 1917, the German Army had used gas in material quantities, but now, in early 1918, including at Villers-Bretonneux, gas had been and was being used in extremely heavy doses and across broad regions.

During the course of April 1918, the impact of mustard gas peaked when some 2411 AIF soldiers on the Western Front were gassed during action. Nelson was one of them. Of those who had been gassed, 74 AIF diggers were poisoned to death.

Boots—the Week before Anzac Day, 1918

Nelson slumped on the platform of the Amiens railway station. A British hospital train screeched to an abrupt halt, discharging large plumes of white smoke from its undercarriage. Hundreds of wounded, mainly Australian soldiers, including Nelson, piled into it.

The train lurched out of the station towards Forte Le Havre. When it arrived there, Nelson and the other gas victims were grouped together. Their eyes were tightly bandaged so they were told to form long lines for boarding a hospital ship headed for England, and safety.

'Put your hand on the man in front of you,' directed the sergeant.

Damaged men shuffled slowly up onto the ship where they were told to sit on long benches stretching on the deck from stern to bow.

Exhausted and cold, Nelson's knees gave way and he fell back hard onto the bench.

The bandages clamped shut over his burning eyes.

As the ship rocked forward to the motherland, the English Channel revealed itself to the damaged soldiers as a long series of high rolling seasickness-inducing waves.

Nelson's bandages were now tightening from the salty air, pressing on his eyes, lancing great pain in them. He leaned forward, dropped his elbows to his knees, and tried to adjust the bandages.

The emerging gap caused further scissor sharp pain, Nelson's eyes now streaming and aching even further from the light and sea salt.

Straining as best he could, Nelson took in the blur of the wooden deck and the rain's heavy sweep. The Channel suddenly assaulted the ship, jolting Nelson against the digger next to him.

As he peered through the small opening between his bandages, Nelson could just make out the form of large old battle-worn AIF boots appearing in front of him.

'I reckon they might be Pomp's boots,' Nelson said to himself.

'They bloody well are,' said Pomp.

The two held each other with all the strength of the AIF.

'Pomp, what happened to you, mate? Where were you? How come you're here?' cried Nelson.

'I was gassed just north of Villers-Bretonneux at Daours, near where they told us to separate.'

'I thought I was going to be in for a grim time going back to England. God's put you on this boat, Pomp. Bonzer.'

'Yeh, I reckon he bloody has, Fergo. I'm so glad you're here.'

The two mates sat on the bench together, taking in the driving rain and the Channel's swell. Pomp adjusted Nelson's bandages, closing out the light for him. The gesture soothed the eyes and quelled the effect of the rolling sea.

'Things will be all right,' Nelson assured Pomp.

'Yeh, not too bad, Fergo. Not too bad from here on, I hope.'

Corneal Lesions

On land, the AIF immediately separated Nelson and Pomp again. Nelson was bundled on to a motor vehicle that took him to Stourbridge, and then on to the University of Birmingham. Another vehicle took Pomp in the opposite direction.

Nelson's car pulled up outside the main hall of the university.

By 1909 it had been equipped as a 520-bed hospital in the event of future war. The hospital had taken casualties from the first month of the war onwards. By the spring of 1915, more buildings had been converted, adding 1000 more beds, and in 1916 another 570 beds had been added. After a wash, Nelson was put into one of those new beds.

'Here we are, Private Ferguson,' the nurse's voice said calmly. 'This is your bed.'

Nelson was gently lowered onto it, changed, washed, and placed under warm soft blankets.

As he lay in hospital, Nelson wondered whether and when he would be sent back to France for further bearing, should that be possible. The army would do its best to make that happen. Fixing broken soldiers as quickly as possible was essential to the war effort.

A short slim man in a long white coat halted by the bed and tapped Nelson on the arm.

'Private Ferguson, I'm the doctor in charge of this gas cases ward.'

Nelson stirred as the nurse pushed pillows up behind his back to get him to sit upright.

The doctor slowly unwound the bandages pulled tight around Nelson's eyes.

'Yes, you have heavy corneal lesions, and I see some corneal ulceration too. That looks significant. But in the short term, your eyes should improve, Private. We will try to get you back with the 15th Field Ambulance as soon as possible.'

'How long will it take for my eyes to come right, Doctor?'

'Your corneas have now been significantly marked by the mustard gas. The pocking may develop over the course of several years. Perhaps longer. You may experience considerable impairment at some later stage. I can't say what will ultimately happen to you. But in the short term, things should improve somewhat. The AIF will, of course, put you back to bearing if you come good on us. My task is to get you rested and well again. We will be doing everything we can.'

'And I see that the hospital's chaplain is in the ward. I will ask him to come over Ferguson.'

'Thank you, Doctor.'

Anointed Eyes

The chaplain calmly approached Nelson's bed from the centre aisle of the ward. The British Government had exempted the 'clergymen, priests, and ministers of religion' from conscription under the *Military Service Act 1916*. Many were performing the Lord's work in army hospitals in England and across Europe.

'How are you travelling then, Private? The doctor thinks it would be good for us to have a talk.'

Yes, I have asked the doctor about blindness but I'm not sure I understand what he's telling me.'

'Well, all I can explain to you is this, Private, just as I have been telling the others. The Almighty has his purposes.'

Nelson nodded.

'You may be aware,' continued the chaplain, 'that in John 9:2–7, Jesus passed by a man who was blind from birth. His disciples asked him: who sinned, this man or his parents? And Jesus replied, and let me quote, Private: "Neither, but that the works of God shall be revealed. And as long as I am in the world, I am the light of the world."'

'Jesus then spat on the ground and made clay, and then anointed the eyes of the blind man, asking him to wash in a pool, which he did, and returned with received sight. And Jesus said that he had come into the world that those who do not see may see, and that those who see may be made blind.'

'Yes I'm familiar with this story, Chaplain,' said Nelson. 'It's in my Bible in my trench coat just over there. My mother gave it to me. I've carried it since I got on the *Karoola*.'

'Very good,' said the chaplain. 'Take store in those words, Private. And in the words of Psalms 146:8 as I recall them to you now: "The Lord gives sight to the blind. The Lord lifts up all who are bent over."'

Nelson sat still in his bed, trying to take in the comfort being given.

'I shall see you again on my rounds tomorrow, Private. Try to rest.'

'Thank you, sir'.

The chaplain continued down the orderly line of damaged soldiers in beds, then turned.

'Remember, soldier. Darkness cannot overpower the light.'

Once lowered back down, Nelson shortly fell into a deep drug-induced sleep.

Another Attack on Villers-Bretonneux—24 April 1918

At 4.45 am on 24 April 1918 the Germans again began firing shells, many of them containing mustard gas, into the Allied positions in and around Villers-Bretonneux.

The German infantry, with 14 supporting tanks, then broke through the British 8th Division which had been badly weakened by German attacks in March, reducing its infantry by half. Much improvement in design had occurred since the mechanical monsters Nelson had first seen in late 1916. Siege warfare had now rendered the tank a necessity.

With these German tanks and infantry pushing hard, the enemy retook the strategically vital town.

But at 10 pm on the same day, 24 April 1918, General Glasgow of the 13th Brigade together with a Ballarat soldier, General HE 'Pompey' Elliott of the 15th Brigade, led a ferocious counter-attack. Elliott had planned the counter-attack while the AIF had been in the reserve position supporting the British. To his dismay, Elliott had seen the British retreat in the first battle of Villers-Bretonneux. Elliott had ordered the Australian officers under his command to shoot any British officer who might show hesitation in the attack.

German machine-gun nests took their toll on the Australians, but they continued the charge, with ultimate success.

As the Anzacs tore into the enemy, flashes from explosions lit up the ruins of the church Nelson and Pomp had visited just a week earlier. The Germans shot red, white and green flares into the air, creating coloured rain. Yet maddened Australians continued their charge. Bayonets lanced enemy throats which witnesses could see from the glare of the flares.

The counter-attack was one of the greatest battles in AIF history but many Australians died or were badly wounded. One of the AIF to die in the battle was Corporal FR Wrigley, whose teaching career, like Nelson's, had commenced in Ballarat. He had been on HMAT *Ballarat* when it had been torpedoed by the Germans a year earlier, on 25 April 1917.

By 25 April 1918, although vastly outnumbered, the AIF had retaken the town. The Australians had suffered a large number of casualties during the course of the night's battle. The Australians, including AV Farrands of the 57th battalion, checked their position, were relieved by others, and took rum.

The withdrawal of the Germans had once again denied them the opportunity to push on to Amiens and then on to Paris.

This victory had unparalleled significance, changing the course of the war on the Western Front. Rare thanks spilled from Field Marshal Haig's special orders.

The Australians now returned the village to its residents. The 51st Australian Battalion placed a large wooden cross on the battlefield.

But the gassing of thousands of young Australian men like Nelson during the month of April 1918, and at other times during the war, would open up a new, and much longer, war of its own. Nelson had seen conflict since September 1916 but he was now entering a new arena in which he would fight.

One involving serious and sustained damage across the rest of his life.

Time for Cake—25 April 1918

When he woke, Nelson's ears were full of hospital chatter spread like butter across the ward.

An Australian nurse stationed at the hospital whispered to him 'It's Anzac Day.' She put fruitcake by his bed.

Although Nelson did not know it, one of his mates, Cecil Bone, of the 15th Field Ambulance, had died earlier in the day in France of meningitis.

Back at Nelson's old medical training facility, Harefield Hospital, a Commanding Officers' Parade of Staff and Walking Patients was being held, attended by some 337 personnel. After inspection by the commanding officer, those present marched through Harefield village to the parish churchyard, headed by the unit brass band. Near the graves of the Australian soldiers, the troops were drawn up in the formation of a hollow square under the Australian flag. Two chaplains conducted the memorial service.

The commander's wife had arranged for the graves to be decorated with flowers. Many ladies contributed from their own gardens. Harefield Hospital had now assumed a large number of hospital functions, including being a centre for eye, ear, nose and throat diseases.

Bronzed Heroes—April 1918

The news of the Anzacs' exploits and courage at Villers-Bretonneux, including the first and second battles there in April 1918, had travelled promptly to Ballarat and all the other cities and towns of Australia via various newspapers. The second battle had been in the news for five consecutive days.

Australian soldiers were being described as 'looking magnificently strong and bronzed' when they arrived at the town. The newspapers reported that the Germans had fled when they had heard that the fearsome Australian warriors were advancing with their bayonets. The Sydney papers did not hold back: one had reported that 'it was a complete reversal of fortune for the enemy, whose bodies lie in heaps.' According to another Sydney newspaper report, the British had been 'weary' but the Australians were 'fresh'.

But the reality for many soldiers was very different; although the Australians, led by Elliott, had courageously retaken the town, there were some 2500 Australian casualties suffered on that now famous night of 24 April 1918.

At the Front Gate—1 May 1918

Nelson's mother pushed the front door open and stepped down past the white prosperous hydrangeas near the letterbox. A short distance away the postman's back rode up Peel Street towards Ballarat's main street at the head of the town.

A brown envelope peeked from the box, the addressee 'Mr J Ferguson'. It had no other markings, official or otherwise.

Lucretia closed the door behind her and pressed herself rigid against the back of the front door, heart pounding.

'Is there mail?' called James from the kitchen.

'Yes, dear, I'm afraid to say. There is a brown envelope addressed to you'.

James moved quickly out of the kitchen and down the corridor to the front door.

'I need to know,' said Lucretia.

'At least it was the postman, not the bicycle boy,' said James.

James and Lucretia knew of the army's notification practices. Ballarat was receiving them daily. In the case of death, the next of kin would be notified by an urgent (pink) telegram, delivered by bicycle. The sight of a boy on a bike put fear and terror into Ballarat families.

However, brown envelopes, like the one now being held by James, were notifications of wounding, dispatched by the army via Base Records, Melbourne.

In the cool Ballarat winter afternoon, James opened the envelope and read out the army's telegram:

Dear Sir,

I regret to advise you that Pte HN Ferguson has been reported Gassed— classed as wounded.

His postal address will be-

No. 9123A Private NH Ferguson

15th Field Ambulance

(late Army Medical Corp Re-enforcements)

Australian Imperial Force, Abroad

In the absence of further reports it is to be assumed that satisfactory progress is being maintained, but anything later received will be promptly transmitted. It being clearly understood that if no further advice is forwarded this department has no more information to supply.

Yours faithfully, Major

Officer in Charge, Base Records, Melbourne, Victoria Barracks

1 May 1918

Parent held parent.

The notification was shocking, but at least it was not on the standard condolence card.

'My God,' whispered Lucretia.

'I imagine it's in the army's interests to get him back on his feet quickly and I am sure they will do so,' said James.

Nelson's father was right. By this stage in the war, the AIF was totally reliant on getting soldiers operational again as soon as possible. Staggeringly, of the 'effective' AIF soldiers that reached the front in France, 60 per cent were so-called 'recovered soldiers'. The Australian

Medical Service within the AIF was not a back-room patch-up function; its work was strategically vital to the war effort and to securing victory. Without these 'recovered soldiers', the AIF simply had no critical fighting mass.

As the message told the Fergusons, to assist the war effort the army asked families to assume their son or father was making satisfactory progress in the absence of further reports to the contrary.

But for the parents of a damaged soldier, whose whereabouts had not even been included in the message, the mere absence of further news could certainly not give peace of mind.

On the same day the Fergusons received the telegram of Nelson's wounding by gas, Private Fenton of the 15th Field Ambulance died. Fenton had been gassed at Villers-Brettoneux on 17 April 1918 (having earlier been wounded at Ypres). Gas from the 5000 gas shells the Germans sent over on that day entered Fenton's lungs and eyes and he had spent time in England for treatment. Before Fenton died, the matron of the hospital ward called for the Church of England chaplain, who saw him there prior to death,

Further News—16 May 1918

On 16 May 1918, Mr J Ferguson received another telegram, delivered to the Ferguson's home:

> I now beg to advise you that Private HN Ferguson has been reported admitted 24.4.18 to the 1st Southern General Hospital, Birmingham, England, gassed (classed as wounded).

However, the AIF repeated its earlier warning to the loved ones of the damaged soldier:

> In the absence of further reports it is to be assumed that satisfactory progress is being maintained, but anything later received will be promptly transmitted. It being clearly understood that if no further advice is forwarded this department has no more information to supply.

Pomp's family too received the same lack of assurance. On 3 May 1918, Pomp's mother, Mrs Scholz, received a telegram in South Australia telling her that the army regretted to advise that Lance Corporal NEB

Scholz had been gassed and wounded. In a later telegram on 22 May 1918, Mrs Scholz was advised that Pomp had been admitted to the War Hospital, Exeter, England, on 26 April 1918, with the description 'Gassed Severe'. The AIF advised Pomp's mother some two weeks later that he was in fact 'progressing favourably' but without providing any further details.

The pressure and resource constraints of engaging in a global war meant the army could not answer even the most desperate questions posed by broken parents. They would have to wait for further news.

But only when the army was ready and able to provide it.

The *Ballarat Courier*—22 May 1918

On 22 May 1918, page 5 of the *Ballarat Courier* reported the following:
Mrs Ferguson of 52 Peel Street south has been informed by the Defence Department that her son, Private NH Ferguson of the 15th Field Ambulance, has been admitted to Southern General Hospital, Birmingham, England.

No further details were given.

Another Anzac Death by Gassing—28 May 1918

The 5000 gas shells the Germans had sent into the region of Villers-Brettenoux on 17 April 1918, severely wounding Nelson Ferguson and many others, and killing Private Fenton, had now taken yet another life. Private Doyle, gassed along with Nelson, Fenton and others, died on 28 May 1918 at the No. 5 British Expeditionary Force General Hospital, France. He was 35 years of age.

The Return to London

After his stay in Birmingham Hospital, the army moved Nelson to London and then on to the AIF's repatriation camps in Salisbury.

By this stage, Nelson had been assessed as a 'B Class' soldier—someone unfit for active duty. The 'B Class' soldier was one the army was trying to restore to fighting strength having been damaged in battle earlier. There were grades within 'B Class'—and Nelson was now slowly working his way up closer towards being able to return to the fighting. He was being rehabilitated medically as best the AIF could with limited resources, undertaking some physical education and other army training. And he was receiving eye treatment regularly. The army told him it would return him to France if his lungs and eyes improved. An assessment was made weekly and Nelson was accordingly rated and then classed as to whether further convalescence was necessary or whether he could return to action.

The army had made at least one thing very clear: he would certainly be told immediately if he could again be 'taken on strength'.

The Allies Get on Top — July 1918

While Nelson was continuing to try to get back to health so that he could again be 'taken on strength', the AIF was making strong gains on the Western Front following the battle at Villers-Brettenoux in April 1918. By mid July 1918, the Anzacs had shown themselves to be a formidable fighting force, pushing the Germans back at regular intervals across the Western Front.

On 4 July 1918, the Battle of Hamel commenced, led by General Monash of the AIF. Monash had combined aircraft, artillery, and armour with the infantry, and in an hour and a half had straightening the Allied line and had taken the town of Hamel from the Germans. The line had been advanced by one and a half miles across a four-mile front with 1600 prisoners taken, and 200 machine guns, trench mortars, and anti-tank weapons disengaged. The Australians suffered 1204 casualties.

In the following month, the Allies launched a massive offensive on the Somme in response to the German Spring Offensive of March 1918. Twenty Allied divisions launched a massive counter-offensive against the German Army, making great gains.

Germany was now being pushed out of France at increasing speed. And out of the war.

The question for Nelson was now a simple one. Would he recover sufficiently to return to stretcher-bearing work at the front before the war ended.

The Wedding and 'the Shellies'— September 1918

It was over two and a half years since Nelson had been stationed at Harefield hospital. It was now a fully expanded multi-faculty hospital doing vital war repair and recuperation work for damaged soldiers on the western front. Every endeavour was being made to get soldiers back up and fighting again.

'Will you have a look at this?' said one of the orderlies, holding the hospital's magazine *The Boomerang*.

'It says here that one of our Anzacs from Ballarat, who's at Harefield hospital now, has just been married to a young Birmingham girl. It says here that the bridal party comprised various members of the AIF stationed at the hospital, including one from the 12th Field Ambulance.'

'Does it say who else went along?' said another orderly.

'Blow me down, it does. It says here that the military guests at the church included all those from Ward 28, the "shell shock" patients, you know, the "shellies". It says here the officer in command gave the bride away, after which the bride awaited a boat to Australia for a new life.'

'Now that's some wedding,' said the other orderly.

'Yeh, and that's some guest list.'

More Footy and the Khaki Girls—28 September 1918

By mid-1918, the local Ballarat community was continuing to develop the Avenue of Honour. In August 1918, the sixth planting, of some 530 trees, had taken place, making 3300 in total. The ladies of Windermere and Burrumbeet Red Cross served tea. A special souvenir booklet was produced with the names of everyone for whom a tree had now been planted.

Now, a new and spirited occasion had been arranged to raise yet further funds to complete the Avenue.

'Come on,' said James Ferguson, 'this will be good for our spirits. We'll be late for the game.'

'Coming dear, coming,' said Lucretia.

Nelson's parents climbed into their neighbour's motor vehicle and headed down to the local oval.

A 'novelty' football match had been arranged as a fundraiser for the further construction of the Avenue of Honour. The 'Khaki Girls' from the Commonwealth Clothing Factory would play the Lucas Factory girls.

To build occasion, the morning of the match had the local residents in a long stream of cars, motorcading the Khaki Girls along the Avenue. And in the early afternoon there was a procession from the intersection of Armstrong Street and Sturt Street to the Eastern Oval—with a brief stop, of course, at the Soldiers' Statue.

'Who are you barracking for?' asked Lucretia.

'The Khaki girls will win this one I'm sure,' ruled James.

'I'm for the other side,' said Lucretia, 'so come on girls!'

The two teams went head-to-toe against each other, cheered on by a large crowd of loyal barrackers who gave generously. The sporting spectacle raised around £530 so that the grand Arch at the entrance of the Avenue could be built. Ultimately, its total cost was £2105.

The Avenue of Honour was now well on its way; at this rate, with good planning and some luck it was expected to be completed before war's end.

The Americans and Fire Power—Last Week of September 1918

While football brought funds for an important Ballarat memorial, the war continued to rage on the Western Front and elsewhere. In the last week of September 1918, the American troops (known by the AIF as the 'bowie knife army'), who were now in vast numbers across France, unleashed hell on the Germans.

In the American offensive in the Argonne Forest, the artillery fired more ammunition than during the whole of the four years of the American Civil War of 1861–65. The shelling cost one million dollars a minute.

If the Allies were finally to push Germany over, this kind of ferocious firepower from the Americans was vital. The other armies of the Allies were now well depleted. The AIF continued providing strategic initiatives on the Western Front in a last drive to quell the Germans quickly.

At this stage of the war, half the British infantry was younger than Nelson and less than 19 years of age.

The Guns Stop Barking

It was now over four years since that very first shot of the war, fired at Portsea, Victoria. The warring nations had literally thrown everything at each other. 'Total war' was now a demonstrated reality. The human losses were in their millions. Countless mothers had lost countless sons. Millions of horses and other animals had been killed, blown to pieces, or shot out of compassion. Of the 1.4 million horses Germany had sent to war, 400,000 would be killed by fire and 500,000 would die from malnutrition-related diseases. Nearly a million horses had been sent to war by the Allies, half of them to the Western Front. Like the cities and towns now empty of men, the farms were empty of horses and mules. Each side was on its knees. By October 1918, the whole of the continent of Europe had worn itself out.

But out of all of the combatant nations, Germany stood out as the one on the verge of total moral, economic and military collapse. German General Erich Ludendorff himself argued with his own government that German defeat was guaranteed, not due to an inferiority in German military might, but rather by reason of the failing 'spirit of the troops'. Others within the German Army blamed the civilian population for failing to contribute all they could to the war effort. The reality was that the whole of Germany had given its all.

Attempts were now being made once again to negotiate peace and to, this time, settle things quickly, if possible.

Word of peace soon covered Europe, even reaching Nelson now in England. His diary entry of 14 October 1918, some one month before the end of the war, recorded: 'Got the rumours about peace.'

The Americans were now prosecuting the war with the force of the most powerful nation on earth. On 2 November 1918 they fired their first mustard-gas shells at the Germans. Hell was now raining down everywhere on German troops.

During the morning of 9 November 1918, demonstrators marched through Berlin in massive numbers. Hundreds of thousands shouted for peace. At the time, Wilhelm II was in Belgium, at the army's headquarters. He declined to step down from the German throne. But Reich Chancellor Max von Baden announced the monarch's abdication in any event, turning the office of chancellor over to the Social Democrats. At 2 pm, from a window of the Reichstag building in Berlin, a new republic was proclaimed.

Germany's people had reorganised their own government, and Germany's army had now surrendered.

On 11 November 1918, the guns on the Western Front and elsewhere stopped barking. A new world order had been created: one now still; one now broken.

Back in Ballarat, a false report from America four days earlier had fired up the public to celebrate. But now, with the formal news that the war was ended, thousands rejoiced in the city and celebrated all night with church bells ringing and wild whistle blowing.

Nelson's unit within the 15th Field Ambulance was still in the field in France on 11 November 1918 and did not know the war was over. The war diary of that unit records:

The Australian Rules football team played the 59th A.I Battalion team in the 15th A.I. Brigade Competition and won the match by 7 points, thus winning the Brigade Cup. Rumours of Armistice being signed are very strong but no official message to this effect has been received.

It was not until five days later, on 16 November 1918, that the 15th Field Ambulance was officially told that the Armistice had been signed.

Nelson's diary entry for that day stated:

Not much excitement here as hotels run out of beer too soon to get Aussies going. A muster parade was held and we were congratulated as part of a victorious army. Sorry that I cannot visit the Strand.

At the end of the month, in accordance with protocol, the 15th Field Ambulance's war diary recorded the medical events and outcomes for the month, but not the end of the war. It merely noted in that regard that: 'Nothing of special interest concerning the ambulance has happened during the month.'

Home Time

It was now time for Nelson, one of the hundreds of thousands of survivors, to go home.

Some 417,000 Australians had enlisted with 318,000 sailing abroad, of whom 59,258 were killed in action, died of wounds or went missing.

Shockingly, the war had decimated the Australian newborns of the late 1880s and 1890s.

Approximately 2300 Australian nurses served in World War I, 29 of whom died in service. Three hundred and eighty-eight were decorated.

Nelson's home state, Victoria, had handed over 114,000 men in the cause of defending the British Empire. Nineteen thousand of those had died. No section of society had been unaffected, including the professions. Of the 19 Victorian barristers who enlisted, five would not return home.

The tally for Ballarat itself was appalling: around 4000 men from the Ballarat district had gone to war, and 800 had been killed. One hundred and twenty-seven of those 800 Ballarat men had lost their lives by December 1915.

Casualties among the initial volunteers were so high that of the 32,000 original soldiers of the AIF who left in August 1914, only 7000 survived to the end of the war.

Gas use had its own unique results. Up to 70 per cent of chemical casualties in World War I were caused by mustard gas. Seventy-five to 90 per cent of all mustard gas injuries had some ocular involvement. By the time of the Armistice, on 11 November 1918, the use of chemical weapons (mustard gas as well as chlorine and phosgene) has resulted in more than 1.3 million Allied casualties and approximately 90,000 deaths.

Of the 121,000 Australian horses sent across wide oceans to assist the Empire, only one would return home.

While Nelson felt enormous relief that the killing had finally stopped, there was now one thing on his mind: to get on the first ship back to Australia. Once there, he could put the ugly nightmare of battle in the past and turn to the future. The long sea voyage home would provide at least some opportunity for restoration, and for reflection on the hell he and Pomp had lived through together for some two years, an experience that would never leave them.

The mates had survived the war. It was now time for eroded returning soldiers to try to survive peacetime too.

There would be many questions for the boys to face.

How would they cope with the transition from the discipline and military purpose which had been imposed on them over the last gruesome several years?

How would they cope in peacetime with what they had seen and done in wartime?

Would their minds and bodies repair from the trauma of war?

What work would they be able to do upon their return home?

Part III
Into Peace

Part III
Into Peace

Arriving Home

Nelson stood on the *Nestor* which was pressed up against the dock. Pomp rested on her high rail. The *Nestor* would depart from England on 12 December 1918, 'boomeranging' them back to Australia with a large number of other lucky diggers.

The journey would be slow but restful for these great mates. With none of the excitement of the forward journey to war, it had all the reward of the return to family and home.

In early January 1919, the bearers passed the Equator, then headed downwards towards Australia.

As Nelson and Pomp looked to the stern and the approach of the end of January 1919, they could now see the 'Heads', the entrance to Port Phillip Bay, the path to home.

Pomp pulled out his diary:

Doctor ordered quarantine and we anchor off Portsea. Excited, no sleep. Read in *The Age* about tomorrow's disembarkation.

Sunday 26 January Each hour expect news that quarantine is off but tonight things sound settled for 7 days.

The quarantine order was to stop the horrendous flu that had killed tens of millions in Europe and elsewhere being brought into Australia.

The small village of Portsea was on the lip of the inlet to Port Phillip Bay, some 60 miles from Melbourne. The men were tantalisingly close to home.

After days of bobbing in the bay quarantined, the ship carrying the two mates planed up Port Phillip Bay towards the St Kilda Pier on the outskirts of Melbourne.

As they approached, Pomp looked down from the bow. Australia's sun glistened on the surface of the bay. Dolphins danced, kicking crystal-blue water onto the hull.

Reunion

The *Nestor* docked at the St Kilda Pier on 1 February 1919, where her cousin, the *Karoola*, had taken Nelson to England in December 1915.

Lucretia studied the enormous ship, and yet more enormous numbers of soldiers, all in khaki, looking exactly the same.

'I can't see him. Where is he?' called Lucretia to James.

'I'm not sure. I can't see him either.'

Suddenly Roy pointed. 'There!' he shouted. 'There, Mum!'

'Yes, I see him. Wonderful!' cried Lucretia.

Lucretia waved wildly to Nelson, now packed against the other returning soldiers, high on the ship's upper deck.

'Here! Here!' called Lucretia.

The ropes out of the ship strangled the wharf's bollards and the *Nestor* moaned against the wharf. A great cheer came up from the crowd, the soldiers volleying back.

Nelson and the other diggers slowly began tramping the plank towards the pier. Streamers tapped high on the ship, then bobbed in the blue bay.

As he stepped towards home soil, Nelson made a keen but cloudy search for family across the thronging pier.

'Over here! Over here!' cried Lucretia.

A Ballarat boy grabbed Nelson's arm, pointing. 'They're down there, mate. I can see your mum and dad with Roy and the others.'

Nelson's eyes scanned again to no avail.

'Here, I'll take you down there.'

The Anzac slowly guided Nelson to the base of the plank and out onto the pier toward the Ferguson family.

Nelson stood there dazed by the bright Australian sun and the overwhelming sense of relief. He then heard the most precious words in the world.

'My beautiful boy, you're home. You are safe.'

Nelson, Lucretia and the other family members now joined as one. Milky eyes sought clear ones. The Army Band now reached *fortissimo* over the top of the crowd's cheers. Jubilant family reunions overflowed the pier.

Nelson and his family swayed, taking all the warmth the high Australian sun could deliver. For now, there was no war. No death. No injury. No mud. No slaughter of young men. The arrival brought only two emotions: sheer relief and pure happiness.

The Future

Nelson telescoped his hands around his eyes, searching back at the ship for the large frame which for two years had held the other end of his stretcher. Still high up on the ship but now steadily disembarking, Pomp planned to catch the train out of Melbourne in the next few days to see his parents back in South Australia.

Pomp's giant boots stomped the old pier's planks and the two men hugged each other hard on Australian soil as if the only ones there.

'Some rendezvous, Pomp!'

'Some place to do it, Fergo! We've bloody well got here, mate. What the hell happens now?' shouted Pomp over the jubilation.

'Not too sure,' said Nelson, 'but I reckon things should be all right now, Pomp. They are going to be all right.'

'I reckon that calls for a beer, or two! And this time it better be chilled Australian beer!' shouted Pomp.

The symphony of soldiers' songs now choired down the pier and filled the hearts and minds of the many awaiting loved ones to return.

'Come on, Nel,' called Roy, 'we've got to catch the train home. I've been practising with the bat while you were gone, Nel. Not sure it will be so even now, big brother.'

'I'm not sure it will either,' said Nelson. 'The army wants me in Melbourne for at least a few days—so we'll have to see, Roy.'

'No worries, Nel—when you're ready.'

Despite the jubilation, the two stretcher-bearers continued to carry the weight of one significant thing.

The future of a returned soldier.

Enemy Aliens

Pomp boarded the train from Melbourne, travelling west to join his parents and siblings back in South Australia.

The Scholz family had been celebrating the whole day and now smiles sat around the dining table.

'So, Mum and Dad, how's our neighbourhood held up during the war?' asked Pomp.

Mrs Scholz turned to Pomp, ashen-faced.

'Many of our friends were called enemy "aliens" during the war, darling. Our little German community here was very hard-hit because we were among the largest European group. Our neighbours were interned. We read in the paper that several thousand of us were interned during the war. The horrible thing was that more than half of them were happy here before the war. Overnight, they were the enemy.'

'Christ!' said Pomp. 'What's happened to them now it's all over?'

'They've been let out of imprisonment, son. They're allowed back into the community.'

'Well if I see them down the street, Mum, I'll make sure they know they're welcome with me. We all have to get on with each other from now I reckon.'

'That's right son, peace. That's all we can ask for. We are lucky here. We are surely too far from Europe to be part of another war.'

'Let's hope so, Mum,' said Pomp. 'I will be doing everything I can to make that happen.'

The Scholz family raised their glasses to Pomp's return. And peace.

Victoria Barracks, Melbourne—Early February 1919

Just as the army had told him to do, Nelson now made his way down to Victoria Barracks to deal with his future. There were two appointments: one with an army doctor; and another about the financial support the government would give him as a returned soldier.

The nurse held Nelson's arm, assisting him into the doctor's rooms.

'Welcome back to citizen life. We need to check you over before I hand you to another part of the administration. It will help you get back on your feet and help you with some finances.'

'Very good,' said Nelson. 'I am still trying to orient myself, Doctor. Maybe the rocking at seas for weeks is not helping.'

'No, I imagine it would not be. Let me have a look then at these eyes, Private.'

The doctor cornered the desk.

'Your eyes are not too bad really. You are doing much better than I had anticipated based on your medical reports from the field.'

'Yes, I can get about with a bit of help,' said Nelson. 'But the eyes are still very sore and gritty.'

'I suspect that that will continue for some time, Mr Ferguson. But to be frank, I am much more concerned about the long-term implications of the gassing and the pock marks I can see on your corneas.'

'What does that mean, Doctor?'

'Well, we don't really know what those marks will do: develop or diminish. But I have to say it seems to me to be likely your sight will get worse rather than better over time. So it's important we keep a good record of how you are going over the next while and we will certainly be doing our very best for you. If the army is good at anything, it is tempering the wind to the shorn lamb.'

Nelson's stomach churned and his lungs gasped in the airless office. His eyes had been troubling him and he had now been told again that he might have significant long- term problems with them.

'Doctor, I am an art teacher. That is my life. Do you think my eyes will eventually come good? It's vital they do.'

'Hard to say. That is a difficult question you raise. We'll give you some immediate treatment. But I will certainly book you in for another consultation in five years, Mr Ferguson. We need to check these things regularly. I am keen to ensure we monitor your progress. In the meantime, could you please make your way to the adjacent office where someone in our administration will talk to you about financial and job support.'

'I'll show you where to go,' said the nurse.

'Oh, one further thing, Mr Ferguson—how are the lungs after the gassing?'

'Not bad, Doctor. Not too bad.'

'Well, we had better have a quick listen. Would you please pull up your shirt, Private.'

Ribs poked from a returned soldier's bare chest.

'Yes, I can hear the restriction. You may drop your shirt. You should let us know if there is any further deterioration. It's good to check regularly in any event. Now you can go to your next appointment if there are no questions.'

Finances

Nelson waited by the door adjacent to the medical room.

'Come in, Private. I am here to advise you on how the government can help you financially and in relation to employment. There is no point being rudderless on your return is there.'

'First, I should mention our new war services homes legislation, which the government passed late last year. It makes provision for you as an Australian soldier and female dependants of Australian soldiers who have returned from active service to acquire a home. Your new home will be arranged through the War Services Homes Commissioner. Through this office a home will be sold to you for a value not exceeding £700. You will be entitled to buy it without having a deposit and, once you have paid not less than one-fifth of the purchase price, the Commissioner will transfer the land and house to you and you will then need to make repayments on the remaining money owing. When the monies have all been repaid, you will own the land and house outright.'

'That seems very fair, thank you,' said Nelson. 'Can I choose where I live?'

'I can't tell you at this stage, Private Ferguson. The establishment of the Commissioner's office and the framework for providing such benefits to our soldiers has only just commenced. But I will certainly be in contact with you in the not too distant future.'

'In the meantime, we will put you up in some satisfactory lodgings. A boarding house in Footscray just north of Melbourne, if that is acceptable to you.'

'I was hoping to stay in Ballarat till I get back on my feet,' said Nelson.

'Yes, certainly you should visit home as soon as possible. But the repatriation officer assigned to you has determined that it is in your best interests to now be retrained as an art teacher at Footscray Technical College. The sooner you start, the better we think you will settle into civilian life again. The boarding house is very near the technical college.'

The government had decided that rehabilitation into civilian life for Nelson would best be achieved by retraining rather than reemploying him straight away. Nelson would spent six months at the Footscray Technical College 're-skilling' himself as an artist and art teacher, in readiness for his return to the workforce.

'Finally,' said the official, 'there's one final payment you are entitled to receive on your return. When you enlisted, like all AIF volunteers, a portion of your pay was held back, for payment upon repatriation. The Commonwealth will, of course, shortly pay it to you.'

'Thank you sir, that would be appreciated.'

A Roll of Photos—Late February 1919

Nelson slowly stepped up to the reception desk inside the boarding house.

'Excuse me,' said Nelson. 'Do you know where I might get this roll of photos processed?'

'Yes, I suggest you go to the top of Collins Street in the city. You will find a photographic studio on the corner of Collins and Spring Streets. They will be able to look after you.'

'Many thanks.'

'Do you want some help getting there?'

'No, I should be fine if I take it slowly.'

The Camera Shop

Heavy boots scraped the city pavement.

When Nelson arrived near the corner of Spring and Collins Streets, a large double-fronted building stood in front of him. Cameras and large photos displayed themselves to the passing public.

Nelson heard the door close hard behind him. He approached the shop counter. A beautiful young woman stood behind it in a pink and blue floral dress.

'May I help you?' said a mellifluous calm voice.

Nelson edged up to the counter. 'Yes, thank you, I have just returned from overseas and have these rolls of film I took in France and on the way back here.'

'Thank you, we can help you with that.'

The assistant reached forward and helped Nelson place the rolls gently onto the counter.

'I'm the studio assistant here. I will ensure that your images are well looked after and processed promptly. They will be ready for you in the next day or so. We have quite a backlog of soldiers' photos. Could I please have your details?'

'Nelson Harold Ferguson, care of 52 Peel Street, Ballarat.'

'Are you staying in the city presently?'

'No, I'm staying in Footscray. The army has put me up there.'

'We have had quite a few of your colleagues in today.'

'Yes, I've only been back in Australia for a few weeks myself. I need to have these processed as quickly as possible for my parents in Ballarat this weekend. I sent some other rolls during the war. Some reached them. This is my latest batch, mainly of my return trip with my mate, Pomp.'

The assistant placed the roll of film into a brown envelope and put it behind the counter.

She looked up to an grey-tinged face with an olive complexion. The assistant could see a deeply damaged returned soldier bearing the strain of a long war. The soldier was extremely thin and frail. Two milky eyes recorded heavy trauma.

'It might be easiest if we were to deliver the photographs to you,' she said calmly.

'Thank you, that would be much appreciated. My boarding house is in Footscray. I can't recall the address, but if you would be good enough to contact Victoria Barracks for me they will let you know where to send my photographs.'

'I will have them delivered, no problem.'

'I'm grateful for that.'

The assistant stepped out from the counter and gently steered Nelson's arm as he turned for the door.

'I should be right from here, thank you.'

Through the glass pane of the door, the assistant watched Nelson press on slowly with his journey back to the boarding house.

As the assistant returned to the counter, the photographer pushed through the curtains at the back of the shop.

'We've just had another returned soldier in. He looks very poorly. If I may, I would like to deliver his photos to him. He's staying at a boarding house in Footscray.'

'Well, we need to keep the shop open during working hours.' The photographer looked toward the assistant. 'But surely that's the least we can do,' he added. 'These boys need all our support. You can do the other deliveries while you are out.'

'Very good,' said the assistant. 'I will deliver them to our customer tomorrow when I can.'

At the Boarding House

The photographer's assistant looked up. A large Australian flag billowed, then emptied at the top of boarding house with peeling paint. She stepped inside.

The reception room was small and unkempt. A small elderly man sat behind a dusty desk. Smoke wafted towards and then away from a clicking fan.

The clerk looked up, turned his head and took another slow puff. 'Yes Miss.'

'I wonder if I might be able to drop this off for a Private Nelson Ferguson. I understand he has just returned from overseas duty with the Australian Imperial Force.'

'I'm afraid he has not returned from his walk into the city, Ma'am. He left some time ago now. Do you want to leave the parcel with me? I can give it to him.'

'Thank you, sir, but, no, that will be fine. He tells me this has his personal war photos in it. I should deliver it to him in person if possible.'

'Very good,' said the clerk. 'If I do see Mr Ferguson, I will let him know you have passed by.'

The Pub, Collins Street, Melbourne

It was just past rush hour for drinks. Tiles on the Flinders Street pub's wall stated 'Young & Jackson' above the main entrance. Groggy returned soldiers relayed 'G'day mate' in and out.

Pomp and Nelson leaned against a bar covered by a rank, wet cloth, finishing off the last one.

'How are you travelling, Pomp, now you're back from seeing your folks?'

'Felt very angry when I got back home, Fergo. Don't know why. But haven't been in a brawl yet, thank God. Trying to keep it that way. Melbourne might be good for work. I had a quick look around but there's nothing in South Australia. People can't get work anywhere, Fergo. The country's gone to the dogs since we left. The army's offered me some re-training here in Melbourne—I might take it too. Just looking around for work's about as much as I can handle at the moment. Even if I got work, don't know if I could actually bloody do it. You?'

'I shuffled up one of these city streets some time ago. Seems a long while now— couldn't seem to make my way back to the boarding house. A digger put me up somewhere overnight, bless him. Still trying to get my bearings, Pomp.'

'But I managed to put our photos in. I can pick them up in a day or two. When we finally get them, Pomp, if they're a bit grainy the handsome one is you mate.'

Pomp laughed.

'That must be some special kind of camera, Fergo!'

The two mates finished the bottom of their beers and placed them on the bar.

'The photographer's assistant had a beautiful voice, Pomp. Can't stop hearing it.'

'What did she…? Never mind Fergo.'

'Her voice made me feel safe, Pomp. It was generous. Not sure what I mean Pomp, but it had harmony.'

'Like your old cornet, Fergo!' joked Pomp.

Nelson paused. 'Like a beautiful hymn.'

'Well don't know about all that for you just yet Fergo. You've got a long way to go to get back on your feet. Take it step by step mate. We have to get back to where we left off before we can take a step forward I reckon. My only job this arvo is to get you back to your boarding house. I'm going to take you there myself when they boot us out of here.'

'You're right, Pomp, this returned soldier is damaged goods.'

Pomp put his hand on Nelson's shoulder.

'One day at a time mate.'

A Call Home

Nelson stood in the pale red phone box in Footscray.

'Where are you calling from darling?' asked Lucretia.

'I'm up the road from the boarding house, Mum. I'm told this is practically the only phone in the suburb. I'm in a phone box.'

'We want to see you very soon if we can, son,' Lucretia said anxiously.

'The army says eye ointment for a few weeks might help, Mum, and they're still looking at my lungs. I still have lots of forms they want me to sign. Then I'll be up home, Mum. Can't wait to be there.'

'We cannot wait either, darling.'

Another Visit

The fan swirled more smoke across the reception room.

'Hello. I came here a few days ago but Private Ferguson was not in. I wonder if I might be able to drop this off to him now.'

'Certainly,' said the clerk, exhaling. 'Private Ferguson's out the back. Someone from the army is putting pads on his eyes after some fancy ointment has gone in. Could you wait here please, Miss, while I see how it's all travelling.'

'If it's not convenient, I can come again later on my next round.'

'No, Miss, it shouldn't be too long. The doctor's been here some time already.'

The clerk rose slowly from behind the desk, prised a tired door from its squeaking frame, then disappeared.

The assistant sat quietly in the reception room. The clicking fan wobbled fast, then slow, then fast again. Returned soldiers and Australian flies came in and out of the front door with the breeze.

A digger on crutches approached the assistant. 'Can I help you, Miss?'

'Yes, thank you.'

'I see there's no-one at reception—are you looking for someone? Have you been waiting long?'

'Yes, I'm waiting for a Private Nelson Ferguson who's staying here presently. I have this for him.'

'Well I know he has his eye treatment in the afternoons, Miss, then he has to lie down and rest to let it take hold. It could be some time. I can check out the back if you like.'

'I think I had better go. My employer will be wondering where I've got to.'

'All right, Miss, that's a matter for you I guess.'

The assistant waited for the fan to journey across the room once more, then rose and turned for the door.

Collins Street—Early March 1919

Trams and old motor cars took themselves up and down the hilly end of Collins Street in Melbourne. Pomp held Nelson's arm as the two mates reached the corner.

'Here it is, Fergo.'

'Thanks, Pomp. Don't know I could have got here without you, mate.'

'It's just up from Young and Jackson's, Fergo, so easy to find as far as I'm concerned.'

Nelson smiled.

'I guess you don't need my help from here, Fergo.'

'I should be right but thanks,' said Nelson.

Pomp pushed open the front door of the photography shop and turned towards drinking turf.

Tea and the Voice

Nelson slowly approached the counter.

The photographer's assistant looked up from her filing. Large blue eyes met cloudy ones and a handsome olive complexion.

'Mr Ferguson, nice to see you. I tried to deliver your photos recently. I'm sorry I haven't got them to you as soon as I had hoped.'

'That's fine,' said Nelson. 'I'm happy to be visiting your shop again.'

'That's kind of you. Please have a seat, Mr Ferguson, while I collect the parcel from out the back.'

'Thank you. I'll rest here, no problem,' said Nelson.

The assistant disappeared into the back of the shop behind the counter and after some time returned with Nelson's photos.

She then sat next to Nelson and handed him the parcel.

'I love photography,' said Nelson. 'I took quite a lot of photos in the war. The photograph records true history.'

'I should introduce myself. I am Madeline Hobbs. I colourise photos once they've been developed. We have had quite a few come in from overseas recently. I've been shocked by what I have seen.'

'Madeline. Is that French?' asked Nelson.

'Yes, I believe it is.'

'The French are wonderful and beautiful people,' said Nelson. '*Tres bon*. They have been through so much. May I look over these?' asked Nelson.

'Yes, of course. They are all there in the parcel, Private Ferguson.'

'Please call me Nelson, or Harold, I don't mind either. May I show you my photos then?'

Madeline opened the parcel for Nelson and handed one to him. He pushed it against his nose.

'This one shows me, and my best mate, Pomp. We're on the *Nestor* on the way back from England earlier this year. I think we are at about the Equator at this part of the trip. Nearly home.'

He handed it to Madeline who looked at it closely. Two soldiers leaned against the rail of the ship on a bright day. 'You seem good friends.'

'We were on each end of a stretcher for more than two years in France. He saved my spirit. And probably my life. I think Pomp did most of the lifting.'

Madeline laughed.

Madeline had been born in Launceston, Tasmania, in 1888. She was now 31. Her French mother, Annie Aspray, had travelled at the age of 22 to England, then sailed on the *Kaikoura* in 1887. After six weeks at sea, she arrived in Hobart in July, marrying Madeline's father in the same month. They were married at 'The House of William Henry Walton', Balfour Street, Launceston.

Nelson pushed another photograph in front of his nose.

'I've just made the tea. It's on the counter there. Would you like some?'

'Thank you, I would like that very much.'

Madeline handed Nelson a cup. 'Here we go. I hope that's all right.'

Nelson paused. Madeline's voice was gentle and soothing.

'Thank you, Madeline,' said Nelson, adjusting his beret.

'You are welcome, Nelson.'

Young & Jackson

Nelson and Pomp sat in Pomp's usual spot for late morning. The barmaid brought one large beer and small change.

'I got a look through the shop window, Fergo. She's beautiful.'

'It's her voice, Pomp. Beautiful. She's kind. We had tea,' said Nelson.

'Well, remember, Fergo, as I said—one step at a time, mate.'

Pomp looked up at his mate. He stretched his hand to Nelson's shoulder, then leaned to Nelson's left ear.

'This is a step you should take, Fergo.'

An Honourable Discharge—March 1919

On 18 March 1919, the AIF formally discharged both NH Ferguson and Norman (Pomp) Scholz from active service abroad.

In the discharge papers the reason given was simply stated: 'Cessation of hostilities.'

Nelson had served abroad for nearly three years. Pomp had served abroad for three years and 97 days. Within that service, they had spent incalculable days at each end of the same stretcher.

Their lives as volunteer soldiers had begun with the signing of an army form and had ended that way too.

For now, there was only the present. Neither Pomp nor Nelson could foresee that one day the peace arrangements which took them out of battle might be the origin of yet another deadly conflict embroiling a further generation of Australians.

An Impression—May 1919

Madeline dabbed pink onto the portrait's cheeks. 'That helps I think.'

The clock told her it was time to reverse the 'Open' sign. As she walked towards the door, she could see through the pane a young soldier gently tapping and waving a small envelope.

Madeline opened the door.

'Can I help you soldier?'

'Are you Miss Madeline Hobbs?'

'Yes, that's me.'

'I am delivering the mail for returned soldiers. I have this for you from a Mr Ferguson of Footscray.'

'Thank you, sir. I am grateful. Please give Mr Ferguson my warm wishes if you see him.'

'I will thanks, ma'am. I'm sorry but it's been with us for some time for delivery but there's been quite a lot to do so I could only bring it now. The army's a bit slow at some things. But we look after our returned soldiers. Delivering their messages is important work.'

After the soldier left, Madeline calmly turned the envelope over as if addressed for another. The scribble on the back said 'NH Ferguson, Footscray.'

Madeline returned to the counter. The bright lamp illuminated the envelope as she opened it and gently pulled out its contents.

Old paper emerged on which Madeline could see a slight and gentle impression of herself as a side portrait, sketched in charcoal.

'That's beautiful work.' She slowly turned over the sketch.

'You are the light. NHF.'

Madeline turned the paper over again. A tear splashed onto the sketch, blending paper and charcoal.

'Are you ready to close up Madeline?' called the photographer from the office behind her.

'Yes I am—in a minute, sir.' Madeline wiped the sketch carefully then returned it to its envelope.

Peace and the Treaty—June 1919

By June 1919, Nelson was still only just getting his bearings in civilian life after war trauma. The world was sorting out its European bearings too.

There was great anger with Germany across the globe. The Prime Minister of Britain, Lloyd George, was in favour of hanging the German Kaiser. But many were not and this was not ordered.

On 28 June 1919, five years to the day after the Archduke had been assassinated, the Allies forced Germany to sign the Treaty of Versailles. Under the 'war guilty' clause, Germany accepted responsibility for itself and its allies for causing all the loss and damage. France's aim was to set the clock back to 1870, thus rendering World War I humanity's largest exercise in waste. The Treaty stripped Germany of 25 thousand square miles and seven million people.

The Treaty obliged Germany to reduce its army so it could not wreck Europe again: to a strength of only 100,000 men (including 4000 officers), comprising 10 divisions only. In 1914, the German army had 3.8 million men comprising some 50 active and 48 reserve divisions. Germany would no longer be able to conscript soldiers from its population, so it could not create a reserve army. The army could not have any aircraft, tanks or heavy artillery above 105 mm. Germany's Great General Staff would be abolished as would the War Academy. Germany's army would only be permitted to control its frontiers and maintain internal order.

But it would not be long before the German Army leadership would seek to circumvent these restrictions. Germany soon introduced a rigorous military training program so that its army would be nimble rather than of large capacity. It also restructured its leadership ranks so that officers could work around the abolition of the General Staff. And moreover, it soon established armaments manufacturing out of the country, together with secret tank and air training centres in the Soviet Union.

Although the Allies had sought to disengage the German war machine once and for all, Germany would soon position itself for the next global conflict.

One that would pull in the next generation of young Fergusons.

The Avenue is Complete—16 August 1919

'Well that's great,' said Pomp, holding the *Argus*. 'It says here that this week the final 600 trees will be planted in Ballarat's Avenue of Honour, the eighth in total.

'I reckon one of those trees will have your name on it, Fergo.'

'Yeh, I think you're right Pomp—Mum told me that was happening.'

'It says here there's only one task to complete in Ballarat now, Fergo: to make the huge 'Arch of Victory' at the start of the Avenue.'

'Yeh, I heard that was going in too,' said Nelson.

Pomp paused.

'That's going to be one fancy get-together and celebration by the town, Fergo. You should think about inviting Madeline to it. That would make it very special.'

'It sure would, Pomp. Let's hope it's not too long away. I reckon I'll visit her again at the photographic studio in the meantime.'

'Let me know if you need a hand passing by Young & Jackson's along the way, Fergo'.

Two mates laughed.

'Will do, Pomp. I certainly will.'

The Prince and Footy—31 May 1920

On 2 April 1920, the Prince of Wales arrived in Australia representing his father, King George V. He had been sent to thank Australians for their participation in the World War I.

But now, some weeks later, it was time for the Prince to turn to lighter and more enjoyable duties.

On 31 May, stepping into one of the grandest ovals in the world, the Melbourne Cricket Ground, the Prince could see over 50,000 Australians cheering wildly, ready for the game.

This would be a match of a very different kind. The Prince was there to see a unique sporting code, Victorian League Football, with 18 men to each side. The league's first premiership was in 1897. Today, the contest would be no ordinary one: the elite of Pomp's home State, South Australia, would play the elite of Nelson's State, Victoria. This was first-class interstate rivalry between two old colonies of Australia.

Pushing into the higher end of the grandstand, Pomp turned to Nelson.

'Come on, Fergo, we're going to miss the start of "where I come from" thrashing "where you come from".'

'I'm right behind you!' called Nelson, a long way back.

As they approached the top of the grandstand, another returned soldier spotted Pomp.

'Hey Scholzie, over here mate, it's me Baker from the pub in Bapaume!'

Pomp turned quickly. His mate was high in the adjacent stand. Each digger saluted the other then waved wildly.

'Hang on a minute, Scholzie!' called another spectator.

'That's bloody German. Get him.'

Jostlers suddenly packed in around Pomp, crushing him up against the edge of the grandstand.

'Take him down!' cried another spectator.

'Yeh, thump that hating Hun down. Throw him over!'

As the crowd swarmed around Pomp, Nelson pressed forward himself, pushing his way through.

'This man's as Australian as any of you bloody blokes. He comes from South Australia,' shouted Nelson, 'and he's been on the end of my stretcher for the whole time I was in the fight in France. Ease up! Ease up!'

'Yeh sure, mate, but if he's a "Scholzie" he's still a bloody traitor!' called another spectator over the thronging mob. 'We locked you bastards up during the war and now we're going to send you over this fucking balcony.'

An enemy of spectators pushed forward, pinning Pomp against the railing. A clenched fist drew aim. A mouth drew phlegm to spit.

Pomp's eyes raged. His large frame pushed back hard and the entangled mob rolled over the stand tumbling on steps and seats like drunks.

'Hey there,' shouted Nelson, 'I reckon you blokes are the traitors if you don't let my mate barrack for his home State. As I said, ease up, just ease up.'

'Hang on, hang on,' called another spectator, 'if this bloke's from South Australia he must be flamin' all right! He's here to watch us thrash the Vics! Give him a bloody go!'

'I reckon it might be the other way 'round!' called Nelson.

The crowd lost interest and dispersed.

'Fergo, the game's only just started mate. Let's head down to the bar first and ease into the match that way.'

'No problem with that Pomp. We can listen to the Vics score go up from down there.'

Nelson was right. Victoria narrowly beat South Australia by five points, 71 to 66.

In the same year, the Richmond football team became VFL premiers at the Melbourne Cricket Ground, defeating Collingwood, another city team, in front of 53,908 obsessed spectators.

The Opening of the Avenue and the Arch of Victory— 3 June 1920

On the morning of 2 June 1920, Madeline peered out through the carriage window. The train was now approaching the magnificent Ballarat railway station. Towering verandahs and a grand façade with a high clock handsomely presented the town to its visitors. Madeline gripped Nelson's hand.

Ballarat was abuzz for the celebration. It was the culmination of three years of work to develop and complete the Avenue of Honour by the planting of trees and the construction of the magnificent Arch of Victory to the north of the town.

Nelson's parents and siblings collected Madeline and Nelson at the station and they all headed north towards the formal celebrations.

As they approached the Arch, 600 girls from the Lucas Factory sat in high tiers constructed especially for them. A large ribbon ran across the entrance to the Arch.

The leader of the AIF forces until May 1918, General Sir William Birdwood, had earlier laid the foundation stone for the Arch, on 7 February 1920, presenting a number of decorations to local returned servicemen and women.

But now the Avenue of Honour with its Arch was fully complete. It had taken some eight separate plantings to complete it between 1917 and 1920. The Avenue now comprised 3771 trees of 23 species, extending over approximately 14 miles. The trees had been planted along the Western Highway in order of the soldiers' and nurses' enlistments. The trees represented the 3912 Ballarat and district men and women who served in World War I—528 of whom had been killed in battle or died of wounds or disease.

The driving rain and wintery conditions had not repelled Ballarat's enthusiasm for this auspicious event. Nelson and Madeline, together with Nelson's family, stood proudly in the dense crowd.

'Nelson,' whispered Madeline. 'The Prince of Wales just arrived.'

A long motorcade of polished cars and prestige horses approached the Arch. The Prince of Wales stepped down out of his carriage and began the regal walk towards the dignitaries and the ribbon.

The locals were now cheering wildly. His Majesty moved on towards the ribbon.

'I now declare this magnificent Arch of Victory officially open,' announced the Prince.

Louder cheers erupted.

Madeline and Nelson now moved closer to the Arch of Victory and towards the Prince.

A break in the clouds brought bright sunshine onto the Arch, beaming its central message to all:

THE AVENUE OF HONOUR
1914 VICTORY 1919

The rising sun emblem of the AIF sat above the words.

'Do you want a photograph, you two?' asked a man standing next to a large tripod.

'Nelson, would that be all right?' asked Madeline.

'Certainly, why not, it's a bonnie day here and I don't think we'll be with the Prince again any time soon.'

Madeline smiled.

The two took up the offer and stood close while the photographer positioned the Arch behind them.

A bright flash struck Nelson's eyes, followed by the word 'Superb' from behind the camera.

'You can pick the image up at my studio in Ballarat tomorrow. Here's my card.'

'Thank you,' said Madeline, 'that will be excellent.'

The Sapling in a Box

Nelson, Madeline and Nelson's parents stepped into the army car. They rode slowly along the Avenue of Honour as part of a larger motorcade. A large number of people from Ballarat, from the surrounding region, and those who had travelled from Melbourne for the day lined the Avenue.

The motorcade made its way several miles up the Avenue. Young saplings lined each side of the road as far as the eye could see. The top of the young trees peeked out of small wooden boxes constructed to protect them from the elements.

Nelson and Madeline's car approached a large hayshed to the right and their driver told them they were nearing Nelson's newly planted sapling. As they pulled closer, Madeline could see the large paddocks on each side of the Avenue full of merino sheep.

'We are coming up to it now,' noted the army driver. He pointed forward. 'Just past there.'

The army car pulled up and Nelson, Madeline, James and Lucretia got out to look closer. In the breeze the small sapling searched the edge of the wooden box which housed it, staked on each corner.

'Would you like a picture?' asked the Private.

'Yes, that would be much appreciated,' said Nelson.

The Private got out a box brownie camera and positioned the Fergusons and Madeline in front of the sapling.

'All done,' said the Private. 'But not for these young ones. This community and the army want them to grow and mature into great timber columns recording contribution to service given. If they grow as we hope, this will truly be an avenue of honour.'

'Very good,' said Nelson. 'Let's also rely on this avenue to remind us to remain in peace. We must never have another Great War.'

'I'm sure the army would agree with that, Mr Ferguson,' said the Private.

The Fergusons now travelled back to the local Returned Soldiers League Hall, a few miles up the road. There was plenty of tea, some cake, and one more necessary ingredient: admiration for work done by the town of Ballarat in recognition of the courageous work the local soldiers had performed thousands of miles from home.

Bat and Ball—3 June 1920

The next day, in the late afternoon, Nelson and Roy sat on the back verandah of the Ferguson house in Ballarat. The winter's rain beat on the tin roof. Roy patted the cricket bat next to him.

'The footy season's a cracker this year but we can't wait till summer, Nel. We need some time again in the paddock I reckon,' reflected Roy.

'Sure Roy, when I come back up to Ballarat this summer, we might head out for a hit like the old times.'

The rain's drum held steady. Brothers studied the back fence.

A City and a Town—First Week of October 1920

'May I welcome all to this important public meeting,' declared the Mayor of Melbourne.

'Please take your seats.'

'As you all know, this meeting is being held at this fine Town Hall to consider the proposal that the town of Villers-Bretonneux, now indelibly associated with Australian history, should be adopted by the citizens of Melbourne.'

On the stage of the Town Hall sat various sponsors of the idea that Charlotte Crivelli had so passionately promoted in support of her home country, France, and the town of Villers-Bretonneux itself. They included no less than Sir John Monash, 'Pompey' Elliot, and Major General Sir John Gellibrand. All used the opportunity to highlight and emphasise the importance of the fighting by the AIF, led by them, in and around the town.

Monash in particular told the Town Hall that he regarded Villers-Bretonneux as the location from which the Allies' counter-offensive had been launched in April 1918, as 'the beginning of the end' of World War I.

'I now call on Councillor Stapley to put the motion,' said the mayor.

'Thank you, sir,' said the councillor.

'The motion is that Villers-Bretonneux be adopted by the citizens of Melbourne in memory of the great Australian victory there in April 1918.'

The motion was carried with thunderous clapping.

The Anzac Name—December 1920

The return of heroes from war had now swelled Australia's developing culture of recognising courage and paying tribute to contributions far beyond any normative standard.

On 2 December 1920, the Commonwealth of Australia implanted that culture permanently by passing the *Protection of the Word 'Anzac' Act* into law. Its provisions were designed to protect the esteemed name 'Anzac' for all time.

The beneficiaries of the legislation and regulations under it would not only be Nelson and Pomp who had served in World War I and all of the other Australians and New Zealanders.

It would include the nations of Australia and New Zealand and all of their citizens present and future.

A Record of Service—March 1921

By March 1921, Nelson was teaching at the Footscray Technical College and renting a house in that suburb. Madeline had just arrived at the house for afternoon tea.

'Maddie, this has arrived. A kind man just delivered it.'

'Let me look over it for you, darling,' said Madeline.

Madeline opened the package and pulled out a large khaki-coloured book.

She read the front page to Nelson:

It was natural to expect that, when the insistent call for service of all kinds came to us with the declaration of war and with the knowledge that the country was in peril, and when such a searching test of the worth of the citizenship of each one of us was therefore being made, none would hear the call more seriously and respond more effectively than the teachers. And the expectation was amply justified. In the heady, exciting weeks of August, 1914, when extra-military organizations for war service were, on all sides, springing into existence, our organization was one of the first to be perfected and to produce results.

From the first, there was no dissentient voice raised. For years, we had endeavoured to demonstrate in our schools the truth that education is development and strengthening of the powers of body, mind and soul, to the end that they may be used in forms of service. We had been training girls and boys for service in the manifold duties of peace; we had now to show that every citizen had even more insistent duties in time of war.

Our country was calling for help. No one was too old to serve in some capacity; no one was too young. Women were serving as well as men; why not girls as well as boys? And so it was resulted that we should band together our schools throughout Victoria, and endeavour to stimulate each and every child to put forth some effort, however slight, for the national cause. The part of the children was to be the relief of distress—to provide comforts for those who were enduring the horrors of the Front Line, to do what could be done to brighten the lives of those who were sick and maimed in hospitals, to care for the dependents left behind.

'It says here too, dear, that of the 752 teachers enlisted, 146 of them died in action. Darling, the book has details of those who served and those who fell.'

'We need to keep this book Maddie. It's very important these teachers have the recognition they deserve. I hope every school keeps one.'

'Yes,' said Madeline. 'This must always be kept.'

Ivory Satin—18 April 1921

Madeline's family had hoped for a Launceston wedding, her hometown in Tasmania. The Fergusons readily agreed.

Tasmania was some 12 hours by rolling ship across Bass Strait, due south from mainland Australia. The Fergusons were all very excited to be travelling 'over the sea' for the special occasion.

As the *Launceston Examiner* recorded:

Palms were arranged on either side of the rostrum, and Easter daisies were artistically used in great profusion. As the bride approached the altar on the arm of her father, by whom she was given away, the organist, Mr. M. Hannagan, played a bridal voluntary. The gown was of soft ivory satin trimmed with hand-made silver tissue flowers; the long train fell from the shoulders with a butterfly bow of silver tissue across one corner. She wore her mother's wedding veil and blossom, and carried a lovely shower bouquet composed of white roses, trumpet lilies, and bouvardia sprays of fern with a waterfall of long narrow satin ribbons.

Madeline's mother wore a costume of plain blue cloth, fuchsia pink hat, vest of the same shade, and she carried a bouquet of fuchsia, pink hydrangea, and autumn leaves to tone.

From the altar of the Patterson-Street Methodist Church, the Reverend W Atkinson declared: 'I now pronounce you man and wife.' 'You may kiss the bride.'

Cheers and family smiles filled Launceston.

As the bride and bridegroom left the vestry the 'Wedding March' was played on the organ, and as they emerged from the church amid showers of confetti.

Afterwards the bride's parents received the bridal party and about 30 guests at Glen Esk. Masses of Easter daisies filled all the rooms. Wedding tea was served, and the tables were decorated with Easter daisies scattered from end to end, and over the bride's table were hung a wedding bell and horseshoe for good luck.

On the recommendation of Madeline's employer in Melbourne, and with the consent of her parents, a fine photographer from Hobart had taken the journey to Launceston to capture the special occasion.

'Now, one other matter,' said the photographer.

'Could we have one final photograph of the bride by herself? Mrs Ferguson, would you mind standing to one side and holding your bouquet just here.'

Madeline stood by the window in her beautiful satin wedding gown.

A bright light flashed the room.

'Very good, thank you for your splendid co-operation. That will be stunning.'

Mr and Mrs Ferguson left by motor car for Hobart. Madeline travelled in a coat and skirt of steel-grey cloth, henna tam hat, and a grey squirrel stole. She also carried a grey suede wrist wallet which, with a pearl ring, was the gift of the bridegroom.

After some time in Hobart, Nelson and Madeline returned to mainland Australia on the ship across Bass Strait. The Victorian Education Department had seconded Nelson to teach art at the old goldmining town of Beechworth, near the border of New South Wales.

Nelson and Madeline would spend some time there, taking clean country air for repair to damaged lungs, and receiving with it the remedy of the calmer rural life.

Repatriation Classes End—1922

The Ballarat councillors returned to their seats.

'Gentlemen, the purpose of the meeting is to determine whether repatriation classes should now finish up. There is an emerging view among councillors that their purpose has been fulfilled,' said the chairman.

'Since their inception over 400 ex-servicemen have been trained in these classes and, with very few exceptions, have been placed in regular employment. The part the school has taken in this national movement will endure among the school's best traditions.'

'Hear, hear,' said a councillor.

'May I propose the following resolution: that the ex-servicemen repatriation classes close forthwith and that all concerned receive the council's deepest thanks and gratitude.'

'Aye,' responded the councillors.

'Finally,' said the chair, 'before I close this meeting may I remind you that our king has graciously now toured the new Commonwealth war cemetery on the Ypres Salient in Belgium. It was as you all know in His Majesty's name that this great country fought in the Great War for the British Empire. The king's words of 11 May 1922 spoken at that cemetery should forever be present in our minds and I commend them to you.'

We can truly say that the whole circuit of the earth is girdled with the graves of our dead. In the course of my pilgrimage to Belgium and France, I have many times asked myself whether there can be more potent advocates of peace upon earth through the years to come, than this massed multitude of silent witnesses to the desolation of war.

Symbols on Chests—September 1923

By 1923, Nelson and Madeline had returned to Melbourne and Nelson was now teaching part-time at a local technical school, in art and design.

Pomp sat at Nelson's kitchen table, tapping his fingers. A brown parcel the size of a pencil case lay in front of Nelson's tea and Pomp's beer.

'Picked it up this morning for you, Fergo.'

'Well, I suppose we should open it and see what's in it.'

Both men already knew.

In 1919, Nelson and Pomp had become entitled to three medals: the British War Medal, the Star Medal, and the Victory Medal.

Nelson had been given the first two when he was discharged from the army in March 1919. At that stage the Victory Medal had not yet been awarded.

But by August 1923, the Base Records Office of the AIF had sought to catch up and issued a circular to returned soldiers. Nelson received this letter:

Dear Sir,

You are hereby informed that all war medals not already issued to members of the AIF discharged in Victoria are now available at Base Records.

W Mackintosh, Captain, Officer i/c Base Records.

Below the circular was a place for returned soldiers to complete their request. Nelson had made one:

I, Nelson Harold Ferguson, desire the undermentioned medal or medals, awarded for service in the A.I.F, to be forwarded to me.

Victory Medal, 1914–19

Signature NH Ferguson, 9 September 1923

On 20 September 1923, the army completed its recognition of Nelson's service in the Australian Imperial Force by sending him the Victory Medal. The Medal Distribution Officer recorded Nelson's receipt of the medal in a register.

Nelson's three medals had three distinct and significant messages.

The 1919 British War Medal marked the end of World War I, recording service given. A member of the AIF qualified if he had entered theatres of war during specified periods or left places of residence and rendered approved service overseas. Nelson qualified.

The next medal, authorised in 1918, was the 1914–15 Star, awarded for service in specified theatres of war between 5 August 1914 and 31 December 1915. The four-pointed star was bright bronze, with a crown ensigned on it. The obverse had crossed gladius, with an oak wreath overlaid and with the cypher of King George V also ensigned. The legend 1914–15 sat on a scroll placed on top of the crossed blades. The ribbon had the red, white and blue colours of the Empire, in shaded and watered stripes. The same ribbon was used for the 1914 Star and the 1914–15 Star.

In 1919 the Victory Medal was authorised, commemorating the Allied Forces' victory. Each Allied nation issued the medal to nationals. A standard ribbon was used but there were different designs so as to reflect national identity and custom. Some had the figure of Victory on the obverse. Australians were awarded the medal as issued by Great Britain. It was awarded to prescribed classes of persons who entered a theatre of war on duty between 5 August 1914 and 11 November 1918. The ribbon had a 'two rainbow' design, with the violet from each rainbow on the outside edges moving through to a central red stripe where both rainbows meet.

Pomp stood over the cutlery drawer and pulled out a large knife, cutting the end of the parcel. He then opened the case that had been inside it.

'This is the last one you'll get I reckon, Fergo,' said Pomp with cheek.

'That's fine by me.'

'You saved so many lives, Fergo, where's the recognition for that?'

'These medals are for general contribution, Pomp, not individual endeavour. We were both just small parts of one large mess.'

'Would you like me to pin it?' asked Pomp.

'No, that's fine. I've got it now and that's enough.'

Pomp handed Nelson the medal.

Nelson pressed his thumb against the face of the bronze object.

Its obverse had a winged figure of Victory. The reverse had the following words all surrounded by a laurel wreath:

THE GREAT WAR FOR CIVILISATION

All of Nelson's three medals were from Britain.

All were service awards for being in a particular capacity in a particular geographical area and time frame, and to commemorate the end of World War I.

The practice of issuing awards and medals to every combatant in war had commenced in England only after the Battle of Waterloo in 1815. Until then, awards and medals had been conferred only for specific acts or achievements during war. Decoration awards required specific acts of heroism or achievement. Because field ambulance stretcher-bearing was a non-combatant role, combatant medals did not apply.

But the position was different in Germany. From as early as 1871, King John of Saxony had instituted a commemorative cross, to be awarded to men and women for services in nursing, and for activities performed at home in connection with the Franco-German war. In that same year, the Germans had instituted an award to women who had earned merit during the war by rendering services in nursing to the wounded or in looking after the wellbeing of the fighting troops.

In contrast, during their time in the 15th Field Ambulance, while hundreds of Australian and other Allied soldiers' and French civilians' lives had been saved, no such act or achievement had been recognised by the army. Nelson's or Pomp's time as stretcher-bearers in the central Allied campaigns in Belgium and France, across the whole of the period between 1916 to early 1918, did not warrant special recognition for outstanding contribution. No Australian medal, either service or decoration, had been or would be conferred on them.

'Time for a different kind of award, Fergo. At the pub,' said Pomp.

'Yes, let's down one before it closes, Pomp.'

Nelson put the Victory medal back in its case.

The bearers headed out for a round of cool ale and reflection.

The Eye Examination—March 1924

It was now some five years since Nelson had returned from war. The army doctor had looked over his eyes upon his disembarkation from the *Nestor* and he had received some short-term treatment with eye ointment. But he had not been formally reviewed since that time. It was now the Repatriation Department's function to supervise Nelson's ongoing medical treatment.

'Step into this consulting room if you will, Mr Ferguson,' said the eye specialist.

'Thank you, sir.'

The specialist looked at Nelson's file.

'I see we are here for our five-yearly check-up'.

'So I believe, Doctor.'

'Well we might start with a basic test then, Mr Ferguson. Could you please look at that chart on the wall over there and start reading from the top. Take your time; this is not a speed test. We are testing for accuracy.'

Nelson read the top line and paused.

'Take your time, Mr Ferguson. As I mentioned, we are checking for accuracy.'

Nelson paused further.

'I see,' said the doctor.

'Let me then turn to a closer look at your eyes. Please take a seat there and sit as still as you can.'

The doctor rolled on his chair and beamed a bright light into the left eye.

'I can see developing signs of deterioration and a few deep pock marks. One eye is much more troubled than the other. You might have observed that already, I would imagine. But on the whole it does not look too bad to me, Mr Ferguson. We can give you some ointment which you should drop into the eye regularly.'

'How quickly will the ointment work, Doctor? My profession is teaching art. It's vital my eyes start working properly.'

'Well, let's see how the ointment goes and we can check on you again soon.'

Thank you, Doctor. Could you also please check the prescription for these glasses? They don't seem right to me. I am having trouble focusing—things seem very blurry. I think if they fix the prescription, things might come right.'

'Well I am afraid that's with the other department, Mr Ferguson, but I will of course refer you back there.'

'Very good, sir, thank you for checking me over.'

'That's fine, Mr Ferguson. I look forward to seeing you on your next review.'

Public Reaction to the Use of Gas

By 1925, gas-damaged returned soldiers from World War I all across Britain, Australia, the United States of America, Germany and elsewhere were continuing to attempt to make a life after the war.

Public reaction across the globe was now universal that gas should not be used again in warfare.

On 17 June 1925 in Geneva, 38 countries signed an international convention, a protocol of which prohibited the use in war of 'asphyxiating, poisonous or other gases and all analogous liquids, materials or devices'. The convention and protocol followed the *1899 Hague Declaration Concerning Asphyxiating Gases* and the *1907 Hague Convention on Land Warfare* which all prohibited the use of poisonous and other gases.

Britain and Australia signed up to the convention, with one important condition: gas could be used as a weapon in retaliation against a gas attack. The ban was accordingly only against 'first use'.

It would not be long, therefore, before countries would recommence manufacturing it, whether as a 'weapon of defence' or not.

A Soldier's Home—Karma Avenue—22 July 1926

Nelson put his hand into the mouth of the letterbox and pulled out an envelope. He had been hoping for a letter from the Commonwealth for some time now.

Nelson anxiously turned the envelope over and put it in front of his nose. The back of it gave the sender: War Services Homes Commission, Victoria. He quickly called out to Madeline. 'Maddie, I think it's arrived. Can you please read it?'

The letter read:

Dear Mr Ferguson,

We are pleased to advise that your application for a war services home loan has been approved and you are now the registered proprietor of the land at 6 Karma Avenue, East Malvern, Victoria.

Your new home will be in the Villers-Bretonneux Estate, in Malvern.

Would you please contact our office to make the necessary further arrangements regarding the above.

Yours sincerely,

The War Services Homes Commission

'Maddie, let's make the appointment with the War Services Homes Commission as soon as we can. Now the government has set aside a block of land we can start to build our house. This is what we've been waiting for,' said Nelson.

'Yes, this is wonderful news, love. I will call them in the morning.'

It was eight years since the Commonwealth had established a scheme under the *War Service Homes Act 1918* for the compulsory acquisition of land, and associated credit loans and house building for returned soldiers. The Commonwealth Department of Repatriation had for some time now been offering attractive housing loans to returned soldiers, nurses, munition workers, soldiers' widows and their children.

Just as Australia had, in the run up to 1914, embedded its army in its civilian population, now too it would embed its returned soldiers there.

Among its many activities, the department had earlier, in 1919, negotiated for the purchase of land in Carnegie and, a year later, in 1920, some 178 allotments and twin reserves (gardens) for plantations in that area had been laid out for use.

The allotments were all within a subdivision in a suburb of Melbourne to be known as the Villers-Bretonneux Estate. The estate was formally declared a subdivision in 1924. The final design of the estate included two gardens, Villers Square and Bretonneux Square. To improve the aesthetic of the subdivision, certain streets within the subdivision had curves rather than the traditional grid of streets.

The choice of street names was an unusual combination of battle sites, such as Villers, Bretonneux and Fontaine, and concepts of Buddhist philosophy—including Nirvana and Karma Streets. These streets had been surveyed in an earlier subdivision before the war, in 1913.

By 1922, some 29 houses had been built and a further 14 War Commission villas had been erected in 1925. After 1925, many of the houses used pattern-book designs issued by the State Savings Bank of Victoria.

In 1926, a further 33 homes had been built. The Fergusons' house at 6 Karma Avenue would be yet another.

The Villers and Bretonneux Squares were just a short walk from the Fergusons' new house in East Malvern. He and Madeline could stroll to them at any time they wished. These squares were some 10,000 miles from the town they were named after in France, where Nelson had been gassed.

The estate was high quality, with wide streets and substantial median reserves. This was in keeping with community expectations that the estate and each house within it should be distinctive, with variation in character of the housing. The estate was unusual in layout so as to avoid the appearance of subsidised, institutionalised housing, presenting a normalised aspect of suburban life.

The estate sat within the City of Malvern, established in 1911. The city was now a quiet, solid and leafy sea of red-roofed brick villas sheltering the more comfortable classes of the greater city of Melbourne. Malvern was the former home of Major Norman John

Bullen, 15th Field Ambulance, a medical practitioner. As Nelson had recorded in his diary on the very day, Bullen had died of wounds in Belgium on 16 October 1917.

Six Karma Avenue would now be the Ferguson family's permanent home. The government was doing what it could to ensure that in consideration of their war service, returned soldiers would live in relative peace and comfort.

Karma Avenue would now provide that opportunity.

But the Avenue would also house the war's recurring darkness. And it could not protect the Fergusons from further trauma brought on by other global events; events they could not at this stage foresee. And ones which would in turn damage their children.

Villers Square—1927

Pomp and Nelson sat quietly in Villers Square just around the corner from the Ferguson home in Karma Avenue.

'You look troubled, mate,' said Pomp.

'I still haven't heard from the college, Pomp, and it has been ages since I put in my application for the teaching job there.'

'Yeh, well they have to take into account your war record, Fergo, so you should be right.'

'That's what I'm afraid of, Pomp. It's been a while now since the Repatriation Department had my eyes looked at by the specialist, and when he did, the news wasn't that good really. And I reckon the department might have sent off the doctor's report to the college.'

'I don't get that,' said Pomp. 'You're a bloody veteran and a bloody good artist and teacher. That ought to be enough, I reckon. If it was me, you'd already be in the job.'

'You say that, Pomp, but not when it's about teaching art. You have to have your senses.'

'Yeh, well the department and the college better come to their senses. They should bloody well speak to me before they decide one way or the other. I'll tell them what they should be doing. And I'll tell it straight, just like the army used to tell us in battle—no bullshit when things are serious.'

'Thanks, Pomp. Let's wait and see what happens. I suppose there are other things I can take up.'

'You mean like gardening, like me. I've been all over South Australia, up to Queensland and now back to Melbourne to find work. It's tough at the moment, Fergo. Pulling weeds is where I've got to, Fergo. Stick to what you're good at, mate.'

'Well, let's hope the college lets me in.'

Pomp looked up. A breeze was rattling the eucalyptus leaves shading the veterans' heads.

'Time to get you back for tea, Fergo. Maddie wants you to come back with me.'

'I'd be fine by myself, Pomp. But like old times, I always feel safer to have you on the return journey home.'

The Menin Gate—July 1927

'Hey, Fergo, we were right there too,' said Pomp, pressing his finger to the newspaper. He then placed a page in front of Nelson on which appeared a photograph of a huge war memorial. Nelson pulled it up against his nose.

'It's the Menin Gate Memorial, on the Menin Road. It says here they've just opened it. That's a bloody decade after we carried blokes there,' said Pomp.

Pomp was right. It was now 10 years since Pomp and Nelson were in hell at the Menin Gate during the Third Battle of Ypres in Belgium. Hundreds of thousands of men had died at Ypres across all of the battles there between 1916 and 1917. Now, the Allies were opening a memorial in honour of those who had fallen.

On 24 July 1927, Field Marshal Lord Plumer unveiled the memorial. British brass bands spoke the sound of sorrow into the large civilian and military crowd. Black flags had been raised in the surrounding area. The Field Marshal declared: 'He is not missing; he is here.'

Carved into the huge memorial are the names of 54,896 officers and men from the forces of Australia, Canada, India, South Africa and the United Kingdom who died in the Ypres salient, for which there is no known grave. The New Zealanders who also died in the salient are remembered on memorials at the Buttes New British Cemetery and at the Messines Ridge British Cemetery. Some 34,888 further names of those with no known grave are on the memorial at Tyne Cot.

'This is for all those who fell,' said Pomp quietly, 'and it's bloody necessary they be remembered,' he whispered.

'You're right, of course, Pomp,' reflected Nelson, 'but the memorial and all the other memorials spread across Europe and in our hometowns also remind me of that other group too. The enemy. So many died on the other side.'

'Yeh, now you mention it, you're bloody right, Fergo. We never build memorials to both sides, or the other side, do we?'

'No, we don't,' said Nelson.

'If we did, we might have a better chance of peace.'

Pomp folded the newspaper into two and the men quietly visited the salient at Ypres for a second time.

Kids and the Sprinkler—December 1928

Now with three kids, the Ferguson family had grown to five: Jessica was seven; John five; and little Meg two.

Every single house in Karma Avenue, and in the streets surrounding it, was now the home of someone in all likelihood very troubled or in pain: a returned soldier. The sorrows of war sat in each home. The Ferguson children, like all the children in the neighbourhood, knew no different. They saw limping and sunken-eyed returned soldiers in the street every day.

The late December heat had hovered over East Malvern for nearly a week now and Nelson had put the water sprinkler on the backyard lawn to try to get brown to turn green.

Young Jess, John and Meg played what they called 'the cooling game'—running through glittering droplets spread by the sprinkler.

As they played, Nelson paused by the wide-open kitchen window. The summer breeze carried laughter and giggles.

But his mind was full of the burden of their future. The way things were heading, he worried whether he could meaningfully contribute to it.

Committee of Selection—Melbourne—January 1929

The recruitment committee of the college had not convened for some time due to a freeze on hiring government teachers. The depression in Australia had assaulted a large part of the workforce and the education sector was no different.

'We have here an application for the position of full-time art instructor in the Art and Architecture Department,' said the chair of the selection committee for the Working Men's College, Melbourne.

'The applicant, one NH Ferguson, has a very good report from the Ballarat School of Mines during his time there from 1912 to 1915 prior to him going to war. It says here he worked as an instructor there. I see he also had a very short period in Warrnambool as a teacher with the Victorian Education Department before joining the AIF in July 1915. And according to this, he's been retrained as part of his repatriation entitlements.'

'Yes,' said another committee member, 'his war record is impressive too. Nearly two years on the Western Front as a stretcher-bearer. It says here the 15th Field Ambulance. It's a wonder he's still with us.'

'Well, I think that may be part of the problem,' said the chair. 'It also says here he has material eye damage from mustard gas. And in this separate report from his local doctor in Carnegie it says he has a hacking cough and damaged lungs, again from the gas. Heavens knows what other trauma this veteran must have suffered and is likely to be still suffering. Sorry, don't know about this one.'

'Do we know how bad the eye damage might actually be?' said the secretary of the committee.

'Well, he had a review done by the repatriation department doctor about five years ago. It says here that the review was "satisfactory" but eye deterioration would be "ongoing", whatever that means.'

'Well, there may be problems, we all recognise that in these veterans—at least it seems like all of them have them. But this college has been giving veterans the benefit of the doubt where it can and so far I have to say that policy has served the college adequately well,' said the chair.

'Well, for my part, I am afraid I could not vote in favour of an offer of a position for Mr Ferguson. At least not without another eye test,' said another member.

The committee fell silent at the prospect of having to deal with a poor result.

'Could I suggest this?' said the chair. 'Let's start Mr Ferguson off provisionally and we will see how he goes in the foreseeable future. I think he deserves that. We can revisit things if he doesn't meet the minimum standard or there is deterioration.'

'All those in favour. Good. Carried.'

Art Instructor—January 1929

'Here, love, it's the letter you've been waiting for. It's from the Working Men's College in Melbourne.'

'What does it say, love?'

'It's a letter about the job you applied for at the Working Men's College. Let me read it. Yes. Yes. It says here you have to report for duty in the Art School on Monday, 11 February 1929 at 9 am.'

'Did I get the position then, Maddie?'

'That's what it says, love.'

'Pomp was right after all. Amazing. This is a new start for me, Maddie. I couldn't be happier to hear this; it's all coming good now. I've just got to make sure these eyes don't get worse, Maddie.'

Madeline looked into milky eyes. 'I'm sure all will come right if that is what is meant to be.'

First Day of Duty—Melbourne—11 February 1929

Nelson reported for duty on 11 February 1929 as the letter had requested. If he passed his provisional period, he would be part of the staff of the Working Men's College for the foreseeable future.

As he stood at the blurry front door to the college, there was only one question on Nelson's mind.

The Repatriation Department—End of 1929

A knock on the front door of 6 Karma Ave brought Madeline to it.

'Hello, madam, my name is Curtain. I am from the Commonwealth Department of Repatriation.'

'Yes, Mr Curtain, how can I help you?' asked Madeline.

'It's just a routine check. We want to respect your Saturday Mrs Ferguson but the department is interested to know how you and Mr Ferguson have settled in to the new Villers-Bretonneux Estate and your home.'

'Quite well, thank you, sir. We're settling in fine.'

'Very good,' said Mr Curtain.

'I was wondering if you and Mr Ferguson would be interested in accompanying me on a short tour of the estate, including a visit to Bretonneux Square, as we have just completed some new seating there.'

Madeline paused.

'Let me check, Mr Curtain.'

Madeline walked down towards the bedroom. She could see Nelson still asleep on the bed. She turned back to the departmental official.

'That's very kind of you, Mr Curtain, but I am afraid my husband is resting. He still finds the full working week exhausting.'

'Very good, Mrs Ferguson. Perhaps another time.'

The official turned and looked out towards the front fence.

'I see you are in Karma Avenue. Very nice. Karma. The force created by one's actions. Yes, very appropriate.'

Madeline nodded.

'Please do let us know if there is anything else the department can do at any time.'

'We will, thank you, Mr Curtain. Thank you for your consideration today.'

Ballarat General Cemetery—2 June 1930

Family and friends dressed in black huddled close together against the driving wind as rain marched down the arc of tilting umbrellas.

Shivering hard, Nelson felt a strong hand steady on his damp shoulder.

'It's raining as hard as in the Old Testament, son. Time to go.'

'I'll come shortly. I just want to spend a little more time here, Dad.'

In front of Nelson's soaked boots lay Lucretia's tombstone within the Church of England section of the Ballarat General Cemetery, just north of the town.

A Great Warrior—March 1931

Within the sweetness of Melbourne's Indian summer, Nelson rested quietly in his lounge room with the radio speaking to him:

It is with great sadness that we now wish to inform the citizens of the State of Victoria and of this nation that a great soldier from the Great War, Major General Elliott, has just passed away. The funeral service will be held at the Burwood cemetery on 25 March preceded by a procession leaving from his home at 56 Prospect Hill Road, Camberwell.

Elliott had commanded Australian troops at Gallipoli. He had also led them at Fromelles, and the places Nelson had seen battle, at Ypres, including Polygon Wood. He had led the now famous charge at Villers-Bretonneux in April 1918.

'Pomp and I need to go to that,' Nelson told himself.

After the war, Elliott had been elected as a Victorian senator in the Commonwealth Parliament. His numerous community causes included the pursuit of welfare for returned soldiers. Elliott had been a student at Ballarat College and retained his affiliation with the town after the war.

The Sword of a Knight—25 March 1931

Nelson and Pomp walked up the road from the Camberwell railway station. A huge cortege worked its way up a leafy, tree-lined street in Camberwell, thronging with thousands of men in military uniform. A large number of citizens were there also, paying their respects to a war hero and statesman.

A full military escort for Elliott consisted of two composite battalions, one under the command of Lieutenant Colonel Lind and the other Lieutenant Colonel Simpson.

After a brief ceremony at Elliot's house in Prospect Hill Road, Camberwell, the coffin was put onto a gun carriage, pulled by horses with resplendent black feathered plumes. The coffin was draped in the Union Jack (the emblem of the British Empire) and on it sat the general's cap, sword and medals. The sword was more than a weapon of war. In the mythology of the ancient and Middle Ages, swords were said to pass mythical powers from one generation to the next. The sword was the attribute of the knight and a symbol of power. It was thus also for Elliot's weapon.

Nelson and Pomp and rest of the sea of mourners, military and civilian alike, walked together to the sound of large regimental bands, towards the small secluded cemetery some four miles away on the hill in Burwood. They encircled the gun carriage upon which rested the soldier's flag-covered coffin. Representatives from the army, navy and government followed in polished motor cars. Former members of the 15th Brigade and the 7th Battalion (a blinded veteran among them) marched with the coffin.

Waiting at the great soldier's grave was a firing party from the 3rd Division Artillery. A roll of muffled drums ushered the carriage into Elliot's resting place. A 13-gun salute pounded Nelson's and Pomp's ears and the eastern suburbs of Melbourne. Local schoolchildren were bustled forward to pay tribute to the revered leader and senator before he was laid to rest.

It was later revealed that Elliott had suffered serious depression, tormented by the deaths, injuries and conditions of World War I. Elliott ended his own life at age 52.

A headstone would later be constructed over Elliot's grave. It reads: Valiant soldier, a great citizen, an upright man.
THIS WAS A MAN

Another Great Warrior Falls—October 1931

'Fergo, there must be hundreds of thousands of people here, mate,' said Pomp, standing behind the public barricade in front of Victoria's parliament building.

'Yes, and listen to that hush of respect, Pomp,' said Nelson.

The two diggers were part of a massive crowd for the State funeral of one of Australia's greatest military leaders—Sir John Monash.

Monash was a true Australian legend. As a young boy he had met the famous Australian bushranger Ned Kelly.

In May 1918 Monash had been made the first Australian Commander of the Australian Corps.

On 12 August 1918, in recognition of his service to the Empire, His Majesty King George V dipped his sword to the shoulders of Monash, rendering him a Knight Commander of the Order of the Bath (a British order of chivalry established some 50 years before even New South Wales had been 'discovered' by Captain Cook and claimed for Britain).

In 1929, Monash had been promoted to General from Lieutenant General, in recognition of his war service.

Monash's State funeral would be the largest in Australia's history. He had been known by the troops as a superb leader, one who gave recognition when it was due.

During World War I, Monash had told the Anzacs, 'fight for yourself, fight for Australia, and the British Empire—in that order'.

One of General Monash's last contributions to Australian society was to conceive the necessary tribute to those Australians who had served, and those who had fallen, in World War I. It would be called the 'Shrine of Remembrance'. It would stand just off Melbourne's St Kilda Road.

And it would be completed just one month after Monash's death.

A Neighbour's Troubles—1933

Suddenly the Fergusons' kitchen window took in loud screaming and shouting from over the fence.

'What's going on, Maddie?' asked Nelson.

'It's next door, love,' said Madeline. 'He's been playing up lately and the family doesn't know what to do. There was shouting yesterday too, when you were at work. War trauma and getting worse.'

'Perhaps I should go over there and see him,' said Nelson.

Nelson rose from his chair. The flywire door slapped closed and Madeline watched Nelson hurry down the narrow driveway and across towards his neighbour's front door.

The Fergusons' neighbour had severe depression after returning from World War I. It had presented in various ways but now violence was emerging as the outlet for his emotional trauma.

Madeline took the washing to the clothesline. As she pegged a shirt, shouting stopped. Madeline peeked over the side fence. On the back steps Nelson sat with his neighbour, whose head was in his hands, hiding hurt. The digger's shoulder received Nelson's arm.

The breeze carried a soft voice within earshot of Madeline.

'You will be all right, mate. It's all right. Things will come good.'

A Shrine of Remembrance—11 November 1934

Nelson and his son, John, stood as little dots among the crowd. John, now 10 years of age, perched himself on a railing and leaned against his dad's chest.

The Shrine had taken years to construct and now it was complete. It stood like an ancient-world grand temple. And now the Duke of Gloucester was at the ready to dedicate it, witnessed by over 300,000 people—a 'massive turnout' from Melbourne's population of one million.

After speeches of praise, the huge military brass band struck up again, drumbeats pulsing into public chests. The enormous gathering milled. Then the Melburnians and others present dispersed.

'Come over here with me, son.'

Nelson took John over to the Shrine's eastern wall.

John peered up. Way above him the carving in the stone read:

THIS MONUMENT WAS ERECTED BY A GRATEFUL PEOPLE TO THE HONOURED MEMORY OF THE MEN AND WOMEN WHO SERVED THE EMPIRE IN THE GREAT WAR OF 1914–1918

Father and son turned away from the Shrine. After some distance, Nelson turned John around to face the Shrine again.

Nelson crouched, his arms now wrapped around the next generation.

'Son, we are on holy ground.

This grand monument is about three things. But only one counts.'

John looked up at the vast structure and then to his dad.

'Peace, son. John there must never be another war. I want you to do everything you can all through your life to prevent war. It is evil. Nothing good can come of it son. It destroys lives. People must be able to work things out together. I hope everyone understands this. You must understand this.'

Father and young son walked to the perimeter of the Shrine site. They crossed Birdwood Avenue and headed for the train to take them home. The avenue had been named after Lieutenant General Birdwood who had led the Australian and New Zealand forces in World War I until 1917. It was said that he possessed the single quality which went straight to the heart of the Anzacs at Gallipoli: extreme personal courage.

Family Life—1936

In 1936, despite continuing trauma and deterioration to his eyes and lungs, Nelson's teaching career was continuing to progress and he was offered, and was now working in, a full-time position as Instructor of Art and Architecture at the Working Men's College, now called the Melbourne Technical College.

Madeline and Nelson's three children were all at school: John now 13 at Dandenong High School; Jessica now 15 also at that school; and little Meg, the youngest, at the local school.

With the family's frugality, the family home at Karma Avenue would soon be paid off.

The burden of World War I, which had imposed itself on the Ferguson family for so long, was appearing to lift.

At least for now.

Another Memorial Rises—22 July 1938

It was now some 20 years since the mustard gas had ripped into Nelson's eyes and lungs, causing deep scarring. The gas had poked Nelson's corneas and was imposing further and steady damage.

In July 1938 Nelson was told there would be a radio broadcast of the opening of a new memorial at Villers-Bretonneux. On that day he sat quietly in the late evening at home, waiting for the ceremony to commence.

Several thousand miles away in France, King George VI's motorcade slowly wound its way to a huge audience in front of a stone memorial sitting in the valley by the town of Villers-Bretonneux.

As Nelson sat deep in his chair, thousands stood still as the royal entourage arrived.

Before the King and Queen of England stood an immense memorial to those who had served in World War I, containing the graves of 1089 British, 779 Australians, 267 Canadians, two New Zealand and four South African soldiers, sailors and airmen. Included in the names on the monument was Bertram Boyce of Ballarat, killed in action on 25 July 1916.

An Australian national memorial now stood in this French cemetery.

Australian eucalypt 'blue gum' trees had been planted in the forecourt of the memorial.

The king looked up at the vast walls of the sacred place, with the names of 10,797 Australian soldiers etched in stone on the walls of the memorial forever. They were the men who had died in the battlefields of the Somme, Arras, the German advance of 1918, and the so-called 'Advance to Victory' by the Allies.

To this was added the names of further soldiers 'known only to God' who would have no known grave.

Nelson leaned toward the radio and made the King of the British Empire louder.

This ridge on which we stand surveyed those hard-fought actions. And the monument that crowns it will commemorate them for all time. Its very surroundings are emblematic of that comradeship which is the watchword of our British Empire. For it looks down on a hallowed field beneath whose soil consecrated by God and of our glorious memory, lie the men who came from every corner of the earth to fight for ideals that are common to the whole Empire. They rest in peace. While over them all, Australia's Tower keeps watch and ward. It is fitting that it should do so and as your King I feel a great pride in unveiling it. Pride and a deeper sense of reverence and gratitude towards those whose last resting place it guards.

With stronger voice, the king explained that the bloodletting at Gallipoli and at Villers-Bretonneux had allowed the new Commonwealth of Australia to pass from 'youth to manhood' and to take its 'rightful place in the community of nations'.

Nelson's radio then sounded the Heraldic trumpets from His Majesty's Grenadier Guards, echoing solemn sounds from the Australian Bell Tower back in France onto the names of the fallen.

The radio then fell silent for one minute, broken only by the steady roll of drums in France and the tick of the hall clock in Malvern.

This was then followed by the hymn 'O Valiant Hearts'.

The radio then explained that the Queen would shortly lay a Flanders poppy, which a child had given her, on the steps of the memorial.

Nelson then heard that the President of the French Republic would speak.

As the President approached the rostrum, solemn trumpets again echoed out over the air waves.

I have expressed the opinion that there is no spot on the whole of the tortured soil of France which is more associated with Australian history and the triumph of Australian soldiers than Villers-Bretonneux.

In Bretonneux Square, just around the corner from Nelson's home, the eucalyptus trees held still.

Between 1916 and 1918, three times the number of Australians served on the Western Front in France than at Gallipoli in 1915. By the war's end, five times more diggers had been killed on the Western Front than at Gallipoli.

Another Night in the Trenches

By now Nelson had been working at Melbourne Technical College for nearly a decade and had built a strong reputation as a dedicated, loyal teacher. His young family was nourished by strong love from both parents.

But the war's incursion into Nelson's life was regular and debilitating. He remained continually vulnerable to its episodic attack on him, its images of violence, and its reminder of the shocking conditions he had been put through. The early morning could be particularly bad if Nelson was rundown from the week's teaching workload.

The sound of early horse hooves told Madeline that the milkman was passing by the front gate. She stirred, tidied the sheets, carefully stretching the cover over Nelson, caressing his face as she did so.

But something was not right. The sheet over Nelson was all wet and he was running a high temperature. As she stood there, he began thrashing in the bed.

A large shell landed by him, spraying his dugout with mud and dirt. It did not explode. Nelson heaved himself up out of his shelter and ran down the duckboards towards the next pillbox. By this time, large numbers of shells were landing around him and he could see sandbags being pocked by machine-gun fire. He could not see any of the AIF and he had no idea in which direction he was travelling. The plume of smoke emerging down and along the trench he was now in engulfed him like a bird flying into a cloud. The trench was rank and stunk. Nelson tripped against a dead German, bloodying his forearm and forehead from the stake jutting from the trenches' supporting beams.

'Love, love, wake up, wake up, it's me. I'm here. Wake up. You are all right. I am here,' cried Madeline.

Nelson's pyjamas were as wet as a tropical storm and he was by this time thrashing even harder, heaving and straining for air. His gasping filled the house.

'Mum, Mum, what's happening?!' cried young Meg from her bedroom. 'Is everything all right, Mummy?'

'I will be back in a second, love,' Madeline whispered to Nelson.

She turned quickly into Meg's bedroom.

Meg sat quietly upright in her bed, scared stiff.

'Everything is all right, Meg. Everything is all right.'

Madeline held little Meg tightly.

'When you get up this morning, I want you to be very quiet, darling.'

'Why Mummy?'

'Your father has had another night in the trenches.'

Young eyes pressed hard against pillow.

The Call Out—November 1941

One late afternoon Nelson put the kettle on for more tea. As the water boiled itself into a whistle, he could just hear the radio in the lounge room.

Suddenly, Nelson's ears pricked to an announcement he had been expecting. He hurried down the corridor to catch it.

We ask that special attention now be paid to the following announcement by the Military Forces of the Commonwealth of Australia.

Would all men born in the following months please report to your local post office where you will be informed of where you must register for the Military Forces.

October, November and December 1923.

Further announcements of this kind will be made at this same time next month.

Nelson's knees folded.

'Maddie, Maddie, come here.'

Madeline moved quickly out of the kitchen, down the corridor, and grabbed Nelson on the right shoulder, steadying him.

'John's only just finished his three-month militia training, and now I've just heard it on the radio. The government's taken the next step. John's been called out. Maddie, he's still an apprentice teacher. And now he's going to war. I told him on the steps of the Shrine that this cannot happen. But it is happening. I can't deal with this, Maddie.'

'Are you sure he will be in the next round, love? Is that what they said then?'

'Yes, I'm sure. It's happening again, Maddie. It's happening again. The army is taking our son.'

John would soon receive a 'call out' notification in the mail. Under Part III of the *Defence Act*, citizens could be 'called out' by any prescribed means, including by month of birth. While a call out did not involve compulsory enlistment, it was the 'expectation' that the men, when called, would volunteer. As with World War I, for World War II Australia's army would comprise of volunteers only.

The Australian War Memorial—11 November 1941

In the month John was 'called out', the nation's Australian War Memorial was officially opened in its capital city of Canberra, on Remembrance Day. Its conception as a museum memorial went as far back as 1916, suggested by Charles Bean during World War I.

Upon its opening, the memorial was widely regarded as one of the most significant of its type in the world.

Another Oath Given—16 December 1941

On a hot summer's afternoon, John headed out of the front door of the Ferguson house and up towards Maben Place, Armadale, about three miles up the road.

When he arrived, John could see young men loitering all over the area, waiting for something to happen. Army trucks and uniformed men were, in contrast, busy and getting busier.

'All right, form a queue here and we will process you all now,' shouted the sergeant.

John lined up and approached the desk.

'As soon as we finish filling in this form, Ferguson, you can file out,' said a Private. The form read: 'Mobilization Attestation Form'. The Private completed the form according to the answers John gave. The form as completed had the following details:

Name: John Reginald Ferguson

Age: 18 years 1 month

Trade or Occupation: School Teacher (Technical) (Apprenticeship)

Married: No

Actual Next of Kin: Mr N.H. Ferguson, 6 Karma Ave, East Malvern.

Just as his father had done on 12 July 1915, John then held a Bible at shoulder height and gave the exact same Oath of Enlistment.

Two years later, after training and soldier work in Australia, as a corporal aged 20, John embarked an Australian ship headed for Papua New Guinea to fight the Japanese. The Australian Army had already been there for many months seeking to stop an invasion. They would be there for some time still.

In all, John would spend 883 days in 'active service' including in the jungles of Papua New Guinea.

PART 3

Australia was fighting for its life. It now had 730,000 uniformed people in the armed forces, and 70 per cent of Commonwealth spending was on defence. In the year of John's 'call out', there were nearly one million American soldiers stationed in Australia in defence of the Pacific.

Moyarra—1941

Madeline looked around the house for Nelson. She stepped outside and into the backyard. Nelson was up near the old studio building, cutting timber to make a frame for one of his paintings.

Madeline put her hand on Nelson's shoulder.

'Love, I have something to tell you.'

'Yes, what is it dear? Is it about John?'

'No, love, it's about Jessica. Her first teaching post after her studies is out at Moyarra, in Gippsland. The department has told her she will be in charge of six classes. The school has only 20 students. The department has arranged for her to stay with the local farmer until she finds long-term accommodation in the town.'

'But why there, Maddie? Why can't she be placed in Melbourne, near us?' asked Nelson.

'The department says that the teacher there at the moment has been called out for war service in New Guinea. They need all the new teachers like Jess to cover soldiers' positions right across Victoria.'

Nelson's saw dropped as he slumped in front of his wife as if in prayer.

'If the government has called that teacher to war, I can understand that Jess will need to fill his place. But that bloody army, Maddie, it is destroying this family. John's already away. Now Jess is going. I can't deal with this, Maddie. I can't deal with it.'

'At least we know she will be safe, love.'

Nelson slumped further.

'I guess you're right, Maddie. It's our duty to help the war effort. But how much does this family have to give, that's what I can't understand. When is this going to end?'

Madeline leaned down and held Nelson. He felt both warmth and strength.

'I don't know what I would do without you, Maddie.'

'And me without you. And me without you,' said Madeline.

Madeline pulled Nelson up and held him securely.

'Let's go and congratulate Jess and get her ready for her posting,' said Maddie.

'Yes, let's do that together, Maddie.'

Toxic War Gas in Melbourne—May 1943

'Hurry up,' called the officer, 'we need to get these bloody drums off this ship as soon as possible and stored safely.'

The officer looked up at blue-funnelled workhorse British cargo ship, the *Idomeneus*. She had sailed from Liverpool to Australia via America in January 1943. Her cargo was war-related and Top Secret. None of the stevedores knew what she was carrying.

'Well it's all very well to hurry us along, sir,' said a stevedore, 'but there's a strange smell down there in the cargo hold and I don't like it at all.'

'Shut up, you bludger. There's no smell. Get on with it.'

The stevedore disappeared out of sight in the hold, then emerged vomiting and shouting.

'Bloody hell, what's down there? We never signed up to carting poison!'

Others were now falling violently sick in the hold. Eyes were streaming and the men started to asphyxiate.

'Hurry,' called out the officer to others on deck, 'let's get these blokes out of there and call a bloody ambulance quick—there's obviously some sort of corrosive substance down there.'

The officer was right. The *Idomeneus* was carrying the last of the mustard-gas shells from England, for use against the Japanese should they attack. The ship had already delivered 3000 mustard-gas bombs 'safely' to Sydney, now stored in a tunnel outside the city. (Locals had unwittingly planted mushrooms in the tunnel for eating.)

The toxic and evil poison which had damaged Nelson's sight and lungs on 17 April 1918 had now followed him across the globe and was now being stored in Nelson's own city of Melbourne and elsewhere in Australia.

A Parcel for Jess—May 1943

It was now some two years since Jessica had moved to rural Victoria as the only teacher in a remote country school in order to support the war effort.

But she was not always away from the family. She had just turned 21 and it was time to be home again at Karma Avenue for birthday celebrations.

'Come on,' said Madeline, 'it's time to join your father and Meg in the lounge room for cake and presents.'

'Let's start, let's start. Come on everybody!' called Meg.

Meg ran into the lounge room, flopping onto the large divan up against the window. The family followed her into the lounge room.

'Jessica,' said Nelson, 'Happy birthday to you. You are a wonderful daughter.'

'Thank you, Dad.'

Happy Birthdays filled the lounge room. Jessica blew hard on the candles. As they went out a great cheer came in.

Just as Jessica began trying on the socks she had unwrapped, the doorbell rang.

'I'll get it!' offered Meg, rushing to the front door.

She returned with a wide, thin parcel.

'It's for Jess, and it says on the back it's from John care of the army.'

'Well, Jess had better open it then,' said Nelson.

Jess untied the string and removed the brown paper.

'Beautiful sketches from New Guinea!'

Nelson pulled out his magnifier. Peering close, he could see John's watercolour of a boat harboured off Port Moresby Bay.

'It is very fine work,' said Nelson proudly.

'Hey, Mum, it comes with a card!' cried Meg.

'It says, "To my wonderful sister Jess, you have lived twenty-one summers".'

'You have too,' said Nelson. 'Always remember the summers, Jessica.'

'I will, Dad. I will treasure this picture,' said Jessica.

'So you should,' said Nelson.

'When will John be home?' asked Meg. 'He's been away too long.'

'He's in New Guinea, Meg, so we won't see him for some time yet,' said Nelson.

The Ferguson family looked at each other. The war's toll so far, and the thought of John fighting the Japanese in the jungles of New Guinea, was unbearable.

'We had better cut the cake,' said Madeline.

'Yeh, let's,' said Meg. 'Let's do it now.'

To Shorten the War, Germany Should Be Drenched with Deadly Mustard Gas—July 1944

By mid-1944, World War II had been raging for some five years. Ways were being sought to shorten it.

An internal war minute from the Prime Minister of England, Winston Churchill, noted that everybody in World War I had used gas, without complaint from either the moralists or the Church. He further noted that:

> On the other hand, in the last war, bombing of open cities was regarded as forbidden. Now everybody does it as a matter of course. It is simply a question of fashion changing as she does between long and short skirts for women.

The minute therefore called for 'a cold-blooded calculation' of how it would pay England to use poison mustard gas against Germany. Churchill requested support from his colleagues for its use. He noted that with permitted use, England 'could drench the cities of the Ruhr and many other cities in Germany in such a way that most of the population would be requiring constant medical attention.' If it were to be done, Churchill considered it should be done 'one hundred per cent'.

Churchill wanted this studied in 'cold blood by sensible people' and not by 'that particular set of psalm-singing uniformed defeatists which one runs across now here now there.'

The proposal was ultimately rejected by the Joint Planning Staff but not because England had signed a 1925 International Convention prohibiting the use of the gas which had damaged Nelson's eyes and lungs. Nelson's damaged eyes and lungs from gas attack on 17 April 1918 held no weight in the consideration of the proposal.

Not because it would cause an equivalent number of appalling injuries and deaths across Europe.

And not because the appalling injuries and deaths of thousands of Allied soldiers from mustard gas in World War I should not be repeated.

It was rejected for one simple reason: its use would slow down the Allied advance into Europe and therefore would not hasten victory.

Archaic Colours—1946

On 25 January 1946, the Australian Army discharged John Ferguson. Nick Papas, his war-time mate, was also discharged.

They had met briefly before leaving Australia for Papua New Guinea, and had become close friends there. By coincidence, near the end of the war they had shared a hospital ward. John had offered his hospital bed to Nick as the army was short of them. John laughed when Nick told him he was so worn out he would be right just sleeping in the corner of the ward, and then did.

The army had, as it had done for Nelson, organised for John and Nick as returned Australian soldiers to undertake 'rehabilitation activities' so they could return to civilian life after the trauma of war. John, having enlisted in the army at 18, had not had the opportunity to complete his art studies. Nick was in a similar situation. Further art studies would now help the boys to return to the workforce in Melbourne.

Nelson now stood in front of his class at the Melbourne Technical College, which housed the art faculty.

In the middle sat John and Nick.

'Right, shall we start?' said Nelson.

'Today I want to talk to you about colour. Without an understanding of it, you cannot become artists or teach art. I need to take you all right back to the Ancient Greeks. The Pythagoreans held that the four basic colours of the ancients, white, black, red and ochre, were associated with the four primary elements of cosmogony: air, water, fire and earth. Empedocles developed the same theory in great detail, maintaining that colours were perceived by the eye through appropriate receptors that "received" the particles that colours emit. For the ancient Greeks and their society, colour constituted a way to characterise various attributes.'

'Hey John,' said Nick under his breath, 'your dad's caught on to the idea that the Ancient Greeks basically were the fountain of all artistic aesthetic, something modern-day Greeks like me are taught from a young age at Greek school.'

'You might be right,' said John, 'but it might still pay to listen to the old man. He is a senior art teacher here and knows his stuff.'

'Of course, Johno, just kidding' said Nick. 'I love listening to your dad. His enthusiasm is contagious. But I will say he's a pretty hard taskmaster.'

'Yes, he is, but that's how we get our artistic standards. That's how it's done if you want to make respected works people will respond to Nick.'

'You're dead right there, Johno,' whispered Nick, 'the Greeks have set the standard from the word go, but …'

'Will you two newcomers tone it down in the middle there,' called Nelson. 'The others here probably want to know what their next assignment is going to be. And you might want to find out yourselves.' The class laughed.

Nelson had by this time been teaching at Melbourne Technical College for some years and continued to hold the position of Art Instructor.

The World War I veteran would go on to teach John and Nick for over a year. Their skills would be refined and developed so they could eventually take up work again, as part of their re-assimilation into civilian life after years at war in the jungles of New Guinea.

Victory Day Parade, Melbourne—10 June 1946

'Here,' said Nelson, 'my old cornet is not getting any work in its case. I wonder whether you might play it in the Victory Day Parade next week.'

'Are you sure that would be all right, Uncle?' said Roy's son Bill.

'Of course,' said Nelson, tapping his chest. 'It was made to be played and I can't do it anymore with these worn-out lungs.'

Bill prised open the small case and carefully picked up the old tarnished cornet. It had been in the Australian brass band championships 40 years earlier. Bill knew its place both in the Ferguson family and in the history of Ballarat brass band eisteddfods.

'I will certainly look after it well, Uncle.'

'As long as it is played with strength and purpose that would be good,' said Nelson.

Bill packed the cornet back into its case and took off down the hall.

'That was good of you,' said Nelson's brother Roy.

'No, it is good of Bill and I am very pleased the instrument will be part of these peace celebrations. I can't wait to celebrate, Roy. When John was away in New Guinea for nearly three years, it nearly killed me. I felt exhausted.'

Nelson's cornet was taken to the Victory Parade on 10 June 1946 and Bill, Nelson's nephew, marched with it down the main street of Melbourne, led by General Sir Thomas Blamey.

Thousands of people attended the parade. The festivities took up the afternoon. Outside the Town Hall, Melburnians cheered the parade and the nearby pubs opened their bars to the thirsty.

World War I was now some 25 years in the past. World War II was now some months in the past too. It was time yet once again for the Ferguson family to hope for a future of long-lasting peace.

The Barber's Chair—1946

The Carnegie shops were walking distance from Karma Avenue. In the main strip was a red and white striped barbershop. Two proud cutting chairs owned the floor space. A smoky mirror doubled the shop's size. The balding barber cut only one style: 'the Continental'—long on top, short back and sides.

It was now a ritual that on the first Saturday morning of every month Pomp and Nelson would go down to have a trim or, if required, the 'Continental' itself.

The two mates sat quietly facing the mirror. The barber jacked up Nelson's chair.

'Excuse me, Mr Ferguson, but I can't cut around your beret. It wouldn't look too good.'

'Sorry, I'll take it off now.'

The barber started trimming.

'We're now at the end of the second one, Pomp,' reflected Nelson.

'Yeh, we are. I feel like I lived through every battle in the newspaper, Fergo.'

'Me too.'

'Having both John and Jessica away during the war nearly killed me, Pomp. I thank the Lord it's now all over.'

'You say that, Fergo, but there'll be another one. I promise. The bloody Huns bullet-holed our memorial at Villers-Bretonneux during World War II—that's not getting it. Those holes in holy ground record the lie of everlasting world peace. Ground where mustard gas took your eyes and lungs, Fergo.'

'Yes, it was appalling what they did, but I reckon the politicians have sorted it out now. They've just created what they're calling the "United Nations", to keep the peace.'

'Yeh, you say that, Fergo, but I read in the paper it just replaces the League of Nations back from 1920—a bloody lot of good that one did. This new one's going to be no better.'

'I reckon it will be this time,' said Nelson, 'the Americans are creating it. Like last time, they're the ones who won the war so they should know how to create the peace I reckon.'

'We'll see, mate. We'll see.'

The mirror showed the barber's progress on the two returned soldiers.

'Make sure mine's as good as Fergo's is turning out,' Pomp told the barber.

'Not a problem,' said the barber, 'the sides will be just as good.'

One of Carnegie's great places of wisdom suddenly filled with laughter.

Learning the Light—Early 1947

Nelson stood at the front of the class on level five of Melbourne Technical College in Swanston Street, Melbourne. The room was full of eager and noisy art students.

'All right everyone. Time to talk about our new subject for this semester. Today you will start learning all about light.'

'There is one grand achievement of every artist—to capture the light truthfully and according to circumstance. If you can't master light, you can't be great artists.'

'And I am going to tell you the secret to that learning. The best and only way is to learn from the masters of it.'

'For next week's lesson I would like you to be familiar with Louis Buvelot's work. He came to Australia from Switzerland, arriving in Melbourne in 1865.'

The audience of students scribbled into their notepads.

'He painted Australian landscapes for 20 years, concentrating on Australian light. He was the forebear to a whole generation of Australian artists who took up the challenge of claiming Australian, as opposed to European, light.'

'I want you all to study his paintings very carefully. How does he get that light into his paintings? How does he invoke that sense of the Australian light which European paintings simply don't have?

'If you can learn the clues of light, capture them, and take command of them in your work, you will all be fine artists indeed.

'I am looking forward to our discussions next week, and to helping you develop an understanding of light, how to embrace it, and how to master it.'

An Opportunity with Windows—1947

By 1947, Melbourne had a population of some one and a half million people. It was, on any view, an advanced city, with well-developed road and public transport, electricity and sewerage systems, large parks, and with a fine university and other educational institutions. The war had taken its toll on the Australian economy but people still lived relatively well.

On his way to another art class at the technical college, John stepped on to one of the main thoroughfares of Melbourne, Elizabeth Street. It joined Melbourne's main train station to its central post office, and was lined with substantial buildings and shops.

As he approached 59–65 on the street, a large sign caught John's attention. 'Positions Vacant'. The sign called for an artist in the stained-glass window-making business of Brooks, Robinson & Co.

'Yes we're open. Do come in,' invited the man behind the counter.

'I've come to ask about the job advertised in the window,' said John.

'Yes, we are looking for someone who will draw what we call the "cartoons" for church and domestic windows to be made from leadlight and stained glass.'

'Sounds very interesting,' said John. 'I'm studying design at the technical college at the moment.'

'Well, if you're interested, bring in a portfolio and we can take it from there.'

'Very good,' said John. 'I would very much like to pursue that. Thank you.'

Brooks, Robinson & Co—1947

In the following weeks, John talked with his dad about it and put together a portfolio of his design work. He had been Dux of Dandenong High School, and first in art.

His portfolio impressed the head of Brooks, Robinson & Co and John was offered a job as a window designer.

'On your first day we want to get you cracking on some designs we have in mind, but I guess I should show you around before that,' said the manager.

'Thanks sir. Before you do, can I introduce you to my mate, Nick Papas,' said John.

'Pleased to meet you, Mr Papas.'

Nick nodded, 'It's a pleasure to meet you too.'

'Nick and I met each other during the war, and we went to art school together after it. Nick would like to talk with you about a job here too if that's all right.'

'Sure, if you have army and art training like John, I'm sure we would be very interested.'

'That's excellent,' said Nick. 'I would like to apply for whatever position you have here. The firm does great work and I would like to be part of it.'

A few weeks later, Nick too joined the firm of Brooks, Robinson & Co, making the windows according to the designs from the design department.

John and Nick worked in the firm for a number of years, John as designer, Nick as skilled craftsman in the construction of stained-glass windows.

Australian War Memorial Windows—1950

Out of the carriage window, still, fat sheep moved quickly past. Flat sun-drenched countryside stretched out to the horizon, framed by stray fences.

'This place must have a million sheep in it, Dad,' said John.

'From the smell of things, I reckon you must be right,' said Nelson. John smiled.

'We're coming into Albury soon, Dad, then we have to get on a bus to finish the trip to Canberra.

It's a long way to see another war memorial, Dad.'

'Yes,' said Nelson, 'but this is the Australian War Memorial. It's been open since 1941 son. It has the Hall of Memory, and now they're opening the Hall of Memory stained glass windows. It's enormous. Fifteen panels, Johno. And it's got an old digger's stained-glass window too, son.'

'How did you find that out, Dad?'

'Well the windows got commissioned in 1937. I've been keeping in contact with the artist, Napier Waller. He was in the war with me son. We were at the same battle together at Bullecourt in early 1917. The poor bloke lost his right arm but learnt to draw. He's worked as an art teacher at the Working Men's College too.'

'He sounds like a great artist, Dad.'

'He sure is. More than 10 years ago I remember he was chosen to create the decorative elements of the Hall of Memory. He told me he wanted to design stained- glass windows for the hall and that there would be three huge and monumental windows on three sides of the hall. Five panels for each window. I'm about to show you them.'

'That must be amazing, Dad.'

'That's why we're going there, son. The windows are of various personnel in the Australian armed forces, showing idealised virtues. He tells me it's all in a sweep of largely blue and grey colours across dim cathedral-like light. At the foot of each window he's put fragments of destruction and war.'

John looked out over more sheep shrouded in yellow dust as the train rattled harder north.

'They sound like masterpieces of light and meaning, Dad.'

The Old Studio—1952

After a number of years, the close mates, John and Nick, decided they could do better and more varied work out on their own. John had recently been inspired by European Modernism to explore the medium, with new designs and fresh techniques. He, along with others, including Alan Sumner, an accomplished designer of windows, became eager to explore fresh directions for the medium.

'I reckon we should start out on our own now, Nick. We're good enough for it, and we can explore newer directions for the medium.'

'I reckon we should,' said Nick. 'Yeh, it's time to go out on our own.'

'Okay, great,' said John, 'but where can we set up the business?'

'Not sure,' said Nick, 'but let's talk to your old man, he might have a suggestion or two.'

'Great idea,' said John. 'I reckon if a bunch of Anzacs can't work it out, no-one can!'

The two mates drove to Karma Avenue to see what John's dad might be able to suggest.

A New Business

'So, Dad, we want to go out on our own.'

'Yes, I can see why you and Nick might want to, son, and the new art forms you have been showing me seem like a fresh direction to go in.'

'We don't have anywhere to set up yet.'

'Yes you do,' said Nelson. He pointed to the old studio in the backyard.

'You can use the old building in the backyard. It's not being used much these days except for me to test my oils. Why don't you use that?'

The studio had been built partly so that John could live out the back when Madeline's mum had come over from Tasmania, and partly so that Nelson could try a bit of painting and woodwork occasionally.

'That sounds great, Dad. We would have to extend it a bit, and put in a kiln to fire the glass. Would that be all right?'

'All right—I wouldn't let you and my son-in-law set up anywhere else!'

Nick had fallen in love with Meg, Nelson's youngest daughter, on one of his many visits after the war. Nelson and Madeline had warmly accepted Nick into the family as John's best mate from the war and Meg's handsome (and cheeky) husband.

'Righto, Nick. Let's get stuck into this. Can you come over on Saturday and we'll start?'

'Sure,' said Nick. 'This will work perfectly for us.'

'Yes, start whenever you like boys,' said Nelson.

'Thanks Dad. This will really set us up.'

The boys headed off into the house for lunch.

As the backdoor of the house closed behind them, a new business opened.

Another Oil in the Making

Jessica opened the front door of the Ferguson home.

'Hi, Florence. How are you? Please come in.'

'This is Jim,' said Florence.

'Hello, Jim, come on in. Nice to meet you.'

'Hello, Jessica, thanks. Nice to meet you too.'

'Thank you, Jim. Come through to the kitchen and I will put the kettle on.'

Florence was an old friend of Jessica's from Dandenong High School in the 1930s. Jess had recently heard Florence had become engaged to Jim and Jess wanted to have the pair over.

Jim held his broad-brimmed hat and the three moved down the corridor and into the kitchen. They waited for the kettle to whistle. Jess poured tea.

'What's that building out there?' asked Jim.

'That's the art studio my brother and brother-in-law have just started working in. They want to make stained-glass windows for churches and houses.'

'No kidding,' said Jim. 'Can I have a look?'

'Of course you can,' said Jessica.

The three strolled out to the backyard and towards the studio.

Through the window to the studio, Jessica could see her dad in front of an easel, patting the palette with a brush.

'Hi Dad, this is Florence and Jim. They've just announced their engagement.'

'Wonderful news,' said Nelson.

'I've heard from Florence you are a wonderful art teacher, Mr Ferguson,' said Jim.

'I don't know about that, Jim, but I do try to keep my hand in with the brushes.'

'He paints still lifes and people, don't you Dad?' said Jessica.

'I try to, love. If someone lets me draw or paint them, that's my privilege.'

'You can paint me anytime, Mr Ferguson. No-one's ever done that, that's for sure,' said Jim.

'Great,' said Nelson. 'Come over next Sunday and we'll start, if you have time. If you think it's good enough, I'll make it a wedding present.'

'That sounds really good.' said Jim. 'Florence and I will be over.'

'Bring that large-brimmed hat, Jim. I'd like to paint you wearing it.'

'No problem. Mr Ferguson, will do.'

The Roof and Danger—1952

Madeline looked up from the backdoor. She could see John and Nick high on the rusty corrugated roof of the old work studio. Tools lay around the studio. An old wooden ladder was propped against the gutter. The roof and the studio were now getting much repair work done as the studio was extended to accommodate the area needed to make the stained-glass windows to be made by 'Ferguson and Papas Stained Glass'.

'Come on, you two,' said Madeline. 'You need to come down from there. It's getting late.'

'We're nearly done,' said Nelson, helping from below.

'Well, you'll be completely done if either of you boys fall.'

'We're fine up here,' said Nick. 'The Greeks know how to make things last.'

'Well I don't want my son-in-law injured up there. Please be safe,' said Madeline.

'All right,' said Nelson. 'The boys will be down shortly I'm sure.'

The Brim—1952

It was Sunday. Jim sat patiently in the studio bearing his large-brimmed hat now slightly down across the brow.

Nelson sat to the side of a large canvas. A range of colours splayed across a palette. Large brushes sprouted from high jars.

'We've been here some time, Jim, but you'll be pleased to know I've just finished. You can have a look now if you like.'

Jim stepped off the stool and came around the side of the canvas.

'It's a beauty, Mr Ferguson! That's me.'

Broad ochre strokes, dark and strong, covered the canvas. Jim's handsome outline centred the work, shaded by a broad brown stripe for a brim.

Jim was an Aboriginal man from the Yorta Yorta tribe in northern Victoria.

First Commission—1953

After some structural and other changes to the studio, it was now ready to house the new stained-glass window-making business.

There was only one thing left to get things going from here: a first commission.

'Hey Nick, it's happened, it's happened!' called John from the kitchen.

'What, did we get it?' cried Nick from the studio, heading over to his partner.

'We sure did, Nick. We're on our way, mate. They even like the slightly modern influence I have put into the drawing. They want us to start straight away on a three- week estimate.'

'Yeh, that's great, but three weeks for the job, not the installation too. Athens wasn't built in a day!'

'Okay, mate, I'll tell them whatever estimate you want to put on it. You're the master when it comes to making and installing.'

'Just kidding, Johno. I reckon we can do it in that time. Let's get stuck into it now.'

'Yeh, let's start now,' said John. 'I reckon this will be the first of many we can put under our belt.'

'Can't wait to tell the old man,' said John.

'Me neither,' said Nick, 'he's going to be very happy with all this.'

Chips and the Darkest Danger—6 October 1953

As the sun set, at the end of St Kilda pier Nelson pulled another long chip from the newspaper wrapping.

'Jesus, Fergo. Can you believe this!' shouted Pomp, unfolding the paper further.

'The heading reads this, Fergo: "Atomic Bombs in Our Arid Lands". Christ!'

Pomp shuffled more of the oily *Sunday Herald*. Chips flew out across old boards as birds flew in.

'Careful, Pomp, our dinner'll go to the gulls if you're not careful.'

'Careful, my arse. The bloody Empire and all that—our government's sold us out. Listen to this.

British genius has developed the atomic weapons and counter-missiles as part of the free world's efforts to defend itself. It so happens that we in Australia have the uninhabited spaces where they can be tried out. In placing the rocket range at Britain's disposal, we are aiding in our own protection and that of the whole British Commonwealth.

This provision of a site is a contribution we are in a unique position to make, and nobody abroad should suppose that we are not making it freely and cheerfully.

'Fergo, they're going to detonate a nuclear bomb any day now, in my bloody home State, the bastards.'

Handfuls of chips were now being pitched at swarming gulls.

'Steady, mate,' said Nelson, waving off birds. 'What else does it say, Pomp?'

Pomp grabbed the paper and tore at it further.

'Well it says here, which I can't bloody believe, that a year ago the

Poms already detonated a nuclear bomb just off the coast of Western Australia. They never bloody asked us, the bloody public, whether they could do that.'

'But cop this,' shouted Pomp, 'it says "We can await with mingled interest and awe the historic tests about to be undertaken".'

'Can't wait!' shouted Pomp, 'I can't wait to kill these idiots. I reckon we should drop the fucking bomb on the Empire. See how they like it in their backyard. Once they drop this one, they'll bloody keep doing it—in the name of testing and development. Some bloody development. It says here the mushroom cloud will be massive.'

Gulls now squawked madly for chips, wildly pecking at each other.

Nelson reached down and wrapped the newspaper over itself. Busy birds flew off.

'Yeh, I guess you're right Pomp. Returned diggers' words can't tilt this world.'

Bretonneux Square, Malvern—Early 1956

By 1956 Nelson had been teaching art at what was now called the Royal Melbourne Technical College for more than two decades. But his sight had failed him some considerable time ago now and he was facing up to what the doctor had described to him as a state of 'legal blindness'. The eyes had essentially lost their essential function.

'Maddie, I'm wondering if we can talk.'

'Of course, love, what is it?' said Madeline.

'Could we get some fresh air first—so I can clear my thoughts?'

'Of course, love.'

Nelson and Madeline walked down Karma Avenue in the cool summer morning.

'I think we should head over to the small park,' said Nelson.

'Bretonneux Square, love?'

'Yes, I don't mind going there now. I didn't like it much at first but now I find it a peaceful place. Pomp and I go there and talk about the old times. It's helped me over the years.'

After a short stroll, Nelson and Madeline arrived at Bretonneux Square, just around the corner from the Ferguson family home.

'Have a seat dear—we can talk here,' said Madeline.

As the pair sat down together on the park bench, a large eucalyptus tree creaked, throwing its canvas over them and giving relief from the sun. Nelson's trench- damaged lungs tasted crisp Australian air.

'I want to talk about my eyes, Maddie.'

'I know things have been bad for a long while now, love,' said Maddie, 'but you seem to be coping well and I'm here.'

'Thank you, Maddie, but I have to tell you that I'm *not* coping. My eyes are gone. I can't see well enough to be the companion you deserve. I can't see well enough to teach and I can't see to help the boys in their new business. I am desperate to help them.'

'I know you are, love. But what you have to do now is give them support in other ways. You're the guiding hand, not the worker—that's been the case for a long time now. Keep that up—it's a tremendous help to them. They're always telling me that. There's always a great deal of help they need around the studio to keep them going during the day.'

'I suppose so, Maddie. I suppose so.'

Nelson squeezed Madeline's hand.

'I need to tell the college, Maddie.'

Madeline squeezed back.

'Yes, you should have a talk to them about your future, Nel. They know your position, I'm sure.'

'The college has been fantastic to me, Maddie, but I reckon I should be calling it a day. I need to let them know how much I have appreciated the more than fair go they have given me. But I have to be fair too.

'When I was in the army, things worked on merit. It had to work that way or people died. I learnt that as a young man, Maddie, and that lesson has stayed with me. I know I can't stay as a teacher now—I just can't.'

Husband and wife rested calmly under the protection of the eucalyptus tree. They then rose together and turned for home.

Royal Melbourne Technical College, Committee of Management—6 February 1956

The principal of the technical college, Mr R Mackay, walked down the corridor of the college building in Swanston Street, Melbourne, and took his seat as chair of the management committee.

'Now to our first agenda item. As some of you may know, Mr Ferguson took up full-time work in 1936 and was appointed to the staff here on 4 February 1942. Our records show that prior to that date, he had been employed with the Education Department since 22 February 1909. He therefore has an unbroken record of some 47 years apart from the war years Mr Ferguson served. During this time he has rendered consistently loyal and conscientious service.

'But I am afraid we have here a letter of 17 January 1956 from the Secretary of the Education Department. He advises that, although he personally has a strong desire to see Mr Ferguson continue on with his teaching duties, he feels he is unable to support Mr Ferguson's continuance at the college due to health matters.

'I have conferred with a number of you recently. It is my strong view that we should write to the department recommending that Mr Ferguson be granted 12 months' sick leave with pay and that at the expiration of that time he be requested to submit himself for a further medical examination to assess whether he can continue. This man has given the college a great deal and he deserves full consideration.

'All those in favour please indicate in the usual way.'

The chair looked out over the committee to arms quickly raised.

A Victoria Cross Gathering—June 1956

In June 1956, Victoria Cross medal holders from throughout the British Empire, including the dominions, travelled to London. No British monarch was yet to visit Australia. The gathering in London was to mark the centenary of the first awarding of the medal by Queen Victoria in 1856.

A party of 37 Australian Victoria Cross holders travelled to the event, including two soldiers from Gallipoli, John Hamilton and William Dunstan, who had received the medal for their bravery at the

Battle of Lone Pine between 6 and 9 August 1915. They were the last survivors of the seven Victoria Crosses awarded to Australians for their courage in the battle.

A great parade in Hyde Park passed by Queen Elizabeth II high on a rostrum, who then made the following address:

> Today, in honouring the recipients for what they did, we pay tribute to an ideal of courage which all in our fighting services have done their best to attain. For beyond this gallant company of brave men there is a multitude who have served their country well in war. Some of them may have performed unrecorded deeds of supreme merit for which they have no reward.

Another Gathering—21 October 1956

Up near the Shrine of Remembrance in Melbourne, a small gathering collected by an English elm. At the base of the tree sat a small plaque about the size of a brick.

John helped his father step across Birdwood Avenue. They had earlier caught the train in from Carnegie to Flinders Street Station in the heart of Melbourne.

As father and son approached, John could see middle-aged men around the plaque, some stooped.

Spring had now decorated the garden beds on either side of the father and son veterans.

They walked down the Shrine's grand steps and took their place to the left beside one of the oak trees there.

'We're here,' said John calmly.

'Thanks son, I reckoned we must be. I can hear some voices of mates from the war.'

The 15th Field Ambulance had earlier written to the trustees of the Shrine, asking if a plaque could be laid on the Shrine grounds. The trustees had agreed and it had been decided that the dedication of the plaque should occur on the anniversary of the departure of the first convoy of ships to Europe carrying troops, horses and supplies from Port Melbourne between 17 and 21 October 1914.

John looked down. The small plaque bore only these words: '15th Field Ambulance'.

The rising sun sat across the top of the words on the plaque.

The names of some of those from the 15th who did not return sit in Nelson's diary.

The complete list of those who died arising from battles in France and Belgium is: Cecil Bone died 25 April 1918 (aged 24), Stanley Bowd died 10 August 1918 (aged 25), Norman John Bullen died 16 October 1917 (aged 30), Edgar Burchell died 27 January 1918, George Byrne died 22 February 1917 (aged 21), Herbert Daley died 20 September 1917 (aged 25), William Doyle died 28 May 1918 (aged 35), Joshua Fenton died 1 May 1918 (aged 27), John Foster died 10 August 1918 (aged 25), Alfred Hopkins died 2 November 1916 (aged 21), Harold Walter Hornby (Snowy) died 15 May 1917 (aged 22), George I'Anson died 24 September 1917 (aged 25), Alexander Jenkins died 2 July 1919 (aged 22), Walter Johnson died 20 November 1918 (aged 28), Arthur Joyce died 2 October 1917 (aged 19), Herbert Mallyon died 29 September 1917 (aged 23), James McClenaghan died 25 September 1917 (aged 27), Roy Quirk died 27 September 1917 (aged 24), Robert Stewart, died 9 October 1917 (aged 32), William Taylor died 8 August 1918 (aged 21), John Thomson died 13 March 1918 (aged 34), Arnold Westwood died 15 May 1917 (aged 21), John Wilson died 9 August 1918 (aged 24), William Wheldon died 25 October 1917 (aged 33).

The Long Run—1 December 1956

On 22 November 1956, the world's eyes were fixed upon one city only: Melbourne. The Olympics had opened at the vast sporting colosseum, the Melbourne Cricket Ground.

Nelson's favourite race, the marathon, had been scheduled to commence on 1 December 1956. It was now starting in Melbourne's typical summer weather, a blistering day of 95 degrees Fahrenheit (35-degrees Celsius). Forty-six competitors from 23 nations would soon brave the heat having been launched off by the starter's gun.

Nelson sat by the radio, entranced.

'They have now left the magnificent Melbourne Cricket Ground and are making their way up St Kilda Road. In the distance peers the grand Shrine of Remembrance, one of the largest memorials to those who served in battle ever to have been constructed.'

The route of the marathon would take the runners right past the Shrine along St Kilda Road and towards Nelson's house in East Malvern.

'Dad, I've checked in the paper—the route will go down Dandenong Road, right past our street. I'll take you down there soon. Zatopek will be running right past you.'

As Nelson knew, Zatopek from Czechoslovakia had won the 1952 Olympic marathon in the Olympic record time of 2 hours and 23 minutes. A large body from Melbourne, and the rest of the world, were hoping for a second victory from him.

'Righto, John, that's a great idea. Let's head down the road soon.'

John was right. The path of the marathon would take the runners right past the corner of Karma Avenue, and it would not be too long before runners would start arriving.

John helped his father down the front steps. The two made their way down the avenue. Neighbours poured out to cheer the runners on.

They approached the corner. Barrackers voiced allegiances on either side of the main route of the race, Dandenong Road. In the stifling heat, many runners had dropped out, and most, if not all, were finding it tough going.

'There he is,' said John. 'Zatopek. Go, go, go!'

Cheers pushed runners harder. Drink bottles flew from sweaty hands. Wobbling athletes came into and out of view.

'Who are you barracking for?' cried John over the drama.

Nelson pushed closer to his son.

'There's only one man in this race as far as I am concerned. Mimoun.'

'Well you might be right, Dad, he's been leading since the halfway mark and he looks pretty strong to me. But there's always Zatopek. I reckon he has Mimoun's measure.'

Mimoun would go on to win the Olympic marathon in Melbourne. Mimoun was a Frenchman.

Exhibition Room—1957

With doors held wide open, a large gathering rolled into the Art Studio on campus. Many were instructors and teachers from the department. Most were noisy students.

'All right, everyone. All right. Good morning to you all. Thank you for coming,' said the Head of College's Art Department.

'We are here to give recognition to and celebrate the wonderful teaching contribution made by Mr Ferguson to this fine institution.

'Many of you may not know that Mr Ferguson began as temporary assistant art instructor in the Art Department here, starting work on 11 February 1929, some nine years after his return from the war.

'When Mr Ferguson joined, this organisation was called the Working Men's College and, later, in 1934, it became the Melbourne Technical College. Last year, "Royal" was added to the college's name.

'I have to say, Mr Ferguson, you are rather like royalty around here, at least according to your students. You are loved and admired by all.'

'Here, here!' cried the students.

'As many of you may know, after joining our full-time staff in 1936, Mr Ferguson was appointed to the position of Senior Teacher of Art in 1942, remaining in that role until 1945, when he was appointed as an Instructor of Art and Architecture. From 1948 to 1955 he was an Instructor in our art teachers' course. That course is recognised throughout Australia as one of the finest.

'We had hoped that Mr Ferguson would be able to continue on with us. Sadly for this institution, its staff and its students, he is unable to do so.

'So now we are here to say farewell and to wish Mr Ferguson the very best.

'Before I do so formally, I ask this question: what does this institution look for when it seeks out new staff? I can tell you it looks for people who are patient with students, who truly want to help them develop their skills and the learning of art, at many levels and depths. It looks for people who will build a new generation of artists, and a new generation of art teachers.

'Mr Ferguson has done this for more than 15 years and we are proud and honoured to have had him in our Art Department for that period.

'May I now say a few words about a unique aspect of Mr Ferguson's life and service to us all. Most of you here will know that Mr Ferguson has been suffering for some time now with significant visual impairment. That impairment was upon him when he joined us in 1929 and has become virtually overbearing in recent years.

'Mr Ferguson's eyesight was badly damaged by mustard gas during the Great War. Despite the profound effect this has had on him, he has shown his students the way to learn and improve their artistic skills.

'On behalf of this learning community, I would like to extend our heartfelt thanks to you, Mr Ferguson, for all you have done for us. We know that there is a next generation of artists out there, and teachers of art, who have been enriched by your teaching. And on behalf of all of us here, may I wish you all the very best.'

The chairman shook Nelson's hand warmly. Applause crowded the room. Teachers gathered around Nelson, embracing him.

'Mr Ferguson, please feel free to say a few words.'

Nelson took a step forward. A sweep of joy filled him.

'My words are mainly to our wonderful students here.'

'The miracle of the eye is a gift. It is nature's prism. You must protect that gift, and you must use it to your best abilities, and with great joy and gratitude. You must apply it by studying the world, wherever you may be, and no matter what may happen to you. And if you can, I ask that you record the world you see, giving it your own interpretation, using the skills and mastery you will have learned at this fine institution.

'If you are able to keep these things in mind when you leave here, then we will have done our job.

'I wish to thank the Head of the Department, all my colleagues who I have worked with, and the students I have taught here. In my life there have been dark earlier times, but here I have enjoyed such happy and bright ones that I am most grateful to you all for that blessing.'

'May I leave you with this. Every endeavour in your life, including struggle, will have an aesthetic moment. Look for it. Cherish it. And in your work, let others re-live what you have seen and be uplifted by it.'

A sustained chorus of applause rang out. Teachers patted backs. For one last time students gathered around the person they had grown to love.

Eye Drops—1957

Nick's firm hand held blade to glass. It screeched down a pre-drawn line, dividing the glass piece. He was now a master at handing the glass, preparing the lead to hold it, and constructing the stained-glass windows as designed and drawn by John. They were a team of expert craftsman and artist.

Nelson arrived at the studio door with tea. As he passed the flywire door, his cardigan caught on a nail jutting from the edge of the workbench. The biscuit resting on the saucer took to the floor. Nelson bent down to feel for it.

'I'll get that Dad,' offered John.

Nelson put the two cups down on the workbench.

'How is it going?'

'Pretty good Dad, the glass is nearly cut and we are about to fire the image in the kiln.'

'I'm sure it will come out just right,' Nelson encouraged.

The workshop door opened gently. Now, at 10 o'clock in the morning, Madeline's kind face was silhouetted by the strong light flooding in from behind her, illuminating the studio workshop.

'We may as well do your drops out here,' Madeline suggested.

Madeline looked over the workbench. Staring intently at it, she studied the emerging shape of a partly formed window which, when finished, would be fitted into a church in the Victorian countryside. It had been commissioned for £50 and would take many months to complete. There, in glass pieces on the bench, sat the partial image of Jesus Christ with outfacing palms and the sun high in the sky behind him. Above him was a white dove.

'It's coming along well,' encouraged Madeline.

In the distance, the workers could hear the house telephone ring.

'I'll get that,' offered John. 'That might be the church in Bendigo I am trying to win work with.'

John passed quickly through the workshop door and out into the backyard towards the house. Through the torn flywire, Madeline held John in her gaze as he walked into the house.

Madeline stood beside Nelson, taking his hand. She gently rotated his wedding ring. The hand was warm but old. It had been put to much work in World War I. The hands of a stretcher-bearer were vital assets for the war effort. They had carried men back from no-man's-land. They had written letters home. They had bound wounds. They had helped the living. But they had also held, and buried, the dead.

Madeline received that history whenever their two hands were one.

Nelson squeezed back, acknowledging his lifeline.

Madeline took a small bottle from the tray. The cap twisted off readily; it had been removed countless times before. Slowly, Madeline removed Nelson's thick glasses. They had three features: they were heavy; they were bent so they would not fall; and they were ineffective.

With her hand gently steadying the back of his head, Madeline put Nelson's beret on the bench and then placed two drops into the left eye.

She looked across it. It was murky, pocked and marble-like. The cornea was rough and full of holes like the 'no-man's land' Nelson and Pomp had rescued countless soldiers from. The scars from World War I were now deeply embedded into nature's miracle. Mustard gas was still the enemy and was still fighting its way further. Nelson's eyes were the record of its impending final victory. To Madeline the damage looked irreparable. The corneal erosion had been slowly and methodically reducing Nelson's sight now for nearly 30 years. Each year the long journey towards the prison of blindness continued.

'There you go,' said Madeline, 'how is that love?'

'A little better, thank you.'

The eye drops had been put into each eye for many years. They provided pain relief but did not perform any repair work, despite the fact that their supply provided hope to many returned soldiers. But the army had not supplied them to enable repair. Created by God but destroyed by war, the eye's rejuvenation was an impossibility. But the army's supply was an unswerving demonstration that it did not give up on those who had served and returned.

Madeline knew much about the injuries, but more than anything her heart knew that Nelson's failing eyesight had a firm destination. However, she knew that the ritual of the drops was important and should not be interrupted, let alone stopped. That would be to deny the hope there might be repair.

'Thank you. I am grateful for this every day'.

Madeline tightened the cap of the bottle and rested it on a piece of rich blue glass on the bench.

'Your appointment with the army's ophthalmologist is coming up, love. He will check things and I am sure he will let you know whether there is anything that can be done.'

'Yes, I am sure he will, Maddie. But if there's one thing I learnt in the army it's that if a soldier is going to see any action, it will abruptly come along only after a long, long period of waiting.'

More Peace Talks—1957

On Sunday afternoon Pomp came over as usual. Pomp and Nelson had shared the Lord's Day for decades.

The lounge room fire glowed across the late afternoon. The old mates welcomed its warmth and each other's company.

'I've pulled up stumps in the teaching position, Pomp. Can't see what I'm doing and there's no justice in that for the students or the staff, or for me for that matter. I got a wonderful send off.'

'Yes, Maddie told me, Fergo, but even as you are, they would have been better with you than if you weren't there.'

'Thanks mate.'

'Things will be peaceful for you now, Fergo. No rushing into town, no classes, no hassle.'

'I could do without the hassle, Pomp, but I do want to press on with my work. It's just that I can't.'

'Well you can, mate, because the boys need you for their glass work. Nick tells me you help a lot.'

'Yes, with the tea!'

The two mates laughed.

'What about you, Pomp? How's the gardening business going?'

'Not too bad until recently, Fergo. I had quite a few clients for a long while. It's tapering off now. The old ladies don't quite seem to take to the handsome worker now. I guess that had to happen. Like you, Fergo, I could do with a bit less work. But I still want to be interested in things, as well as being at least a little bit interesting too—if you know what I mean.'

The two mates laughed harder.

'Anyway,' said Pomp, 'sooner or later everyone's kingdom will end.'

'You're right, Pomp. It's going to be more peaceful now for both of us, whatever that means. Did you hear any more about those atomic tests, Pomp?'

'Nah, the papers never said much more about that. They never knocked it either. Bastards.'

'For me, as long as there are no more bloody bombs, no more bullets, no more stammering machine guns right in my bloody ear, no more mud, no more mown-down men and sprayed death everywhere, no more gusts of gas, and no more bloody orders, I'm happy!' said Pomp. 'The war brought out the primitive in man and I never want to see that again.'

Nelson stared into the fire. 'It was the stained red operating table which got me. One after the other. And when I was told to go out and put hands and feet in a large bucket to keep up Unit morale. I can't believe I did that.'

'How is it Pomp, that we went through all that together yet both sides read the same Bible and prayed to the same God? Doesn't make sense to me.'

'Armies and wars don't resolve conflicts. They only stop them temporarily. There shouldn't be a contest about that. We found out the hard way—peace, even when you have destroyed the evil of the enemy, never lasts. Why is that Pomp?'

'Fergo, it's a fool's mind that having a bigger and better army means bigger and better peace. We saw so much waste, from both bloody wars, and so much wasn't learnt that could have been. For God's sake, no-one's bloody well learning it now!'

'I reckon it's not how *they* work it out, Pomp, it's how *we* all work it out. It has to start from us. I've been telling my students that since after the war.'

'Yes, and I've been telling my old gardening clients that too, but I guess the message falls on deaf ears when it comes from an old fart.'

The problem is, Fergo, people don't remember hard enough. All they can remember is that the conflict eventually stopped. They need a bloody good jolt to tell them it shouldn't have bloody started, it didn't bloody stop, and it hasn't bloody stopped because there will always be conflicts.'

Pomp poked the fire and it flared abruptly then died down.

'You're right, Pomp. These memorials to war. They're memory markers of what happened. They tell us what went on, they recognise contributions made. I guess they need to remind us of those things. But I reckon they also need to remind us of more. To *stay* in peace. Like our Sunday arvos. People should be talking things out, Pomp.'

'I reckon the whole problem is that peace is invisible but war isn't. So people don't value it the way they should.'

'It's a wonder to me that no-one bloody listens to us old-timers. We bloody well went through it all, more than once. I don't understand why no-one gets the message and I never will.'

The room cooled in the late afternoon. Pomp fed fresh fuel to the fire. The brighter, warmer glow embraced the old bearers. The sound of sipped tea and a crackling fire broke the afternoon's pause. The hall clock patiently ticked down Sunday.

Pomp leaned forward and looked at his lifelong mate.

'Here, Fergo, I reckon they need a good clean, old chap.'

He carefully removed Nelson's heavy eyeglasses and rubbed them with his sleeve.

'Don't know how you see through these, Fergo.'

'I can't see with them or without them, Pomp.'

Pomp carefully handed clean glasses over.

'Yeh, Fergo, I know.'

Windows and Light—Late 1950s

By now, the Ferguson and Papas stained-glass firm was booming. Orders were frequent and significant works were being commissioned. There was now an 18-month wait for any church or other organisation wanting a window. Large masterpieces of light were being created and installed across a number of churches, not only in Melbourne but also in rural Victoria, including Ballarat and Bendigo.

Nelson's role as mentor to the boys continued but, increasingly, his major role was to make strong tea and plain lunches.

Part IV
Providence

Part IV

Providence

A Continuing Military Commitment—1960

It was now some 45 years since the Australian Army had first given Nelson its commitment to look after him until the end.

That commitment was real and continuing. He was still living in the same house which had been funded in part by a returned soldiers' war loan granted in 1926. He was on a part war pension which was supplementing his teacher's pension. And he was still getting regular medical assistance as required through the repatriation department of the Commonwealth of Australia. The army had after both world wars, and other military engagements, continued to provide pensions, facilities and treatment to returned soldiers. The Australian Services League, and other organisations such as Legacy (an offspring of the Remembrance Club founded in Hobart in 1923 by Major General Sir John Gellibrand, who had landed at Anzac Cove on 25 April 1915), were also providing very considerable financial, social and emotional support.

But the army knew, because it had kept the records, that the cause of Nelson's now failed sight was the mustard gas used in World War I, and that his lungs were fragile as a result of it, and becoming more so.

The army's slow but deliberate support over many decades had helped a great deal. But its enduring challenge remained: to provide the opportunity to remedy the damage, not just ameliorate it.

If the army had the power and resources to put Nelson into battle some 45 years earlier, it might just, even at this late stage, be able to help pull him out of the current one as well.

But if the opportunity for that were to occur, a great many things would need to happen first.

An Entitlement Card—1960

'The Repatriation Department has written to you again, love,' said Madeline.

'Do they want me to check in again for a review of my eyes?'

'Perhaps, let me see.

Well, according to this letter, you are entitled to have your eyes treated. It says here the Repatriation Department will pay for it. Look there's also an "Entitlement Card" with the letter. This is wonderful, love.'

'What do they mean by "entitlement", Maddie?'

'I am not sure. Let me read it carefully.'

Madeline held up a small square card, labelled 'Entitlement Card'. It read:

REPATRIATION DEPARTMENT

ENTITLEMENT CARD

Name: FERGUSON, Nelson Harold – 6 Karma Avenue, East Malvern

Regtl No. 9123A Rank Pte Unit 15th F.A.B.

DISABILITIES DUE TO WAR SERVICE

SCARRING OF CORNEA

ENTITLED TO TREATMENT (AT REPATRIATION EXPENSE) FOR

SCARRING OF CORNEA

'It says here we need to make an appointment with the department's eye specialist, Mr Glassford.'

'That sounds very exciting, love. Let's see what the specialist can make of my condition. There might be something more they can do. They've been pretty good to me so far, Maddie, but if more can be done I'm all for it.'

The Specialist—September 1960

'Please take a seat, Mr Ferguson.'

'Thank you.'

'Tell me how your sight has been in the last little while.'

'Well, Doctor, it's been the same for some time. I can only read with great difficulty by using a magnifier.'

'Let me make an assessment then, Mr Ferguson.'

Glassford's equipment revealed the following readings:

L.2/60.

R.5/60, improving with glass to 6/36.

'I see that your Entitlement Card reads 'scarring of cornea' but I have to say I consider this a mustard-gas keratitis.'

'Yes, Doctor, the damage is from the mustard-gas attack on 17 April 1918 at Villers-Bretonneux. I remember that day like yesterday. Pomp remembers it too. Sorry, I realise he's not here.'

Glassford nodded, then scribbled on his clinical report:

His incapacity is unaltered at 90% (ninety per cent).

'That is all we will be doing today thank you, Mr Ferguson. The Repatriation Department will be in contact with you again I'm sure.'

'Very good, thank you Doctor.'

A Call for a Cure—January 1962

Mr Glassford had referred his review of Nelson's eyes to the Repatriation Department. The file sat with the department for over a year. It had been Nelson's whole life experience that the army might take a long while to finish a task it had set itself and so he had waited patiently to hear back about whether something could be done for his eyes.

Over the kettle Nelson could just hear the phone ringing down the corridor. He shuffled to it in time.

'May I speak with Mr Ferguson?'

'Speaking.'

'Mr Ferguson, I am Mr Samuel from the Repatriation Department. Your file has now come on to my desk. We want to have you appear before the Assessment Appeal Tribunal to determine whether you should have eye surgery to correct damage you may have suffered due to your war service.'

'Yes, I was wondering where Mr Glassford had got up to with things. Very good,' said Nelson. 'Would you like me to come in?'

'Thanks, Mr Ferguson, could you please attend at the tribunal in two weeks. The appointment will be on 6 February at 10 am. The members of the tribunal, who are medical officers at the Victoria Barracks, will further assess your eligibility then.'

'Very good,' said Nelson. 'I'll arrange with my wife to be there.'

Assessment—6 February 1962

'Mr Ferguson, I am Mr Anderson, today's chair of the tribunal. With me is Mr W Duncan. We are both medical members of the tribunal. Could you let us know how you are getting along with your eyesight?'

'I manage to do a little woodwork these days. I help my son and son-in-law a little with their stained-glass window business. I mainly make the tea and sandwiches for lunch. Sometimes soup. My eyes are pretty out of action. I can't read music, but I can make out the headlines in the paper if I use a magnifying glass.'

'Yes, our earlier clinical assessment shows significant corneal scarring in both eyes consistent with what you have told us.'

The medical officer looked at the written report from the assessment. It read:

VR without correction 2/60. VL without correction 1/60.

VR with correction 6/18. VL with correction 4/60.

The numbers revealed that Nelson's eyes had virtually failed him.

'We suggest that corneal grafting be considered perhaps with the advice of those experienced in its use. We propose to award an entitlement to the treatment for corneal scarring at the expense of the department. How does that sound?'

'Yes, I'd be very interested to see whether that might be possible. Many thanks.'

'Thank you, Mr Ferguson. Could you please wait outside?'

Assisted in doing so, Nelson left the room.

'There are significant risks but I have to say I think we should recommend that this veteran be able to take up his entitlement as soon as possible. This man's eyesight is finished unless we attempt treatment for him.'

'I agree,' said Duncan.

'Let's see if Mr Glassford can make a further and more detailed assessment of Mr Ferguson in a few weeks. Glassford can then report back to the tribunal.'

'Yes, I agree with that approach too,' said Duncan.

'We need to get this man seeing again if we can, as soon as it may be able to be achieved. This man's duty to country has now taken its full toll and I want us to move on this now.'

Another One—22 February 1962

Madeline held Nelson's hand, steering him into the ophthalmologist's office at 2 Collins Street, Melbourne.

'Come in please, Mr and Mrs Ferguson.'

'Yes, thank you, Mr Glassford, we understand you are acting for the Repatriation Department in the further assessment of my husband's eyes.'

'That is correct,' said Glassford.

'Can I see the Entitlement Card?'

'Certainly—here,' said Madeline, handing it to him.

'Thank you for showing me that,' said Glassford. 'You may keep it.'

'Now let's have a careful look so I can make a more formal assessment for you.'

Glassford put on small spectacles with attached long miniature magnifiers. He pressed forward and peered into Nelson's left, then right eye. A bright small light pieced the curve of the eyeball. He then took up the medical report the tribunal had prepared and read it carefully.

Glassford pushed back in his chair.

'Mr Ferguson, you may already know much of this and therefore please excuse me if I am repeating what you've been told already. A cornea is a tissue that covers the front of each eye. In its normal condition it is clear. Light entering your eye first passes through the cornea, then your pupil, the dark spot at the centre of your coloured iris, and then your lens.

'The cornea must remain clear for you to see properly. However, a number of problems can damage the cornea, affecting your vision.

'In your case, I am afraid that the damage to the corneas is acute. Your eyesight has been extremely poor now for a considerable time as a result. To address this, we would need to conduct what is known as a penetrating or full thickness corneal transplant. This involves transplanting all the layers of the cornea from a donor. In other words, we take off the damaged film over your eye and replace it with better quality material from a donor's eye.

'There are many obstacles. First, a suitable donor might not be able to be found. Second, there is a very material risk that the grafting of a new cornea may be rejected. If you decide to proceed and that risk eventuates, you may lose the limited sight you currently have in the eye sought to be cured.'

The room fell silent as a church.

'What I am saying is that you only have one potentially repairable eye. If we try to fix that with a corneal transplant which does not take, you will be left with nothing. I am sorry to put it in those blunt terms, Mr and Mrs Ferguson, but that is where we stand today.'

'Can you tell us what risk that might be?' asked Madeline.

'All I can tell you is that it is a serious risk because the eye is sensitive to foreign material and a new cornea is exactly that.'

'Do I understand you are recommending against the operation then, Doctor?' said Nelson.

'I cannot say that you should proceed with it. The risks are very material. If it does not work, you will have nothing.'

'Thank you for explaining that, Doctor,' said Madeline.

'I'm not sure what we should do,' said Nelson.

'I suggest you discuss this between yourselves and then just let me know your decision when you are ready. But if you decide to proceed, you should tell me sooner rather than later.'

'Hearing your opinion, sir, I think it might be better if I stayed with what I have,' said Nelson.

'Yes, if the risk is as you have identified, I think my husband might be right,' said Madeline. 'That seems the best course. We have learned to cope with his condition reasonably well and we would not want to be put into more trouble than need be.'

'Very well,' said Glassford, 'I will write to the tribunal on that basis and let them know your decision. I think that your decision is probably the best one in the circumstances.'

The alternative warned of was unimaginable to the Fergusons.

'Thank you for coming in today, Mr and Mrs Ferguson. I know this is difficult for you both. I will put a note on the file to indicate that your decision should be reviewed in approximately five years, for good order.'

'Thank you, Doctor, that would be much appreciated.'

The Fergusons stepped into Collins Street. The late-morning sun warmed their backs. Madeline steadied her husband's steps. But the assessment had put a chill through them both. The silent walk back to the train station brought deep thought, and deeper sadness.

Advice Given—22 February 1962

'Could you please type the following?' said Glassford.

'A letter to the Medical Assessment Tribunal regarding Mr NH Ferguson.'

Re. Ferguson N.H. M 45590

As suggested by the Tribunal, I have examined the abovenamed ex-member.

Gas keratitis cases have proved to be a very 'bad risk' as regards visual improvement from a corneal graft.

I discussed this with him, at length, and he has decided to accept my opinion as negativing an operation.

E. Gordon Glassford.

On 27 February 1962, the chair of the tribunal, Anderson, merely wrote 'Noted' on Glassford's letter.

Frustration—February 1962

The Ferguson family sat around the dinner table, eyes downcast.

'The doctor seemed quite sure that the risk was not worth it,' said Madeline.

'Yes, he seemed pretty sure to count it out,' said Nelson.

'But, Dad, I thought the army had given you an entitlement card for the operation and that it was to be paid for by the department,' said John. 'I thought they were telling us that the operation would go ahead and they thought you deserved it to go ahead.'

'There is no doubt about all that, John, but the specialist himself has discounted it, and we've accepted his advice,' said Madeline.

The dinner-table light held dim.

Ants and Eyes—1967

As midday approached, Nelson began his now regular job of making the boys' lunch. The business had been growing for over a decade and had a mature client base of churches and institutions. Works out of the firm Ferguson and Papas, were on back order for many years.

'Won't be long now, chaps,' he called from the verandah.

'Righto,' said John, 'take your time Pop.'

'I'll make some tea too'.

'Goodo.'

'We'll be in soon, Dad.'

'Don't worry, son, I'll bring it out.'

'If you're sure you're okay with that, Dad, great!' called John.

Nelson returned to the kitchen and began slicing stale bread left on the kitchen table. He took some butter from the small fridge and jam from the pantry, generously smearing it with a blunt knife.

Clutching a large tray, Nelson walked carefully out into his well-worn track towards the studio. The carry was sandwiches, tea and a big smile. He pushed open the flywire door of the studio with his foot, stepping in.

'Great, Dad,' said John, 'I'm starving.'

'Thanks,' said Nick.

'No worries, hope you enjoy it boys. Let me know if the tea is too cold,' offered Nelson.

Out of the studio now, Nelson made his way back to the kitchen.

The boys looked down. An army of black dots crawled across the sandwiches. Some were now embedded in the jam.

'Sorry Nick, next time I'm in, I'll throw the old jar in the bin. We'll get some fresh jam later.'

'Doesn't worry me at all,' said Nick generously. 'Your dad's support is incredible and always has been. We all know the old man is the mainstay of this business, and always will be.'

'Yeh, thanks Nick, too right,' said John, 'too right.'

The two mates smiled at each other.

Blade cut glass and pencil marked paper.

A Statue at the Shrine—25 April 1968

'Right, Dad, time to go.'

'Fine, son, let's head off.'

John closed the passenger door for Nelson and then got in the car. He eased off the handbrake and took off slowly down Karma Avenue, then turned right into Dandenong Road.

After some time they approached the Shrine. A modest mob lined St Kilda Road. John could see diggers and bands heading up to the Shrine.

'Dad, after the ceremony, we need to head up the steps and into the Shrine itself. There's something in there I want to describe to you when we get there.'

'Sure, son, that sounds interesting.'

Later, after the ceremony, John directed his father up the stairs of the Shrine, passed enormous stone columns, and continued deep into the monument.

Once inside, John took his father along a number of long corridors. They then turned into a darkened room. The Crypt had a high vaulted ceiling. Flags shot from the walls.

In the middle of the Crypt stood a large bronze statue, resting on a stone plinth. While working on a window design in his studio, John had heard that the Governor of Victoria had unveiled it on 7 April and that the public was now invited to view it.

'Dad, we are now looking at a statue of two soldiers, facing away from each other. One is wearing a World War I uniform, the other a uniform from World War II. The World War I soldier is in the battledress worn by the troops who fought in France. I can see the puttees over the shorter trousers and they are bound down to the ankle boots. The other soldier is wearing the uniform of the troops who fought in the jungles of the Pacific. He wears canvas American-style garters replacing the puttees, and has a slouch hat.'

'That sounds like us, son,' said Nelson.

'Dad, the plaque under the statue says this:

These figures of father and son honour the courage and sacrifice which links two generations of Victorian service men and women who served in the World Wars 1914–1918 and 1939–1945.'

The two soldiers stood alone in front of the statue, the dim Crypt airless.

'We have given a lot in war, son. I hope no-one has to give to it again.'

'Yes, we have,' said John, 'but you have given even more in peacetime, Dad, and I am grateful forever for that, and so are hundreds of your students.'

'Thank you, son. No medal for a chest can beat those words.'

John took his father's hand as they stepped down out of the Shrine and on to the stone landing. The eternal flame outside burned opposite them, representing eternal life.

As John began to guide his father down yet further steps towards the car, they passed over large brass words embedded into the stone landing:

LET ALL MEN KNOW THIS IS HOLY GROUND

At the Clothesline—1968

Madeline reached for another peg and then up to the clothesline. The handle of the line had rusted and cranking it was proving difficult work. As the line reached as far as it would go, Madeline rocked dizzily as if on a rolling ship. She quickly knelt down, gripping the basket, then regained her balance.

After a slow walk to the kitchen and a cuppa she started feeling much better.

'I must be right now.'

Another Look—February 1969

Mr Hardy Smith's ophthalmology waiting rooms in the wealthy Melbourne suburb of Hawthorn were large and bright. Nelson and Madeline sat patiently with other patients.

'Hello, Mr and Mrs Ferguson, I am Peter Hardy Smith. Please come with me to my room.'

Hardy Smith was a gentle man with a soothing voice and a kind face. After medical school and further specialist training, he had remained an eye specialist his whole professional career. He had just returned from England where he had been studying advances in eye surgery.

'The Repatriation Department has referred you to me, Mr Ferguson. As it is now more than five years since your last review, we should have another look at those eyes.'

'Yes, Doctor, it's been quite some time. I would be grateful to know if there is anything that can be done. My eyesight gave up on me some time ago. I can't read even if I use a magnifier and glasses.'

'Yes, I understand. The report I have from 1962 states you were 90 per cent incapacitated back then.'

'Let me first have a look at that left eye,' said Mr Hardy Smith.

Mr Hardy Smith carefully pulled his chair towards Nelson and drew a bright lamp over Nelson.

'Yes, it looks in bad shape all right. I would imagine you have virtually no sight through that cornea. But I am certainly going to refer you for the new corneal scan we can now do. There is a new machine in Melbourne and I can get you in in two weeks if that suits, Mr Ferguson.'

'Yes, I guess I can tell the boys I will be away on that day,' said Nelson.

'Very good, I will book you in then. The scan will help us determine our ability to replace the failed cornea. If the scan results are satisfactory, I will be recommending that you have a corneal graft done. You are 76 years of age, Mr Ferguson, but that should not hold us back this time.'

Hardy Smith rose from his chair and assisted Nelson to the door. He then accompanied Nelson and Madeline back to the waiting room where he requested that his receptionist call a taxi.

The Doctor's Room, Carnegie—1969

For Madeline, things were still not right. The dizzy spell at the clothesline had recurred and she was troubled by it. She sat alone in the waiting room listening to her heartbeat.

'I'm afraid I'm not feeling very well at the moment, Doctor—anxious about things. It seems to have come over me in the last while. My husband and I have been managing until now,' said Madeline.

'Yes, well I see from this card that you are now 79, Mrs Ferguson,' said the doctor.

'Well, I have been able to look after my husband for more than 40 years but now it all seems to be an increasing struggle. I want to help him so much but he has virtually lost his sight now and that has made things quite difficult for us really. I don't want to trouble him with my concerns, but…'

'Yes, I can well understand that, Mrs Ferguson. Let me just take your blood pressure then and we will see what is going on.'

The doctor wrapped a tight band around Madeline's left arm and pumped it up. He then listened to her heart. The blood pressure was high and the pulse low.

'I'm afraid you have signs of what is called hypertensive cardiac disease. I will prescribe you some medicine for it. Things should settle down over time with the medication, which you must keep taking, but you should also rest much more, Mrs Ferguson.'

'Thank you, Doctor. I am sorry to be any trouble but I have been worrying about things a great deal recently. It is just that so much has happened in our family over the years.'

'Take this prescription to the chemist up in Carnegie. Two pills twice a day. I would like to see you again in three months. Please make the appointment on the way out.'

'Thank you, Doctor. I will do so.'

Madeline rose slowly from the chair. She paused, then approached the door, and then paused again.

'I will be right from here. Many thanks again, Doctor.'

'Please ensure you get the medication and start taking it right away, Mrs Ferguson.'

'I will. Thank you, Doctor.'

Contemporary Light—1969

Nick stood on the last step of an enormous ladder climbing a high wall in St Paul's Anglican Church, Canterbury, a suburb of Melbourne.

'I see you're nearly done,' said John, 'I reckon we are about due for a tea break when you're ready.'

'Righto, good idea,' said Nick.

Nick stepped down carefully off the ladder then looked back.

'She's a modern beauty.'

'Yes, the light is streaming in now,' said John.

The boys had been working on the installation of magnificent new windows for the church made possible by two legacies from the estate of Flora Forsythe Smith. The Smith and Ballantyne families had been founders of the church.

John had earlier written to the church to explain the designs:

The Nave windows are more contemporary in style than I had intended. Their meaning is as follows—the long lines descending from the top of the left frame panel represent the veil of the tabernacle which is drawn aside to reveal the figure of Christ. From him grow the fishers of men whose nets reach down past the open tomb and into the roots of the modern city, whilst over the latter hovers the Shepherd's crook and the sacrifice of Calvary. In the trefoil you will find the Passover lamb, *Oeku Mene* (Gk. ecumenical) or ship and peace dove.

The windows were later dedicated by Bishop Sambell of the church.

In the Night—16 February 1969

Melbourne's summer evening held calm and warm. Maddie and Nelson sat drowsily on their back verandah taking its advantage. The occasional light warm breeze visited. The sun had just taken itself to another place.

'I reckon I could just about sleep out here on these old boards tonight, it's so balmy,' said Nelson. 'I'm sure you could, love, but it might be best if we head in now and start to get ready for bed.'

'Yes, you're right, Maddie, let's head in soon.'

It was now some 50 years since the two had first met in the photographic shop in Collins Street. There would soon be a 48th wedding anniversary. Their marriage had seen the trauma of two world wars, severe disability, and now failing health. But for now, the warm calm evening had taken that history far into the distance.

After a short while, Nelson followed Madeline into the house and sat down gently on the edge of the bed, tucking his slippers under it.

Madeline lay sleeping. Nelson switched off the light and slowly lifted the old sheets. He then carefully lay down next to her, as he had done since after World War I.

After some hours, Nelson woke. The warm air from the open window tickled the curtain. The pink dawn light had begun to enter the room and birds were now taking to song.

But Nelson could feel the bed was cold; and it seemed as if it had been for some time.

'Maddie, wake up. Maddie, wake up.'

Something was terribly wrong. Nelson grasped and then held.

Madeline lay still.

From the hallway, Nelson dialled frantically. The ring felt like eternity.

'John, it's Dad. Can you come straight over, son. I've just woken and found Mum. She's died in the night, son. She has only just died. Can you come now? Come now.'

The telephone's cord dangled. Nelson returned to the bedroom. The hall clock ticked impatiently.

Madeline had died suddenly and quietly of a coronary occlusion.

A returned soldier's lifeline had gone.

Bretonneux Square, Malvern

The eucalyptus trees stood like drooping statues, sorrowfully bearing the heat of Melbourne's late summer.

Nelson sat by them alone, folded on the park bench.

A different silence filled the square.

'You are the light, Maddie.'

Keeping an Appointment—15 March 1969

'Come on, Dad. It's time for us to leave for your eye scan.'

'I'm not sure I'm up for that, Johno. Things have got me down just now.'

'I know last month was very hard, Dad, hard for all of us, but this appointment needs to be kept. We need to see if there is going to be a next step to getting you to see again. Mum wanted to see what could be done with these new medical procedures. There's no reason to stop now. You need to go along and see what they can do.'

John grabbed his father's coat and the men took themselves down the front steps towards the eye scan facility.

The Green Light—15 March 1969

A large white machine hovered over Nelson in an antiseptic room.

'Don't move Dad,' said John.

'Yes, please stay completely still, Mr Ferguson.'

The scanner ran slowly over the top of Nelson's left eye. The scanning specialist studied the printed image.

A second scan then printed.

After some time, a lab-coated specialist appeared from the adjacent office.

'I have some rather good news for you, Mr Ferguson.'

The specialist's pen recorded the result:

Nelson Harold Nelson, Age 76, 6 Karma Ave, East Malvern. Telephone 2117134.

Previously advised by eye specialist to have corneal graft. It is now possible for him to go ahead and have the operation. General condition on examination: Active. Alert.

A Memorial to all from the City of Footscray— Early April 1969

The old Combi wagon smoked its way up the narrow driveway. John and Nick jumped out. Nick started untying the old wooden ladder from worn roof racks.

'I was wondering where you fellas had got to this arvo,' said Nelson.

'Hi Dad, we've just finished putting in a huge window at a church in Footscray.'

'Footscray is where I met your mum, Johno. The army put me up in a boarding house after I got off the ship from England with Pomp. God bless that boarding house.'

'Well Dad, this window is a memorial to the servicemen and women from where you stayed. It features the Garden of Gethsemane, but we put emblems of the army, the navy and the air force in there too. They're in the window itself.'

'Sounds just right, Johno. I would love to see that one day.'

The window was at the Parish of St John the Evangelist, Footscray. The minister of the church had fought in the 14/32 Infantry Battalion, which had seen action in Papua New Guinea. He had suggested that the battalion members might like to donate a memorial stained-glass window to the church. After the funds had been raised, the window was commemorated to all of Footscray's servicemen and women.

The window was dedicated on 27 April 1969 at the Anzac Day service, two days after Anzac Day.

Weeds and Wise Words—May 1969

Pomp pulled a hefty weed from the garden bed and pitched it over his shoulder.

'Steady!' said Nelson. 'I'm right behind you, old chap.'

'Sorry, Fergo. Forgot my pile was behind the other shoulder.'

'No worries,' said Nelson, 'I may as well be under it.'

'You can't be like that,' said Pomp. 'I know we have just lost Maddie, but you've still got a lot to get on with and enjoy if you can.'

'What would that be Pomp?' queried Nelson.

'Well, John tells me they gave you the go ahead from the scan. Your operation is practically booked in, Fergo, and you better go through with it or I'll take you there on the back of my old bike myself and wait there till it's been bloody well done. The sun needs to rise on this great Anzac and just has to happen, I'm telling you.'

'You're a good trooper, Pomp, but I don't need it now.'

'But, Fergo, I've seen those sketches from the war, I've seen what you've done for the students for the last 35 years, and I've seen what's been made by John and Nick in your own bloody backyard. Incredible. You need to go and have a look. If the surgeon is all they say he's cracked up to be, that's all out there for you.'

'Let me think about it,' said Nelson.

'Well don't think about it too much, Fergo. Us stretcher-bearers can do the carry for a long while, but not forever.'

Both men knew Pomp was right. World War I had taken much from these old soldiers over their lives yet there were still last opportunities to be taken.

Nelson stood quietly, listening intently to the birds in the garden. And to Pomp's words.

'I think you might be right, old mate,' said Nelson.

'And I reckon I'm also right I need to finish off this bloody weeding, Fergo, I've been here all day!'

Army Transport—27 July 1969

Nelson shuffled around the bedroom, searching, then bumping.

His hands stretched under the bed. 'Ah, there they are.'

'Yes, I reckon you have everything you will need now,' said John. Nelson handed John his slippers who put them into his small bag.

'We have to catch two trains, Dad, so we better get going.'

'Very good, son. Lead the way.'

John locked the front door and father and son stepped down onto the pathway and out towards the street.

As they approached the letterbox, a long green car turned the corner and pulled up.

The driver got out with the engine running.

'Mr Ferguson, I am Private Collins. I have come to take you for your eye operation today at the Repatriation Hospital.'

Collins was referring to the Repatriation General Hospital in Heidelberg, a suburb of Melbourne. After World War II the hospital had been handed over by the army to the Repatriation Commission. The Commission and the Department of Veterans' Affairs operated the hospital, caring for Victorian war veterans from all campaigns.

'I didn't realise you were coming. I'm happy to take the train if the car can be used for someone else,' said Nelson.

'Mr Ferguson, the army wishes to provide the necessary transport for you to the hospital, and we will of course take you home after it as well.'

'What do you think, John?'

'Well I think we might take up this kind man's offer, Dad. Is it all right if I come along too?'

'Of course,' said Collins. 'The army will do whatever it can to assist with Mr Ferguson's medical procedure tomorrow. Please accompany Mr Ferguson should you wish to.'

The Right Donor Needed—27 July 1969

Nelson had by this time been approved for eye surgery. The cost would be to the department's account.

But the operation was dependent on a donor for the cornea to replace the one World War I had destroyed. Donors were rare; usually they were the victims of fatal car accidents.

'Mr Ferguson, thank you for coming in. We need you to change into this gown and then rest on this bed. We will come back to you shortly for the next stage of the procedure.'

Nelson sat upright in the bed for some considerable period before Mr Hardy Smith appeared.

'It's good to see you look ready for the procedure, Mr Ferguson. But I am afraid I have just determined that the donor material is incompatible. The operation will have to be deferred to another day.'

'What does that mean?' said John.

'We will have to wait until we receive a compatible donor before we can do the operation.'

'I understand, Doctor. We can't go ahead today. That's all right,' said Nelson. 'You see Mr Hardy Smith, ever since basic training at Broadmeadows when I joined up, I have understood that it pays to be patient in the army. I know that because it can be a very long while before anything happens. But when it does, hold on for the ride. That's the approach I'm taking here.'

Hardy Smith nodded.

'It shouldn't be too long, Mr Ferguson. I will do everything I can to ensure that you are given the best possible chance in the best possible time.'

Another Chance—3 August 1969

In the early hours, on a dark distant road in rural Victoria, a high-speed car swerved too late and struck a tree, fatally injuring its driver.

Several hours later, the phone rang at 6 Karma Avenue.

'Mr Ferguson, I'm from the Heidelberg Repatriation Hospital. You need to come in urgently. We will send a car for you straight away. Please inform your next of kin the procedure will be undertaken very very shortly.'

In the Barber's Chair

'The Continental again, Mr Scholz?'

'Yes thanks,' accepted Pomp.

'Where's Mr Ferguson today?'

'He's just gone off to hospital.'

'I hope he's all right. He's been coming here for 40 years.'

'Yeh, he's got a strong ticker. It's not his heart. It's his eyes. They're going to try and give him a new one using a new fancy procedure. The other one can't be fixed. A doctor trained in London is having a go at him this morning.'

'Well that sounds fantastic. All the years I've known Mr Ferguson and his condition, and now this.'

'Well you say that, but they're pretty big risks for Fergo. He's an old man, not a young buck like me. The doctors are worried about him. But no-one's more worried than me. Even if the operation works, how is Fergo going to cope? He's had so many years like he is. I told him to get stuck in and have the operation, but I reckon there's a good case for just letting him be.'

The barber paused and sprayed more water on a balding head.

'Well I reckon he made the right call to go ahead with it. He deserves a break. He's a great veteran and a good man,' said the barber.

'Well, you might be right. But I can't bear it to go wrong. And they reckon there's a good chance it will.'

The barber pointed to the empty chair next to Pomp.

'He'll be sitting right there next month, I bet.'

Pomp whispered to himself.

'Sorry, Mr Scholz, I didn't catch that.'

Pomp looked up at the barber in the mirror.

'Karma.'

In Theatre—4 August 1969

The nurse looked at the chart and the band on Nelson's wrist. 'We have here, Nelson Harold Ferguson of 6 Karma Avenue, East Malvern, Victoria.'

Nelson lay on the operating table in a white gown. A bright white light lit his face and the top part of his shoulders.

'Very good, Nurse, that's me all right.'

'How are you, Mr Ferguson?' asked Mr Hardy Smith.

'A little anxious but as good as the Ballarat gold-rush,' said Nelson.

'As I mentioned to you this morning, Mr Ferguson, we will be performing the procedure very shortly.'

'The corneal graft will be undertaken while you are awake as the eye is inert and the risk of complications from the anaesthetic is not justified at your age. I will be cutting your cornea out and then stitching the donor's on in its place. The procedure will take some time and then you will be sent to recovery. Do you have any questions?'

'No, Doctor. Many thanks. Go ahead.'

Mr Hardy Smith studied the left eye. He could see heavy pock marking across and into the cornea. The marking had effectively left Nelson blind and unless the cornea was replaced, Nelson would stay that way.

There was some risk that the new cornea would not take, and there was also an infection risk. Mr Hardy Smith had carefully weighed those considerations and had told Nelson about them.

A steady hand appeared across Nelson's face. At this distance, Nelson could make out the blur of moving objects up very close.

'Don't move,' said Hardy Smith.

'I won't, sir.'

The nurse gently placed her hand on Nelson's arm.

The scalpel made its cut, removing the cornea slowly and methodically.

After removing the damaged cornea, Mr Hardy Smith took the fresh cornea from a small jar and placed it on Nelson's eye.

The nurse handed Hardy Smith a needle with an invisible thread.

The stitching of the cornea onto the eyeball would be slow and required incredible sureness of hand.

The surgeon put the needle into the eye and then pulled it back, completing the first stitch. The eye grabbed, then released.

As Hardy Smith worked his way around the new cornea, the patient remained calm and surgeon sure.

'We are nearly through,' said Hardy Smith. 'I have just one or two more stitches to make.'

The surgeon then pressed a circular pad on to both the eye with the new cornea and the irreparable one.

White bandage strips were then wrapped tightly around Nelson's head to keep the pads on.

'Are those Pomp's boots?' Nelson muttered.

'What was that Mr Ferguson?' asked Hardy Smith.

'Nothing thanks, Doctor, all good.'

'We will keep these on for approximately four weeks, Mr Ferguson'.

'Very good, Doctor, as long as it takes is fine with me.'

'You need to keep as still as possible for a considerable period of time. I will come and see you soon and explain this further.'

'Very good, Doctor.'

The operating table was wheeled out towards the recovery ward.

The nurse pulled the blinds, darkening the room. She then elevated Nelson to the sitting position.

'Are you comfortable, Mr Ferguson?'

'Yes, thank you, I am very comfortable here. Not sure how I will find my slippers.'

'We will look after all that for you, Mr Ferguson. You are in good hands at this hospital. We care greatly about our returned soldiers. Your bandages will need to remain on until we say so. For now you must not move unless we tell you you can.'

'No problem, I can do that. I'm good at following orders.'

'The order of today is to put things right if we can, Mr Ferguson,' said the nurse.

Reflections—Mid August 1969

Nelson had by now been in hospital for a couple of weeks, minimising movement as requested, and resting. Much to Nelson's delight, Pomp had used the opportunity handsomely. Pomp's visits could not come often enough. There was plenty of time for the two men to remind each other of the good times, and some not so good, of the last 50 years.

'How'ya travelling, Fergo? You look pretty good to me,' said Pomp by Nelson's bed.

'The left eye is troubling me, Pomp. One eye's weeping but they change the pads pretty well. Otherwise, I'm fine. Lost track but it's been some time since the operation I reckon.'

'Well if anyone can do it, it's Hardy Smith. As soon as I met that bloke I knew he was special. He asked me heaps about our stretcher-bearing in the war and the gassing,' said Pomp.

Pomp paused, then leaned closer to Nelson.

An old bearer's strong hand rested on the other's arm.

'Time for the next step I reckon, Fergo.'

The Ribbon of Hope—Late August 1969

'I'm sorry, Mr Scholz. I would be grateful if you would step out for a moment,' said the nurse.

'If I have to, Nurse, no problem,' said Pomp. 'I'll just be around the corner, Fergo.'

Mr Hardy Smith pushed up against Nelson's bed.

'We are going to take off the bandages now, Mr Ferguson.'

'Very good. I am ready,' said Nelson.

Mr Hardy Smith leaned forward, unclipping the safety pin at the back of Nelson's head. The tightness around his eyes eased.

The surgeon's calm and sure hands slowly unwound the first circle of white bandage. More then fell away, and still more. The long white ribbon of hope then took yet another journey around.

'I think we need to pause here, Mr Ferguson. You will shortly know whether the cornea has taken,' said Hardy Smith.

'You may feel a level of disorientation or pain—please remain as calm as you can as we need to protect the corneal graft from any sudden movements.'

By God

The nurse grasped Nelson's hand firmly. The surgeon slowly unwrapped the remaining length of the white bandage.

Suddenly, Nelson began to see intense brightness peek through, and then flood in. Nelson squinted hard, trying to make sense of what he was seeing. His eyes streamed wildly.

Intensely irritated eyes now fought impulse and will. The nurse dabbed each eye frequently, calming the veteran with her hand on his arm.

'By God!' breathed Nelson.

Suddenly the ward was immersed in colour and sharp focus. Nelson looked to his left and was struck by a rich red vein of light piercing through the ward's window. The floor was full of rubble. As Nelson lifted his head an enormous stained glass window came into view and he stumbled towards the door of the church.

'Pomp, where are you?'

'Mr Ferguson, are you all right? Please just stay very steady for us for now. We are nearly through. You are safe here with us,' the nurse said, trying to calm him.

Continuous dabbing dried weeping eyes. The room then cleared.

On his lap Nelson could see discarded bandages and a silver tray with shiny medical instruments.

He could see his surgeon's hands and now the room beyond them.

For more than 50 years the evil of mustard gas had invaded Nelson's eyes, lungs and life. Now, at this very moment, it had finally been defeated, conquered by combined forces: resilience, love, the miracle of science, and a surgeon's brilliance.

Restoration

'We need to take the sutures out now, Mr Ferguson.'

'Certainly, go ahead, Doctor. I am sorry about before—I got a bit disoriented.'

'It's going very well, Mr Ferguson. You are in the home straight.'

The cornea had taken to the eyeball and now the surgeon's task was to cut away the stitches he had earlier put into the eye.

As Nelson looked up he could see a steady and strong hand tug on the stitches in his left eye, slowly releasing them one by one from the cornea.

'How does that look now, Mr Ferguson?'

Nelson looked up at the surgeon. Then across to the nurse. The room was intensely clear.

'Incredible. Better than amazing, sir. You have restored my life.'

The nurse dabbed the eye one more time and then half drew the curtain.

'We might allow some time for the eye to settle and then we will have an army car take you home, Mr Ferguson. You still need to rest for some time and you need to ensure you do not make any sudden head movements until we are sure that the graft has completely settled down.'

'I will be happy to do that,' said Nelson.

'I am very satisfied with the procedure, Mr Ferguson. There is nothing further I can do for now. I must continue on my rounds,' said Mr Hardy Smith.

A Parcel

As the surgeon approached the exit to the ward, a wiry elderly man in an old checked shirt passed back in.

'May I come in, Nurse?'

'Of course, Mr Scholz. Mr Ferguson would love that I'm sure. He's not allowed to move his head so please sit close by him.'

'Will do, Nurse. Will do.'

Pomp approached the bed, carrying a parcel behind his back.

'Hey, Fergo, it's me, over here.'

'Pomp, my eyes are streaming so you're a blur, but a bloody beautiful one. I can't tell you how amazing it is, and that you are here now, mate.'

'Wouldn't be anywhere else, Fergo.'

'The surgeon has done a fantastic job.'

'Yeh, this should give you a new lease on life, Fergo, no worries.'

Pomp leaned closer to Nelson's bed and pulled the parcel from behind his back.

'Open it when you get home, not now,' said Pomp.

'OK thanks,' said Nelson.

'What's in it, Pomp?'

'Open it when you get home.'

'Thanks Pomp, no worries.

Pomp sat down by Nelson's bed. The two old bearers took each other back into yet more fond memories.

'I'm afraid it's time. You will have to finish up now,' said the nurse.

'Don't worry,' said Pomp, 'I've been thrown out of much less salubrious establishments than this!'

'Yes he has,' said Nelson, 'but he's usually managed to make his way back in.'

'Well not this time, I'm afraid,' said the nurse.

'Very well,' said Pomp. 'Fergo, great to see you. We'll catch up later in the week, mate, when you're back home and settled in.'

An Image—September 1969

In the late afternoon, Nelson and John arrived home in an army car. The front yard was full of the joys of spring. Blue and white hydrangeas were now emerging from their winter hibernation.

'If you're right now, Dad, just want to check something in the studio and then we'll have a cuppa.' said John.

'That's fine,' said Nelson, 'I'll put the kettle on.'

Nelson walked to his bedroom and sat on the bed. He pulled out Pomp's parcel and slowly unwrapped the brown paper. It was a framed picture. He sat looking at it for some time, before opening the supporting bridge behind the frame and placing the photograph on the small table next to the bed.

Standing to one side was a beautiful bride in an elegant satin gown. Every aspect of the image held one constant: love.

Next to the photograph sat another framed image. A tear drop had been rubbed from it 50 years earlier.

Nelson wept.

No Worries—4 June 1970

'Please take a seat,' requested Mr Hardy Smith.

'Thank you, Doctor.'

'Now it's nine months after the operation, I just want to have a look at how you're travelling. Your son has noted that you have been reading with a magnifier and thought your sight might be going off.'

'From my perspective, I am very happy with how it's going,' said Nelson.

Mr Hardy Smith looked closely into each eye. The bright light penetrated as the doctor thoroughly inspected the miracle organ.

'I can tell you your eyes are in remarkably good condition now.'

'Could you please read the chart, Mr Ferguson?'

Nelson read the bottom line.

The surgeon then wrote on the repatriation review card:

Getting on very well. No troubles.

Graft crystal-clear.

'Yes, I don't think there is much more we need to do here. I will make a small adjustment to your glasses' prescription for music reading,' said Dr Hardy Smith. 'You will be all right from here'.

'Thank you Doctor. I want to take in all I can from now on. There is a great deal to see and do.'

'Yes I'm sure there is for you, Mr Ferguson. With those crystal-clear results you'll be able to see a great deal of what has gone on in the last while,' said Hardy Smith respectfully.

'Those are very wise words, sir,' said Nelson.

Colour—1970

Nelson looked up at the enormous coloured stained-glass window recently installed behind the nave of the church.

'What do you think, Dad? She's a beauty isn't she? It took Nick and me more than three months to make it. It took us four days just to install it!'

Nelson's eyes wandered all over the huge colourful image. As his eyes pored over it, the sun suddenly struck its light onto the halo above Jesus, bathing father and son in a golden glow.

Nelson stood transfixed.

'Look at that, Pomp. Incredible.'

'It's me, Dad.'

'Sorry, son, of course it's you. This is brilliant work. The light will come into this church now as never before. As I have just seen it, as long as this church stands. This is a real testament to you and Nick, son.'

The side door of the nave creaked open, followed by measured footsteps on the marble floor.

'Thank you for coming, Mr Ferguson. May I say, we are so happy with John and Nick's work,' said the priest, turning to the window in admiration.

'And we are very grateful also for your work, Mr Ferguson.'

'I just make the tea, Reverend!' said Nelson.

'Well, that may be right, Mr Ferguson, but my understanding from talking with the boys is that you are the spirit behind these windows. We would like you all to come to this Sunday's service.'

'That would be very nice,' said Nelson, 'but for my part, seeing it now is all that I need.'

'Thank you also, sir,' said John, 'but we're happy for the congregation to receive the window in the usual way. Please let them have our best wishes for Sunday,' said John.

'Very good,' said the priest, 'I will let them know you have all been here and I will convey those wishes.'

John and Nelson turned into the aisle and headed down the steps of the church.

'For a moment I thought I was on the other side of the world, John. Villers- Bretonneux.'

'I am sorry about that, Dad.'

Nelson turned to John. Both stopped on the steps of the entrance to the church.

'No son, I'm not sorry. The beauty of the church window I saw there 50 years ago I have also seen here now. A lot of things have happened and changed, but those two windows to the world are the same; they provide the light of life. The colour of life. And hope for a peaceful life.'

John nodded.

The old VW Combi wagon smoked its way back to Karma Avenue and the afternoon took itself towards dusk.

Brushes

From the studio John could hear Nelson's call.

'Johnno, come and have a look at this.'

'Righto, Dad, coming now.'

Nelson pulled the oil painting from where it had been leaning and held it at arm's length.

'John, just finished it last night. What do you think?'

'Very nice, Dad. You have got the peninsula's rocks and beach just right, I reckon. The colours look spot on to me. This shows great detail.'

John admired a small work Nelson had painted on an old piece of canvas, now hand-framed by him out of boards from a pile behind the old studio in the backyard.

'It's for the surgeon, Mr Hardy Smith. His hands are a miracle.'

'Your eyes are the miracle, Dad.'

John held the picture for Nelson. He could see on the back a pencilled message from Nelson to the surgeon.

Dear Mr Hardy Smith

Please accept this as a token of my esteem for your work.

Because of your courageous recommendation to have the surgery, and your immense skill and care, I have now returned to active duty.

This time with brushes.

Nelson and John headed for Carnegie station and then on to Chrystobel Avenue, Hawthorn, to deliver a work which until now had been impossible.

Artichokes and the Old Glass Pile

After a hard stint in the studio to make up time for a newly commissioned window to be fitted next month in a large church in the country, Nick and John had called it afternoon teatime.

They sat in the kitchen looking out to the backyard. Right up against the back fence they could see Pomp and Nelson, digging and fossicking like old goldminers.

'What *are* the old boys up to now?' asked Nick.

'Well, as far as I can tell,' said John, 'Pomp is digging for artichokes. The diggers loved artichoke soup during the war and Pomp and Dad just can't wean themselves off it. I reckon it tastes awful myself.'

'What about your dad? What's he doing up there on top of the old pile of glass offcuts from our windows?'

'He told me he wants to make a small table to put tea cups on, with a top made from old coloured glass pieces. Sounds pretty interesting actually.'

'Yeh,' said Nick, 'wouldn't mind one myself from the old glass soldier.'

The two World War II mates looked at the two World War I mates and smiled.

'I wish we had that much energy!' said Nick.

'You're right,' said John. 'We've learned a lot from those two old bearers, and there's plenty more.'

'Too right, John, too right.'

The Shrine of Remembrance and Peace—24 April 1971

On a cloudy Saturday afternoon, Pomp and Nelson sat in the pub just off Dandenong Road in Carnegie. While the publican was serving down the other end of the bar, Pomp reached over and 'borrowed' his newspaper.

'Will you look at this!' shouted Pomp, slamming the paper down hard on the bar.

'Someone's written bloody PEACE right across the columns of the Shrine of Remembrance. Bloody hell. How could anyone do that?!'

'Let's see,' said Nelson.

The pub gathered around the newspaper.

In the paper a large picture revealed the Shrine of Remembrance with each letter of the word PEACE written on each front column.

'That's a bloody disgrace!' cried a drinker, 'I'll bloody kill whoever did that, the bastards! Tomorrow's bloody Anzac Day!'

'It says here that early in the morning, four young men attacked the guard at the Shrine causing injuries requiring hospital treatment. It says the bastards then painted the word 'Peace' and various peace signs on the walls of the Shrine. That's right, look at the picture! It says it's a demonstration against Australia's involvement in the Vietnam War. It says here we've been involved since 1962 and we've sent more than 50,000 Aussies over there. It says more than 500 of our own have bloody died there!'

By now the advanced drinkers had become raucous and hostile and were tearing the paper to pieces and spilling beer all over the place.

'All right!' said the publican, 'you can fix the bastards who did it if you want to, but don't fix up this joint for nothing.'

'Righto, righto,' said another drinker, 'we'll calm down. But that's not the only thing going on. Other bad stuff has been happening too. I was up in Ballarat the other day and I was told the Cadet Training

Depot in Ballarat was set on fire. Anti-war slogans were painted on the outside walls. What the hell is going on?'

'Yeh, let's try to work out how we find the bastards who are doing all this stirring and we'll straighten them out,' said another.

'Wait on, boys,' said Pomp, rising from his bar seat, 'the message these jokers have put on the Shrine is actually right. It's just that they're desecrating sacred ground and I agree that's just not on.'

'Yeh, well I don't care for all that,' said another drinker, 'I'm going to bloody kill those bastards if I can. Come on boys, let's head down to the Shrine and see what we can find out!'

Loud shouting and wolf whistles filled the pub as everyone exploded with raw rage for retribution, charging out of the pub.

Except two.

More Colour—Late 1974

A large blue truck filled Karma Avenue, heading for Nelson's home. It pulled up outside his letterbox. Two burly men emptied the cabin and dragged a large cardboard carton towards the front door of the house.

The bell rang and Nelson opened the door.

'Sign here, Mr Ferguson. This is for you.'

'Nice truck boys. What's in the box, gentlemen?'

'It's a television. Your daughter Jessica has sent it to you. She's paid for the TV and delivery. It's colour. Where do you want us to put it?'

'That's fantastic. I have no idea where it should go. I have a radio but no television, let alone colour. Thanks for delivering this. Perhaps you could put it in the lounge room for the time being.'

'Sure, Mr Ferguson. We'll even unpack it for you and plug it in if that helps.'

'They're playing colour programmes on the box every few days, Mr Ferguson. You might be lucky tonight with one.'

Colour television broadcasting commenced in Melbourne in October 1974. The broadcasters alternated colour programmes with black-and- white ones as part of the changeover.

The men opened the box and carefully placed the colour television into the corner near the piano. A long lead led into the wall socket.

The miracle now in the corner of Nelson's lounge room invited him to test it.

Nelson leaned forward and switched it on. The bright screen amplified the room and then colour flickered on the screen.

The men pulled a chair behind Nelson and he leaned back into it.

'Thank you, men. Incredible!'

'That's fine, Mr Ferguson. Anything else we can do?'

'No, boys, you have done a great job to get me started.'

The delivery men took themselves to the front door and drove off.

Nelson pulled out his sketchpad and some charcoal. After some endeavour, a newsreader began to emerge on the sketchpad.

Nelson looked up at the TV and then back at the sketch.

'Not bad.'

The Fig Tree

Propped by a cushion, Nelson rested in an old cane chair on the back verandah at Karma Avenue. The late afternoon sun would shortly pierce the lip of the back fence.

Nelson looked down at his boots and could see leather shoelaces surrounded by the heads of rusty nails, which had been punched into old floorboards.

'I didn't know there were that many,' Nelson muttered.

The long grass surrounding the washing line swayed easily in the evening breeze; Nelson wondered at the tiny dancers in front of him.

'John, have a look at this will you?'

John opened the flywire door and stepped out of the kitchen, perching himself on the stool beside his father.

'Have a look at the way the grass moves.' The two men admired nature's waving fingers.

'And will you look at that,' said Nelson, pointing to the grand old fig tree occupying the end of the yard, now burdened by its produce.

'John, I saw it budding some time ago and knew the summer was near.'

Nelson pointed up to the top of the tree.

'Would you like one, son?' asked Nelson.

'Yes, Dad. I can give you a hand.'

'No thanks, son. All good this time.'

Nelson stepped off the verandah and headed over to the tree. He took a long wooden ladder from the wall of the studio workshop, prised it open at the base, and placed it in front of the tree.

'I can see two real beauties up the top!' called back Nelson.

Near the last step, he turned to see John and, beyond, his old house. The ladder wobbled.

'Take care up there, Dad.'

Nelson stretched forward at the top, breaking off two large ripe figs from the branch out to his left. The late sun poked rays through the leaves.

Nelson gently threw the first to John.

He could see John holding the fig and gently swinging his underarm back and forth.

'Dad, are you up for this?'

'This old soldier is good for it I reckon, son,' said Nelson.

After several more swings, John carefully threw the fig high and back over to Nelson.

Nelson's eyes readily followed the fig's path to him high across the backyard.

'I reckon you might be out son!' he called.

'And glad to be caught by you, Dad, if you can.'

From the top of the ladder Nelson stretched his hand out as far as he could. The fig struck the centre of his open palm.

Then fell to the ground.

Now down from the ladder, Nelson picked up the fig and returned to the verandah. He pressed himself back into the old cane chair.

Father and son sat close, watching the sunset illuminate the back of the beautiful old fig tree.

John then tasted the tree's prize.

'The figs are bittersweet, Dad.'

'Yes they are, son.'

Time for an Important Ride—1975

Down along Karma Avenue, lyrical episodes of birdsong began to open up the early Sunday morning to the local community. It would not be too long before old World War I soldiers would sip tea and start getting ready for church.

But the sudden roar of an old motorbike took the vocalists from the trees and stirred the old men earlier than usual.

A tall, slim, but slightly hunched rider in a worn shirt pulled up outside Number 6. He ripped his large goggles off his face and stretched them around the front light, giving the throttle one last jab for good measure. The rowdy engine raced up, then cut out. Smoke billowed, then disappeared.

Pomp hopped off the bike, exposing a gleaming red-bellied chassis. His checked sleeve gave it one last proud polish.

The house's flywire front door swung open. In pyjamas, Nelson looked from the top of the steps out to the street in amazement.

'Hey Pomp, where's that old beauty from?!' called Nelson.

'I picked up the old Indian at the Carnegie local motor auction. It's taken me months to put it back to its original 1915 condition but have a look now! See the sidecar too. I've fully restored it. Couldn't wait to show you.'

Pomp pointed: 'That's where you sit.'

'Fergo, it's time for a ride.'

'Okay, I'll get dressed. I think I know where we might be going. Won't be long, Pomp, I've just to get something from the boys' workshop out the back.'

Mustard Seed

The bright red bike hauled the two mates out of Melbourne and down along the old Ballarat Highway. Pomp pressed on the throttle again and the old engine pushed them further along the long road towards Nelson's hometown.

Leaning forward in the sidecar, Nelson's large clear goggles pressed tightly against his face, protecting him from the wind and obstacles, giving him a vivid view of the open countryside.

The blue sky's canvas covered the bearers on their two-hour journey towards a sacred place. Nelson's eyes fixed on the rural images which had formed and been retained in his memory from a young age.

The bike roared up Sturt Street, Ballarat, past the old Engineers' Hall where Nelson had first performed with the championship Prout's Brass Band and later his rifle brigade band.

The stretcher-bearers then flew past Clarendon College, the great soldier 'Pompey' Elliott's old school.

The two old mates now roared up towards the beginning of the Avenue of Honour.

'We are coming up to the Arch of Victory,' shouted Pomp.

'Yes I can see it now,' called back Nelson.

They raced under the grand structure Nelson had been at with Madeline and the Prince of Wales after World War I. On its expansive face, Nelson could see 'The Avenue of Honour. 1914. Victory. 1919.' written in large classical letters. The rising sun sat above the words.

As the old Indian purred, remembrance trees whipped by left and right.

Pomp took his hands off the handlebars, pointing. 'Hey, Fergo, look over there!'

'Sure, mate, but how about looking here!' called Nelson, gesturing down the road.

The road took the old bearers along the long avenue of trees planted after World War I in recognition of a whole generation's contribution to the nation.

The stretcher-bearers sped down the Avenue. Pomp and Nelson could see some 3000 soldiers' trees: for those who had returned and for those who had not.

As Pomp eased the throttle back, the engine tired.

Now several miles north-west of the town, the motor exhausted itself and cut. Pomp reached across, helping Nelson slowly from the sidecar.

Both men stood near upright and looked straight down the tree-lined road. Pomp's arm reached to Nelson's shoulder.

The mates stood as one in the centre of the Avenue, framed by a parallel line of trees as far as they could see.

'Up there,' said Pomp.

Nelson stepped slowly along the road.

'I'm going to leave you in peace, mate. Yours is No. 3167,' said Pomp, pointing.

As Pomp rested by the bike, Nelson's weary steps took him along the Avenue. He paused by a plaque with a single star, recording a Ballarat boy's ultimate sacrifice.

Nelson looked up the slight but long hill. He could see a large haystack off to the side of the road and then the flow of more trees. As he walked down the middle of the Avenue, the breeze stilled and the air cooled.

Nelson quietly turned back to Pomp.

'I've found it, Pomp. It's here.'

'Yeh, you're in the right place now, Fergo. You have arrived.'

Nelson stepped closer to his tree until it was in front of him. As he scanned to the top, he admired the old oak, now fully grown. Its branches and leaves strong and mature.

A plaque, made from gun metal, rested diagonally by the base of the tree. It read:

NH Ferguson No. 3167 15th F.A.

Nelson slowly bent down, perching himself against the trunk. The rusty barbed wire nearby, separating the adjacent farm from the Avenue, had taken the weather but was still protecting sacred ground.

Nelson reached for a small book in his coat pocket. His thumb ran through the old Bible. It had stayed with him through every day of the war since he had recovered it from under the rubble in the church at Villers-Bretonneux in April 1918.

The thumb suddenly stopped, revealing the passage he had pencil-marked more than 50 years earlier:

The Kingdom of Heaven is like a grain of mustard seed, which a man took, and sowed in his field: Which indeed is the least of all seeds: but when it is grown, it is the greatest among herbs, and becometh a tree, so that the birds of the air come and lodge in the branches thereof.

Matthew 13:31–32

The leaves above Nelson flickered. He removed his beret and lifted his eyes to the blue Ballarat sky. White cockatoos released themselves from the tree. Nelson watched them soar across golden swords of light sourced from glorious white clouds.

Epilogue

Epilogue

On 25 September 1976, Nelson Harold Ferguson died at the Repatriation Hospital, Heidelberg, Victoria. He had been admitted with a blood clot in his leg. He died a week later in his sleep. The honourable soldier had given his life to his community, to his family, to his students, and to his nation.

May he rest in peace, God willing.

Not all of him shall die.

* * *

The man on the other end of Nelson's stretcher, 'Pomp' (Norman) Scholz from South Australia, died one year after Nelson, aged 85. There is no tree for him. However, he is listed on the Riverton Methodist Church Honour Roll of Congregation and Sunday School Members who served in the Great War, erected by the Girls Guild. The small brass plaque that bears his name is affixed to a wooden backing board in the nave of the Uniting Church in the town.

There is also a small Scholz Park Museum in Riverton, Pomp's hometown. In the museum is a small cabinet dedicated to his war service.

The two bearers' mateship was forged in war but sustained by their love for peace.

* * *

Roy Ferguson, Nelson's younger brother, became an art teacher and taught at Collingwood Technical School, in Melbourne, for many years.

Two of Nelson's other siblings, John and Hilda, were also art teachers. The fourth sibling, Alice, worked in design.

* * *

The Ferguson and Papas stained-glass firm made windows to be installed across not only Victoria but also other parts of Australia, including windows with war dedication. Their work included the windows at the All Saints Chapel at Lavarack Barracks, Townsville, Queensland, depicting 'The Morning Light' and 'The Evening Light', completed in 1980 and the windows at St Marks Memorial Chapel, in HMAS *Cerberus*, Westernport, Victoria. A list of windows is included later in this book.

* * *

In 1985, the tiny town of Robinvale in far northern Victoria and Villers-Bretonneux became twin towns. They are about the same size (some several thousand people only). Both have horticultural interests. The relationship was inspired by the death of Lieutenant Robin Cuttle MC, resident of Robinvale, who was killed near Villers-Bretonneux on 9 May 1918.

* * *

Up until 1990, John Ferguson, Nelson's son, continued with his stained-glass art. Nick had retired and John's boys, Peter and Andrew, assisted the old master. John often wore an old beret.

In 1990, John Ferguson and his wife, Nancy, were hit by a drunk driver in another car. Both survived the accident but were both heavily and permanently disabled. John did not make another window. Just prior to his accident, John had completed windows at St Martin de Porres Church in Avondale Heights, a suburb of Melbourne. The National Trust of Australia deemed them 'as being of State level significance' and 'an outstanding representative example of Modernist art as interpreted for a religious setting and a late twentieth century audience.' During installation, the priest told John the windows on the west were receiving a bright glare from the sun, blinding readers at the lectern during summer. After careful consideration, John decided to darken the sheep on the Good Shepherd's shoulders at the centre of the window. The priest later noted how right that decision was—

the Lord's words from the lectern continue through summer, yet the window remains magnificent.

The sons of John Ferguson (grandsons of Nelson Ferguson), Peter and Andrew, have taken on the stained-glass window-making business. It continues today.

In the same year as John's accident, those grandsons installed a large stained-glass window in the Saint John the Evangelist church on Soldier's Hill, Ballarat. At the base of the image appear the words: I WAS BLIND. BUT NOW I SEE. (John 9:25)

* * *

Since World War I ended the innate urge to commemorate courage and sacrifice has stayed strong.

Each year the town of Harefield ensures that it never forgets the Anzac diggers who changed the face of their community some 100 years ago. The first formal British recognition of Anzac sacrifices was in August 1915 when King George V and Queen Mary visited the Harefield Hospital. The Anzac Day ritual has been happening there for nearly all that time. Each year, schoolchildren from the town lay flowers on the graves near St Mary's Parish Church at Harefield. The churchyard contains the graves of over 100 Anzacs who died in the service of the Empire. More than 50,000 Anzacs passed through the hospital between 1915–19.

* * *

In January 2007, the Melbourne Symphony Orchestra toured Europe.

The brass section travelled by train from Paris, north to Villers-Bretonneux.

On the steps of the Australian War Memorial there, Geoffrey Payne, the principal trumpet of the orchestra, lifted Ferguson's cornet. The 'Minstrel Boy' sounded out over sacred ground. Payne was accompanied by his wife, Julie, and other section members; Derek Guille of ABC Radio; and Nelson's grandson David, also a trumpet player. Another grandson, Donald, listened via telephone back in Melbourne.

Payne's great-uncle had served in the AIF's 30th Battalion on the Western Front. He had been killed in action near Villers-Bretonneux on 16 April 1918, the day before Ferguson's gassing. He is buried in the Adelaide Cemetery outside the town of Villers-Bretonnuex. That is the very cemetery in France from which the body of an unknown Australian soldier was recovered and transported to Australia, which body was interred in the Hall of Memory at the Australian War Memorial, Canberra, on 11 November 1993.

The local representative of the town of Villers-Bretonneux stood on the steps holding Payne's sheet music, and wept.

The town had promised in 1919 that it would 'never forget the Australians' (*N'oublions jamais l'Australie*) who liberated it on Anzac Day the year before. That promise has been kept.

Each musical note Payne played on Ferguson's cornet and from the other instruments gave recognition of that undertaking and recognition to those who had served and fought, and those who had paid the ultimate sacrifice, including Payne's great-uncle.

But the music made that day was also in acknowledgement of the contribution made to the community by returned soldiers, and to those who supported them upon return, without which the fabric of new and peaceful societies could not have been woven.

* * *

In 2007, the Melbourne Villers-Bretonneux Brass Ensemble was formed. It comprises world-class brass players and other musicians. Through narration and song, together with pieces from the period of World War I, the story of the Glass Soldier is told in performance. To date, it has been performed many times, including at the Cooma RSL Club, New South Wales; at the Port Fairy Music Festival near Warrnambool; at St Michael's Boys School, Sydney; at Camberwell Grammar School (attended by Nelson's great-grandsons, Jim and Andy); at the Melbourne International Brass Festival; at the Australia Club, Melbourne; at the Hamilton Performing Arts Centre; at BMW Edge, Melbourne, in collaboration with Genazzano FCJ College; at

Ballarat's Her Majesty's Theatre; at the Melbourne Town Hall as part of the Shrine of Remembrance Annual Dinner; at the ABC's Iwaki Theatre, Southbank Studios; at the Whitehorse Theatre, Nunawading; at Scotch College, Hawthorn (Sir General Monash's school); and at the Shrine of Remembrance Melbourne itself.

* * *

The Glass Soldier is a play by one of Australia's most eminent playwrights, Hannie Rayson. The Melbourne Theatre Company performed it in 2007.

* * *

The Glass Soldier Suite was composed by Australian composer Nigel Westlake. It has been recorded by the Melbourne Symphony Orchestra. The world premiere of the piece was performed by the Australian Youth Orchestra in 2014. It was also performed in 2015 by the Hopkins Sinfonia, Melbourne, as an Anzac Tribute.

* * *

In 2015, schoolchildren across Australia donated gold coins to help rebuild a dilapidated school in the village of Pozieres, France, where thousands of Australian troops died in fierce fighting in 1916.

The project was endorsed by the French President Francoise Hollande, and by South Australia's Margaret Forbes, 86, the daughter of World War I soldier Arthur Blackburn who was awarded the Victoria Cross for his bravery at Pozieres.

All participating schools were acknowledged on a plaque at the school in Pozieres.

In 2015, a school in the town of Pozieres, Queensland, received a casket of earth from the battlegrounds of the Somme: a gift from the citizens of Pozieres, France, in sacred memory of the Australians who lost their lives on the Somme. It is held at the Returned Soldiers League Building, Stanthorpe, Queensland.

* * *

In February 2017, after the planting in 2003 of an additional 30 trees in the Avenue of Honour, Ballarat, taking the number of commemorative trees to 3801, the Garden of the Grieving Mother was officially opened, completing Ballarat's iconic Arch of Victory precinct.

* * *

Nelson's daughter, Jessica, married the author's father, John Law Farrands, a returned soldier (captain) from the fighting in Papua New Guinea in World War II. In 1971, Dr John Farrands became the Chief Defence Scientist of Australia, and later the Head of the Commonwealth Department of Science. He was an eminent Australian in defence and scientific matters for which he was awarded a CB and an AO. Four out of John's four uncles volunteered for the AIF and three saw battle: Leslie Robert, Albert Ernest, and John Hazen Farrands. LR Farrands enlisted on 28 August 1914 with the 3rd Battalion AIF. He was in the second wave of small boats which breached Anzac Cove, Gallipoli, at dawn on 25 April 1915. He lost his right eye from battle on 22 May 1915. AE Farrands (1st Battalion) fought on the Western Front as did JH Farrands (aged 19 on enlistment, 4th Pioneers), who was wounded in action on 11 August 1918. The fourth uncle, Bruce Farrands, volunteered two weeks before the end of the war, on 31 October 1918 (aged 19). His mother, a widow of eleven children, had objected to the AIF' s enlistment, the basis being that three sons had fought, one had returned having lost an eye, another (Harold Rawlings Farrands, the author's grandfather) was living elsewhere, and Bruce was the only son then at home. The AIF did not call up the son for duty. The cousin of these brothers, Alfred Victor Farrands, was killed in action on 8 August 1918 at the Battle of Amiens, near Villers-Bretonneux and is buried in the Heath Cemetery, Plot: II. E. 18, Harbonnieres, Departement de la Somme Picardie, France. The rising sun sits at the top of his tombstone.

Notes to Part I

Towards War

Australia—Early 1900s

Australia's wealth had come essentially from three sources: gold, wheat and wool. The gold rushes of the 1850s and following years had permitted the development of the banking system; enabled grand buildings to be constructed, including those in Nelson's hometown of Ballarat; and led to a vast influx of immigrants, which in turn enabled further economic development. As for wool, Australia had some 50 million sheep as far back as 1902 (even with the preceding eight-year drought). Australia was also a world supplier of wheat and had nearly 8,500,000 acres under harvest in 1914, producing over 100 million bushels.

The primary production powerhouse of Australia was severely affected by a drought at the turn of the century and the great depression of the 1890s, resulting in a collapse of the financial sector. The depression also caused major emigration and a huge slowdown in immigration—between 1875 and 1890, Australia's net gain through migration was 500,000 people; in the following fifteen years, the gain was only 8000.

At the turn of the century Australia had not yet been industrialised; BHP's first iron furnace in Newcastle would not be opened until after the war had begun.

Australia's rural areas were largely unregulated; most of the vast countryside of New South Wales had no local government until 1906.

And the influence of Australia's primary-production-based population could be seen in its under-developed education system: as late as 1900 there were still only three state secondary schools in Australia—all in New South Wales. As late as 1911, in the whole of Victoria there were only around 1000 university students. Formal education for Aboriginals was practically non-existent: by 1912, in

Western Australia all Aboriginal children had been expelled from, and were forbidden entry to, state schools.

The Birth of the Australian Army—1885 to 1910

For several decades before Australia's Federation in 1901, the colonies had supported British conflicts. In January 1885, the Australian colonies had provided 750 infantry to the Empire to assist Britain's reverses in its Sudan conflict. In 1899, from its young volunteer defence force, Australia offered and sent 16,632 soldiers (in five waves) to support Britain's endeavour in the South African War, on 'suggestion' from the British War Office. Australian troops had been organised into six different colonial forces for the six different colonies. Following Federation in 1901, the forces that departed for South Africa were organised into Commonwealth regiments. The Australians had returned in 1902 with a wide reputation for dash and daring, and with a good dose of wildness when unengaged. Except for patriotic private funds, those who returned were unsupported irrespective of their level of disability.

Ever since the 1880s, it had been a commonly held view that Australia should have its own national defence force. Russian ships on local shores had added emphasis to that idea. By 1902, with the new nation some two years old, it was time to build the necessary legal architecture for a national defence force designed to protect the Commonwealth and the States. On 22 October 1903, the *Defence Act 1903* did just that. Australia would for the first time have its own defence force. There would be naval and military forces; the latter divided into permanent (full-time) and citizen forces. The citizen forces would in turn be divided into militia (paid), volunteer (not ordinarily paid) and reserve (essentially rifle club members) forces. All male inhabitants of Australia (except exempt persons) between 18 and 60 years of age were 'liable' to serve in the militia forces. Nelson and the 17th Rifle Brigade Brass Band members were accordingly 'reservists'.

The King of England's representative in Australia, the Governor-General, could raise, maintain and organise such forces as he deemed necessary for the defence and protection of Australia. Those ultimately engaged in an active force during war had to swear an oath to the 'Sovereign Lord the King'.

The defence force was intended for fighting in Australia. Australian forces were for Australian, not foreign, wars; wars were 'any invasion or apprehended invasion of, or attack or apprehended attack on, the Commonwealth or any Territory under the control of the Commonwealth, by an enemy or armed force'.

But the King of England could still directly access Australian fighting troops; and the Australian Governor-General (as agent of the king) had the power to put the Australian forces under the orders of the Commander of the King's forces. And members of the Australian force could 'augment' the king's forces by volunteering.

This legal framework remained until 1909. In that year, Australia decided it should have its own navy rather than relying solely on the British Navy. (The colonies had been paying subsidies for its use for some time.)

By a new and significant process established in 1909, the Australian Army could be bolstered in number and competency by expanding the reserve forces. This would be achieved by the Governor-General of Australia calling upon all persons liable to serve in the citizen forces to enlist and serve (known as a 'calling out').

Further, from 1909, all male inhabitants of Australia had to undergo military training between the ages of 12 and 25. At the end of it they would then be assessed as 'efficient' or 'non-efficient' and if need be undertake additional training. Males over 25 were required to join the reserves.

But this new regime did not apply to Australians 'not substantially of European origin' and so Aboriginals could not form part of any army raised to protect Australia.

There were serious consequences for non-participants. Those who, without lawful excuse, evaded or failed to receive training committed an offence.

By these mechanisms, from 1909 every male of fighting age in Australia (apart from Aboriginals and other non-Europeans) had to be trained for war, and committed a crime if they did not participate.

Nelson had been part of this military regime since he turned 18, joining the reserve forces and training accordingly.

The Australian Government recognised that Australians wanted an army for Australian defence purposes only; and that it should not, except if required by an emergency, be shaped to be a British force; or for that matter even principally directed to Britain's problems.

Nevertheless, young Australians like Nelson, along with those in the rifle brigade bands, remained in the British War Office's sights. That office had planned for some time that as far as possible Australia's defence force (and those of the other dominions) should be organised and trained specifically along British lines. That would enable them to be interchangeable and, if necessary, combined, with provision for an Imperial General Staff as the leadership. That would provide the necessary bridge to permit young Australians to fight abroad in aid of Britain, should it need extra 'resources'.

Within this framework, from 1909 the Australian Army was formed for home service only *but* modelled on British Army doctrine and, if need be, integration.

In 1910, the British again put their guiding hand on Australia's adolescent army. In that year, Lord Kitchener visited the new nation to inspect the Australian defence capability. His Lordship recommended that 215 military areas be established, including the area surrounding Nelson's hometown of Ballarat. The recommendation was accepted by the Australian Government. The establishment of the 17th Rifle Brigade Nelson was in before World War I was a direct result of the Kitchener visit.

By 1910, there were already 45,000 in the Australian Army, mainly youngsters between 19 and 21, such as Nelson, who had been trained 16 to 25 days a year and organised into brigades. A further 35,000 mainly older men such as farmers were in various rifle clubs. A government factory in the Blue Mountains near Sydney had begun to supply the necessary rifles.

By these means, young Australia, including Nelson and his Ballarat mates in the band and the brigade, was steadily readying to protect itself but also to support the mother country should it call for help.

The Ballarat 17th Rifle Brigade would be one local contribution in what might one day be a global conflict.

By careful design and long-term planning, the British had been building their access to competency and resources for war out of the young men, including Nelson, of this new nation and of other dominions of the British Empire.

By 1911, Australia had just turned 10 years old and therefore it was still an adolescent nation. This permitted the mother country to take a critical role in setting the purpose of Australia's defence policies and systems. The purpose was dual in nature: for the protection of both Australia and the British Empire.

But due to its location and remoteness, in 1911 Australia was virtually free from possible invasion. The biases and flexibility that had been built into the Australian Army were now primarily directed to one thing: providing resources (men) to the Empire should they be needed.

A hundred years earlier, Britain had sent its criminals out of the sight of the mother country (some 160,000 by the end of transportation in 1868). Now, their descendants, more recent immigrants, and white Australians would protect the great Australian continent. But the new defence measures had also now established a mechanism by which those resources could be accessed for a different continent, if and when Britain or its allies got into strife and called for help. That call was in fact made in July 1914.

The Birth of the Australian Nation—1901

Nelson Ferguson was only a young boy of 10 when Australia became federated in 1901. Although New Zealand had decided not to participate, by a new Australian Constitution (a schedule to an Act of the British Parliament) all of the colonies of Australia, as settled by the British Empire, would be 'commonwealth'.

The realisation of Federation in 1901 and therefore the creation of the nation of Australia was of huge significance to all those in the colonies. Celebrations of the birth of the nation had taken place on New Year's Day 1901. Mounted Australian troops, recently returned from assisting Britain in the Boer War, gathered in Sydney's Domain for the celebrations. They were accompanied by Australian lancers, infantry and cadets, together with colonial troops and detachments of British troops and many other notable military men.

But these were not the only ones present at this ushering in of the new nation: there was a large gathering of shearers and other figures iconic of the Australian character, all decorating the celebrations. Sixty Aboriginal men, women and children also participated in the celebration, even though the new Constitution itself stated that on a reckoning of the number of people in the nation, they would not be counted and that, further, the Commonwealth could not make a law with respect to the Aboriginal race in any State.

Even Nelson's primary school, in the tiny town of Waubra, some 30 miles north-west of Ballarat itself, had held a special event for the children.

The European Race to War—1900 onwards

Since 1900 Germany had, through its Second Naval Law, been building a fleet capable of engaging the British Royal Navy in battle. England regarded this as an unjustified threat to their century-old command of the open sea. Napoleon himself had placed a trade embargo upon England and had forced his allies to take part in economic warfare against the mother country. Britain's Navy had been the island's saving grace and supremacy at sea had been a central tenet of military policy ever since the Battle of Trafalgar. From 1906, Britain's most important foreign policy initiative was to outbuild Germany in battleships.

But that was just on sea. By 1904, all European armies had long-laid military plans.

Germany was now leading the race towards war. That race was being developed under the so-called Schlieffen Plan. Schlieffen was the chief of the German General Staff who had from 1905 onwards been developing a plan to deal with what was emerging as a bifurcated Europe: Germany, Austria and Italy on the one hand (the Triple Alliance), and Britain, France and Russia (the Triple Entente) on the other. Schlieffen considered France to be Germany's serious opponent. He thought Germany should seek to defeat France first because Russia would take a number of weeks to mobilise against it.

In essence, it was Schlieffen's view that a massive short and successful attack on France would encourage Britain to stay out of a continental war, and allow the German Army to transfer troops by train to take on Russia in a second phase. Germans had already timetabled some 11,000 trains within the proposed mobilisation period. Since May 1912, France too had plans to concentrate some 7000 trains for mobilisation of its troops.

Schlieffen's plan to invade France was bold because it required Germany to attack France via Belgium, yet Britain had since 1839 said it would guarantee its neutrality. Therefore, the plan necessarily assumed Britain would pull out of supporting Belgium—yet it might not. Although small, both in area and population, Belgium was an important hub of commerce, with the sixth largest economy in the world.

As Europe approached the end of the first decade of the 20th century, it appeared to many in England and elsewhere that a general war in Europe would be inevitable. Lord Haldane of England had in 1908 informed Sir John French that Sir John would probably be required to command the British expeditionary force if it were sent to the continent. The British and French armies had in fact already been in close and secret consultation for some years prior, collaborating on details such as where British troops would ultimately de-train at stations across France in the event of war. The troops' safe passage would be dependent on the British Navy keeping the English Channel free; now the challenge to the security of the Channel was also real. It was true that Britain and France had been at war in 1793, and that France had attempted to invade Britain in 1797. War had flared again in 1803. But now they were allies, and close ones.

The formation of the Triple Entente between France, Britain and Russia in 1907 and the subsequent spectre of German's 'encirclement' by them had now rattled the German psyche and it continued to build its army accordingly. But Germany's ascent as a powerhouse in Europe had already been building for some 30 years. And by 1913, Germany was also expanding its influence elsewhere, colonising in far-off lands; it held territory and naval bases in north-east China and island possessions including Nauru and Western Samoa, and was also colonising parts of New Guinea north of Australia.

France was not in this position. It had for many years suffered a serious manpower problem compared to its virile neighbour, Germany. For this reason, France had earlier commenced fortifying the Franco-German frontier. The strategic plan, based on a fortification of the frontier, was initially to be defensive, followed by counter-offensive steps should Germany penetrate the fortification zones. However, a change of military strategy meant the fortifications were never built; General Joffre of the French Army thought that defensive strategies were not part of the French 'national character'. An offensive strategy against Germany had therefore been developed after 1912. The weakness in the plan, however, was that if the German Army moved through Belgium, and held its ground, the French would crumble. The original defensive plan (now abandoned) would have enabled France to meet German aggression much more readily. This was now not possible.

By 1913, as part of this 'aggressive' defensive plan, France had sought to bring its soldier numbers up as close as possible to those of Germany, even though France's population was only two-thirds of Germany's. France had been outraged by Germany's earlier demands to cede eastern French provinces, and nursed the humiliation of the German Army surrounding Paris on 19 September 1870, with Paris capitulating on 28 January 1871. In the armistice of that year, France had ceded Alsace and part of Lorraine, and had agreed to pay indemnities to Germany. French military policy reflected this determination not to tolerate such humiliation.

There had been high-scale activity on the continent for nearly a decade by now, with Britain keeping more than a watchful eye on developments. It knew for some time now that there might be a need to call on the dominions to support it in the brewing European hostilities. Kitchener's visit to Australia in 1910 had made Australia well aware of that.

Now it was time for another visit. On 13 February 1914, Sir Ian Hamilton, Inspector General Overseas Forces of the British

Government, visited a small town outside Melbourne. There at Lilydale, some 100 miles from Nelson's hometown of Ballarat. Sir Ian observed drills performed by some 3000 officers and soldiers from the 13th, 46th and 51st Infantry Brigades and the 13th Army Services Corps and 13th Army Medical Corps. The commander of the camp was Colonel John Monash (later Lieutenant-General Sir John Monash). (Some 150 tons of firewood had been secured for the local army camp, for cooking.) Massed brass bands at the drill and the encampment brought triumphant sounds to the Australian bush. The local newspaper noted that Sir Ian Hamilton had commented during the drills that it was 'a lovely spot for manoeuvres'. Sir Ian later commanded the Gallipoli campaign.

These developments were all part of the European heavy industry of creating soldiers. In the first decade of the 20th century, all major European nations were putting their young men through military training. In the German Army, a conscript was required to spend two years of adulthood in uniform, and thereafter was required to return to service to keep his soldier hand in. The equivalent of this scheme existed in France, Austria and Russia. Europe was, by these systems, building and maintaining an array of submerged and invisible military forces, aggregating to millions of men, ready to take up weapons and march to war on notice.

It was true that Europe had seen significant-sized battles in its history, including the biggest encirclement battle to date on 3 July 1866 when some 180,000 Austrians and 200,000 Prussians faced off against each other, involving some 1500 artillery in the Austro-Prussian War.

But the current approach to war would be of a larger order of magnitude.

The 'all in' approach to conflict was inaugurating what would become an exercise in mass slaughter; European powers had been competitively planning large-scale warfare for years.

Flashpoints, then War—July 1914

By mid-1914, the European trouble Britain had long feared was significantly escalating. The earlier fragmented stew of conflict was continuing to consolidate itself into something globally significant.

As summer approached in Europe, Britain continued its long-term policy of supporting its ally, France, against German aggression in support of Austria. According to many in Britain and elsewhere, Germany's desire and readiness to make a bid for supreme world power had been evident for decades and was now open and in ascendency. By a confluence of individual relations and friendships, Russia and other countries also fell into this impending international conflict.

On 28 June 1914, the Austrian Archduke and heir to the Austro-Hungarian imperial throne, Franz Ferdinand, and his wife, were assassinated in Sarajevo. This did not immediately signal the outbreak of war. It would be another month before Austria-Hungary would declare war on Serbia on 28 July.

Before that declaration had been made, in mid-July Britain had called up its Royal Navy reservists from all over the country. Britain had gathered its most powerful armada of some 180 warships for exercises off Spithead. For some six hours, the ships sailed past the salute of King George V. On 29 July, the core of the fleet, which would comprise an 18-mile line of battleships and cruisers, was ordered north to a naval base.

On 31 July, Germany sent Russia an ultimatum, declaring war on it the next day. Under the Franco-Russian Convention of 1892, both France and Russia were required to mobilise and, if either were attacked by Germany, to go jointly to war against her. France accordingly mobilised against Germany and on 3 August 1914 Germany declared war on France too.

When Russia mobilised, posters announcing the fact were put up in the streets of St Petersburg and all major Russian cities. In fact in all of the major combatant countries, ordinary people were ecstatic at the news of war. Virtually all British, French, German and Russian citizens rallied to the cause of the war.

In France, formerly notorious anarchists suddenly brandished the tricolour with the same enthusiasm as the most ardent of patriots.

In St Petersburg, an enormous crowd congregated and, upon the Emperor's appearance, knelt to sing the Russian national anthem.

In Berlin, the Kaiser also appeared on his palace balcony, telling the tumultuous crowd that the sword was being 'forced' into Germany's hands and asking them to go to church, kneel before God and pray for the safety and success of Germany's gallant army.

From this point, things happened quickly. On the morning of 4 August 1914, German cavalry crossed into Belgium and by nightfall the heads of German columns of troops were some miles over the border. The German conception of violating Belgium neutrality could be traced back as far as 1892 as part of Germany's offensive plans for Russia and France. Those plans had now become a diplomatic reality for Britain, a long-time guarantor of Belgian neutrality.

At 11.00 pm on 4 August 1914, in support of its ally France, Britain officially declared war on Germany. The British Cabinet had earlier met and rejected (12 to 6) the guarantee of British troops being sent to France, but the German violation of Belgian neutrality had changed that. The Prime Minister of England, Asquith, had not much earlier written to a colleague stating that there seemed to be no reason why the British people should be anything more than 'spectators'. That belief had now been shattered by Germany's unrelenting aggression and the domino effect of ally upon ally joining the fray.

Britain had not known a major war for a century, and on the continent there had not been a war between the great powers since the Franco-German war of 1871. Europe was about to be tipped upside down with well-prepared violence. Relative peace for almost 50 years was now being shattered.

On 5 August 1914, German forces reached Liege in Belgium. Only one day later, on 6 August, the Germans entered the town and its fortress was besieged by German soldiers. Steel-helmeted soldiers had invaded a small country without provocation. German war atrocities were soon committed, enraging the international community and sparking further anti-German sentiment across Europe and beyond. The German flag, coloured black, red and gold, could be seen across the town. They had been the colours of national unification and freedom since 1814, and were declared the colours of the German confederation in 1848. From that time, it had been known as the war and trade flag.

These events were outside the consciousness of the crowds gathered in London and Paris on the same days demonstrating their patriotic belief, to sing God Save Our King, and to trumpet the Marseillaise from proud throats.

Britain's army was itself now mobilising. On 12 August 1914, less than 10 days after war had been declared, the first British troops started across the English Channel toward the new enemy. Germany had hoped to avoid conflict with England until France and Russia were out of the way but that would not be possible now. Nevertheless, statistically, in manpower it had an advantage over England of some five to two in infantry and three to one in cavalry, not to mention vast superiority in heavy ordnance. On 14 August, troops moved forward by train to the area of concentration between Maubeuge and Le Cateau.

Germany had also initiated vast train movements in the first month of the war: between 2 and 18 August 1914, some 2150 fifty-four wagon trains crossed the Hohenzollern Bridge over the Rhine.

There had, in fact, been no delay by any nation from the starter gun onwards. The pace of war was likely to be quick, and strategy, at least in the early stages, conventional.

By late August 1914, the full weight of Germany's power began to be felt as it moved from the planning to the execution stages of war. Nearly a whole month of invasion had been underway.

But there was one major power missing in the sprawling frenzy of the overture to mass warfare. America too had subscribed to the thinking that globally deployed military power might be important one day. In 1907 it had, on President Roosevelt's initiative, sought to demonstrate growing American military power and so-called 'blue-water' navy capability by sailing some 16 battleships around the world. The fleet visited Melbourne, Australia, on 29 August 1908, staying for some five days. In 1914 it was President Wilson who had to decide whether to place America in the flare of conflict erupting in Europe. Although he loved England, Wilson soon made it clear to the combatant nations that America would 'stand above' the war so that it could shape the peace when it ultimately arrived.

Aside from that philosophy, there were some eight million people in America who had been born in Germany, out of a total population of 105 million. That was enough cause to keep out of the fray. At least initially.

Australia's New Cause Arrives—July 1914

The events of late June and July 1914 had certainly alarmed Britain. It had, since 1911, focused its Imperial Defence force on naval spending rather than on building an infantry. It had held the view that the major battles of the war would be in the North Sea, and that its Home Fleet (later renamed the Royal Fleet) would prevail.

And unlike the major European powers, Britain had resisted introducing conscription and had kept an army of only a handful of divisions at home. It was by that strategy both vulnerable as regards ground troops and limited in capacity to provide immediate manpower to its allies, France and Russia, should they call on Britain for land-based support. It had only a small capability of artillery equipment: a mere 60 aeroplanes. In contrast, each of Germany, France and Russia had in excess of 100 planes.

The impending war threat stimulated Britain to consider warning the dominions, including Australia and Canada. The term 'dominion' had first been used during the 1660s to identify certain parts of America, and its first collective use for Australia and Canada was at the British Colonial Conference of 1907. At that conference, Britain and Australia had agreed to receive 'a signal' of this kind should Britain consider it necessary to send it.

Although such a communication had been contemplated as far back as 1907, successive Australian Defence Ministers had previously refused to allow contingency planning for the Australian Army for war between Britain and Germany. However, from June 1910, recognising that assistance might well be called on and, if so, that it should be orderly and well managed, the Director of Military Operations for the Australian Army, Brudenell White, requested approval from the Defence Minister to work out such a plan. In November 1912, the minister approved talks between Australia and New Zealand. The heads of each army agreed that a composite force of some 18,000 men (12,000 of whom would come from Australia) would be an appropriate contribution to Britain should it request assistance.

On 30 July 1914 Britain sent a telegram to each of Australia, New Zealand and Canada: war was 'imminent'. The 'warning' on 30 July 1914 was a call for support in the form of men. The dominions did not disappoint and a warm response came swiftly. On 31 July, the first offer of a force of men came in from Canada—given on the basis 'if the need arose'. On the same day, Australia's Opposition Leader, Andrew Fisher, promised that under his government, if elected, Australia would support the mother country to 'our last man and our last shilling'.

Soon after, the Australian Government offered to dispatch 'a force of 20,000 men of any suggested composition to any destination desired by the British Home government, and to maintain it there'. The earlier figure of 12,000 had been bumped up to 20,000 by the British-born Australian Prime Minister, Joseph Cook. Brudenell White, then the acting Chief of General Staff, told Cook that a divisional formation of that size could be organised in about six weeks.

The British accepted the offer. From that very moment, Australia was a willing participant in the fray Britain now found itself in. The Australian Government knew that in all probability the new nation's involvement would become increasingly thicker and deeper if the impending conflict escalated.

At the broader level, Britain and Australia were now together attempting to work out how best the new nation could provide support. Owing to pre-war planning, the decision as to what to do with the Australian Navy was relatively straightforward; it would be placed under the authority of the British admiralty.

As to the army, Britain and Australia ultimately agreed that the Australian support would not be split up among the divisions of the British Army but rather that there would be a dedicated and compact Australian force. The source of this force would have to come from the youth of Australia, principally those in their first or second year of training under the scheme established by Kitchener following his trip to Australia. By 1914, some 45,000 men aged 18 to 25 formed the Australian Militia Force.

But as the *Defence Act* precluded conscripts from being sent overseas, a special force by enlistment from the whole population would now be created. The name, the Australian Imperial Force or AIF, was chosen by its first commander, Brigadier General WT Bridges, signifying its dual Australian and Imperial mission. Bridges would use White's mobilisation plans; together they worked closely, creating the arrangements to preserve the separate identity of the Australian force within the British Army. White then created a Charter to guide the AIF throughout the war and develop its culture.

By these arrangements, the young nation agreed to veer from the task of progressive nation building that had preoccupied its first decade. It would now apply itself virtually exclusively to the job of defending Britain and its allies, and, of course, herself. From at least one perspective, this stood to reason; more than half a million of the nearly five million strong Australian population were British born, including Australia's then Prime Minister, Joseph Cook. And apart from that, the Australian High Court itself had said in 1906 that an Australian nationality as distinct from a British one was a 'novel idea' to which it was 'not disposed to give any countenance'.

The declaration by England of war against Germany meant the now 13-year-old nation of Australia was also at war. It had launched itself into the demands of a global war at a time when its population was just under five million people. This meant, according to official estimates, that there was a potential pool of up to around 820,000 men of 'fighting age', between 19 and 38.

Because of the provisions of the *Defence Act*, that pool specifically excluded Aboriginals. (The 'assimilation' program commenced in 1913 for them to join white Australia, which might ultimately make them eligible, but not for now.)

In consequence of the declaration, on 7 August 1914, regiments around Melbourne, including Nelson Ferguson's 70th Infantry Brigade(Ballarat Regiment) under the command of Lieutenant Colonel William Bolton, were mobilised and headed to the army fort at Queenscliff, ready to take further orders pending the formation of the volunteer force to be known as the Australian Imperial Force.

Nelson's regiment was sent to Fort Queenscliff for 14 days' guard duty and further training. Bolton then travelled to Victoria Barracks in Melbourne to meet some of the officers he would work with, including a Ballarat boy, Harold 'Pompey' Elliot, of the 58th Infantry (Essendon Rifles).

For the Victorian regiments, and elsewhere across Australia, theory had suddenly turned to enactment.

It was not only enactment for Victorians. On 7 August 1914, the French consul in Australia announced in the local *Courrier Australien* that Frenchmen in Australia were required to rejoin their military corps in France and, if without means to do so, would receive a requisition for a French ship to take them home. The ship would take them to Marseilles. On 22 August 1914, the SS *Malwa* sailed from Sydney to Marseilles, carrying 21 French reservists.

By 8 August 1914, Bridges and White had presented to the Minister for Defence plans as to how the AIF would be structured: there was both an Australian infantry division and a light horse brigade.

On 10 August 1914, less than a week after Britain, and as a consequence, Australia, had declared war on Germany, recruitment for the AIF officially opened. The general consensus of the Australian population was that recruitment should be broad and from across the vast new nation. Consistent with that, the first Australian infantry division would be made up of a brigade each from New South Wales and Victoria, and a third supplied by the other States of Australia. The division would include light horse, artillery, field ambulances and horse transport, making up a total of 18,000 young men. The light horse brigade would be nearly 2000 strong. The total force that Prime Minister Cook had contemplated, namely 20,000 men, would soon be met from Australia's finest volunteers. They would come from the elite of young Australia; and true to the young nation's egalitarian culture, they would be paid the average worker's wage.

Australia had been settled by the British little more than a century earlier. There had been frontier battles between settlers and Aboriginals that had endured until a few decades before Federation. But Australia had had little demonstrable national military heritage upon which to pin its emergent nationalism. It was true that in 1854 British troops had stormed Australian goldminers and others, at Eureka (near Ballarat), killing 30 people. While the lost battle had started political reform in the colony of Victoria, it was not 'international' in character. But now, Britain's declaration of war with Germany had given Australia the opportunity to establish the presence of a 'nation' on the world stage.

This was not just a fight for Britain. Australia itself had critical national interests at stake; if Britain got into trouble, so did Australia. The British Royal Navy was in effect Australia's major defensive shield against the rise of Japan and Germany's imperial ambitions in the Asia-Pacific including in nearby New Guinea. Australia's coastline would not be defendable if that navy were deployed elsewhere for too long.

Within several weeks, at the British Government's request, Australian naval and military forces landed on the eastern coast of the Gazelle Peninsula. They took control of a German wireless station and an administrative centre at Rabaul. Six Australian soldiers died in the engagement, the first of the war. Australians patrols pressed into the German-controlled territory.

On 1 November 1914, enthusiastic, fit and strong young men, having gathered from all over Australia, now being the 1st Division, sailed from Western Australia for war. Nearly a third of them were in fact British-born. They were headed for Egypt for further training and then onwards according to England's particular war needs. However, they would first need to travel to Rabaul to destroy the important German wireless station there so that Germany's naval reach, possibly heading for Sydney or Melbourne, would be diminished or annihilated.

The First Five Months of World War I—
August to December 1914

The Schlieffen Plan had been enacted as Schlieffen himself had designed, with Germany attacking France via Belgium.

Revised and refined over time, Schlieffen had studied and restudied the logistics and planning of an attack on France. With customary German precision, Schlieffen had concluded that Germany would take only 42 days to defeat France.

This was nearly the case.

By mid-August 1914, the Germans were proving they could be very swift as invaders. Brussels fell on 20 August 1914. The way to Paris was now open.

On 24 August 1914, the whole of the British force found itself outflanked by the Germans and Sir John French, the commander of the British Army, ordered a major retreat.

By late August 1914, the German Army was only 22 miles from Paris. The French dismantled bridges across the Marne. Grazing cattle and hay were put on racecourses at Longchamp and Auteuil for possible future use. Desperate attempts were made to protect Paris. The government announced it had moved to Bordeaux, and the military governor of Paris commandeered 700 small taxis to transport thousands of soldiers in record time to attack the right flank of the German invaders.

Despite their advances, Germany had itself withdrawn a critical number of troops to deal with what was expected to be a significant threat on the eastern front, in Russia, leaving Germany exposed in France. Whether the Germans would be able to take Paris remained an open question.

By September these events had merged into one of the first of numerous major battles, known as the Battle of Marne. There, the British and French were able gradually to halt the German advance on Paris, at a cost of half a million casualties each.

As the Germans could not make it to Paris, they went north, and each enemy then sought to turn the other's western flank to achieve a knockout victory. These manoeuvres in October and early November gave rise to the First Battle of Ypres, in Belgium.

By the end of 1914, a quick and conclusive victory by Germany, or France, or by Britain, or anyone else for that matter, was completely out of the question.

The warfare in France had revealed one thing: Britain's resourcing for war was almost completely out of alignment with the resourcing needed to be an active participant in the emerging concept of 'total war'. Things would have to change, and quickly, if Britain was to assist France in any meaningful way. It would have to focus on the western front in France, and on how to bolster manpower for that costly stalemate.

Britain's reaction was to recruit further volunteers, and urgently. To achieve this, on 11 October 1914, Britain lowered the minimum height for a volunteer from 5 feet 8 to 5 feet 5. By the end of October 1914, Lord Kitchener had called for a further 300,000 British volunteers.

This course was shortly further supplemented: on 5 November 1914, after some further 30,000 casualties, it again lowered the height to 5 feet 3 inches.

Not only was the time scale and manpower requirement miscalculated by virtually everyone, by the end of 1914, although the war had only been going for four months, the amount of wastage was staggering: some 300,000 Frenchmen were dead and 600,000 wounded. This was from a population of some 20 million men, of which 10 million were of military age.

For Britain too, the carnage was overwhelming. In the first months of the war, officer casualties alone were 4270 dead and wounded. The British prediction that the war would largely be waged in the North Sea was proving to be seriously wrong and the infantry was now suffering incredible losses.

Germany too had suffered unthinkable losses of men in its 'six-week' assault.

Apart from men, animals were also suffering huge casualties, in particular horses. Although trucks had been used extensively as part of mobilisation, the combustion engine remained unreliable and, in the case of the German Army, some 60 per cent had broken down in some fashion or another. The consequence was that horses were being used in their millions to pull equipment and supplies, including food. However, they too required fuel: hay. The problem was that the several million pounds of feed required per day was not available. German horses began eating unripened French corn, causing tens of thousands of deaths.

These were not the only new and staggering dimensions to war. New battlefield tactics were emerging, even in the first few months.

In particular, in October 1914, the Germans had used poison gas at Neuve-Chapelle, near Ypres. The gas was contained in small irritant canisters inserted into shrapnel shells which were fired on the French troops. It had had virtually no effect. But it had introduced the idea that gas might be developed and used to devastating mass effect.

And there was yet one further, now functionally requisite aspect to this modern warfare: the trench. The trench was not new; it had been deployed in the American Civil War and in the Boer War. But since November 1914, a permanent trench line had been dug from Nieuport on the Belgian coast right through to the Swiss border, including the now notorious Ypres Salient within it. The trench system was now enormous. Trenches were long excavations in the ground, enabling soldiers to stay relatively protected from infantry attack and machine gun fire, and facilitating the movement of troops along and to and from the front in relative safety. If trench systems were to be breached by the enemy, they would need to be destroyed. This need gave rise to a massive build-up of artillery power on all sides of the war. The first Christmas of the war saw absolute deadlock across the trench system. The war on the front would soon bog down into a 'game' of stalemate, each side waiting for the other to attack, and being unable to dislodge the other. In effect, from early on the war had become one of attrition—the process of reducing the enemy's strength through sustained presence and endurance.

The stalemate of the trench had been brought about by the culmination of the following dynamics: huge artillery power, which could smash any oncoming attacker on a grand scale; advances in machine-gun efficiencies, which could eliminate large numbers of infantry quickly; and poor logistics (the supply of military equipment and food). It was entirely logical therefore to dig these large slits into the earth and take shelter in them.

By the close of 1914, 52,516 Australians had enlisted in the AIF (similar per capita to the Canadians). No Aboriginals were supposed to be included in that number; recruiting regulations prohibited it. However, two 'half castes' had in fact enlisted under the discretion of recruiting officers.

As with the other dominions, white Australian volunteer enlistments had not yet been engaged in the main theatres of war, only 'sideshow' campaigns. But the building up and training of substantial expeditionary forces was well underway and major engagements using them would soon be inevitable.

The War by Early 1915

On the European continent, the new year of 1915 remained grim. The British had repeatedly failed to break the German line despite releasing huge numbers of infantry, with the cavalry in pursuit. The Germans had taken some 19,500 square miles of French and Belgian territory and were managing to hold it. The British had recaptured eight square miles, at a cost of some 250,000 casualties.

The short period of the war so far had demonstrated a number of harsh realities.

First, the purposes of the war as ascribed by each side permitted no compromise and therefore the war would be much longer than might have been foreshadowed. The Germans had planned to take Paris within six weeks—this objective was now long gone.

Second, the scale of battle would not only be across a large number of nations; it would, for the first time in any war, be fought on air, land and sea.

And third, it would be waged on the level of what could only be described as wholesale, industrialised violence. The cavalry charge had become an anachronism; so had the British officer's sword, now jettisoned after only six months of fighting.

But in the immediate human dimension, namely the welfare of men and women, there was one more harsh reality of the most serious kind: anyone who came within the maelstrom would be likely to be damaged, and probably irreparably, either physically or mentally or both. The first four months of the war had demonstrated that it was naive to believe there might be any form of moderation to this new kind of warfare.

By 1915, these realities were likely to be best demonstrated on the Western Front in France. The Commander-in-Chief of the British

Army, Sir Douglas Haig, had made it very clear in March 1915 that the Allies could not hope to win the war until the German Army had been defeated in the place where it counted: France and Belgium.

Stalemate—Mid-1915

It was now some three months after the landing at Gallipoli by British, Australian, and New Zealand troops on 25 April 1915.

On 12 July, the day of Nelson's medical examination, British forces at Helles on the Gallipoli peninsula had launched an attack known as the Action of Achi Baba Nullah. Some Turkish trenches were captured but no significant headway was made. One unit—a battalion of the Kings Own Scottish Borders—lost more than 300 men killed and 200 wounded. At the end of the day, one British commanding officer wrote that the troops in one sector 'could not be induced to go forward'.

In France, the war had already bogged down. Generals on both sides remained impotent to affect a result. According to military doctrine, the art of winning decisively and quickly lay not in the destruction of soldiers, but in rendering the enemy incapable of further effective action. This was usually achieved by destroying the enemy's communications and then overwhelming their forces. But the system of fighting since August 1914 had already settled into trench warfare across France. Enemy communications could only be taken out if trenches could be breached. That would require a full-scale frontal attack.

To date, no side was achieving any success and tens of thousands of young men were dying in the course of failure. This was likely to continue into the foreseeable future. The Central Powers were opposed by Russia in the east and by the British, the French and the Belgians in the west. Although the German forces now marshalled were immense, they were not sufficiently strong to carry out offensive operations on both fronts, and so Germany had decided to hold one front, the west across France, and take an offensive stance on the other, the east near Russia. Australia's contribution to defeating that offensive eastern stance had been to send troops to Gallipoli. This, however, was having little or no effect.

However, the defensive position of the Germans in the west had given the French an opportunity at the end of 1914 to launch an offensive operation in the Champagne region. But by March 1915, this had achieved no real result. The British, too, had gone on the offensive in those months but they had made little progress either.

And during April and May 1915, the Germans had also decided again to go on the offensive, attacking at Ypres, a Belgium municipality, located in the Flemish Province of West Flanders. Ypres was no stranger to battle; the Romans had raided it as far back as the first century BC. Ypres and the French frontier were only several miles apart and for hundreds of years the town had been occupied by invaders, including the British in 1385 and again in 1680. By 1905 it was a quiet residential area having largely been deserted by commerce. Nevertheless, Ypres had a large number of beautiful buildings erected in the Middle Ages, including a rich Gothic architectural jewel, Cloth Hall. The whole Ypres region was now subject to competing military objectives and therefore crucial tactical battles.

The German attack on Ypres achieved some tactical success. This was due chiefly to the surprise use of poison gas as a weapon of warfare. However, the main strategic advantage of the Germans was that the battle was cloaking the movement of troops from the west to the Russian front.

Not only did the battle at Ypres have the distinction of using gas as a weapon, a new type of warfare was now coming of age: wholesale destruction of everything within range by a massive hail of shells from artillery power, including mortar fire. This was followed by the infantry taking and then occupying ground. For the first time in military history, the artillery would take the lead ahead of the infantry.

This change in the scale of warfare brought big problems for the Allies on a number of levels. Only heavy guns, not field guns, could destroy modern entrenchments and the enemy's munitions and armaments from as far back as the front. But the Germans had one heavy gun for each field gun, compared to the French, who had one in four, and the British, who had one in 20. The Germans were producing 250,000 rounds per day, compared to France at 110,000 and Britain at 22,000.

The war was being waged on a scale and dimension never before seen—and by mid-1915 the Germans held the upper hand.

The Allies had a further major problem. The French calculated they would reach the summit of their capacity by the autumn of 1915, but this meant the whole of the male population would be working for the war effort. In contrast, Britain's mass contribution was only just beginning and was not expected to be at full strength until the spring or summer of 1916, nearly a year away.

In consequence, the Germans were able to hold the Western Front defensively, while smashing the Russians in the east.

The radical changes to the machinery of war, and the extent of the now industrialised violence, was resulting in indiscriminate damage to an enormous number of men. It was also producing rampant disease and other ailments among the soldiers.

On the Western Front in France, no Anzac had yet arrived.

But with the acute shortages of manpower the British were now suffering, Australian boots would be marching that way, and soon.

Morale and War—1915

In May 1915, French Lieutenant Colonel Rousset wrote in Paris's most popular daily newspaper, *Le Petit Parisien*, that French troops continued to march into battle as they would 'to a party'. Another lieutenant asserted that the troops looked forward to the new offensives as they would a holiday: 'They were so happy! They laughed! They joked!' Another wrote how he could not conceive of life after war and affirmed that casualties and death were the exception in life at the front. The highly censored French press continued with a colourful array of inane and largely inaccurate platitudes to describe the continued failed offensives, appalling conditions and dwindling morale on the front.

On the home front in Paris, to many the war seemed almost distant. The primary concern for most Parisians was the cost of living, which had increased sharply since the outbreak of war. Concern for military operations was secondary, but this was largely due to a general confidence in a favourable outcome.

If the war felt distant to the Parisians, it was a world away for Australians back home. Yet every soldier's family knew that with the excitement of war came adversity and despair. The reports of major casualties at Gallipoli were already causing great concern across Australian society. A large number of Ballarat boys had already been fighting there and the casualty count was mounting. The town had already given a lot of its young men to the campaign. If they did not return, or returned damaged, this would have a profound effect, not only on the families, but on the whole rural region.

Gas and Other Weapons of Terror—Late April 1915

Although the Australian and New Zealand troops who had taken themselves out of the small rowboats and onto the rocky shores of Gallipoli did not know it, the Germans had in the same week of April 1915 discharged a new lethal weapon on the Western Front: chlorine gas from cylinders in order to hinder the British prior to the German attack at Ypres, Belgium. The attack, now the second at Ypres, saw German artillery bombardment followed by an infantry advance of some three miles.

Despite the use of the appalling gas, and the early gains made by its use, a lack of infantry reserves once again slowed the German advance.

Gas was not the only new weapon now under active consideration and use: the Germans had begun to use flamethrowers as tools of terror.

Each enemy was now in the business of exploiting huge manpower, with consequential mass wastage of life, and inventions for destruction had emerged. Anyone coming into this global fray would be punished by their deployment. And probably punished permanently.

Gas Use by the British—July 1915

By September 1915, the British had decided to attack the Germans at Loos. On the 15th of the month, six divisions went forward. But before that, the British had sought to put the Germans into disarray not only by the customary artillery barrage, but by the use of what was being described euphemistically as 'the accessory' weapon—cylinders which released chlorine gas.

This tactic backfired; much of the gas blew back into the British trenches.

As part of the attack the British had also used another form of missile launched at the Germans. The 1st British Battalion of the 18th London Regiment kicked a football toward the enemy lines while attacking. This was the first feat of so-called 'football bravado' recorded by the British.

The six British divisions were subjected to slaughter and the attack was called off after some 11 days of folly, adding 60,000 British casualties to the tally.

The commanding officer of the British army, Sir John French, had visited the troops several times during the weeks of battle at Loos. He travelled on a white horse, visiting the injured at first-aid stations.

More Men Needed—October 1915

By October 1915, Britain was short on volunteers and so the British Government introduced conscription, to commence in early 1916. Britain's society had run out of the 'willing'.

And by that same October, the British War Office was also calling for a new 'supply' route of men from the dominions: indigenes. On 8 October 1915, all Governors-General of the dominions, including the Australian Governor-General, received a confidential memorandum from the Colonial Secretary asking for a report 'as to the possibility of raising native troops'. The request asked for an estimate of the number which could be raised, the length of time needed to train them, and an opinion 'as to their fighting value'.

The next day, the French issued a decree offering war contracts to all French indigenous colonials for the term of the war.

Some of the dominions immediately commenced action to provide a meaningful response and contribution to Britain's request. Australia did not. There had been moves earlier in 1915 to create Aboriginal units but the military authorities had flatly rejected the idea. No Aboriginal would be fighting as part of the AIF until 1917.

Support for Returned Australian Soldiers—Early 1916

In February 1916, the Premiers of each State of Australia, together with their Ministers for Lands, held an interstate conference to consider draft plans for soldier settlement after the war. The money for the settlement initiatives was to be raised by the Commonwealth and lent to the States, who would take the benefits of the successes, but bear the burden of failures, in particular returned diggers who could not meet their loan repayments for any reason. Some saw an opportunity to use the thousands of 'diggers' who would inevitably return to establish new industries or resuscitate old ones. Others advocated the revitalisation of shipbuilding or the manufacture of china, tiles, cement, glass and similar products. Forestry activity was also promoted, in particular where soldiers would guard against pests and fire. It had even been suggested that broken and weary soldiers could take up the culturing of herbs, seeds and berries as women had already shown that they could make a success of this activity.

Whatever ultimate form of support would be decided on, the governments of Australia (Commonwealth and State) knew that there would be some very heavy lifting to be done to support a huge number of returned soldiers when the war ended. And the emerging central theme would be land settlement schemes, particularly in Nelson's home state, Victoria.

But there was also a more immediate problem with soldiers who had already begun to return home. Volunteer recruiting had to be continually stimulated to enable Australia to keep up its 'commitment' to the supply of able men for the war in Europe. There were two strategies employed to encourage recruits: one was to ensure that there was little or no sign of unemployed, destitute or troubled returned soldiers; the other was to demonstrate that, upon return, soldiers would be given some material rewards, such as land, either in rural areas or in the cities. This, together with promises of reinstatement to old jobs, or the provision of government jobs, and, as appropriate, generous pensions, would, so it was hoped, ensure that large numbers of volunteers would continue to show that the significant demands being made on Australian males would be met.

The grant of land was a large drawcard for recruitment. The early proof was that a large percentage of returned soldiers—some 6000 by the end of 1915, one-third of which had returned to Victoria—had indicated a desire to settle the land with the assistance of land grants.

The British Government had by 1916 become well aware of the Australian proposals for land grants which would permit returned soldiers to settle on land after their return. As far as the British were concerned, it was desirable that these support schemes permitting land grants should also apply to British soldiers. Accordingly, Sir Henry Haggard had been sent to Australia to persuade the State governments that British servicemen should qualify for land settlement entitlements after the war. At the conference of State Premiers in 1916, it was resolved to treat returned British soldiers in a manner similar to that in which returned Australian soldiers would be treated. Britain would, of course, under the proposal, provide funding for such activities.

The War and the Sea—31 May 1916

The war since August 1914 had largely been fought on land, although fighting in the air was becoming increasingly frequent and extensive. Despite Britain and Germany possessing two huge armadas, the two nations rarely faced each other at sea because the war was essentially land-based.

On 31 May 1916, the great two navies met in the North Sea. It would be the largest naval conflict in the war. Two hundred and fifty ships positioned themselves, and then attacked each other in what became known as the Battle of Jutland; although it lasted only two days, it was the greatest sea battle the world had then seen even though no submarines or aircraft took part. With its supposedly superior fleet, Britain had expected a second 'Trafalgar'-type victory, but this did not happen principally because the destructive power of its navy was enormous but its communications were antiquated—the British admirals insisted on using blinking lights and flags instead of the newly installed wireless devices. Fog caused the following collisions: two battle cruisers ran into each other; one battleship collided with a merchant ship; and three destroyers smashed into each other. Although the British fleet had sunk and damaged a number of major German ships, it could not claim victory. Germany had likewise inflicted more losses but could not rightfully claim victory; the Kaiser soon declared otherwise.

These sea battles were a long way from where Nelson would ultimately spend time in battle across France and Belgium but they were nevertheless highly relevant to his future. The Germans had failed to break the British blockade of supplies into Germany. Its navy remained therefore desperate to achieve blockades of supplies to Britain. Each nation was literally trying to starve the other. For as long as each army was undernourished and short of supplies, the will and capacity to wage a decisive offensive campaign would be difficult, if not impossible. Yet there was one important dimension to Germany's naval endeavours; Germany had in the same month as the Battle of Jutland agreed not to torpedo American passenger or merchant ships on their way to Britain and France. It kept its word until early 1917, when it began sinking merchant and passenger ships, bringing America into the war.

The Battle of the Somme—July 1916

In July 1915, a strategic conference of Allied leaders had been held at Chantilly in France. They had decided that only concerted and simultaneous attacks on the Germans would deprive them of their strategic advantages. And they had also decided that this should be done on the Somme.

But in February 1916 the Germans disrupted this plan with their surprise and massive attack at Verdun. Warfare had never before been so furious, with the initial shelling by the Germans lasting some nine long hours.

The Battle of Verdun would ultimately last several months, petering out in December 1916. The battle lasted 299 days. It left the French Army demoralised and, in some places, mutinous. The French had suffered 337,231 casualties with 162,308 missing soldiers, presumed dead. The Germans had suffered almost as much. By the end of the battle, the combined total was over 700,000 casualties. For that carnage, the lines had barely moved from February to December 1916. The main objective had been been *Blutabzapfung* (to bleed France white)—this had been achieved.

The 'distraction' of Verdun had caused the Allies to reassess the plan for the Somme offensive and it was reworked into a tactical offensive with a strategically defensive operation. This would force the Germans to fight on two fronts, and would provide some relief for the French from the trauma of the Verdun campaign.

The British High Command considered that more troops were needed for such a push and so summoned the Australian 1st and 2nd Divisions, and the New Zealand Division, together known as the 1st Anzac Corps, from Egypt, with the Australian 4th Division crossing the English Channel to join in.

The Allies' preliminary bombardment in the Somme region opened on 24 June 1916, with the British shelling the German defences for eight days. The British fired a million and a half shells on the enemy, using 1537 guns. In the last hour, the barrage reached fortissimo at nearly 225,000 shells into the German-held territory. Although it was out of earshot of Nelson at Harefield, the residents of Kent could hear the rumble.

Three times the number of British troops used at Loos, namely half a million men, had gathered along a front stretching 18 miles. A quarter of them would attack on 1 July 1916. Preparations had been extensive. Communications would not be the problem; some 70,000 miles of telephone cable had been unrolled in the lead up to the initial engagement.

The enemy's position was very different. No major German attack had occurred for a year and a half on the Somme sector of the front; they had stuck to the business of building defences for that whole period.

On 1 July 1916 the artillery shifted to more distant targets and 11 British divisions climbed from the trenches. The infantry moved forward in waves to the assault across a 23-mile front.

The first Battle of the Somme was underway. The British had mounted a seven to one infantry advantage over the Germans.

Haig, a deeply religious man, had written on 22 June 1916, before the attack: 'I feel that every step in my plan has been taken with the Divine help.'

The attack again took in the now established British convention of kicking a football towards the enemy. On 1 July 1916, Captain WP Nevill, a company commander in the 8th East Surreys, brought four footballs to battle, one for each platoon. He offered a prize for the platoon who at 'jump off' first kicked the ball to the German front line. The captain was killed instantly.

The Germans, even with only six divisions, were up to the task of holding their position. They rose from their deep dugouts and with machine guns soon ready, began hosing down the British infantry. Of the 110,000 British attackers, 60,000 were killed or wounded on the first day. The day of Britain's greatest single day of bloodshed had arrived: 21,000 soldiers had perished by the end of that day. Haig had scribbled in his diary: 'This cannot be considered severe in view of the numbers engaged, and the length of the front attacked.'

In the several weeks before, an Old Etonian dinner of British officers had been held at the Hotel Godbert in Amiens. One hundred and sixty-seven had attended; of those, more than 30 had died on the first day of the battle. The artillery bombardment's more distant targeting had broadcast the infantry's every move, and this hopeless lack of surprise had produced mass carnage.

After the first week, Haig received intelligence assessments of progress. On 9 July 1916, he was assured that if the offensive were maintained for six weeks, the Germans would ultimately run out of infantry reserves.

Those assurances were in fact false. The attempts to break through the German lines on the Somme continued and lasted many months. The Allies mustered 750,000 men, of which 80 per cent were British and the rest French. Twenty-seven Allied Divisions fought 16 German divisions. Multiple attacks by the British and French were met by multiple counter-attacks by the Germans. The German Chief of Staff had told the German infantry that not one foot of ground was to be lost. That objective was ultimately met.

In the initial stages, the Australians were still on their way to Europe from Egypt and so did not take part in the shocking early days of the battle. However, by July, the 1st, 2nd and 4th Divisions and the New Zealanders had arrived, in considerable numbers: 40,000 Australians and 18,500 New Zealanders. They marched down from Armentieres and joined the attack on the ridge at Pozieres on the Somme. The

5th Division, with its 15th Brigade and 15th Field Ambulance, had already seen battle at Fromelles. Although they had not been used at Gallipoli, the Australians were now issued with steel helmets for a different kind of warfare: mass destruction by mass artillery fire.

Even though the majority of the AIF was now in France, the Allies remained permanently short of men. It was therefore inevitable that the British would seek as much further Australian and New Zealand manpower as they could get their hands on. It was also inevitable that once they had arrived, those additional resources would be deployed at the Somme.

Notes to Part II
In War

Conscription in Australia—1916

The voting form Nelson Ferguson filled out in October 1916 reflected the patriotic groundswell for conscription back in Australia although there was in fact significant opposition from certain religious groups, in particular the Catholic Church, and the labour movement. By mid-1916, the Prime Minister of Australia, Billy Hughes, having returned from England, was convinced of the manpower difficulties of the Empire. He was determined to follow the example of Great Britain and introduce conscription for military service. Hughes was backed by Universal Service Leagues across Australia who were demanding the introduction of the policy, and the principal newspapers were strongly in favour of it. And by this time, the recruiting figures were declining, after some 200,000 men had enlisted in the 12 months following the Gallipoli landing in April 1915. Politicians and the public recognised that the annual quota of 198,000 men being asked for by Hughes could not be obtained by voluntary enlistment alone.

Back in Australia, the referendum for the conscription bill was held 10 days after Nelson voted, on 28 October 1916. Nelson Ferguson's home state of Victoria, together with Western Australia and Tasmania, voted yes (totalling 1,087,557), the other States voting no (totalling 1,160,033). The vote was accordingly defeated. Many in Australia had thought that the spirit of the Australian soldier as a willing combatant defending liberty would be defeated by conscription; others were appalled by the casualty rates so far and could not bear further damage being done to a whole generation of young Australians.

The question of conscription would remain on the agenda, despite proving itself a political liability: Hughes's attempts ultimately ensured that he was expelled from the Labor Party and the question ultimately split the labour movement.

Unlike the other Allies (aside from South Africa) Australia was maintaining the voluntary nature of its army.

Australians and Gas—Late February 1917

The Germans and the British were not the only ones to use gas. In late February 1917, Major General Monash of the AIF ordered that smoke and gas shells be used in preparatory bombardments of divisional artillery around Ypres, Belgium. But when the AIF attacked, only smoke shells were in fact fired. This meant the attacking Australians would not be affected but the Germans would be tricked into keeping their gas masks on, making them the less effective enemy. Eventually, both sides deployed this tactic.

The Health of New Australian Recruits—March 1917

On 30 March 1917, Major General Howse of the AIF wrote to General Fetherston, also of the AIF, complaining of the unsatisfactory result arising from the lowering of the enlistment standards. (Howse was a significant figure in Australian military history—he had been conferred the Victoria Cross for his services in the Boer War, the first such recipient serving in the Australian armed forces.)

Howse had been given command of Anzac medical services in September 1915 and in November of that year became director of the AIF's medical services, with the rank of surgeon-general. When the AIF moved to France, Howse had taken up a position in London, overseeing medical services in France, Egypt and Palestine.

Fetherston had volunteered for active service but on 15 August 1914 the Commonwealth appointed him director-general of medical services, based in Melbourne, with the task of raising the medical service for the AIF.

Howse wrote:

I am trying to arrange transport for two or three thousand 'B' class men; they are absolutely unfit for service. Many of them do not disclose any organic disease upon a carefully conducted clinical examination, but are in and out of hospital, and are quite useless for front line, and practically useless for Home Service…Far better no reinforcements be sent from Australia as they do no duty, and only cause congestion in our hospitals and Command Depots. The class of reinforcements you are sending are not up to the old standard. Headquarters AIF Depots report that 20 per cent are unfit for the front line.

The lowering of the height standard from 5 feet 6 inches to 5 feet 2 inches, the reduction in the required standard of vision, and the acceptance of men with minor defects had given the AIF significant problems operationally. For special units additional lowering had been approved. Men for railway sections and mining corps could be up to 50 years of age. Men needing glasses were allowed to enter the Australian Services Corps (ASC), Australian Medical Corps (AMC) and ordnance corps. And men with minor and curable conditions suitable for operation could be taken into a military hospital for treatment if they agreed to enlist for general service and to being discharged if the treatment did not work, and not to claim compensation or a pension. This method was ultimately abandoned because so many men pleaded disability from the operations and were discharged.

Overall, approximately three per cent of AIF reinforcements sent to France were being assessed as unfit to begin active front-line service and were now being turned around and sent back home to Australia.

Nelson was not in this 'B' class group. For someone who had been in the trenches and stretcher-bearing for some six months now, he remained relatively lean and fit. The war had not destroyed his immune system yet and he was capable of surviving and being productive despite the horrendous conditions he was living and working in.

Time to Recruit a New Class—March 1917

With the failure of the vote in October 1916 for conscription, and the return of 'B' class men back to Australia, the Australian Government was continuing to look for ways to bridge the shortfall in volunteers. Australian forces had suffered nearly 50,000 casualties between July 1916 and April 1917, 27,000 of those in the Somme offensive.

Recruiting was significant in 1915 at 165,912 and in 1916 at 124,355 volunteer soldiers, but the numbers from the beginning of 1917 had dropped off significantly.

In March 1917, although there had been no amendment to the *Defence Act* which prohibited Aboriginals participating in the defence force, a memorandum was issued by the AIF stating that 'half-castes' may be enlisted, provided that the medical authorities were satisfied that one of the parents was of European descent. Shortly after that, a further change permitted Aboriginal recruits who were closely associated with white Australians, including those raised in white families.

Despite such inclusion, the war would not see the formation of any Aboriginal unit.

America Joins the Fight—April 1917

By early 1917 the French were not the only ones in dire straits. By early April 1917, things were extremely serious for the Germans.

They had withdrawn to the Hindenburg Line in late 1916 to recover from the intense fighting in the Somme which had commenced in July of that year. While they had somewhat regrouped in the Somme by early 1917, the Allies had damaged the German Army badly.

That was, however, not the only dramatic change which had gone against Germany. Despite having agreed in 1916 to cease sinking passenger ships (which was putting Americans at risk) in early 1917 Germany resumed all-out submarine warfare. It was now once again sinking ships on sight, without warning, including passenger and merchant vessels bound for Britain and France. This was in direct breach of Germany's undertaking to America made in May 1916.

On 4 February 1917 America had shown its disdain for Germany's actions by severing diplomatic relations with Germany. This was fantastic news for the French. At a performance of *Madama Butterfly* at the Paris Opera Comique, the second act commenced with 'Yankee Doodle Dandy' when the US ambassador took his seat.

But with the sinking by Germany of further ships in March and early April 1917, America had had enough. On Good Friday, 6 April

1917, America declared war on Germany. Not only had war been declared, but now a further and more fundamental declaration was being made—the leadership of America had tasked itself with ensuring that 'the world would be made safe for democracy'.

All participants recognised this as a turning point in the war. But Germany's hope was that it could still win major contests, and ultimately defeat the Allies before America had time to gather military momentum (which would take many months). Although many nations suspected that America could build an unstoppable army in the foreseeable future, it was starting from a very low military base. The question being asked by both the Allies and the Central Powers was: could America get to Europe in time?

None of these events, including America's declaration of war, were pencilled into Nelson Ferguson's diary.

The Allies Deteriorate Badly—Spring 1917

In the spring of 1917, things deteriorated dramatically for the Australians and British on the Western Front. This was due to one incredible and largely unforeseeable event.

Since the beginning of the war, the French Army had borne the brunt of the offensives on the Western Front. But by now it had taken all it could bear and morale had simply collapsed. Almost three years of low pay, meagre rations, poor leadership and appalling physical conditions had taken its toll. In addition to an enormous mobilisation of men, France had suffered the additional indignity of being partially occupied throughout the majority of the war. For the French, it was a total war, akin to those fought during the Revolution, when every citizen was mobilised for the war effort. This too had taken its toll on civilians.

In the lead-up to the last days of April 1917, the new French Commander-in-Chief, General Nivelle, had ordered an offensive on the Chemin des Dames. The first large-scale tank attack, followed by some 52 French divisions, was on 38 German divisions, capturing a few miles of ground, and taking some 20,000 German prisoners in the first few days. But still there was no breakthrough. This seriously demoralised the French—so much so that on 29 April 1917 things came to a head. Mutinies began across the French Army. There were roughly 250 incidents of mass insubordination—68 divisions out of 112 reported 'acts of collective indiscipline'—with the most common action being soldiers refusing point-blank to take up positions and instead staging anti-war demonstrations. The desire to advance against the German Army had, at least for a short time, left the French soldier.

For the British and Australians, however, this meant one thing: they would be called on to do yet further heavy lifting in battle so that the French Army could recuperate and rebuild.

French Recovery—May 1917

By mid-May 1917, the French leadership had taken its first step towards restoring its army. It sacked General Robert Nivelle and replaced him with General Philippe Pétain. Pétain was a somewhat more intuitive and pragmatic leader who quickly made some positive reforms in food distribution and leave policy, satisfying many of the concerns of a large number of the French troops. More importantly, Pétain made it clear that there would be no further ill-conceived, poorly planned offensive campaigns that had merely succeeded in demonstrating to the infantry that the upper command considered it to be disposable.

Over the next several months the French Army would slowly rebuild its capability to fight alongside the British, Australian and other Allied troops. Until then, however, the Allies would be expected to shoulder both attack and defence. Both activities caused damage and death. And therefore both activities would involve Nelson.

A New Allied Offensive on the Western Front— 7 June 1917

The early work on the Avenue of Honour in Ballarat had commenced in mid-1917 in expectation of an eventual peace, but across the globe the war continued to rage, and plans for further long-term warfare were well underway.

By mid-1917, General Douglas Haig had transferred his focus to Ypres, Belgium, even though this was not within the zone of strategic operations originally intended. There were major areas of the Somme where communications had been devastated. German submarines in the English Channel, North Sea and elsewhere upon vital British supply routes were causing food shortages in Britain, and the Second British Army would soon be stationed at the nearby Messines-Wytschaete Ridge.

The Ypres initiative was intended to have the Germans concentrate on the British, so that the French Army, whose morale had collapsed, could recover. Pétain, the head of the French Army at the time, had earlier appealed to Haig to take over almost the whole burden of the Western Front so the French Army's morale could be rebuilt.

There were other reasons for the proposed Ypres offensive. It would enable the Allies to address the German submarine crisis. And the British Army would also attempt to penetrate all the way to the railway system through Liege.

On 7 June 1917, the offensive commenced. The objective was to take Messines Ridge, south of Ypres. In the preceding two years, not less than 19 tunnels had been dug beneath the German positions, which were now filled with explosives. These were discharged as the offensive commenced.

The Germans were demoralised by the biggest explosion in the history of warfare. They were pushed back some 2000 yards, their trenches being taken by a relentless push by the Allies.

The French Army received the relief it needed, with only two soldiers per yard of the front line compared to the German's six. This enabled it to recover its fighting spirit, but the British suffered severely under atrocious and abnormally wet conditions.

The British in turn were also looking for relief and in that regard there was also expected to be a revival of fortunes lying ahead for the Allies; the first contingent of American troops were due to arrive in France very shortly, in late June 1917.

Another Vote—December 1917

In April 1917, Australia had taken yet further steps to keep its volunteer numbers up. It had in that month, for the third time since the war started, reduced its height requirement for eligibility into the AIF. It was now 5 feet, from 5 feet 2 inches.

But by late 1917, Australia's contribution to the war effort by the provision of its generation of young men (and in some cases, their fathers) had continued to stall. The government felt it needed to act. In order to seek to boost the vote, it had repatriated 'B' class men from Europe, on the basis that this might improve the likelihood they would vote in favour.

And in December 1917, the Australian Prime Minister, Billy Hughes, once again put a plebiscite to the Australian people, seeking compulsory enlistment of all those who could fight. Those born in foreign countries could not vote even if they had taken out British citizenship; nor could their children. They would not be allowed to wreck the vote.

The Prime Minister was frenetic in his attempts to achieve an overall 'yes' from the public. On 10 December 1917, he spoke at a rally at the Melbourne Cricket Ground. Eggs, road gravel and glass bottles were thrown at him and the rest of the dignitaries, including the speaker, at the rostrum.

As with the first vote in 1916, the Australian people gave a decisive 'no' vote; more so than they had the first time. There would be no further debate and, accordingly, no further vote. The AIF would remain, as it had been since the start of the war, an entirely voluntary military force.

The Allies Restructure—Early 1918

In February 1918, General Ferdinand Foch, who had been recalled as the Chief of the General Staff of the French Army in 1917, took the chair of a new Executive Military Council comprising a French, a British, an American and an Italian general. Its establishment was in lieu of the appointment of a single Allied Commander-in-Chief. The restructure failed to ensure unity of military effort.

The Russians, under Bolshevik leadership, had by now pulled out of the war, negotiating a treaty with the Germans. Accordingly, no Russian representative sat on the council.

By March 1918, the situation had become critical and the Allies agreed to abandon the council; instead of the council's workings, Foch would 'coordinate' the Allied Forces.

One month later, Foch was appointed the Commander-in-Chief of the Allied Armies in France and Belgium (excluding the Belgian Army).

This single leadership structure was the first in the war for the Allies. And it was the first stage of a number of leadership initiatives that would change the course of the war.

The German Spring Offensive—March 1918

Throughout the winter of 1917–18, following the collapse of Russia, German troops had been streaming from east to west, resulting in an increase in German numbers by some 30 per cent on the Western Front. Trains carrying four newly freed German divisions rolled westwards. By March 1918, the Germans had superior numbers there. This gave the Allies serious problems, not with offensive operations, but with seeking to establish defensive measures. The Allies had simply not had the time or the men to construct major defensive zones to push the Germans back.

As a consequence, and taking into account that the Americans were arriving in increasing numbers on the Western Front, the Germans decided to launch a new major offensive in early 1918.

Of the three areas considered, the Germans selected the Arras–Le Fere area, hoping to break through between Arras and Peronne and drive the northern Allies back towards the sea, attacking the French using mobile forces.

Arras was 30 miles due south of Peronne (the distance between them being the pathway the Germans would take) and Amiens (their target) was 30 miles to the east of Peronne.

On 21 March 1918, the Germans attacked across a 74-mile front on the Somme. They emerged from the safety of the Hindenburg Line at dawn. The air was filled with smoke and gas, the German infantry continuing to wear their gas masks for some 12 hours. The preceding creeping barrage was epic in its scale, with the firing of some 6400 guns and 3500 mortars on the British positions, combining high explosives with gas shells. More than a million shells were fired in a five-hour period.

The attack had been expected for some time and the Minister of Munitions, Churchill, had decided to visit divisional headquarters to see the event unfold. He described it in the following eyewitness, yet removed, terms: 'Exactly as a pianist runs his hands across the keyboard from treble to bass, there rose in less than one minute the most tremendous cannonade I shall ever hear.'

The onslaught of artillery fire for such an extended period, followed by German infantry attacks, forced the British and French to cede ground. It did not help that Haig had, just before the attack, granted leave to some 88,000 British troops. There was a further reason for the Germans' success: instead of long lines of advancing infantry, the army had been retrained to act in small units of seven to 10 soldiers, as 'storm troopers'. Low hanging fog had assisted that initiative even further.

After four days, Germany had reached the old 1917 trenches and Peronne and Bapaume, where Nelson and Pomp had been bearing, was retaken.

By 24 March 1918, the Germans had pushed forward 14 miles, the farthest of any force since 1914. Paris itself came under artillery fire on 25 March.

It was a stunning victory but at great cost to all; there were some 150,000 British casualties, 77,000 French casualties, and 250,000 German casualties. British casualties over the next several days rose to 300,000.

The Germans met some resistance but less so in the south and therefore the army at the left side of the front was reinforced to take advantage of the progress made there, directing the reinforcements (the 18th army) at Amiens and beyond.

The German advance had put Amiens in danger, and the German Army was now heading towards the small town of Villers-Bretonneux and would soon be there if they proved able to take tactical advantages early.

The German offensive continued yet further into Allied territory. On 28 March 1918, the Germans attacked near Arras, seeking to drive to the Channel coast at Boulogne, where Nelson had first disembarked from his channel crossing. Following a ferocious barrage, nine German divisions attacked four British ones, who were nevertheless able to repel the invader.

Villers-Bretonneux—Early April 1918

In early April 1918, the German offensive and the various advances made as a consequence continued to cause the Allied leadership great concern because, should they have gained momentum, the Germans might well have been able to push on to Paris. As a consequence, the British Forces and the AIF attempted significant moves to halt recent gains by the German Army across the region of the Somme. It was in fact the 5th Division of the AIF that would act as reinforcements, including the 13th Field Artillery Brigade, arriving at Amiens after several days' travel.

By early April 1918, the Germans had advanced some 40 miles and were, as a consequence of the depth of their positions across 30 miles, now holding an additional 1200 square miles of invaded French territory.

The Germans now pursued their drive towards Villers-Bretonneux. The Germans attacked the centre and to the left of the French First Army, which initially fell back, but counter-attacked. British and Australian troops of the 14th Division, the Australian 35th Battalion and the 18th Division held the line from north to south.

By 4 April, around Hamel the German 228th Division attacked the 14th Division and it fell back. The 9th Bavarian Reserve Division was held off by the Australians whilst the British held off the Germans. But the Allied forces pulled back because the British 14th Division retreated.

The Australian 15th Brigade reinforced the line west of Hamel but the Germans pushed the 18th Division in the south. It seemed Villers-Bretonneux would ultimately fall to the Germans.

Although the Germans came within 440 yards of the town, on 4 April the 35th Battalion and others made a surprise counter-attack. As they advanced using section rushes, the Germans were pushed back. Two German divisions were force to retreat from Villers-Bretonneux.

By the end of the German offensive on 5 April 1918, 90,000 British and French soldiers had become prisoners.

The retreating British Army bore heavy casualties. The British Secretary of State for War dutifully wrote to the parents of the dead:

The King commands me to assure of the true sympathy of His Majesty and the Queen in Your Sorrow. He whose loss you mourn died in the noblest of causes.

The message appeared on a standard condolence card.

The shortage of British soldiers since just after the beginning of World War I was unabated. The solution for the present was to move more divisions from Palestine and Italy to the Somme. And there was yet two further initiatives put into place: the minimum conscription age would be lowered to 17½ years; and conscription would be extended to Ireland.

Villers-Bretonneux—A Long History of Invasion —April 1918

The town had a long history of conflict. The Villaria, which gave its name to the first part of the town's name, was crossed by the Roman road between Amiens and Saint-Quentin. The second part of the town's name refers to the Breton Mercenaries the Romans had posted there as auxiliary soldiers.

From the earliest times, its geographical location had placed the town inexorably on the road of invaders. The Normans had ravaged the entire region in 853; it had been pillaged many times by the English during the Hundred Years' War. In 1417 it was destroyed by the Burgundians; in 1636, the Croatians of the Spanish army Aet houses and castles on fire; in 1815 during the Napoleonic Wars, the Cossacks indulged in systematic pillaging; and they were followed by the Prussians in 1870.

Although the Germans had not taken the town this time, the British and their Allies knew that it was considered to be strategically significant, if not vital, to Germany's push to Paris via Amiens, with its rail and commercial links. If the Germans took Villers-Bretonneux, they could fire on Amiens with heavy artillery and then attack that with infantry. If Amiens fell to the Germans, so too might Paris itself.

By early 1918, the Germans were readying themselves to launch another attempt to take Villers-Bretonneux. This occurred in two waves in April 1918.

The Red Cross and Gas—April 1918

In the first week of April 1918, the International Red Cross had tried to assert its influence to restrict the use of poison gas against troops and civilians. The French Government at once intimated to the Red Cross that they would be willing to give up using poison gas if the Germans were also willing to abandon it.

But in that same week, on 6 April 1918, Winston Churchill, the Minister for Munitions, wrote to the French Minister for Munitions, Loucheur, in the following terms:

> I am much concerned at the attitude taken by the French representatives at the Conference held last week on the Red Cross suggestion of the willingness of the German Government to abandon the use of poison gas. Apparently France is strongly in favour of our offering to give up this form of warfare, or at any rate of accepting a German offer. I do not believe this is to our advantage. I hope that next year we shall have a substantial advantage over them in this field. Anyhow I would not trust the Germans' word. They would be very glad to see us relax our present preparations, allow our organisation to fall into desuetude; and then after an interval, in which they had elaborated new methods, they would allege that we had broken the arrangement and, perhaps even without this pretext, resume gas-warfare on the largest scale.
>
> I am on the contrary in favour of the greatest possible development of gas warfare, and of the fullest utilisation of the winds, which favour us so much more than the enemy...

The Allies did not use mustard gas until November 1917 at Cambrai, France, after capturing a stockpile of German mustard-gas shells. It had taken the British more than one year to develop their own mustard-gas weapon, but now they were good at it and Churchill did not want it stopped.

Churchill's view prevailed. In the month following his letter, over one-third of the shells fired by the British Army were gas shells. Between

April and August 1918, the production of gas shells increased by over 100 per cent. By the end of that period, Britain was manufacturing some 795 tons of shells a week.

The Germans were not ready to down tools on the use of poison gas either. The strategy to maim, displace and demoralise soldiers through the use of gas reached its crescendo in April and May 1918.

Women and Munitions—1918

While Australians at Harefield hospital and at home were celebrating the third Anzac Day, on that very day, 25 April 1918, the House of Commons in the English Parliament was receiving a munitions update.

Although around 1000 heavy guns and 5000 machine guns had been lost or destroyed since 21 March 1918 when the major German 'spring' offensive began, out of the factories of Britain there had been produced more serviceable guns than the ones lost, and more of practically every calibre. The same was true of aircraft. Further, every tank lost had now been replaced by newer and better models.

The House was further told that despite this level of make-up, the present problem for England was a shortage of manpower. Since May 1917, the Ministry of Munitions had released some 100,000 men for use by the army, and since the German offensive on 21 March 1918, the release of men from munitions-making had increased to 1000 per day. In other words, men were moving from munitions manufacture to fighting and this was causing shortages in munitions supply. The solution, the House was told, was for men in England to volunteer as munitions workers.

The House was told that this process had in fact already occurred of sorts when some 1500 firms had provided workers over the Easter holidays for armaments-making. The House was most grateful to hear this.

But there was even more praise in the House for the significant number of women munition workers who had now taken up the cause. In particular, some 750,000 English women were now being employed in the Ministry of Munitions. In fact, by April 1918 more than nine- tenths of all workers making shells were women. They were now providing the labour force necessary to ensure the continuing power and terror of the British artillery—even though virtually none of them had even seen a lathe before the war. These were not the only British women who were contributing to the war effort. The Women's Army Auxiliary Corps had been established in December 1916 (later renamed Queen Mary's Army Auxiliary Corp), after a War Office investigation had shown that many jobs done by British soldiers in France could be performed by women.

By the end of April 1918, the violence across Europe continued to be seemingly inexhaustible as governments remained determined to use whatever means available to keep the supply of deadly weapons up to the front lines, including deploying mothers and daughters to make killing equipment. This endless activity of war was resulting in two things: mass destruction and mass killing.

The Allied Offensive—Mid-1918

By mid-1918, the Allies were engaging in a major offensive against the German Army, which was largely in retreat. American involvement was both substantial and crucial.

The Americans had not been put off by the sea of reports regarding the carnage on the Western Front. Recruiting was from the time of conscription by America in 1917 strong and continuous. It was, for the young American, just as for the young Australian, an opportunity for adventure and heroism, one that could not afford to be passed up.

Since January 1918, the number of American troops into France had escalated at incredible rates: in January, 13,000; February, 17,000; March, 19,000; April, 24,000; May, 33,000; June, 41,000; July, 54,000. And in August and September the numbers would be yet higher. By autumn 1918, four million Americans were serving in the armed forces. Half of these young soldiers were boots on the ground in France.

As to the standard of fighting expected of them, according to one report, when asked by a Digger 'Are you going to win the war for us?' the American replied: 'Well, we hope we'll fight like the Australians.'

The arrival of the Americans in huge numbers was a godsend to the British. In July 1918, Churchill described it in these terms:

When I had seen during the past few weeks the splendour of American manhood striding forward on all the roads of France and Flanders, I have experienced emotions which words cannot describe. Britain's reward for answering the appeals of Belgium and France in 1914 was not territorial or commercial advantage but the supreme reconciliation of Britain and the United States. We seek no higher reward than this supreme reconciliation. That is the reward of Britain. That is the lion's share.

For Churchill the wind was in the Allies' sails. He considered that with America's might now present in France, the war would necessarily be won. It caused him in July 1918 to reflect on Britain's path to that point:

I am persuaded that the finest and worthiest moment in the history of Britain was reached on that August night, now nearly four years ago, when we declared war on Germany.

The AIF were involved in attacks along the Morlancourt Ridge, culminating in the capture of Hamel, and then in the major Allied offensive in August, when they captured Mont Saint-Quentin and penetrated the Hindenburg Line.

In these attacks, the AIF had been used as 'shock troops'. According to Haig's Chief of Staff, 'There were certain divisions which if given a thing to do would do it. All the Australian divisions are in that category.' In the last offensive, although the Australian Army Corps represented less than 10 per cent of the whole of the British divisions engaged on the Western Front, they were able to capture 23 per cent of the guns and prisoners taken.

Apart from the raw courage displayed by the Allied and American troops, the Americans were also providing an additional vital element to victory: enormous raw artillery firepower.

Simultaneously, the British Army advance was taking place near Saint-Quentin–Cambrai and the Belgians too were advancing near Ghent. By this time, half the British infantry was less than 19 years of age.

Losses from World War I

On 11 November 1918 the guns on the Western Front and elsewhere stopped barking. Between 1914–18, on that front, more than 700 million artillery and mortar rounds had been fired.

The losses across England, France and Russia, and other warring nations, were immense.

The British losses are recorded on a tablet in virtually every cathedral in France:

To the Glory of God and in memory of one million men of the British Empire who died in the Great War and of whom the greater number rest in France.

About 12 per cent of all British soldiers who participated in World War I died. It was 19 per cent for peers or sons of peers. Of those young men who graduated from Oxford University in 1913, 31 per cent were dead.

By the war's end, Britain had thrown at the war effort nearly all its men capable of fighting; only 20,000 would refuse conscription.

By the end of the war, British clearing stations had admitted 160,970 gas casualties, of which 77 per cent were from mustard gas.

France lost nearly two million: two out of nine who marched to war. The majority of them were from the infantry, which had lost 22 per cent of those enlisted. Half of the French soldiers between the ages of 20 and 32 were dead. By the end of the war, there were 630,000 French war widows. Amongst the unspeakable tragedies of the war were the nearly one million French orphans.

More than two million Germans died in the war, or of wounds after it. More than 35 per cent of those between the ages of 19 and 22 had been killed. Serbia, whose population was five million, lost 125,000 soldiers but more than 600,000 civilians succumbed to disease and other influences, making up 15 per cent of the total population.

Of the over five million wounded in the war, several hundred thousand, known as 'grands mutiles', had lost limbs or eyes.

Overall, the war had cost the Central Powers some three and a half million men, and the Allies, five million.

On 11 November 1918, there were 95,251 AIF soldiers on the Western Front out of a total of 178,426 in the AIF, with 58,365 in England on that day.

By the end of the war, the AIF's casualties by theatre were: Mediterranean expeditionary forces/Gallipoli: 8159 (deaths), 17,924 (wounded), 102 (prisoners of war); Western Front: 46,960 (deaths), 131,406 (wounded), 3853 (prisoners of war); Egyptian expeditionary force: 1282 (deaths), 2617 (wounded), 129 (prisoners of war); United Kingdom: 1938 (deaths), 1 (wounded), n/a (prisoners of war).

Between April 1916 and the end of the war, 11.8 per cent of battle casualties were from gassing.

The 15th Field Ambulance formed part of the 5th Division within the AIF. By the end of the war, the 5th Division's casualties were: killed in action: 5716; died of wounds: 1875; other deaths: 684; prisoners: 674; wounded: 23,331; total: 32,180.

By the end of the war, chemical weapons had lost much of their effectiveness against well-trained and equipped troops. Nevertheless at Armistice, chemical weapon agents had inflicted an estimated 1.3 million casualties.

Around 420,000 Australians had enlisted for service in World War I. When the war broke out, the British Empire comprised some 400 million people. Australia had therefore contributed a mere one-tenth of one per cent of that figure to the war effort. But it had been asked to do some extraordinarily heavy lifting as a nation—its individual contribution represented a staggering 10 per cent of its population overall, and moreover some 38.7 per cent of the male population aged between 18 and 44.

The Australian contribution was in those terms 'generational' in scope.

The official record is that some 580 Aboriginals fought in the AIF, of whom 83 were killed, 125 wounded and 17 were prisoners of war. Casualty rates were only two-thirds that of white Australians who fought, as Aboriginal recruitment began after the major campaigns of mid-1916 to early 1917, and because around a third of Aboriginals were in mounted units which had lower casualty rates than the infantry.

For those who gave the ultimate sacrifice, only one soldier's body would be returned home to Australia. It was that of the man who founded the name the 'Australian Imperial Force', Major General William Throsby Bridges. He had been killed by a sniper's bullet at Gallipoli in May 1915. Initially buried in Alexandria, Egypt, he was later reinterred at the Royal Military College, Duntroon, in Canberra.

Australia had thrown its shoulder to Britain's call for manpower in a supreme way. Its initial contribution of 20,000 men in November 1914 had increased some twenty-one fold.

Britain's initial strategic reliance on the navy had proved to be ill-directed. By reason of the positioning of Germany and, in turn its arch foe, France, the war was always going to be a manpower fight, overlaid with massive artillery power. Britain had not figured on material air force participation, but its initial fleet of 60 odd aircraft at the start of the war had grown to 22,171 aeroplanes by the end. And Britain's manpower contribution to the war in France had ultimately been pulled from two sources: conscription from British civilians; and a calling out for participation by the dominions, principally Australia, New Zealand, Canada, and South Africa. The British Army had grown from 730,000 men and five divisions to some 3,560,000 and 50 divisions, drawn from initial volunteers, the so-called Territorial Army in 1915, Kitchener's New Army in 1916, and conscripts in 1917 and 1918. Of Britain's total population of 46 million in 1914, six million had mobilised and five million had served in the theatre of war in some fashion or other.

Britain's officer ranks alone had soared from 12,000 at the beginning of the war to some 124,000 by the end. Hundreds of thousands of British men had died in the war. Of those, the single greatest soldier tragedy was that over 300 of them had been shot by the British themselves, principally for desertion. The Germans shot fewer.

By its multi-resourcing strategy, Britain had been able to assist in giving France what was needed to push over the Germans. Australia had punched above its weight. Nelson was part of the heavy lifting, as were some 420,000 other Australians, let alone those who had supported the war effort from home.

The dominions had provided enormous manpower resources to Britain when called on to do so, ranging between eight to 13 per cent of their total populations.

Of all the other Allies assisting the cause, including New Zealand, Canada, India and elsewhere who had made immense contributions, it was the Americans who had finished off the job of defeating Germany; it had put millions of men into Europe in 1918 and that sheer number of troops had overwhelmed the Germans both physically and morally.

British and Commonwealth soldiers would now lie in 400 cemeteries across the Somme battlefield, along a 20-mile avenue.

These numbers of dead and injured across dozens of countries were huge but yet insignificant in one tragic respect; for every dead or injured soldier, nurse or other participant in World War I, there would be family members who would have to endure heartache over what had happened to their loved ones and the demands injury might make for years to come, if not a lifetime. And those loved ones were in the tens of millions.

From War to Peace—1919

The sounding of the bells across Europe and in England on the eleventh hour, of the eleventh day, of the eleventh month had caused Nelson and his digger mates to reflect on past, present, and possible future deeds.

As he waited for Big Ben in London to tell that the war was over, Churchill himself described the minutes before that time through the Empire's prism as he then saw it:

My mind strayed back across the scarring years to the scene and emotions of the night at the Admiralty when I listened for these same chimes in order to give the signal of war against Germany to our Fleets and squadrons across the world. And now all that was over! The unarmed and untrained island nation, who with no defence but its Navy had faced unquestionably the strongest manifestation of military power in human record, had completed its task. Our country had emerged from the ordeal alive and safe, its vast possessions intact, its war effort still waxing, its institutions unshaken, its people and

Empire united as never before. Victory had come after all the hazards and heartbreaks in an absolute and unlimited form. All the Kings and Emperors with whom we had warred were in flight or exile. All their Armies and Fleets were destroyed or subdued. In this Britain had borne a notable part, and done her best from first to last.

There was no direct mention in this reflection of the heavy lifting that the dominions had performed. No mention of the dominions having engaged some 10 per cent of their entire population directly in the fighting. No mention of Australia having handed over nearly 40 per cent of its young men to the war effort, most of whom had already or would soon return damaged and broken in some shape or form. No mention of Australia having one of the elite fighting armies of all time. And no mention of Australia having provided the leadership on the Western Front which would ultimately be a significant cause of the enemy's collapse. Issues of this very kind applied to the other dominions as well.

The reason for the silence lay not in any fundamental leadership failing to give due recognition for the immense support the dominions had given. It was this: the dominions were legally, culturally and therefore intrinsically regarded as part of the British Empire.

The end had brought a new beginning, and with it difficult questions:
My mind mechanically persisted in exploring the problems of demobilisation. What was to happen to our three million Munitions workers? What would they make now? How would the roaring factories be converted? How in fact are swords beaten into plough-shares? How long would it take to bring the Armies home? What would the soldiers do when they got home?

The last question posed by Churchill was a critical one, not only for Britain and its soldiers, but for all of the soldiers of the dominions, including Australia.

The soldiers would be entering a no-man's-land of a different kind. The phrase had not existed prior to January 1915. It had been picked up by the French, who had used *la terre neuter* (neutral ground) initially but switched to *le nomansland* during the war; and by the Germans, who had used *vorfeld* (the ground in front) but had switched to *der niemandsland.*

Economic Parameters of War—1914 to 1918

World War I pushed Australia's economic development on and on. Britain had effectively funded a war-related boom; the demand for wheat and wool during the war meant that Australia's current account was in surplus, due principally to customs and excise receipts. Britain had subsidised various markets with the guarantee of prices in excess of those prevailing within the United Kingdom or within Australia's domestic markets. And beginning in 1916–17, London had bought the entire wool clip of Australia and New Zealand at a price 55 per cent higher than before the war.

But the war had still cost Australia a staggering £333.6 million. Funding for it had come essentially from three pockets: the Australian Government had borrowed £43.4 million from Britain (the mother country had felt obliged to make this loan even though Australia's economy was largely self-sufficient); the Australian Government had also borrowed £188 million from Australian families (in six war loans spread across 1914–18); and finally it had introduced estate duty in 1914, income tax in 1915, and a war profits tax in 1917, so that by 1920, £71 million in revenue had been raised from these taxes for war-related purposes.

Funds had also been raised for other purposes. Within Australia during the war a number of patriotic funds and appeals had been established to send money and goods to France. The French Red Cross Society of Victoria had been established in 1916 by a French citizen resident in Melbourne, Charlotte Crivelli. The society distributed 'comforts' to French soldiers. Fundraising by the society had raised in the order of £80,000 during the war. Overall, Australians raised some £700,000 for the French apart from the goods and other in- kind donations out of various other patriotic funds. France was not alone; the Belgians received £320,000 from Victorians alone.

The net effect of the war on Australia's economy was negative. Real wages were five per cent lower in 1918 than in 1915. For Britain's part, the war had taken a heavy toll on its finances. Its external debt at the end of the financial year 1918–19 stood at £1364.8 million, of which £1162.7 million was owed to the United States and Canada.

The British and French war effort in 1918 had been dependent on American finance; each country would have gone broke if the United States had not provided substantial loans. Up to March 1917 alone, Britain borrowed a staggering US1.5 billion from America. But the loans were not a one-way street. As early as the beginning of 1917, if not before, the United States had realised that the inevitable consequence of a bankrupt Europe would have been the end of trans-Atlantic trade, and with it dire financial consequences for the United States itself. From 1917 therefore, even without the increasing introduction of the enormous American Army into the battlefields of Europe, the fortunes of both Britain and the United States had become inseparable: the former out of sovereign survival; the latter out of economic imperative.

The Prime Minister of Australia, Mr Billy Hughes, attended the Peace Conference held by the Allies and others after the war. He had told those organising it that the dominions should attend not only as part of the British Empire but also as contributors to the Allied victory in their own right. He duly attended in those capacities. He told those present that he represented the 'sixty thousand dead', more than those lost to America. Hughes claimed every Australian who had purchased a war bond was entitled to reparations and claimed £464,000,000 from the Germans, including £264,000,000 for actual war expenditure. Australia was ultimately paid £5,500,000.

But the overall penalties imposed on Germany were staggering and would have long-lasting effects upon the economy, society and national morale. The desire to impose severe penalties had been growing for years prior to the Armistice. That desire had been expressed by Churchill in July 1918 in these terms:

Germany must be beaten; Germany must know she is beaten; Germany must feel she is beaten. Her defeat must be expressed in terms and facts which will, for all time, deter others from emulating her crime, and will safeguard us against their repetition.

Churchill went on to say that once the war was over, the German people must be treated with 'wisdom and justice'. However, this aspiration would, by November 1918, be forgotten by the victorious Allies.

Notes to Part III
Into Peace

Anzacs Returning Home – 1919

Thirty-two thousand, four hundred and twenty soldiers and others returned to Australia from the conflict in the first quarter of 1919. Eventually, a total of 264,373 soldiers returned home. Of those, the army had classified over 102,000 as sick or wounded.

According to the army the military task of returning the soldiers was 'superior to anything with which we were connected during the war'.

A Marking of the Standstill—1919

Shortly after the end of the war, many European countries commenced the process of marking out significant battlegrounds and sites. Others commenced the making of memorials and monuments to victory.

Marshal Pétain, the leader of the French Army at the time of Armistice, was an early initiator. In 1919 he directed that metre-high marking stones be imposed into the ground to record the points at which the German advance had been stopped.

Such stones were placed around the Ypres Salient and at 'Hell Fire' corner itself.

On each of the stones was inscribed, in three languages: 'Here the invader was brought to a standstill 1918.'

A Perpetual Assurance Given to Australia—July 1919

In other parts of Europe, memorials were being conceived in memory of those who fought, those who died, and those from other countries who had made significant contributions to the Allied cause.

In mid-1919, the ruined town of Villers-Bretonneux lay within the Somme, ruined by war.

Shells around the town continued to explode without warning, killing and maiming locals. Australians continued living in the area into 1919, carrying out grave work. The battlefields remained devastated.

But powerful memories remained of what the Australians, including the 5th Division, had done there.

On 28 June 1919, the combatants signed a Peace Treaty at Versailles. In Villers-Bretonneux, the residents held a Peace Ball. The mayor of the town presented a memorial tablet to the diggers present, telling them the memory of the Australians 'will be always kept alive' by the townfolk. He told them 'the burial places of your dead will always be respected and cared for'.

The memorial tablet in remembrance of Australian soldiers who had been killed there read:

The first inhabitants of Villers-Bretonneux to re-establish themselves in the ruins of what was once a flourishing little town have, by means of donations, shown a desire to thank the valorous Australian armies, who with the spontaneous enthusiasm and characteristic dash of their race, in a few hours chased an enemy ten times their number … soldiers of Australia, whose brothers lie here in French soil, be assured that your memory will always be kept alive, and that the burial places of your dead will always be respected and cared for.

Spirits Enlivened—the Anzacs—1920

On 2 December 1920, and some six months after the grand opening of the Arch of Victory at Ballarat, the *Protection of Word 'Anzac' Act* of the Commonwealth of Australia came into force.

Regulations were subsequently made under the Act to the following effect.

By operation of law, use of the word 'Anzac' or any word resembling the word 'Anzac' was prohibited in connexion with any trade, business, calling or profession or in connection with any entertainment or any lottery or art union or as the name or part of the name of any private residence, boat, vehicle or charitable or other institution, or any building in connection therewith, unless the minister authorised it.

It was prohibited to use the word 'Anzac' on any goods manufactured, produced, sold or offered for sale and as the name or part of the name of any firm or company registered in Australia. Trademarks and designs could not be registered if to do so would offend the prohibition.

However, the word 'Anzac' could be used for so-called 'entertainment' if it was held on 25 April in any year or on consecutive days.

Similarly, a name of a street, road or park could not use the word 'Anzac' or any word resembling 'Anzac'. This did not apply to public memorials relating to World War I (later this included World War II). However, streets, roads or parks that contained the word 'Anzac' or any word resembling the word 'Anzac' prior to the new prohibitions could keep their names.

By these and many other means, the Commonwealth of Australia had set about ensuring that the reputation and esteem of the name 'Anzac' would be protected for all time.

By reason of World War I, Australia now had a national military heritage upon which to pin its nationalism and its culture. The Australian Government had now determined that that nationalism and culture should be enshrined in legislation to apply across the vast continent.

The Anzac spirit, having originated on 25 April 1915 at Gallipoli and confirmed on 25 April 1918 at Villers-Bretonneux, now had legislative force intended to ensure that that spirit and its sentiment, upon which the blood of so many young Australians had been spilled, could never be misapplied. The Gallipoli campaign, together with that at Villers-Bretonneux, although not far-sighted in design, had created a nation and the spirit of it was now being perpetually recognised within five letters.

With the coming into being of the legal structure protecting the sanctity of the Anzac spirit, it would not be long before the Australian Imperial Force would be disbanded. On 1 April 1921, it officially ceased to exist. But it would not be long before each State of Australia would declare Anzac Day a public holiday, for commemoration and reflection.

But there was yet another spirit to be honoured and enlivened too. After August 1912, Australia had not played a cricket test match. With the war at an end, that inevitably would change. In December 1920, England, under the auspices of the Marylebone Cricket Club, toured Australia in a five-test series. Australia won the series five–nil. Equivalently, an AIF cricket team successfully toured the United Kingdom after the war.

Whether an Anzac or a cricketer, with effect from 1 January 1921 onwards, every Australian would be deemed a 'British subject' by operation of the Commonwealth *Nationality Act 1920.*

Funds for Villers-Bretonneux—July 1921

By now, there were huge demands on the public purse for the support of a large number of war-related relief and charity initiatives. The Victorian Villers-Bretonneux Fund which had been established in 1920 had hardly got started.

The promoter of the Villers-Bretonneux cause in Melbourne, Charlotte Crivelli, was now seeking to raise substantial funds for the orphans, mothers, little children and old people of the town. Rather than being a Melbourne fundraising effort, the fundraising would now be State-wide. The funds would go to the 'tortured soil of France'. A strong fundraising set of initiatives was undertaken, including meetings between the Lord Mayor of Melbourne and other mayors across Victoria to encourage the arrangement of fundraising activities.

By August, there was considerable force behind the fundraising. Some £22,000, above the target of £20,000, was reached, much to Crivelli's pleasure. Over £10,000 came from the public, the rest from the Victorian Department of Education.

Major General Sir John Gellibrand, now the President of the Fund, declared that Villers-Bretonneux would now 'remain a place of pilgrimage for all Australians'.

Other Patriotic Funds—1922

But the Melbourne Villers-Bretonneux Fund was not the only fund for providing relief from the effects of war.

As far back as August 1914, when the war had first broken out, the Victorian Education Department, which Nelson was then serving in, had established its own Patriotic Fund. The fund enabled staff and students across Victoria to contribute to the war effort from the home front. The fund would provide comfort for Australian soldiers abroad, assist returned soldiers, and provide relief from distress among Allied nation civilians.

During the war, some £422,000 was raised for these purposes, and in 1922 there remained almost £100,000 in the Fund.

Frank Tate, a director of the department and chairman of the fund, had since 1921 been a big supporter of the Victorian Villers-Bretonneux Fund as a beneficiary of the department's fund. In particular he had proposed a specific and worthy object for funds: the reconstruction of the Villers-Bretonneux school, which had been destroyed in 1918.

A number of Australian soldiers had in fact begun rebuilding the school in 1918 but they had returned to Australia, and there had been no funds to enable the reconstruction to continue. Now this would be solved. The Education Department's fund would provide the very considerable grant of £10,000.

Church Stained-glass Windows in Remembrance of Service—1920s onwards

Prior to the end of World War I, and into the 1920s, it had become popular for Victorians to invest in stained-glass windows in remembrance of sons and fathers who had given the ultimate sacrifice in World War I.

Their history as an art form had not been a uniform one but the medium was now well established in Australia.

They had flourished across the great churches of the 12th to 14th centuries in Europe but by the 18th century it was almost extinct as an art form. It was only by reason of Britain's so-called return to 'true principles' in the 19th century that a new awareness of the importance and value of stained-glass windows emerged. This had been pioneered by Gothic revivalists: Ruskin, Pugin, Barry, Pre-Raphaelites and William Morris, the great interior designer of Britain.

This Gothic church revival of stained-glass windows had been transported to Australia along with the arrival of the first free settlers in the first half of the 19th century.

By the late 1850s, gold production in Victoria was globally significant and the tent and shantytowns of the early goldmining towns were now being replaced with significant residential and commercial buildings.

The building boom included new and substantial churches, which looked to install stained-glass windows if able to be sourced. Churches initially turned to well- established British firms. But the opportunity for local production presented itself and, shortly after their arrival in 1852, two Scots, James Ferguson and James Urie, established their own stained-glass business in Melbourne.

Their windows were largely based on established glass patterns from English designers; however, Ferguson and Urie took in a new partner, John Lyon, who began to develop designs himself.

As Melbourne and its surrounds continued to grow and prosper into the 1870s and beyond, stained glass was enlisted to display the position and status of wealthy businessmen and land- owners.

But Ferguson, Urie and Lyon were not the only business in Melbourne. By the late 1860s, another firm, Brooks, Robinson & Co, was providing significant competition. Henry Brooks had arrived in Australia in 1853, at just 24 years of age, intending to be an agent for his father's glass and china exporting business in London. Edward Robinson joined him in 1869 and they promoted their business as among other things 'importers of plate and sheet glass'. By around 1882, the firm was producing stained glass. The firm would later be selected to install windows in the significant St Paul's Anglican Church in Melbourne. On that occasion, the windows were in fact imported from Clayton & Bell, London. The firm was one of the largest importers of historiated glass windows.

By 1891, Brooks, Robinson & Co had expanded their business and had premises at 59–65 Elizabeth Street, Melbourne.

But it was not only glass that was needed. The glass pieces were joined together using lead, and, by 1864, the Melbourne leadworks operated by J McIlwraith & Co was rolling lead for local glass firms.

But by the time of Australia's Federation in 1901, new architecture, including the Federation-style bungalow house, no longer required a great staircase and windows. Instead, decorative leadlight was all that was required. Nevertheless, there were still at least seven firms around Australia, employing up to 40 people, producing stained glass.

But now that World War I was at an end, widows and families of men killed in action in Turkey, France and elsewhere deserved commemoration, and stained glass would become the desired medium for meeting that need. The tradition and sacrosanctity associated with stained glass appealed to those who wished to mourn formally and reflect openly.

The first commissions for memorial windows had commenced even before the Anzacs' Gallipoli landing in April 1915.

But now, with the war over, commemorative windows began to be constructed all over Australia. Many of them reflected Australia's close ties with the mother country and saints such as St Alban, Britain's first martyr-saint, as well as the patron saint of England, St George. These would represent the best of the British soldier and, as a consequence, the Australian soldier too.

The windows themselves became a form of headstone and were unveiled with great formality. Windows could thereby be used as places of pilgrimage and private prayer if need be.

Later, parish and community stained glassworks became more dominant in lieu of works dedicated to individuals.

The work output of the stained-glass-window making firms was significant. Apart from Ferguson, Urie and Lyon, and Brooks, Robinson & Co, the firm of William Montgomery produced some 80 windows for Victorian churches from 1915 to 1927.

In 1915, Trinity College in Melbourne retained Montgomery to design a window in memory of Captain O'Hara, on behalf of O'Hara's father. The captain had died in France on 13 February 1915, the first of more than 20 former Trinity scholars killed in action.

Another memorial set of windows was commissioned by Geelong Grammar School in Victoria; each of the individual windows was a memorial to former students killed during the World War I. The windows were designed and produced according to the messages of St Luke and St Mark (in 1918), St John and St Matthew (also in 1918),

St Stephen and St James (in 1918), St Michael and St Gabriel (in 1919) and St Andrew and St Patrick (in 1920).

Yet another major window was designed and installed by Montgomery in St Columb's Anglican Church in Hawthorn, a suburb of Melbourne. It was unveiled on 14 November 1920, the Sunday after Armistice Day's second anniversary. The service began with 'God save the King'. The window was unveiled by Lieutenant General Sir Harry Chauvel, who had held a significant role at Gallipoli and who had commanded the Australian Light Horse in Egypt. Chauvel declared the window 'to the soldiers of this Church who died in the Great War'. The messages on the window depicted service, sacrifice, and victory.

Other windows with war motifs were installed into large Melbourne buildings. These included a large three-light window at Melbourne Teacher's College, dedicated in 1920. The window features an Australian digger, flanked by a long list of names of all of the college men and women who had volunteered, and those who had paid the ultimate sacrifice. An Australian flag billows out behind the soldier. The rising sun badge shines above the soldier's head, halo-like in form. Originally conceived as a window that would feature a medieval knight or Roman soldier, the designer, William Wheildon of Brooks, Robinson & Co, chose the Australian soldier as the expression of the ideal of courage. The window did not sit within a church, but rather a large college. It depicts Australia's involvement in World War I at Gallipoli as part of the mythological development of Australia's nationhood.

At the top of the window is the college's motto: *Non omnis moriar* (Not all of me shall die).

The figure of the Australian digger was later accepted in religious settings including church windows in other parts of Victoria, including Heyfield, Geelong and at Malvern.

Soldier Settlements—1919 and following

Many suburbs of Melbourne had land allocated within them for returned soldier homes: East Malvern, Hampton, Spotswood, West Coburg and Surrey Hills.

An area of Hampton comprising 67 acres was acquired by the War Service Homes Commission in 1919, with the estate largely complete by 1929. In Hampton, the street names include Amiens, Villeroy, Passchendaele, Imbros, Rouen, Hamel, Lagnicourt, Favril and Avelin.

The area in Spotswood was 49 acres and in West Coburg, 77 acres.

The Surrey Hills area forms party of a leafy eastern suburb. In August 1920, a small subdivision was completed for war homes. The streets in the subdivision were named: Amiens Street, Lille Street, Marne Street and Verdun Street. By 1925, soldiers had started to live in those streets and, several years later, the 51 war service houses were occupied.

Shortly after the war, soldier settlements occurred in other States of Australia, including in Queensland, south of Toowoomba. Some 40 families took up soldier settlements there. On 16 June 1921, a small school was established there: Pozieres State School, with 17 pupils. The towns of Pozieres and Amiens are joined by the Amiens Road (which joins with the Bapaume Road), all south of Toowoomba, Queensland. The Passchendaele State Forest is adjacent to these towns.

The School at Villers-Bretonneux—25 April 1927

The fighting on 25 April 1918 at Villers-Bretonneux had left not only the town itself, but also its boys' school, in ruins. By 1927 the Victorian Education Department's Fund grant of £10,000 had been spent and the rebuilding of the school was complete.

The new school's inauguration was on Anzac Day 1927.

The school would have a new name from that day on: Victoria College.

And the school hall would permanently record the obligation the school had imposed on itself: 'Never forget Australia.'

It was opened in the presence of a large assembly of French, British and Australian ex-servicemen, the Australian High Commissioner (Sir Granville Ryrie), and the Agents-General of the Commonwealth. The Imperial War Graves Commission was also represented. Hundreds of schoolchildren participated in the dedication ceremony in which Australian flags took a prominent part, hanging from many windows.

Poppies and the Menin Gate Memorial—July 1927

The year 1927 was some 10 years after Nelson had been part of one of the largest and deadliest battles in World War I, the third battle of Ypres, in Belgium. He had been in that maelstrom from September 1917 until early November of that year.

Hundreds of thousands of men had died at Ypres in the three major battles there between 1915 and late 1917. The poppies that had sprung up from the Ypres battlefields, immortalised in the poem 'Flanders Fields', would later become a symbol for lives lost in war.

The Australians, New Zealanders and other Allied soldiers, including Nelson and Pomp, had accessed the battlefields of the third battle of Ypres via the infamous Menin Road, on which sat the also infamous Menin Gate itself.

The battles in and around that area had caused mass harm and death to the Allied soldiers and those of the Central Powers. It had been from the Menin Gate itself that hundreds of thousands of men had set out on the Menin Road for the front line.

Now the site of the Menin Gate would be the place for a memorial for those soldiers who had died in battle.

On 24 July 1927, Field Marshal Lord Plumer unveiled the Menin Gate Memorial, designed by Sir Reginald Blomfield with its sculptures by Sir William Reid Dick. British and Belgian brass bands sang the sound of sorrow into the large civilian and military crowd. Black flags had been raised in the surrounding area. Plumer told those assembled that it could now be said of each one in whose honour those present were assembled that here today: 'He is not missing; he is here.'

The Menin Gate is a classical victory arch together with a mausoleum. Carved into the Memorial are the names of 54,896 officers and men of the forces of Australia, Canada, India, South Africa and the United Kingdom who died in the Ypres salient for whom there is no known grave. As originally designed, Menin Gate was not ultimately large enough to record the names of those who died, and accordingly the record ends as at 15 August 1917. New Zealand casualties who died on and prior to that date are commemorated on memorials at the Buttes New British Cemetery and at Messines Ridge British Cemetery. The names of a further 34,888 men who died between that date and the end of the war and who also have no known grave appear on the Tyne Cot Memorial.

The Menin Gate recognises all the warriors from many nations who had paid the ultimate sacrifice. But it, like all other war memorials, including the 2500 British war cemeteries in France and Belgium, would also ventilate the existence of that other group of men so central to war matters: the enemy.

Support for Those Who Returned—1931

By 1931, the number of people receiving AIF pensions peaked at 283,322. Less than one-third of these were for returned soldiers; the other two-thirds were for wives, widows and children of the dead or disabled servicemen and women. Over 74,000 soldiers had applied for vocational training, of which over 27,000 had completed their courses. The children of soldiers who had been fatally wounded or wholly incapacitated were educated at public expense. Ultimately, under the *War Service Homes Act*, over 37,000 soldiers, including Nelson, were able to buy or build homes after the war. There were virtually no arrears owed by the servicemen and women some 20 years later. The settling of soldiers on the land was much less successful. Often the land was ultimately considered to be unsuitable or too highly assessed in value compared to its economic output. Nearly one-third of the soldiers who took up rural land schemes failed on the land. An enquiry into the stress and failure rates caused the government to write off large loan balances. Returned Soldiers' League, the Sailors' Imperial League and Legacy were among many community-based organisations which assisted returned soldiers and their families to cope with the aftermath of war.

The Aboriginals had effectively been excluded from the land grant schemes of the State governments as established at the end of World War I. Some Aboriginal reserve land was in fact seized, or reduced in size, with the Aboriginal residents being relocated in order to provide land to white veterans. Of the 580 Aboriginals who served in the war, only one, from New South Wales, was allocated land under soldier settlement schemes.

Closing Out Britain's Long Reach—1931

In the same year as the death of two great Australian soldiers, Pompey Elliot and John Monash, Britain decided it should free Australian federal laws from the supremacy of British law. Under the *Colonial Laws Validity Act (UK) 1865*, British laws overrode colonial laws, and later federal laws of Australia, if inconsistent. Now, with the passing of the *Statute of Westminster (UK) 1931*, this regime would no longer apply to Australian federal laws. This change required Australia's assent, which would not be given for another 10 years. But the serious vestige of the Empire embedded into Australian federal law was now on its way out.

But at this time the laws of the States and Territories of Australia continued to be subject to British law.

At least federally, Australian laws governing Australians would no longer be dependent on British law. The nation had taken yet a further step towards independent adulthood.

The Ablest Australian Soldier Goes—13 August 1940

On 13 August 1940, a small plane flew over Canberra, the capital of Australia since 1913. At 11 am, it crashed near the aerodrome, killing all onboard, including one of the soldiers who had landed at Gallipoli on 25 April 1915, Brudenell White.

White was one of the founders of the Australian Imperial Force, its tactical and administrative commander in all but name. No single man had done more to form and develop the AIF than White, and now one of its creators and key sponsors had gone.

Charles Bean, the prolific Australian historian of World War I, called White 'the greatest Australian he had ever known'. General Monash described White as 'far and away the ablest soldier Australia ever turned out'. Sir Robert Menzies, the Prime Minister of Australia, described him as the 'very model of everything that an Australian should be'.

In the year of his death, White had been recalled from retirement to become chief of the general staff of the Australian Military Force in defence of the nation in World War II.

As rain fell, the 150 motorcars in the cortege moved from Middle Creek, White's residence, to Buangor Cemetery, 180 kilometres west of Melbourne. Returned soldiers from Ararat and Beaufort preceded the hearse, followed by dignitaries from the Commonwealth and from the local area.

White was on any view one of the greatest Australians of the 20th century. His contribution to the defence of Australia was immense.

Stained Glass—1947

Stained glass had fallen into heavy demise by 1940 as it was considered non-essential to the war effort (one firm, Yencken, having closed down in accordance with a government directive). However, after hostilities had ceased, there began a resurgence of interest. Following the end of World War II, the firm of Brooks, Robinson & Co, established in 1882, was producing a significant body of glassworks. In particular, there was now a strong demand for traditional designs and repair work that had not been attended to during the war. And there was also a heavy demand for war memorials of glass and windows to celebrate the centenaries of many country towns. The firm had a large number of employees, including glass painters, designers, draughtsmen, cutters, puttiers, glaziers and outside workers. This worker group was able to produce not only traditional windows but large commercial leadlights, including for shops.

Notes to Part IV
Providence

A New Gallipoli Medal—March 1967

In March 1967, the Commonwealth of Australia, with the New Zealand Government, instituted the Anzac Commemorative Medallion.

It would be awarded to surviving members of the Australian and New Zealand forces who served on the Gallipoli Peninsula, or who directly supported the operations from close off shore, at any time between the first Anzac Day in April 1915 and the date of final evacuation in December 1915. Next of kin or other entitled persons would be entitled to receive the medallion on behalf of their relative, if the relative had died on active service or had since died.

The obverse of the medallion depicted a great Australian at Gallipoli, Simpson, and his donkey, who carried wounded soldiers to safety during the campaign. This was bordered on the lower half by a laurel wreath above the word ANZAC. The reverse (the back) showed a relief map of Australia and New Zealand superimposed by the Southern Cross. The lower half was bordered by New Zealand fern leaves.

No equivalent medal was issued for the campaigns on the Western Front, including those for the diggers who had fought at Villers-Bretonneux.

Aboriginals and the Constitution—27 May 1967

On 27 May 1967, Australia held a referendum, following which its Constitution was amended. Now Federal Parliament could, for the first time since 1901, enact laws for the 'Aboriginal race in any State' and Aboriginals would be counted in the census.

Historical Matters

Australian Cricket

Cricket is a sport much loved by Australians. The first recorded cricket match in Australia was in 1826.

The first cricket match between the colonies of Victoria and New South Wales was held in March 1856. The winning team, New South Wales, had all but one player Australian born. In contrast, the Victorian team had only migrants.

The first English side toured the country in 1861–62, playing only against odds. In 1868, an Aboriginal cricket team was sent to England, the first organised tour of any Australian cricket team to be sent overseas. The Aborigines played 47 games, with 19 draws and an equal number of wins and losses. Each match was followed by a round of 'native sports', spear and boomerang throwing.

The first match on equal terms in 1877, played at the Melbourne Cricket Ground, resulted in a win for Australia. In 1882, the Australian victory at the Oval in England had prompted the lament that English cricket was 'dead', and that only its 'ashes' remained to be carried to Australia.

In Ballarat, cricket had been played since its establishment as a town. The town had in fact hosted international and interstate matches as early as 1862 when the first English touring team captained by HH Stephenson of Surrey played a XXI from Ballarat. In the 1911–12 tour by England of Australia, England had won the series 4–1, based on six ball overs and timeless match lengths. Many of the Ballarat locals had taken the train to Melbourne for the Melbourne Cricket Ground test held in February 1912.

The History of Stretcher-bearing

The history of stretcher-bearing could be traced back to the Napoleonic forces. They were the first to start the early systems for caring for the wounded in battle. The *brancardiers* (French for bearer) removed casualties from the battlefield and, later, ambulance wagons were introduced. The British also established field hospitals, emphasising hygiene with and among soldiers as part of early medical practices in warfare. The Battle of Waterloo in 1815 showed signs of these developments, but casualty evacuation still remained non-systematic. At that time bandsmen brought the wounded to surgeons (although this did not include drummers). The bandsmen were untrained in medical procedures and stretchers were rare, apart from makeshift ones.

Later in the 1800s, animal-drawn stretchers appeared, as did chairs carried between two mules, known as cacolets, which were used in the Crimean and American Civil Wars. In the Union Army in America wooden handheld stretchers were widely used. During the Civil War, more than 50,000 of these had been engaged.

There were two types of stretcher-bearer in the AIF.

The first were non-medical corps, namely regimental bearers, who wore on their arms the letters 'SB'. These were classed as combatants, part of a fighting unit. Their job was to go to the wounded in the field, give first aid to those who could not take cover, and take them to Regimental Aid Posts. There, a regimental medical officer would give pain treatment, rest, food and water, and sort the men according to the degree of wounds. A ticket describing the soldier's condition would be tied to him and he would then be sent back to an Advanced Dressing Station (known as an 'ADS') close to the front of battle, or Casualty Clearing Station, a Main Dressing Station, or a hospital.

The second type of bearers were men from the ambulance units. Unlike the regimental bearers, the ambulance bearers were from the Australian Medical Corps. They each wore on their left arm a red cross on a white background. A field ambulance unit comprised some 224 men, including 112 bearers. Their task was to carry wounded from the Regimental Aid Post near battle, to the next form of relief, such as an ADS. From there, often wheeled transport, cars or other equipment, and sometimes horses, would carry the wounded further back. Relay posts some 400 yards apart were often dotted along the route from the battle line to the Regimental Aid Post.

Both regimental and ambulance bearers often came under heavy fire. Gallipoli had already shown this to be a danger.

There was one fundamental but largely theoretical difference between the regimental and ambulance bearers; the former were combatants, the latter were not. Therefore only ambulance bearers received the protections afforded under the *Geneva Convention*.

The tradition, starting at Waterloo, of using bandsmen as stretcher-bearers continued for the British Army and within the AIF. This was particularly so for regimental bearers, but also ambulance bearers too. Music could stir the troops to battle, but was largely redundant in the thick of war. Ambulance bearers could also spread their time between music practice and bearer training. Musicians were also often better educated and therefore could receive medical training more readily.

The Role of the Field Ambulance

The overriding strategy of an army is not to kill the enemy; it is to render it ineffective. In seeking to do so, an army must avoid rendering itself ineffective by self-harm. This can take two forms: insufficient preventative medicine, including the hygienic practices necessary to keep the men fit; and not having adequate facilities to enable the injured to return to fitness quickly so the fight could be continued by them. An effective army was one that understood and applied these 'preventative' and 'return to fitness' strategies better than the enemy. Field ambulance work was at the core of these strategies; the army simply could not function without them.

The job of the field ambulances was to take the wounded back to casualty clearing stations; small hospitals generally located at a railhead or similar transportation hub in forward areas. The clearing station would provide emergency treatment and move casualties back to the stationary and general hospitals.

The AIF was in the process of learning that in any great battle some two to five per cent of all battle casualties (other than from gassing) would, if lives were to be saved, require special arrangements for ensuring early and effective first aid, if not on the battleground then at 'field' hospitals. For the rest, success in their treatment was largely determined by an exact and early categorisation of them into stretcher cases, 'sitters' or 'walking wounded', and then making special arrangements for the transport and treatment of each class accordingly. The Australian Medical Corps had developed a basic principle of ensuring successful evacuation of the wounded under all conditions and irrespective of circumstance. Another basic principle lay in adapting arrangements to address all physical, physiological, and pathological wounds and illnesses no matter how they arose in all types of warfare and in every battle.

Port Phillip Bay

Port Phillip Bay had been discovered in 1802 by Matthew Flinders. In that year acting Lieutenant John Murray, commanding HMS *Lady Nelson*, had taken possession of Port King (as it had been earlier called) in the name of His Sacred Majesty George of Great Britain and Ireland. Near the mouth of the port, later named Sorrento, Murray had hoisted the Union Jack for the first time. The Union Jack became a symbol of Australia's early democracy, maturing 50 years later, at the Eureka stockade just outside Nelson's hometown of Ballarat.

By 1803, Lieutenant Governor David Collins of the British Admiralty had been charged with establishing a penal colony within Victoria. Collins ordered that Aboriginals must not be killed or wounded, and that violence to Aboriginal women would be punished by death. The colony had started off well.

However, by 1804, without a ready supply of drinkable water, Collins had relocated his settlement to Hobart, Tasmania. The British did not return to Port Phillip for some 30 years, until 1835, when a settlement of Tasmanian civilians gave rise to the establishment of the city of Melbourne.

Pomp's Home State—South Australia

The first site of British settlement was in 1836, on Kangaroo Island, some five months before the city of Adelaide had been established. The State came into being under the British *South Australia Act 1836*.

Britain had earlier claimed the area of the State in 1788 as part of the colony of New South Wales. Under the Act, the State was to be convict free, Aboriginal land ownership was acknowledged, and the Aboriginals were guaranteed occupation and enjoyment of lands actually occupied. South Australia was in these terms a progressive colony. It proved that case by granting women the vote, and enabling them to stand for Parliament, in 1894, a world first.

Alien Germans in Australia

Despite the fact that many men of German heritage were keen to enlist in the AIF, and did so, the continued presence of those with German heritage in Australia was nevertheless used as a method of propaganda in order to foster enthusiasm for the war.

In 1914, the Defence Department had initially set up internment camps to detain 'enemy aliens' and prisoners of war, who for the most part were the crews of German commercial ships that had been apprehended upon the declaration of war. However, the scope of this policy was soon expanded as the military began to arbitrarily arrest those of German descent with whose conduct 'they were not satisfied'.

South Australia, in particular, had a large German community at the time and a Spartan camp was set up on Torrens Island in Port Adelaide to house those under suspicion. Brutality at Torrens Island was notorious and ultimately led to its closure in 1915, while its commander Captain Hawkes was investigated. This anti-German feeling was systemic, ideological and continuing: South Australia would ultimately ban the teaching of German in schools, and towns with German names would have their names anglicised. In some cases Germans were deported back to the country from which they had emigrated. German businessmen were interned under the *Trading With the Enemy Act 1914*.

The Quarantine Station at Portsea

The quarantine station was in fact adjacent to the Portsea fortification Nelson had sailed past on his way to war in 1915. The station was 70 years old. With the discovery of gold in 1851 the steady flow of immigrants sailing into the Port Phillip District became a flood. Within a year nearly 100,000 people had arrived in Melbourne by sea. Due to the crowded conditions on board, ships were breeding grounds for disease. Cholera, smallpox, typhoid, influenza and measles occurred in epidemics in the 1800s and caused many deaths. To control and prevent the spread of these diseases Point Nepean was opened in 1852 as a maritime quarantine reserve. Ships carrying passengers with infectious diseases were required to land all cases there. Now it included returning soldiers.

Medals

For some soldiers, if they paid the ultimate sacrifice, yet another commemorative medal would be delivered: a 'dead man's penny'.

It would come with a letter from King George V stating:

I join with my grateful people in sending you this memorial of a brave life given for others in the Great War.

The 'penny' was in fact a memorial plaque, issued after the war to next of kin of all British and Empire service personnel killed. The plaques were made from bronze, like the penny. In all, 1,355,000 plaques were issued across the British Empire, and continued to be issued into the 1930s to commemorate people who died as a consequence of the war.

The image on the plaque was of Britannia holding a trident and standing with a lion. In Britannia's outstretched left hand she holds an oak wreath above the rectangular tablet bearing the deceased's name cast in raised letters. The name did not include the rank so no distinction would be made between the sacrifices of different individuals. Two dolphins swim around Britannia, symbolising Britain's sea power. A second lion tears apart the German eagle. The reverse is blank, making it a plaquette.

Around the picture the legend reads:'HE DIED FOR FREEDOM AND HONOUR'.

For the 600 plaques issued to commemorate women:
'SHE DIED FOR FREEDOM AND HONOUR'.

But not all Australian families were happy to receive the commemorative medallion; some returned them in protest for the loss of their loved ones.

As a unit, the 15th Field Ambulance received no battle honours during World War I. However, medallions for specific acts of gallantry were awarded to specific stretcher-bearers and others.

But it remained unclear for some time whether the highest award, the Victoria Cross (VC), could be conferred upon stretcher-bearers. The first direction issued by the British high command in late August 1916 prohibited it. In that month, Australians in France were told that instructions had been received that in the future the Victoria Cross would only be given for acts of conspicuous gallantry which were materially conducive to the gaining of a victory, and therefore that cases of gallantry in lifesaving, however fine in nature, would not be considered for the award of the Victoria Cross. A further direction, however, in September 1916, stated that in future the Victoria Cross or other immediate award would not be given for the rescue of wounded, except for those whose duty it was to care for such cases. A further clarification was issued in November 1916 by the Commander-in-Chief himself, Sir Douglas Haig. The historical record is that, although British bearers received the VC in the World War I, no Australian bearer did.

While medals and decorations remained important symbols of recognition for work done, the coveted award most sought by bearers could not be given out but had to be earned: the highest place in the estimate of comrades.

Of the 580 Aboriginals who served in the war, three were awarded the Distinguished Conduct Medal, nine the Military Medal, three the Mention in Dispatches award, and one the Military Cross. A quarter of the Aboriginal soldiers did not fight on the Western Front, where 50 per cent fewer decorations were awarded compared to those conferred in the other theatres of war.

Sir John Monash

Prior to World War I, Monash had been an engineer and a lawyer. Before that, as a young boy he had met the famous Australian bushranger, Ned Kelly.

A naturalised child of Prussian Germans, in September 1914 he had been appointed commander of the 4th Infantry Brigade with the rank of colonel rather than brigadier general.

He was the most celebrated soldier of the AIF. He had been at Gallipoli in 1915.

Monash had been part of and responsible for major victories on the Western Front, consolidating the Australian divisions, rendering them invincible. He was aware of the enormous courage of the Australian soldiers, and was well known for giving due recognition for it. He had told them to fight 'for yourself, Australia, and the British Empire', in that order.

Moreover, he had led the Allies to overall victory on the Western Front from mid-1918 until the end of hostilities. Earlier in that year, on 31 May 1918, Monash had been promoted to Lieutenant General and made the Australian Corps Commander, a position accepted with enormous enthusiasm for the AIF divisions on the Western Front. Monash's fundamental goal was to protect the infantry to the maximum possible extent by use of mechanical resources and to advance with as little possible impediment. His planning, strategy and use of all of the resources of the army available to him rather than the use of the infantry as the primary attack weapon, had resulted in significant and recurring battle victories.

Monash had led the Battle of Amiens offensive on 8 August 1918, breaching the Hindenburg Line and thereby crushing the Germans, 30,000 of whom became prisoners. It was later described by the German High Command as the 'Black Day of the German Army'. On 11 August, at an unplanned gathering of senior Allied generals and politicians at Villers-Bretonneux, Monash and Lieutenant General Sir Arthur Currie of Canada were congratulated for their work.

During the course of the following 60 days of battle, the AIF, led by Monash, acted as the spearhead of the British Army, producing a rolling run of victories.

And Monash's esteem had grown even further as a result of his efficient and empathetic approach to the repatriation of some 160,000 Australian soldiers, almost entirely within eight months.

General Monash's health too had suffered significantly from the burden of war. He was unable to march at the 1931 Anzac Day parade in Melbourne but took the salute on horseback as the soldiers passed by.

After the war, Monash had led the development of Victoria's electricity network, and had been responsible for the conception of the monumental Shrine of Remembrance to be built in Melbourne, on St Kilda Road. At the time of his death it was still under construction. There were calls to have him buried there but his stated wish was that 'the Shrine should be no man's tomb'. This had been respected.

At 66, the strain of war caused a fatal heart attack and, on 8 October 1931, Monash died.

The day before his State funeral, Geelong played Richmond in the Grand Final of the Australian Football League at the Melbourne Cricket Ground, with a crowd of some 60,000. The Ground was Australia's colosseum. As a mark of respect, the players wore black armbands and the huge crowd held one minute's silence. Monash had been to the Melbourne Cricket Ground in 1929 to watch Donald Bradman, the world's greatest cricketer, bat for Australia.

Monash received a State funeral. Like Elliot's, Monash's coffin was draped in the Union Jack, and placed on a gun carriage. Fifteen thousand diggers, sailors, airmen and nurses marched with Monash to the cemetery. Later, the military escort joined in, including Monash's old school cadet corp. And there was Monash's white charger, with boots reversed in the stirrups. A massive crowd of 300,000 lined the streets. Over 60,000 gathered at the cemetery.

In summing up the man, this had been said of Monash: that of life's varied and often tragic entanglements, he could see the practical heart of what was vital to be done, and then did it.

Britain and Australia's Ties to It

In 1986, the Commonwealth and British Parliaments passed legislation that removed the United Kingdom's right to legislate with effect in Australia, and to be involved in the government of Australia. Further, all appeals to a British court from any Australian court were abolished. Australia's sovereignty had by those means become virtually complete. Britain had become a 'foreign power' under the Australian Constitution; a British national could not be a member of the Commonwealth Parliament.

In 2003, the High Court of Australia confirmed that the legislation amounted to establishing 'Australian independence' as at 3 March 1986, when the legislation took effect.

It had taken some 70 years since Nelson Ferguson's gassing for Australia to detach itself from the legal controls of the British Empire.

The Victoria Cross

In 1991 Australia replaced the 'Victoria Cross' honour, which had been established in 1856 by the British, with the 'Victoria Cross for Australia'. Ten years later, in April 2001, a senator of the Australian Government introduced the *Award of Victoria Cross for Australia Bill 2001* for the purposes of awarding the Victoria Cross for Australia to three members of the Australian forces. The awards were intended 'to raise the profile and recognition of three ordinary Australians, who displayed outstanding bravery'.

The awards were to be made posthumously to three soldiers in World Wars I and II: John Simpson Kirkpatrick, Albert Cleary and Teddy Sheean for their acts of valour.

Simpson was a stretcher-bearer with the 3rd Australian Field Ambulance, Australian Army Medical Corps at Gallipoli during World War I. On 25 April 1915 he landed at Anzac Cove and with his donkey began carrying wounded from the battle line to the beach for evacuation. He continued doing so for three and a half weeks, often under fire, but was killed.

Simpson had not received a Victoria Cross for his conspicuous valour. Nevertheless he and his donkey appeared on the obverse of the Anzac Commemorative Medallion, first issued in 1967.

On 13 April 2011, the Federal Government announced that 13 cases of valour would be examined posthumously by the Australian Government's Defence Honours and Awards Appeals Tribunal. The Tribunal first debated 'the eligibility of the 13 to receive the Victoria Cross, the Victoria Cross for Australia or other forms of recognition', and then discussed the individual cases.

On 6 February 2013, the inquiry advocated to the Australian Government that no awards be made, which the government accepted.

It remains the case today that no stretcher-bearer or other member of any field ambulance in World War I has received the highest award for valour in the presence of the enemy.

List of Churches

Stained glass windows made by the Ferguson and Papas stained glass business include those in the following churches.

Church of England, Parish of Mordialloc, Aspendale and Edithvale, Victoria

St Martin de Porres Church, Avondale Heights, Victoria

St Margaret's Presbyterian Church, Balaclava, Victoria

St John the Evangelist, Soldiers' Hill, Ballarat North, Victoria

St Thomas More's Catholic Church, Belgrave

St John's Anglican Church, Blackburn, Victoria

St. Bartholomew Church, Burnley, Victoria

Canterbury Baptist Church, Canterbury, Victoria

St Paul's Anglican Church, Canterbury, Victoria

St Mary's Church, Caulfield, Victoria

Lumen Christi Parish Church, Churchill, Victoria

St Joseph's Church, Coleraine, Victoria

Our Lady's Church, Deepdene, Victoria

Uniting Church, Diamond Creek, Victoria

St Andrew's Uniting Church, East Malvern

Presbyterian Church, Euroa, Victoria

St John the Evangelist Anglican Church, Footscray, Victoria (war motif)

St Paul's Anglican Church, Frankston, Victoria

St Stephen's Anglican Church, Gardenvale, Victoria

St Paul's Anglican Church, Gisborne, Victoria (war motif)

Christ Church Anglican Co-Cathedral, Hamilton, Victoria

St James Church, Ivanhoe, Victoria

All Saints Church, Kooyong, Victoria

Brighton Congregational Church, Middle Brighton, Victoria

St Margaret's Anglican Church, Mildura, Victoria (war motif)

St Margaret's Uniting Church, Mooroolbark, Victoria

The Catholic Parish of the Holy Family, Mount Waverley, Victoria

St Luke's Anglican Church, North Brighton, Victoria (war motif)

St Stephen's Presbyterian Church, North Williamstown, Victoria
Holy Trinity Anglican Church, Port Melbourne, Victoria
All Saints' Anglican Church, Preston, Victoria
Holy Trinity Anglican Church, Rochester, Victoria
Uniting Church, Sale, Victoria
All Souls Anglican Church, Sandringham, Victoria (war motif)
Holy Trinity Anglican Church, Stawell, Victoria
St Matthews Presbyterian Church, Stawell, Victoria
The Uniting Church, Stawell, Victoria
All Saints' Anglican Church, Tatura, Victoria
Toorak Uniting Church, Toorak, Victoria
All Saints Chapel, Lavarack Barracks, Townsville, Queensland
St Michael's Catholic Church, Traralgon, Victoria
St Luke's Church, Vermont, Victoria
St Augustine's Church, Wangaratta, Victoria
St Mark's Memorial Chapel, HMAS Cerberus, Westernport, Victoria
(war motif)
St Stephen's Church, Wodonga, Victoria

Bibliography

Note: There is nearly a universe of material written on World War I and other matters related to the events and issues dealt with in this book. In the course of my research for this book, I have found the following references particularly relevant.

Arthur, Max, *The Faces of World War I*, Cassell Illustrated, London, 2007.

Australian Imperial Force unit war diaries, 1914–18 War, Medical, Dental and Nursing, 15th Field Ambulance, Australian War Memorial website.

Ballarat Tramways Museum Inc, *Fares Please*, October 2014 edition.

Bean, CEW, *Anzac to Amiens*, Penguin, Ringwood, Vic., Australia, 1993.

Bickerton, Ian, *The Illusion of Victory: The True Costs of War*, Melbourne University Press, Carlton, Vic., 2011.

Blainey, Geoffrey, *The Story of Australia's People (The Rise and Rise of a New Australia)*, Penguin Random House, Australia, 2016.

Brown, Malcolm, *The Imperial War Museum Book of 1914: The Men Who Went to War*, Pan in Association with the Imperial War Museum, London,2005.

Blainey, Geoffrey, *The Causes of War*, Macmillan Publishing, South Melbourne VIC, 1988.

Burness, Peter, *Villers-Bretonneux to Le Hamel: Australians on the Western Front—1918*, Dept of Veterans' Affairs, Canberra, 2008.

Dennis, Peter, and Jeffrey Grey, *Victory or Defeat: Armies in the Aftermath of Conflict: The 2010 Chief of Army History Conference.* Big Sky, Sydney, 2010.

Chataway, Lieut T. P., *History of the 15th Battalion AIF 1914-1918,* The Naval & Military Press, East Sussex, 2010.

Derham, Mark, *Brudenell White: An AIF Legend*, Oryx Publishing, St Kilda, 2015.

Derham, Rosemary, *The Silence Ruse: Escape from Gallipoli; a Record and Memories of the Life of General Sir Brudenell White*, Cliffe, Armadale, Vic., 1998.

Downing, WH, *Digger Dialects, a Collection of Slang Phrases used by Australian Soldiers on Active Service*, Lothian Book Publishing Co Pty Ltd, Sydney and Melbourne, 1919.

Downing, WH, *To the Last Ridge, the World War One Experiences of WH Downing*, Grub Street Publishing, London, 2002.

Egan, Ted, *The Anzacs 100 Years On: In Story and Song: Australia and New Zealand in World War 1*, Wild Dingo Press, Cheltenham, Victoria, 2014.

FitzSimons, Peter, and Jane Macauley, *Victory at Villers-Bretonneux: Why a French Town Will Never Forget the Anzacs*, William Heinemann, North Sydney, NSW, 2016.

From the Australian Front, September 1917, Australian Imperial Force publication, Cassell and Company, Ltd

Fussell, Paul, *The Great War and Modern Memory*, Oxford UP, New York, 1975.

Gilbert, Martin (Historiker), *World in Torment: Winston S Churchill 1916–1922*, Mandarin Paperbacks, London, 1990.

Ham, Paul, *Passchendaele, Requiem for Doomed Youth*. A William Heinemann Book, Australia, 2016.

Hochschild, Adam, *To End All Wars – A Story of Protest and Patriotism in the First World War*, Pan Books, London, England, 2012.

Hughes, Bronwyn, 'Remembrance: Victoria's Commemorative Stained-glass Windows of World War I' (2015) 96 *The La Trobe Journal* 182–195.

Hughes, Bronwyn, 'The Art of Light: a Survey of Stained Glass in Victoria' (2012) 90 *The La Trobe Journal* 78–98.

Johnston, Mark, *Stretcher-bearers: Saving Australians from Gallipoli to Kokoda*, Cambridge University Press, Melbourne, Vic., 2015.

Jones, Simon, *Yellow Cross: the Advent of Mustard Gas in 1917*, Simon Jones Historian website, published 14 February 2014, https://simonjoneshistorian.com/2014/02/14/yellow-cross-measures-to-protect-against-mustard-gas/.

Keegan, John, *The First World War*, A. Knopf, New York, 1999.

Keneally, Thomas, *Australians: Eureka to the Diggers*, Vol. 2, Allen & Unwin, Sydney, 2014.

Kolata, Gina Bari, and A Verghese, *The New York Times Book of Medicine: More Than 150 Years of Reporting on the Evolution of Medicine*, Sterling Publishing Co Inc, US, 2015.

Kramer, Alan, *Dynamic of Destruction: Culture and Mass Killing in the First World War*, Oxford University Press, Oxford, 2007.

Kyle, Roy, and Bryce Courtenay, *An Anzac's Story*, Penguin, Camberwell, Vic., 2003.

Lake, Marilyn, *The Limits of Hope: Soldier Settlement in Victoria, 1915–38*, Oxford University Press, Melbourne, 1987.

Lovell, Chen, *Surrey Hills and Canterbury Hill Estate Heritage Study*, Surrey Hills War Service Homes Residential Precinct Citation, 2012.

Lycett, Tim, and Sandra Playle, *Fromelles The Final Chapters*, Viking an imprint of Penguin Books, 2013.

Macdonald, Ian, Catherine G Burke, and Karl Stewart, *Systems Leadership: Creating Positive Organizations*, Ashgate, Burlington, VT, 2006.

Macdonald, Lyn, *Somme*, M. Joseph, London, 1983.

Manne, Robert, and Chris Feik (eds), *The Words that Made Australia—How a Nation Came to Know Itself*, Black Inc. Agenda, 2012.

McMullin, Ross, *Pompey Elliott*, Scribe Publications, Carlton, Vic., 2002.

Neiberg, Michael S, *The Military Atlas of World War I*, Chartwell Books Inc., New York, 2014.

Newton, Douglas 'We Have Sprung at a Bound: Australia's Leap into the Great War, July–August 1914' (2015) 96 *The La Trobe Journal* 6–27.

Parliament of Australia, Parliamentary Research Paper, Anzac Series, April 2016.

Pedersen, Peter A, *Villers-Bretonneux Somme*, Pen & Sword Military, Barnsley, 2004.

Perry, Roland, *Monash: The Outsider Who Won a War*, Random House, Milsons Point, NSW, 2007.

Plunkett, Geoff, *Death by Mustard Gas: How Military Secrecy and Lost Weapons Can Kill*, Big Sky, Newport, NSW, Australia, 2014.

Reynolds, David, *America. Empire of Liberty*, Penguin, US, 2009.

Steele, Alan B, *The Western Front: A General Outline*, Arrow, Melbourne, 1930.

Stephens, David, and Broinowski, Alison, *The Honest History Book*, NewSouth Publishing, Sydney NSW, 2017.

Strachan, Hew, *Financing the First World War*, Oxford University Press, Oxford, 2004.

The Harefield Park Boomerang Magazine, Vol II, No. 10, October 1918.

The Queen's Commission: A Junior Officer's Guide, Royal Military Academy Sandhurst, 2006.

Todman, Daniel, *The Great War: Myth and Memory*, Hambledon, London and New York, 2005.

Tsouras, Peter, *The Greenhill Dictionary of Military Quotations*, Greenhill, London, 2000.

Wade, Linda, *By Diggers Defended, by Victorians Mended: Searching for Villers-Bretonneux*, Thesis, University of Wollongong, 2008.

Winegard, Timothy C, *Indigenous Peoples of the British Dominions and the First World War*, Cambridge University Press, New York, 2011.

Zimmer, Jenny, *Stained Glass in Australia*, Oxford University Press, Melbourne, 1984.

✠ I WAS BLIND